W9-DDJ-075

Designing Hard Software

Designing Hard Software

DOUGLAS W. BENNETT

MANNING
Greenwich
(74° w. long.)

For electronic browsing of this book, see:
    http://www.browsebooks.com

The publisher offers discounts on this book when ordered in quantity.
For more information, please contact:

    Special Sales Department
    Manning Publications Co.
    3 Lewis Street
    Greenwich, CT 06830

    Fax: (203) 661-9018
    email: orders@manning.com

©1997 by Manning Publications Co. All rights reserved.

No part of this publication may be reproduced, stored in a retrieval system, or transmitted, in any
form or by means electronic, mechanical, photocopying, or otherwise, without prior written
permission of the publisher. The C programs herein have been carefully tested, however, neither the
publisher nor the author may be held responsible for any damages arising due to the use of these
programs.

♾ Recognizing the importance of preserving what has been written, it is the policy of Manning to
have the books they publish printed on acid-free paper, and we exert our best efforts to that end.

Library of Congress Cataloging-in-Publication Data

Bennett, Douglas W., 1947–
    Designing hard software : the essential tasks / Douglas W. Bennett.
      p.   cm.
    Includes bibliographical references and index.
    ISBN 1-884777-21-X (hardcover)
    1. Computer software—Development.   I. Title.
QA76.76.D47B457   1996
005.1'2—dc20   96-25892
                                      CIP

 Manning Publications Co.
    3 Lewis Street
    Greenwich, CT 06830

    Copyeditor: Margaret Marynowski
    Typesetter: Aaron C. Lyon
    Cover designer: Leslie Haimes

Printed in the United States of America
1 2 3 4 5 6 7 8 9 10 – BB – 00 99 98 97 96

Contents

Preface   xiii

Introduction   xv

    The Situation in Software   xv
    The Situation in Hardware   xvii
    Software as a Hard Product   xix
    The Audience   xx
    Structure of the Book   xxi
    Conclusion   xxii

Chapter 1   Hard Structure for Software   1

1.1   Architectures of Software   1

1.2   Software Architecture in the Software Industry   4

    1.2.1   Architecture in Research Publications   4
    1.2.2   Architecture in Popular Methodologies   8
    1.2.3   Software Architecture in Practice   9
    1.2.4   Patterns and Bottom-up Architectures   9
    1.2.5   What Now?   10

1.3   Questions about Software System Architecture   11

    1.3.1   Basic Principles of (Software Design) Evaluation   11
    1.3.2   Which Elements to Include?   12
    1.3.3   Which Notation Should Be Used for Software Architecture?   15
    1.3.4   What Do We Do With the Other Elements?   15
    1.3.5   How Do We Evaluate Alternative Architectures?   16

1.4   A Definition of Software System Architecture   17

    1.4.1   Notation   18
    1.4.2   Tangibility   19

1.5   Using the Architecture in the Software Life Cycle   19

    1.5.1   Addressing the Emergent Properties of the System   20
    1.5.2   Viewing the System   20
    1.5.3   Reuse   20
    1.5.4   Implementation Assignments and System Integration   21

1.6   Summary   22

Chapter 2   Essential Tasks in the Development Process   25

2.1   Introduction   25

2.2   Basic Principles of Evaluation   26

2.3   Essential Tasks   29

2.4   Essential Tasks in the Larger Process   31

2.5   Current Development Processes   31

    2.5.1   Current Software Development Processes   31
    2.5.2   Current Hardware Development Processes   32

2.6   A Proposal for a Software Development Process   34

    2.6.1   Cross Product Processes   34
    2.6.2   Product Life Cycle Processes   35
    2.6.3   Project Processes   36

2.7   Defining Essential Tasks   38

    2.7.1   The Essential Tasks   40
    2.7.2   Document External Requirements   40
    2.7.3   Addressing the External Requirements   41

2.8   The Architecture Task Chunk   43

2.9   Summary   44

Chapter 3   The External Requirements Tasks   47

3.1   Introduction   47

    3.1.1   Who has the Requirements?   49
    3.1.2   The Run-Time View   49
    3.1.3   The Build-Time View   50

3.2   What are the Requirements?   51

3.3   Evaluating the External Requirements   52

    3.3.1   Semantics   52

3.4   Documenting the External Requirements   53

    3.4.1   Run-Time Requirements   53
    3.4.2   Evaluate the Nominated Actors, Roles, Use Cases,
            Interfaces, and Constraints   60
    3.4.3   Documenting the Build-Time Requirements   61
    3.4.4   Requirements Notations   67

3.5   Requirements Task Summary   68

Chapter 4   External Requirements Example   71

4.1   Run-Time Requirements   71

    4.1.1   Scope of the System   71
    4.1.2   Goals and Expectations   72
    4.1.3   Actors and Their Roles   72

4.1.4 Use Case Names and Descriptions   73

4.1.5 Control Interfaces   78

4.1.6 Information Interfaces   79

4.1.7 · Rules and Algorithms   79

4.1.8 User Constraints   80

4.2 Build-Time Requirements   80

4.2.1 Project Scope and Goals   80

4.2.2 Role the Product Will Play in the Development Organization   80

4.2.3 Instances of Growth and Change   80

4.2.4 Development-Sponsor Constraints   81

Chapter 5   The System State Task   83

5.1 Introduction   83

5.1.1 Which Properties Are Being Designed?   83

5.1.2 Evaluations   85

5.1.3 Notations   85

5.1.4 Develop Evaluation Criteria   86

5.2 Notations   87

5.3 System State   88

5.4 Evaluation   90

5.5 Carrying out the Evaluations   91

5.5.1 Semantic Level   91

5.5.2 Sufficiency of the Models   91

5.5.3 Efficiency   92

5.5.4 Extensions and Additions   93

5.6 Summary   93

Chapter 6   System State Modeling Examples   95

6.1 Derive the Criteria   95

6.1.1 Extract Access Requests   96

6.1.2 Extract System State Change Cases   98

6.2 Derive State Elements   99

6.2.1 Nominate State Elements, Attributes, and Relationships   102

6.3 Evaluate the Nominations   103

6.3.1 Using an Access Request for Evaluation   104

6.3.2 Elevating an Attribute to a State Element   104

6.3.3 Adding New State Elements   105

6.4 Evaluating Three Versions of the Model   107

6.4.1 Evaluation Against Likely Extensions   114

6.5 Fixes   116

6.6   Completing the System State Model   119

6.7   Summary of the Example   120

Chapter 7   **Behavior Identification and Allocation Task   121**

7.1   Introduction   121

    7.1.1   What Properties Are Being Designed?   121

    7.1.2   Kinds of Components   122

    7.1.3   Evaluation   127

    7.1.4   Variations   127

7.2   General Approach   128

    7.2.1   Nominating Components   129

    7.2.2   Identifying and Allocating Behavior   131

    7.2.3   Evaluation   132

7.3   Techniques   133

    7.3.1   Interaction Model   133

    7.3.2   Develop an Interaction Diagram   135

    7.3.3   Evaluation   139

7.4   Collaboration-Responsibility Model   147

    7.4.1   Notation   147

    7.4.2   Develop a Collaboration-Responsibility Model   148

    7.4.3   Evaluation   149

7.5   Service Modeling   152

    7.5.1   What Are Service Components?   153

    7.5.2   Nominating Service Components   155

    7.5.3   Service Components from Use Cases   155

    7.5.4   Service Components from Increments   156

    7.5.5   Nominating Increments of Development and Enhancement   157

    7.5.6   Evaluation   158

7.6   Summary   159

Chapter 8   **Behavior Allocation Examples   161**

8.1   Interaction Model   161

    8.1.1   Nominating Components from Scratch   161

    8.1.2   Nominating Components Using an Architecture Diagram   162

    8.1.3   Building an Interaction Diagram   163

    8.1.4   Issues about Allocation Decisions   172

    8.1.5   Evaluating the Results   175

    8.1.6   Implementation Increments   182

8.2   Collaboration-Responsibility Model   189

    8.2.1   Nominating Responsibilities from Scratch and Allocating Them   189

    8.2.2   Evaluating the Collaboration-Responsibility Model   196

8.3   Service Model   201

    8.3.1   Deriving Service Nominations from Various Sources   201
    8.3.2   Evaluating Service Nominations   208

Chapter 9   **The Software System Architecture Task   211**

9.1   Introduction   211

    9.1.1   What is Being Addressed?   211
    9.1.2   How to Measure System Architecture   212
    9.1.3   Handling Variations   213
    9.1.4   Developing Evaluation Criteria   213
    9.1.5   Notation   213

9.2   Architecture Templates   214

    9.2.1   Two-Layer Architecture   217
    9.2.2   Four-Layer Architecture   220
    9.2.3   Five-Layer Architecture   222
    9.2.4   The Generic Architecture Template   224

9.3   Develop a System Architecture   225

    9.3.1   Draw the Boundary   226
    9.3.2   Identify the Ports   226
    9.3.3   Nominate Subsystems of the Architecture   227
    9.3.4   Refining an Architecture   235

9.4   Allocating Behavior to Architecture Subsystems   237

    9.4.1   Deriving Subsystem Interfaces   240
    9.4.2   Organizing Messages into Channels   243
    9.4.3   Summary of Allocating Behavior   245

9.5   Evaluate Architectures   246

    9.5.1   Change Case Evaluation Involving Platform and Peripherals   247
    9.5.2   Change Case Evaluation Involving Presentations   248
    9.5.3   Making the Changes   249
    9.5.4   Evaluation Summary   249

9.6   Allocation across Hardware Boundaries   250

    9.6.1   Interface Machinery   251
    9.6.2   Placing the Boundaries   253
    9.6.3   Allocation to Non-Hardware Subsystems   255
    9.6.4   Summary of Allocation to Hardware   256

9.7   Architecture Summary   257

Chapter 10   **Architecture Example   259**

10.1   Specifying a Boundary and Ports   260

10.2   Nominating Subsystems   261

    10.2.1   Interface Subsystems   261
    10.2.2   Presentation Subsystems   261

10.2.3 Model Subsystems 263

10.2.4 Dialogue Subsystems 265

10.2.5 Service Subsystems 267

10.3 Evaluating the Preliminary Architecture 270

10.3.1 Completeness 270

10.3.2 Evaluating against User Requirements 270

10.4 Allocating Model Components to Architecture 274

10.4.1 Organizing Channels 278

10.5 Evaluating the Detailed Architecture (Boxless) 286

10.5.1 Portability Evaluation 287

10.5.2 New Configurations, Reuse 287

10.5.3 Extensions 288

10.5.4 Integration 289

10.6 Allocating Architecture Subsystems across Hardware Boundaries 295

10.6.1 Workstation Architecture 296

10.6.2 Server Architecture 300

10.6.3 Evaluating Traffic Between Nodes 304

10.6.4 Allocating to Tasks in a Node 304

10.6.5 Summary of the Subsystem Allocation Process 308

10.7 Implementation Increments 309

10.7.1 Project Sequence 312

Chapter 11 The Behavior Description Task 315

11.1 Introduction 315

11.2 Behavior Description 316

11.3 Constraints 316

11.4 References 318

11.5 Evaluation 318

Chapter 12 Conclusion 319

12.1 Summary 319

12.2 The Critical Ideas 323

12.3 The Big Picture 324

12.4 Next Steps 324

Appendix A Summary of Essential Tasks 327

A.1 The Essential Tasks 327

A.1.1 User Requirements Task 329

A.1.2 Development Sponsor Requirements 330

A.1.3   System State Task   331
A.1.4   Behavior Identification and Allocation Task   332
A.1.5   Behavior Description Task   333
A.1.6   Architecture Task   335

Appendix B   Methodology Comparison   339

B.1   Software Methodologies   339
B.2   Methodologies and the Essential Tasks   341
    B.2.1   Structured Analysis and Structured Design   343
    B.2.2   Responsibility-Driven Design   344
    B.2.3   Object-Oriented Analysis (Shlaer-Mellor)   344
    B.2.4   Object Modeling Technique (OMT)   345
    B.2.5   Objectory   347
    B.2.6   Summary of the Comparison   347

Bibliography   349
Index   351

Preface

I wrote this book because I believed the advertisements that PPI (later Stepstone) Corporation published. PPI was an early player in the object technology market. Their ads promised wonderful things to the users of object-oriented programing languages: reuse, quick development, robustness in the face of change, and ease of extension. I went to work for PPI and found that those benefits were not automatically appearing in products written in the company's programming language. Why not? I thought, it must be the methodology. Software methodologies were a little thin at the time, particularly in the area of object-oriented design. Around 1987, Ivar Jacobson had just started publishing articles on his proprietary (at the time) process for developing software. He was saying good things about the importance of making sure that designs matched the needs of the users. So, I took what I could from the articles on Objectory, filled in the missing pieces, and went out into the world to preach the gospel of object-oriented design.

Before I left Stepstone, Brad Cox, one of the PPI founders, said two things that I believed then, and still believe. The first was that software was in the same position that gun manufacture was in before the development of gauges to measure tolerances: we have many tools for production but very few tools to measure the results. There was no "reuse" in the gun industry until measurement tools were introduced. The second was, "There is no such thing as object-oriented design, just good design and bad design." These two ideas grew in my training and consulting practice until they overwhelmed the cookbook approach to the methodology I was preaching. I had seen the light: software could be treated like other engineered products. I had some confidence that this was a good light because I could make software design look like the chemical plant designs that I had done as a chemical engineer. The evaluation of work products against external requirements has provided a way to objectively resolve many of the differences of opinion about software design issues. The discussions about those differences can sound like the discussion of angels on pinheads rather than the design of a high technology product.

The combination of the evaluation idea with my belief in the myth that software can be built from reusable components led to the elevation of the software system architecture from its somewhat obscure position in current practice to the central role it plays here in making software "hard." A key advance for me came when I realized that the benefits being claimed for object-oriented programming were not benefits to the system users but to the people who paid for the development, the development sponsors. The system architecture could serve as the focus designing in extensibility and all those other wonderful "ilities."

The result is that this book is not a methodology book; nor is it a book about object-oriented design. It was my intention to write a book about "good design" of software systems. I hope that readers will find that to be the case.

We never do anything alone. This work has been supported and contributed to by many people. Brad Cox and Ivar Jacobson have been generous in sharing their ideas with me. Their influence can be seen throughout these pages. It has been said that if you want to learn, teach. That has certainly been my experience. Preparing courses and presenting them to professional developers has been a great education. Being a consultant has given me the chance to see many software products and organizations. My clients have been patient teachers as we worked on the challenges they faced in delivering products.

My editor at Manning Publications, Marjan Bace, has been a gentle, but persistent nudge. His habit of claiming ignorance about software matters before asking pointed questions about how and what I was trying to say has contributed much to this effort. My wife, Pat, has been a very helpful reviewer and a source of support and encouragement. The foibles, errors, and inconsistencies are, of course, all mine. For the good ideas I owe much to the people who have shared their time, energy, and ideas with me.

Introduction

THE SITUATION IN SOFTWARE

Software, which does so well in standardizing and automating other industries, is having trouble repeating that performance on its own turf. The growth of productivity and product quality has been lower in software as compared to, say, electronic hardware or automobiles. Why so? Some answers that have been voiced over the years include the following: software is intrinsically complex, software is an art, or software requirements change too quickly.

If we look into how people develop software, we can see some things that contribute to the view that software is complex and not at all like those other kinds of products. Some comments and observations that I have heard include the following:

- "Those methodologies and all that design documentation just get in the way of the real work."—a programmer
- "Have you started coding yet?" and "When will the code be finished?"—a manager
- "The development team for a system that will be implemented on a client-server hardware architecture is responsible for everything, from nested case statements to ensuring that the system achieves the required transaction throughput rates."—a project plan
- "I can code it from scratch faster than I can figure out what the existing component does and modify it to do what I need."—a programmer
- "Our system architect has an advisory role on the project."—a developer
- "We don't have a system architect, but we encourage the various development groups to talk to one another."—a project manager

Software developers who hold the views implied by these comments produce software that can be accessed only through its source code or as a running system. Programmers looking at source code can only see programming language constructs. These constructs—functions, instances of classes, etc.—are quite small relative to the size of most systems, so looking at a software system in terms of its code makes it very difficult to see any larger scale structures in the system.

Looking at just the trees makes it hard to see the forest.

I believe that the lack of a view of the larger scale structures of software systems is a major contributor to the apparent complexity commonly ascribed to software systems. Residential house design and construction would look intrinsically complex if they were viewed from the level of hammers and nails. Most carpenters, of course, work to a plan developed by an architect. They can easily see the larger structure of the house in the architect's plans. They even have the luxury of being able to step back and look at the complete structure. A software developer working without an architecture diagram does not have that luxury. The result is that much software looks like a house built without a plan by several carpenters who did not talk to one another.

When most software development organizations wish to improve the quality of their products and the economics of their process, they often turn to software development methodologies. Methodology writers, or their case tool vendors, promise wonderful things to those who use the methodology. Yet, it appears that some people in the organizations believe the promises, given the time and money invested in selecting and deploying a methodology in some organizations. There is often considerable energy invested in selecting which one will be used because the methodologies are mutually exclusive. A shop that uses structured analysis can hardly be expected to use Booch at the same time.

It's hard to cook a banquet with just one recipe.

There are indications of problems with the process of adopting a methodology. These problems have to do with the apparent inflexibility of most methodologies. Thumb through the pages of any book on software methodology and you will see that a great many diagrams and documents are needed. Listen to an enthusiastic adherent of the methodology and you will get the impression that all the documents should be produced in every project. However, if you compare the number of different documents called for in most methodologies with the much smaller number of document types actually produced in most development organizations, you will see one of the problems with adopting a methodology.

On the other hand, there are problems with the ability of software methodologies to adequately describe the process of developing software. As I will show in the chapters on the architecture and development processes, software systems are composed of a hierarchy of products and subproducts. Each product needs its own set of multilevel processes. Software methodologies sound much like a single level, single thread process.

So, we have a situation where the sources of guidance for process improvements that organizations turn to, methodologies, do not appear to be well suited to provide that guidance. On one hand, the process they describe is too far from the current practice of software development to be readily adopted. The experience of the Total Quality movement in the manufacturing industries tells us that large step changes in process and culture are not feasible. On the other side, a single methodology cannot adequately describe the multiproduct, multiprocess development universe needed to deliver complex software systems.

THE SITUATION IN HARDWARE

In the discussion of differences between software products and other kinds of products, I will refer to the other products as hard products. Hard products seem to have some advantages over software in the areas of manageability of both the complexity of the products and of the processes for developing them. Experience with hard product development indicates that, if hard products were treated with the same processes and practices used in software, then hard products would also appear to be intrinsically complex, product quality would be highly variable, and the process would be expensive and labor intensive. I believe that the converse is also true. If software were treated with the same processes and practices as are used in the hard product industries, beginning with the essential tasks I will describe in this book, software would begin to look more like a hard product and be more manageable.

How do those other guys do it?

It is interesting to ask what hard products have that software products do not. There are three things that are common in hard product development that would be very valuable to have in the software industry. These are a tangible representation of the product structure, flexible development practices, and measurements to determine if the desired attributes have been designed into the product.

Product Structure

If you ask a building architect about his current project, you will be shown a few drawings of floor plans and elevations of a building. The diagrams will define the static structure of the complete building. The architect will be able to describe how the occupants of the building and their equipment will be facilitated in doing their jobs by the building structure. The architect's drawings will not show the occupants, the structural steel, the mechanical, or the electrical views of the building, but there will be room in the structure for all those things. The architectural diagrams of the building define the single structure that will be built. All of the uses and views of the building are accommodated within the physical structure.

Flexible Development Practices

New products, like a reduced instruction set for chips, carbon composites in aircraft frames, or ceramic engines in cars, start out as ideas. When an idea is proposed it is often investigated with informal design studies to uncover feasibility problems and to determine the economic potential of the new product. If the economics look good, but there are feasibility problems, a prototype may be designed and constructed to resolve the problem. More detailed design studies may be carried out to get a better handle on costs and risks, and finally production prototypes may be designed and built to work out production details.

A whole cookbook of recipes.

Engineers of hard products have a well-stocked tool box of design tools like notations and the techniques to apply them that they can use as the situation warrants. These techniques range in formality from back-of-the-envelope techniques to formal, mathematical simulations of the product design. If the question to be answered is along the lines of, "Is it bigger than a bread box?" then informal techniques would be appropriate. If the question is, "Can we reduce the weight by 2% and still provide the safety margins?" then a very different, more formal set of techniques would be used. Having this set of techniques means that questions that arise at any stage of the product's life cycle can be answered effectively and efficiently.

Measurements

The term *reuse* is not used in the hard product industries like the integrated circuit and aircraft industries. Instead, subsystems are bought or built. Standard components, from light bulbs to jet engines are *used*. This was not always the case. Consider the problems that designers faced when they were trying to develop reusable machine parts. Brad Cox has pointed out [COX89], that Eli Whitney tried and failed to produce reusable parts for guns. Congress tried for 50 years to get interchangeable parts for their guns. These and other efforts failed until gauges were developed to compare the tolerances of the parts during manufacture with the tolerance specified in the design.

Two things are needed for measurements to contribute to reuse and other attributes of product quality: one is a way to measure the property of interest, the other is a guideline for which values of the measurement are acceptable. Having tolerances for parts and a way to measure those tolerances was essential for developing "reusable" machine parts. Lately, more esoteric properties of hard products have become important, such as maintainability. Having acceptable levels of this property in hard products requires that the product be explicitly designed to be maintained, that measures are available to confirm that the maintainability is expressed in the design documents and is manifest in the product.

Goals, building tools and measuring tools.

These three features of hard product design: a way to represent the physical structure of the complete system; a flexible set of design tools; and design goals for specific properties and measures of those properties, would be very useful if applied to software product development.

SOFTWARE AS A HARD PRODUCT

The *Hard Software* in the title comes from applying these three features of hard product development to software design practices. In fact, it is possible to treat software development like hard product development and end up with a product that is tangible, visible, and amenable to the same kinds of design goals and evaluations that are used in hard products. Many of the techniques and diagrams for doing this already exist in the software development domain. We need only a few additions and a slight attitude adjustment to make the change.

Goals, building tools, and measuring tools work in software, too.

Software System Architecture

In Chapter 1, an architecture for software systems is proposed that consists of subsystems, channels, and the boundary of the system. To make the subsystems tangible, they are enclosed in existing implementation containers. The different levels of implementation containers have a strict contained-in relationship with one another, so that the software subsystems have the same contained-in relationships with each other. This software system architecture definition provides a medium for designing in the *emergent* properties of the system. Emergent properties include extensibility, maintainability and any others that depend on the whole system for their expression. The subject of software architecture definition is discussed in Chapter 1, and the process of developing the architecture diagram is discussed in Chapter 9.

A Tool Box of Design Techniques

The problems of methodologies appearing to be both too big and too small to describe an effective process are addressed by separating the individual design techniques from the application of those techniques. A set of tasks based on the category of work product they produce is proposed. Together, these task categories, called the Essential Tasks, are sufficient to document the design of software systems from need through the system architecture. They address all of the essential properties desired in a finished product. The definition of Essential Tasks and their relationship to methodologies and to real practice are covered in Chapter 2. Each of the individual tasks gets its own chapter and a chapter of examples.

Measurements and Evaluations

As you recall from the earlier discussion, measurements were the missing element that, when developed, enabled machine parts to be reusable. Software developers are struggling with quality and reuse issues right now, probably for the same sorts of reasons that Congress and Eli Whitney struggled with reuse: the lack of measurements. Having complete, quantified goals for all the properties desired in a system and measuring the design documents to see that the properties are, in fact, designed in, are critical to delivering software systems that express the properties. To that end, a set of Basic Principles of Evaluation are described in Chapter 2. These principles are used to guide the application of each of the Essential Tasks. In the chapter on Essential Tasks we will see how application of the Basic Principles could lead to a structure of software products that looks just like the structure of electronic hardware: individual products defined at a single level of implementation unit.

Documenting external goals and using those goals as explicit evaluation criteria for design documents represents the biggest departure in this book from current methodology instruction. It is also the most important idea in the book. If you only take one thing from this book, make it the idea of evaluations against external goals. If you have these measures in your design practice, you can detect and fix problems of inappropriate notations and bad design decisions. Without these measures, you will have no way of knowing whether those elusive properties of maintainability or reuse are actually present in your design.

This book describes the tools in the engineer's tool box and how to use each one individually. The topic of applying the appropriate tools in useful sequences in various situations is mentioned briefly in the Essential Tasks chapter, but the details are outside the scope of this book.

THE AUDIENCE

Developers, engineers, and managers.

The intended audience of this book includes the people I have dealt with in my training and consulting work. These people are professional software developers and their managers who work for, usually, large organizations. They are responsible for the form, content, and production of the software products on which their organizations depend. Their current development practice is rather informal. The managers and the developers of the organization recognize the need to improve the quality, economics, reuse, maintainability, and flexibility of their software products. There is widespread agreement that an important aspect of improving the product is to improve the process and practice of designing the software. But there is widespread disagreement on which procedures to change and how much time should be devoted to the changes.

For designers and engineers, this book can help them improve how they carry out their design tasks. In particular, I think that the evaluations could profitably be added to most existing tasks. Any of the Essential Tasks that are not part of the current practice could be added.

For managers concerned with improving an invisible process, I believe that the evaluation aspects of the tasks provide an opportunity to make the development process, itself, more visible and tangible. The details of which diagrams get drawn are less important than the demonstration that the decisions documented in the diagram effectively address the external requirements.

For methodologists selecting the "corporate methodology" the Essential Tasks offer a basis for comparing and integrating existing methodologies. The Essential Tasks help one get beyond comparing methodologies, using names of the steps and diagram types.

STRUCTURE OF THE BOOK

The chapters and their contents include:

- *Hard Structure for Software*   Chapter 1 includes a brief survey of the literature on architecture of software systems. It then defines a single, physical architectural structure for software systems in terms of hierarchies of subsystems, each contained in a physical boundary. The subsystems are defined with existing implementation components such as OpenDoc, heavyweight process, processor, board, node, and cluster of nodes. This representation of the software architecture corresponds directly and tangibly with the physical software system.

  What is architecture, and how should we evaluate it?

- *Essential Tasks in the Development Process*   Chapter 2 describes the practice universe as all the things that must be done to deliver economical, timely, and successful software systems. There are hierarchies of activities and processes. Down toward the bottom of the hierarchies are the practices and processes associated with the engineering of single software systems. Below that are the Essential Tasks that inform and constrain those engineering practices as shown in the figure.

  Use separate levels of tools and practices.

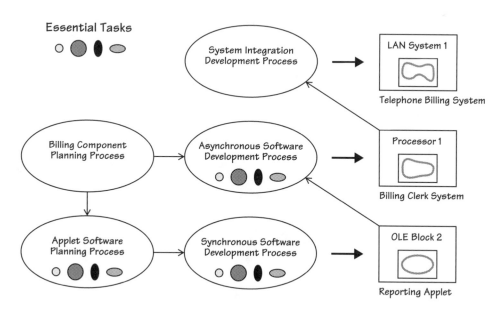

In this chapter, the Essential Tasks are described and their role in the practice universe is discussed. That role includes serving as a basis for comparing and unifying existing methodologies. How they can be applied in developing common architectures across related products is described. Common architectures are the necessary prerequisite for component reuse.

- *The Essential Tasks*   A chapter of examples follows each chapter. The remainder of the chapters contain instructions and examples for each of the essential tasks. The tasks follow in order, dictated by their information dependencies. They are as follows:
  – Chapter 3: The External Requirements Tasks
  – Chapter 4: External Requirements Examples
  – Chapter 5: The System State Tasks
  – Chapter 6: System State Modeling Examples
  – Chapter 7: Behavior Identification and Allocation Task
  – Chapter 8: Behavior Allocation Examples
  – Chapter 9: The Software System Architecture Task
  – Chapter 10: Architecture Example
  – Chapter 11: The Behavior Description Task

CONCLUSION

The tasks fall into two groups: documenting the external goals and properties the system is to provide (Chapter 4), and making decisions about how the system will do that (Chapters 5, 7, and 9). As you can see, each chapter is followed by a chapter that illustrates the concepts using an extended example. The extended examples contain useful illustrations of notations, and discussions of evaluation processes.

CHAPTER 1

Hard Structure for Software

CONTENTS

1.1 Architectures of Software   1
1.2 Software Architecture in the Software Industry   4
1.3 Questions about Software System Architecture   11
1.4 A Definition of Software System Architecture   17
1.5 Using the Architecture in the Software Life Cycle   19
1.6 Summary   22

1.1 ARCHITECTURES OF SOFTWARE

While it was originally called *software* to distinguish stored programs from the machine that executed them, software has earned its reputation of being "soft" in a variety of ways. It is not visible when it is running. It seems to change all the time, both when it is running and when it is being built. The pictures drawn to represent a software system seem to focus on only one specific aspect of the system, like functions, data, or domain objects, and those pictures often do not correspond with what is actually built. In other words, there is no widely known way to describe the structure of a complete software system in the same way that the structure of a complete building, an airplane, or a chemical plant is described. Nor do many of the well-known software analysis and design methodologies provide notation for describing the structure of the complete system.

1

This "softness" has led to the situation where only the people who write the code can "understand" the system. Since granularity of programming language constructs is very small, large systems look very complex because of the large number of small pieces involved. This in turn has led to the idea that software is "intrinsically complex," and is best handled by small teams of people. Is software really fundamentally different from other products that have "hard" structures? Is it possible to deal in a concrete way with "invisible" software structures?

The answers to those questions are: no, software is not intrinsically complex; and yes, it is possible to deal with software in a concrete, tangible way. To make it so, we need a definition for software structure that is connected to the physical structure of software systems. We also need notations that make the structure visible and accessible, and processes for handling software that accommodate the physical structure. In this chapter I will introduce the architecture of software systems. In the next chapter I will address process issues.

The word *architecture* has many meanings both inside and outside the software industry. One thing all the meanings have in common is a connection to form, shape, and structure. If we talk about the architecture of an office building, images of plans and elevations, perspective renderings, or a 3-D model come to mind. These documents describe the form, shape, and size of the building, as a whole. They do not describe all the details of the building, but they show the whole shape and the outside surface, the boundary between the building and the rest of the world. The primary job of the building architect is to determine a form, size, and shape of a single building that will meet the needs of its occupants, will be safe to build and use, and can be built for a reasonable and predictable cost.

Here is a portion of a poem by John G. Saxe, *The Blind Men and the Elephant*, about six people:

To learning much inclined,
Who went to see the elephant
(Though all of them were blind),
That each by observation
Might satisfy his mind.

The first approached the elephant,
And, happening to fall
Against his broad and sturdy side,
At once began to bawl,
"God bless me! but the elephant
Is very like a wall!"

The second feeling of the tusk
cried: "Ho! what have we here
So very round and smooth and sharp?
To me 'tis mighty clear
This wonder of an elephant
Is very like a spear!"

This story in the poem is funny because the storyteller and the reader can see that all the blind men "see" the same elephant, as designers and programers without an architecture "see" the same software system. This is a apt analogy for software, but the software story is not funny, because there is no story teller who can tell us that there is only one elephant.

Other views of the building focus on specific aspects of the structure. Some of these views include structural steel, electrical wiring, plumbing, air conditioning, or controls. None of the special views account for the whole building; nor is the building just the sum of the special views. There is a single representation of the complete, physical building and this representation subsumes all the other views. The representation of the complete, physical building tells us things about the building that are not contained in any of the other views. Rechtin [REC91] put it nicely. He defines a system in two parts:

> 1. A system is a complex set of dissimilar elements or parts, so connected or related as to form an organic whole.
> 2. The whole is greater in some sense than the sum of the parts, that is, the system has properties beyond those of the parts. Indeed, the purpose of building systems is to gain those properties.

One physical structure in other products

That single, physical structure of the building must provide room for all the pieces that make up a building, like the steel that holds it up, its walls, the plumbing, the air conditioning, places to store cleaning supplies, places to put the telephone wiring, and on and on. In addition, the building must look good, must not blow down in the storm of the century, must be pleasing to its occupants, and must allow them to do what they're supposed to do. The term I would like to use for this view of the physical form and shape of the complete building is *architecture.*

Architecture is always of something.

Everything, of course, has a form and shape, so we can say that everything has an architecture; it is important to identify the architecture to which we are referring. The architecture of the building is different from the architecture of the structural steel, or the plumbing system. None of this is a problem when talking about buildings. Separate people handle each of the different views. Architects talk to owners and design the single building to meet all of the needs of all of the parties that have an interest in the building. Structural engineers, on the other hand, design the steel; mechanical engineers design the plumbing, heating, and air conditioning; and electrical engineers design the power system. The magic in all this is that the one structure described by the architect provides for all of the requirements of all the views of the building.

The ideas that, first, there is only one building being designed and built, and, second, that the one structure must combine all the specialty views and meet all of the requirements, are well established in industries that build hard products like buildings, but they are not well established in the software industry. As the next section will show, this lack of a single, physical representation of the architecture of the complete software system is a major contributor to software's reputation of being more complex than other products, and it contributes to many of the problems that plague the software industry.

1.2 SOFTWARE ARCHITECTURE IN THE SOFTWARE INDUSTRY

There are many segments of the software industry, and each has its own focus and concerns. The structure and architecture of software systems is one of those concerns that is common to many parts of the industry. To provide a context for the discussion of architecture in this chapter and its treatment in this book, I would like to look at how architecture is treated in three areas of the industry: 1) research publications, 2) popular software analysis and design methodologies, and 3) commercial software development organizations.

1.2.1 Architecture in Research Publications

Software architecture is a major area of activity in software research. The state of this activity is indicated by three recent publications: Mary Shaw's new book, *Software Architectures* [SHAW96], the *Proceedings of the First International Workshop on Architectures for Software Systems* [GAR95], and the architecture theme in the November 1995 issue of *IEEE Software* [IEEE95]. The architecture workshop proceedings provide a very good summary of current activity in the field. The Workshop Summary is quite succinct, so I will quote it, here:

1 What is the importance of Software Architectures?
- To reduce risk, cost, and time-to-market.
- To increase predictability, reliability, and quality.
- To provide early identification of potentially very large reuse opportunities.
- To leverage experience by using the architecture to document design knowledge and to train.

2 What is the importance of Software Architecture evaluation?
- To make sure one is using "good" ones.
- To ensure good fit to requirements.
- To ensure implementability of system.

3 What is the state of the practice of Software Architecture evaluation?
- Most evaluation approaches are ad hoc.
- They are experience-driven, and people based; smart, experienced people do their stuff.
- Most approaches lack rigor in their methods and notations (there exist empirical proofs of "goodness," but not formal proofs).
- Most analysis is bottom up: patterns are an example of this,
- Most evaluations are based on incomplete and inconsistent architecture descriptions.
- There are no consistent evaluation criteria (especially of the "ilities").
- Many practitioners are beginning to use design patterns that encapsulate architectural guidance although they typically omit evaluation criteria.
- Often analysis is "bad practice"-based (the architecture is compared to ones that have failed).
- The suitability of an architecture is often based on similarity to existing solutions of similar problems.

4 What is the state of research of Software Architectures?
- Some ADL's (architecture description languages) exist, but they are not very mature.
- There is limited analysis capability.
- Practitioners don't know how to use the tools.
- Patterns are a ray of hope for standardization of how people informally characterize architectural elements.

5 What are suggested research topics to support Software Architecture evaluation?
- Representation: requirements, architecture, transformations, heterogeneity.
- Analysis: evaluation criteria, metrics, empirical validation.
- Cataloging/classification.
  - Problems, architectures, patterns.
  - Connector types and their characteristics.
  - Experiences.
- Process.
  - Requirements to architecture to implementation.
  - Justifiability of steps.
- Training curricula.
  - Component-based system engineering.
  - System architecture design.

Some issues that came up regularly at the workshop included: views, layers, and the definition of software architecture; styles; and notation, patterns, and ways to evaluate architectures.

While the idea that the software architecture is composed of several views was mentioned by many of the authors, there was little agreement on what constituted an adequate set of views. Sets of views mentioned include the following:

- Static Software, Data, Distribution (to hardware), and Development [EME95]
- Static, Logical, Dynamic, and Physical [KRU94]
- Conceptual, Module Interconnection, Execution, and Code [HOF95]
- Functional, Structural, and Allocation [KOZ95]
- Functional, Reuse, and Delivery [MEZ95]
- Logical, Process, Physical, and Development [KRU95]

Krutchen summarizes the relationship among views when he states, "The various views are not fully independent. Elements of one view are connected to elements in other views, following certain design rules and heuristics[KRU95]." Many authors mention coordinating the different views as a current concern. They would agree that architecture is defined as the elements that make up the system, but from the combinations of elements mentioned in the list above, it is clear that there is little agreement on what those elements should be.

The question of which elements constitute an architecture is also addressed in the notion of architecture style. A style consists of the design elements used in the architecture, a set of configuration rules that guide the configurations of the elements, a semantic interpretation of the compositions, and analyses that can be

Figure 1.1
Architecture
notations

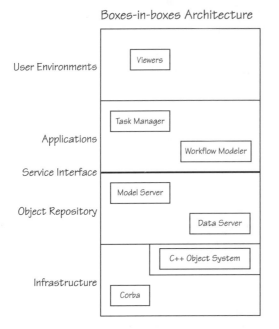

Boxes-in-boxes Architecture

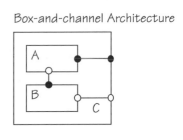

Box-and-channel Architecture

performed on systems built in that style [GAR95]. Some styles (defined by their main elements) include: Pipes and Filters, Object-Oriented, Event-Based, Domain-Specific, Layered, Repositories, Rule-Based, Process Control, Distributed, Main Program/Subroutines, State Transition-Based, and Heterogeneous [GAR93].

Can one house be a drywall-oriented house and another be a two-by-four-oriented house?

The state of style thinking was nicely summarized by Shaw, who notes that styles differ in the aspects of the system on which they focus [SHAW95]. Each style, as described above, addresses some issues and is silent on others. This is a serious problem, in my opinion, because in the field, the end user of a system is counting on all of the issues having been successfully addressed.

Notations for representing software architecture were not included in very many papers, but two forms of notation appeared in several. One is what I will call the boxes-inside-boxes notation, and the other is the box-and-channel notation. Examples of each are shown in Figure 1.1. The boxes-inside-boxes notation is more common, but, in my opinion, much less useful for defining a software system structure.

Patterns are an increasingly popular concept in the object-oriented community. They will be discussed in more detail later. One paper in the architecture workshop explicitly addresses patterns [PAUL95], which are solutions to specific, recurring design problems described as a set of components and their internal connections. The concept of patterns attempts to address structure issues, but is limited in its effectiveness by addressing only a very small subset of the "system problem," and by not having an enclosure for the pattern.

From this brief survey, it is apparent that the science of software architecture is in a very fluid state right now. Having consistent ways to evaluate any given notation or design would help, but consistent evaluations, as we will see in the methodology discussion, are rare in software practice. Authors of papers on architecture have a considerable range of opinions on evaluation. Van der Linden [VAN95] describes a building block approach to software architecture that is quite close to the approach that I advocate. When describing evaluation of the designs, he states that, "Because building blocks are self-contained, they are easily replaced." This approach to evaluation, which is very common, can be summarized as follows: because certain components are present in a design, or certain procedures are used, the resulting product will have the desired properties. There is no evaluation called for to demonstrate that the properties are actually there. This represents one end of the evaluation spectrum.

Moving toward the other end of the evaluation spectrum, you will find a call for explicit evaluation against external requirements. Chung et al.'s position is summed up in their architecture workshop paper title: "Using Non-Functional Requirements to Systematically Select Among Alternatives in Architectural Design" [CHU95]. Gacek et al. support this, suggesting that a software architecture should consist not only of the system components and connections, but also the stake holder's requirements, and demonstrations that the requirements are met by the components and connections [GAC95]. Evaluation against external requirements, particularly the build-time requirements, is central to the architecture design techniques described in this book.

To measure or not to measure, that is the question.

In summary, the research community is almost unanimous in its conviction that software architecture describes something about the structure of the system and that it plays a vital role in determining the system's emergent properties. They are much less than unanimous on the questions of which elements should be included in the architecture, how to coordinate different collections of those elements (views), and how to evaluate the architecture against the external requirements.

There is a great deal of activity involving software architecture in the research community, but it has not produced very many firm recommendations for practice as yet. However, I will recommend and follow some practices. For example, I recommend that the subsystem structure, described with a boxes-and-channels notation, be defined as the architecture of the software system. I follow the practice that the subsystems will be defined in terms of physical implementation units and that all other views are subsumed by the collection of subsystems that make up the system. Explicit instances of build-time changes will be documented as part of the requirements and will be used to explicitly evaluate the architecture structure for extensibility and changeability.

For the banquet you're hosting, here's a recipe book, measuring cups, and an oven thermometer.

1.2.2 Architecture in Popular Methodologies

Many methodologies have been published in books and articles, but I would like to focus on the methodologies that are well known in the development community, that is, the popular methodologies. By a popular methodology, I mean one described in a book, whose author is well known to members of the development community, which is supported by one or more case tools. These methodologies for developing software are the most common and influential source that organizations turn to when trying to improve their process. Some of these methodologies will be examined in more detail in the next chapter, but for now, I would like to look at how software system architecture is treated in these methodologies.

The question of architecture's position in methodologies can be answered by looking at the main work products called for in each methodology and how much attention each gets in the descriptions of the methodology. The work products for several methods are shown in Table 1.1.

Table 1.1　Work products for several methodologies

Name	Structured A & D	RDD	Shlaer/Mellor	Objectory	Unified Method	OMT (original)
Reference	[YOR89]	[WIR90]	[SHL92]	[JAC92]	[BOO95]	[RUM91]
Work				Use cases	Use cases	Problem statement
	Entity-relationship	Hierarchy	Information model	Entity object model	Class diagram	Object model
Products	Dataflow	CRC cards	State model	Analysis object model	Message trace	Dataflow
	State transition	Class specification	Process description	Interaction diagram	Object message	State model
	Structure chart			State model	State mode	
	Processor model	Subsystem collaboration	Subsystem model	Subsystem structure	Module (file) diagram	
	Task model		Domain model		Platform diagram	

Methodologies are drywall and two-by-four oriented.

The allocation of emphasis in the methods can be summed up by saying that the primary emphasis in all the references is on the information and functional aspects of the system (the top five rows of work products). One or more large chapters are devoted to producing each of these work products. Subsystems (except in RDD) get a page or two. Allocation to hardware gets even less. There is very little guidance offered to help anyone actually design the subsystem structure of the system. The bottom line is that the structure of the system, as a physical product, gets very little attention in the most widely known software methodologies.

1.2.3 Software Architecture in Practice

I want to discuss two aspects of software architecture in the practice of developing software. One is the issue of definition, similar to the definition issues in research. The other is the practice of developing a subsystem structure for a system, whether or not it is called the architecture of the system, from the bottom up. Both issues hinder the development of effective architectures for software.

In the last year, or so, I have noticed a large increase in the use of the architecture words in conversations with clients and students and at conferences. There is widespread recognition that the architecture of a software system is very important in determining the properties of the system. The phrase *architectural approach* is used to describe almost every work product in the life cycle. When people refer to the software architecture, I often ask what they mean by architecture, or what picture they would draw. The answers are consistently vague. I have heard architecture variously defined as a collection of the regular design documents, as a set of rules for constructing the system, as the hardware the application runs on, and as the initial block diagram of the system.

Software gets built, but the final system is usually a surprise.

For the people and organizations I have encountered, the architectural situation is the same in practice as it is in the literature and in methodologies described previously; architecture is recognized as being important but there is little agreement on what architecture is.

1.2.4 Patterns and Bottom-up Architectures

The approach to developing an architecture that will be described in this book is a top-down approach. That is, we begin with the "ility" properties that the system is supposed to have, and shape the structure of the system to provide them. There is another approach that is well-established in practice: begin with small elements of the system and group them according to some internal criteria into larger structures. This is the bottom-up approach. There are two places where this approach is recommended. One is in software methodologies where it is the recommended technique for identifying subsystems. The other is in object-oriented programming practice. Here, groups of instances of classes are called patterns.

The technique described in Wirfs-Brock [WIR90] is representative of the bottom up approach to subsystem identification in methodologies. All of the objects from the behavior model are laid out in a single diagram, and all the connections for the required collaborations are shown. See Figure 1.2. Lines are drawn around groups of objects based on some internal criteria. Example criteria include grouping to minimize collaborations across the subsystem boundary and grouping by functional, data, or interface coupling. Subsystems identified in this manner are usually considered to be "logical groupings" of smaller components, rather than physical components of the system.

Figure 1.2
Collaboration
graph with
subsystem
nomination

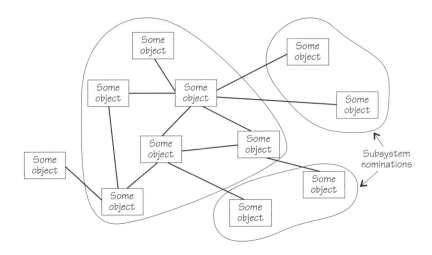

Patterns in object-oriented programming are very popular right now. They are also an example of a bottom-up approach to systems structure. A design pattern is defined in the book *Design Patterns* [GAM95] as being a problem, and its solution is described in terms of the elements that make up the design. Those elements are always instances and classes in object-oriented programming languages. They are identified by observing patterns of objects in existing programs. Patterns would be candidates for low level subsystems, but there is no effort made to enclose the pattern inside any boundary.

Everything must be built from the bottom up, but we don't have to design from the bottom up.

The bottom-up approach is certainly workable, but it makes it difficult to explicitly address the issues that can only be seen from the top. Of course, any subsystem nomination can be evaluated for its ability to satisfy any criteria, regardless of how it was derived. It is much easier to design the building and then arrange the bricks to make the building, than it is to arrange bricks and then see if the arrangement is a building. Likewise, it is easier to arrange the subsystem structure of a system to deliver the desired properties, than it is to group objects and then look to see if the resulting system has the desired properties.

1.2.5 What Now?

The position of software system architecture in the industry practice can be summed up with the following statement: it is important, but not very well defined. We are the blind men with no story teller to remind us that there is just one elephant. So, what are we to do? There are systems to build, needs to satisfy, and returns on investments to make. We need a definition of architecture that will help us design systems with the desired levels of portability, extensibility, and reuse.

I believe that a suitable definition can be given. Many good ideas have been proposed in the literature, and there are abundant sources of analogy with architectures of other kinds of products. If we recognize that we are trying to deliver certain properties in the finished product, and develop ways to measure those properties in our designs, we will have evaluation criteria for architecture definitions and for notations for specific architectures for a system. Notations and techniques that help deliver the properties are good; those that do not should be discarded. With evaluation criteria in hand, the problem of defining a software architecture becomes a matter of trial-and-error, or perhaps *cut-and-fit* would be a more positive way to put it.

Work backward from the goals to discover what software architecture should be.

1.3 QUESTIONS ABOUT SOFTWARE SYSTEM ARCHITECTURE

The questions before us are, which elements are included in the definition of a software architecture, what do we do with the elements of the system that are not included in the architecture, how do we evaluate alternative architectures, and what kind of notation should we use? All of these questions have been posed and answered in the literature on software architecture, but the difficulty arises from the fact that there have been many different answers given.

1.3.1 Basic Principles of (Software Design) Evaluation

Some basic principles to help guide our selection of the techniques would be helpful. I have formulated five principles that I have found to be useful in doing designs myself and in evaluating software methodologies. These principles will appear again in the next chapter with more explanation, but I would like to list them here because they will be helpful in formulating a definition of architecture.

Basic Principles

1   Document what the external goals are for each activity and measure the output of the activity against those goals.

2   Evaluate all engineering decisions against the goals those decisions are supposed to address.

3   Always evaluate the results of any engineering decision before those results are used in another decision.

4   Use run-time requirements to evaluate behavior and information. Use build-time requirements to evaluate allocation of that behavior, the structures, and architecture of the system.

5   All items that are to be evaluated together must be visible at the same time in the design documentation.

1.3.2 Which Elements to Include?

In various places in the literature, almost every construct in the software development life cycle has been nominated as a constituent of the software system architecture. The situation is similar to that in the story of the six blind men and the elephant. Each has a separate view of the elephant. Each view is valid, but the elephant is more than the sum of its views. There is one physical entity that is the elephant, which includes all the specialized views. Saying that the architecture of a software system is all of the current, specialized views is like saying that the elephant is merely the sum of its views: there must be something that represents the single physical entity that is the system.

The big properties should be designed while looking at the big picture.

We can turn to the issues that need to be addressed for guidance as to what to include in the definition. Accounting for the information and behavior content of the system is already addressed in the information, object, and behavior modeling techniques that are a prominent part of most methodologies and of actual practice. The properties that are not well addressed are things like extensibility, maintainability, and reuse. These "ility" properties are determined by the collective properties and behaviors of the whole system, from edge to edge. The "ility" properties emerge from the entire system. If the architecture of a system is to describe the whole thing, then our software architecture should include the whole system, including the edges.

The architecture should account for the "ility" properties. These properties, like extensibility, maintainability and reuse, are not visible when the system is running, but become visible when the system is down and the hood is opened. They are build-time properties of the system. If the architecture is to allow us to address these issues, it should include the build-time components of the system. The ultimate form of reuse is to assemble systems from "reusable" components, so the elements of the architecture should be those reusable components. Something that can be "plugged into" a system should be a physical thing that can sit on the shelf, that can be sold and installed.

This line of reasoning has led me to nominate the physical units of implementation as the elements of the software system architecture. By definition, a system is composed of subsystems, so the elements of the architecture are subsystems. The physical elements of the construction view of a software system are units of hardware and software that are "bigger" than elements of programming language. They have complete enclosures. In fact, the physical elements that make up software systems already exist. They include clusters of LAN systems, client-server systems connected by a LAN, computer boxes, boards, processors, memory boundaries of heavyweight tasks, asynchronous enclosures such as threads, and synchronous enclosures such as OLE, OpenDoc, and DLLs. All of these elements, except the threads, have the common and desirable properties of a complete enclosure and a specified interface that may hide its internals from all users of the element.

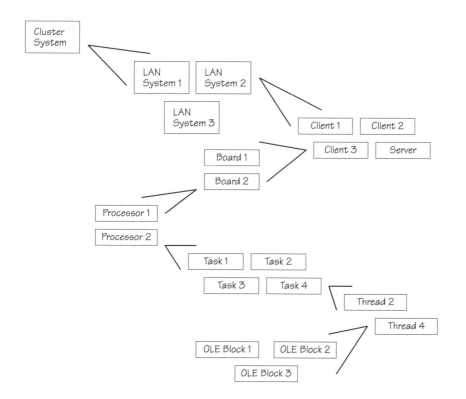

Figure 1.3

Contained-in relationships of implementation components

Our software system elephant contains all of the parts and views that anyone can see or use.

As Figure 1.3 shows, the elements of the software system architecture are arranged in a hierarchy of *contains* relationships. The contains relationship among the physical components of the hierarchy is quite strict in that a processor, for example, is completely contained within its board. There is never any suggestion that a processor can be "distributed" between more than one board. The software subsystems that are contained in each hardware subsystem have the same contained-in relationship.

Software is chunked by its hardware containers.

Some of these architecture elements are clearly elements of hardware. Some of them are clearly software components. I can state, without fear of invoking controversy, that the hardware elements are part of the hardware architecture of the system. The software elements, from heavyweight task down, are not part of the hardware architecture, and labeling them as part of the software system architecture is not common. The assertion that I am making is that each instance of each level of implementation enclosure defines the boundary of an element of the software system architecture.

Figure 1.4
**Software
loads inside
the imple-
mentation
components**

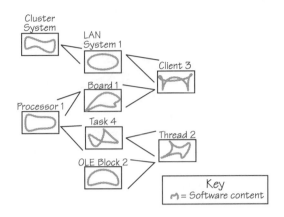

Why should this be so? Because each of the elements in the architecture hierarchy has a software load that must be installed in it before that element can do anything, and the installed software cannot cross the implementation enclosure boundary. This connection of the hardware and software implementation enclosures to the elements of a software system architecture is valid because there is a strict containment relationship between each implementation enclosure and the software that animates it. If we consider software to mean a unit of executable code, then a single piece of software cannot exist outside a single memory space, or any other boundary that restricts access by anything outside the boundary. A piece of software can no more be "distributed" across, say processor boundaries, than a chip can be "distributed" across board boundaries. Thus, terms like *distributed data, distributed objects,* or *distributed software* may accurately describe the functional view of a system, but they cannot be applied to the physical implementation or to the architecture of the software system. Each implementation enclosure has a boundary that must be explicitly recognized by the software contained in the enclosure. Therefore, the physical building blocks of any software system architecture are necessarily the same as the physical implementation enclosures. The hierarchy of software architecture elements exactly matches the hierarchy of implementation enclosures, as shown in Figure 1.4.

This definition of software system architecture is only a slight extension of existing usage. It is common to define the software architecture to be the collection of subsystems that make up the system. The extension offered here is to associate each software subsystem with a physical implementation subsystem.

Two more elements are needed in the architecture specification before it can play the role we have assigned to it. They are the connections between subsystems and the edge of the system. Connections between subsystems are a part of many of the definitions of software architecture. Indeed, reuse and plugging subsystems together require that all parties agree on the connections. That agreement must include everything about the connection, from its physical media to the logical form and content of the things that are exchanged over the connection. This need for connections makes the choice of representation easy; the boxes-inside-boxes notation does not show connections.

The edge of software systems is a somewhat neglected topic in software system descriptions. Rechtin said in *Systems Architecting* [REC91] that, "the greatest leverage in system architecting is at the interfaces." As we will see in the Chapter 2, most of the utilities and infrastructure components connect the application-level components to the outside world. That connection crosses the system or subsystem boundary. Having the boundaries appear explicitly in the architectural notation provides a place to put the utilities. It also provides a way to show everything in the architecture diagram without showing all the detail. The bottom line is that the boundary should appear in all software architecture diagrams.

1.3.3 Which Notation Should Be Used for Software Architecture?

Basic Principle 5 suggests that a sufficient notation is one that enables the necessary evaluations to be made. Of the two notations commonly used to describe systems, subsystems, boxes-inside-boxes, and box-and-channel, the box-and-channel notation is the clear winner. Being able to see the channels is essential to evaluating the impact of a change case on the system and to defining reusable components and architectures. If we include a boundary on the box-and-channel diagrams, then the interfaces to the outside world will be explicitly visible.

A software system architecture diagram shows the system boundary, the subsystems that make up the system, and the channels that join the subsystems and connect subsystems to the boundary. If the architecture is supposed to show "everything," then how do we handle the hierarchy of components? I will offer the same answer that is used in describing the architecture of hard products: a single architecture diagram shows only a single level of the component hierarchy. A few small examples are shown in Figure 1.5.

One picture is worth a million lines of code.

1.3.4 What Do We Do With the Other Elements?

The drywall and the 2 x 4s are all part of the house.

The elements of the architecture are the physical components from which a software system is built. All of the other components and views are contained in, or are provided by, the set of subsystems that compose the system. The other elements and views, such as dataflow, (function) structure charts, object models, timing, scheduling, and the rest, have the same relationship to the software architecture that structural steel, plumbing, heating, electrical, and human traffic flow have to a building architecture. The form and shape of the building, as defined in its architecture diagrams, provides for all the other views. Indeed, the architecture specification

Figure 1.5
Hierarchy of
architecture
diagrams

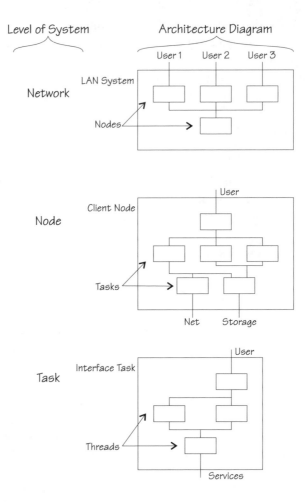

of a building, or of a software system, is the elephant. It is the one, physical thing that provides for all the views that anyone can have of that thing. In the techniques described in this book, the elements designed in the other views, such as those focusing on information or behavior, will be explicitly allocated to the subsystems that make up the system architecture.

1.3.5 How Do We Evaluate Alternative Architectures?

The answer to the question about how to evaluate software architectures is that they should be measured on their ability to satisfy the external requirements that emerge from the system as a whole. In particular, architectures should be evaluated on their ability to satisfy the build-time requirements of the system.

I have formulated the basic principles to help answer the question of evaluation. The principles remind us that we should have explicit goals for each work product, and that we should evaluate each work product, including the architecture diagrams, against goals for that work product. The architecture diagram represents the physical structure of the entire system. Principle 4 indicates that we should use build-time requirements to evaluate that structure. Those build-time requirements should be stated as specific instances of growth and change that the system should support, which I will call *change cases* in the next chapter. If we can demonstrate that a given architecture can support the change cases better than any alternative structures we can think of, then that architecture is sufficient.

The measure of an architecture design is how well it provides the big "ilities."

There are several run-time attributes of a system that do not manifest themselves until all of the subsystems that make up the system are working together. These attributes include reliability, performance, throughput, and availability. The architecture should be evaluated against the specific levels of each of those run-time "ilities" (the other half of Principle 4). That is easier said than done. The process of evaluating a system for reliability and performance is a large task, often involving large simulations or trials on working systems.

The preceding discussion functions as a rationale for why I have chosen the particular definition of software architecture that I use in my practice and describe in this book. I have examined the question of what to include as elements in the software system architecture. Guided by the five basic principles, I have shown the importance of including subsystems with boundaries, the system boundary, and the channels that connect subsystems to each other and to the system boundary (indicated using a box-and-channel notation). The software subsystems of each system have the same, strict "contained-in" relationship that hardware subsystems have with their system. I have also looked at evaluation, pointing out how to measure a system architecture to determine if the "ility" properties are really present. I now turn to a detailed discussion of the definition itself.

1.4 A DEFINITION OF SOFTWARE SYSTEM ARCHITECTURE

This definition of software architecture is based on the definition of architectures of conventional products. Because of that analogy, the software architecture can play the same role in developing the software product that architecture plays in conventional products: it is the medium we use for looking at and handling the product. Here is the definition:

> A software architecture specifies a set of implementation units and a way to connect them, such that when those units are created and connected as per the specification, the system will run.

More specifically, an architecture specification always consists of the following elements:

- A physical border or boundary
- Ports or connections that cross that boundary
- Fixed and stable subsystems that compose the system
- Communication channels that connect the subsystems

1.4.1 Notation

The forms and shapes of the software house.

I have selected the box-and-channel notation for the architecture because of its ability to support the evaluations. I first encountered box-and-channel notation in Mascot [MAS87]. A very similar notation is used in the ROOM method and tool [SEL94]. Similar notations were used by Vickers [VIC95] and Magee [MAG95]. The Mascot notation consists of subsystems with named ports and windows that are defined in terms of the channel types they provide or require. The enclosure is complete; both send and receive ends of the channels are part of the subsystem specification, and the channels themselves are named and typed separately as parts of the architecture specification. Figure 1.6 shows a sample Mascot box-and-channel specification.

Figure 1.6
Mascot diagram with key to notation

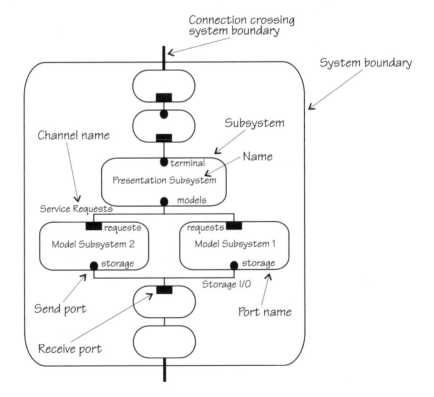

HARD STRUCTURE FOR SOFTWARE | CHAPTER 1

This notation is sufficient for describing the structures of complete software systems and for evaluating those structures against the build-time requirements. It is sufficient for informal evaluations of the overall run-time behavior of the system. More detailed evaluations of run-time emergent properties, such as performance and reliability, require more specialized views.

The floor plans, elevations and perspective renderings of the software house.

1.4.2 Tangibility

The definition of software architecture requires that the subsystems be fixed during operation of the system. That is, they are created when the system starts up and they exist for as long as the system runs. Indeed, they are the system. If one of the subsystems is removed, the system will either break or it will be a different system. This definition provides important benefits. It makes the diagram of the system exactly match the implementation of the system. It makes the software architecture analogous to structures of other hard products.

Architectures of other hard products are specified in terms of fixed implementation units. For example, in a building architecture, the walls, floors, and roof are part of the architecture. People, furniture, and equipment that the building must support are not shown in the architecture specification because they are not part of the structure. The reason for putting the building up in the first place is to house and support the people, furniture, and equipment, but these transients are not part of the architecture. The architecture drawings and specifications of the building describe what gets built and what will be available to support the transient things that use the building.

A software architecture defined in terms of fixed subsystems brings the same tangibility to software that buildings enjoy. The distinction between what is "fixed" and what is "transient" is based on what must be put in the system, or installed, in order for it to run. This is not to say that the transient things in software systems are not important or that they do not have to be designed and implemented. They do. They are just not part of the system architecture. In software, the transient elements are described in the system state and behavior models.

It is very hard to nail jelly to anything.

1.5 USING THE ARCHITECTURE IN THE SOFTWARE LIFE CYCLE

At this point we have an architecture defined in terms of subsystems enclosed in various kinds of implementation components. Now, what can we do with it? There are four places in the software life cycle where this type of architecture definition is useful. The architecture plays a role in: 1) addressing the emergent properties of the system, 2) viewing, 3) reusing components, and 4) allocating development assignments to different groups. The architecture diagram should also be the basis for estimating the size and cost of the system. That, however, is a problem for another day.

1.5.1 Addressing the Emergent Properties of the System

An edge-to-edge view of the system, including the edges, is an essential prerequisite to designing in properties that emerge from the entire system. I have said this before, but it bears repeating. The build-time properties of extensibility, maintainability, configurability, and reusability all depend on how the entire system is partitioned and connected. The architecture view proposed here provides that edge-to-edge scope. We will see in the chapter on doing architecture, how to design and evaluate those properties.

The run-time properties like performance and reliability also require an edge-to-edge view of the system. Designing and evaluating for those properties require more information than is provided in the architecture diagram proposed here.

Developing systems with good "ilities" is necessarily a top-down process. The structures of systems designed to be extensible and reliable will be profoundly different from structures of systems designed to be, say, small and fast. The structural implications will impact every aspect and level of the system, so that drilling down to code before defining a system architecture that will provide the desired emergent properties in the system, is wasting time and money.

1.5.2 Viewing the System

When the question is "What does the system look like?" or "How big is the system?" the answer is provided by the architecture diagram. It should account for or have room for, all of the services and utilities that make up the system. The architecture is an appropriate medium for managers to use in viewing and managing the system development.

1.5.3 Reuse

Since this book is concerned with the engineering design of systems, we will focus on the technical issues around reuse. Appropriate architecture is a key link in the chain that leads to effective reuse, but it is not the whole chain.

In order for a component to be reused in more than one system, two criteria must be met. The first is that the same communication interface for the component must be used in each of the possible sites of reuse. The second is that the behavior allocation used to define the component must also be used in all sites of reuse. I will offer an example of these two requirements being met in the domain of home audio components.

If you wanted to design and sell a speaker that could be "reused" in everyone's audio system, you would need to have a constant interface and consistent behavior allocation in all home audio systems. These criteria are met because all audio systems use a low-voltage, analog, electrical signal in a two-wire medium. Behavior allocation is consistent because all audio system manufacturers have agreed that speakers will house only the voltage-to-sound transducer and nothing else. If some manufacturers had decided to use a frequency modulated signal on a coax cable as the interface, or if some manufacturers had decided to put the power amplifier in their left speaker, attempts to "reuse" your speakers on those systems would fail.

Assuming we are interested in reusing more than one component, these two criteria lead to a very important conclusion: having consistent interfaces and consistent behavior allocation across multiple systems requires consistent system architectures, as defined here. I believe that there will be no widespread reuse until architectures of systems are explicitly stated in terms of components and their interfaces, and the architectures of systems reusing the components have the same form.

The architecture notation proposed here is a good basis for design for reuse, but it is not the reuse solution. The type of subsystem proposed here, with complete enclosures and all channels that cross the enclosure explicitly identified, is an essential prerequisite for effective reuse of software components. The fact that the subsystems have a physical implementation as part of their specification makes buying a component off the shelf possible, but it is important that the system structure be described using the same notation and conventions used in describing the components that are to be reused. Having the system architecture defined in terms of physical implementation components enables the architect to explicitly use allocations and interfaces that will be compatible with the components available for reuse. Design for reuse is not a single project activity. As will be seen in the next chapter, design for reuse is two levels up the process hierarchy from the techniques described here.

Reuse needs physical components with visible interfaces: chips with pinouts.

1.5.4 Implementation Assignments and System Integration

The elements of the architecture are enclosed boxes with well defined and explicit interfaces. If we can assume—or better, demonstrate—that the components and their interfaces are good, then the elements of the architecture would make ideal units of work assignment, testing, and integration. As long as each development group adheres to the interface design for the boxes they work on, integration of boxes developed by different groups should look like plugging Legos™ together. The subsystem specification should also provide adequate input to the process of designing and developing test harnesses.

These four benefits, of getting help with emergent properties, visibility, reuse, and development assignments, do not come as a free lunch. Once again, there are implications for process and sequence. Having firm components and interfaces before parallel development assignments are made implies that enough engineering work was done on the system as a whole to arrive at those good components and interfaces before making the assignments. This means a fairly complete pass through the essential tasks. How much completeness and rigor is required depends on the cost of having an error in the subsystem specifications. If the cost is high, larger initial engineering efforts can be justified.

This approach requires a top-down, multipass approach to the design. The early passes develop the architecture in enough detail to allow effective increments to be proposed. Subsequent passes design for the specific increments. Incremental development is a very powerful technique for avoiding the risks of the all-or-nothing delivery of big systems. Subsystems of the system architecture are the appropriate elements of the increments. The specific increments should be added to the list of change cases that the system is to support and the system architecture should be "designed to be incremented" (more on change cases in the next chapter).

1.6 SUMMARY

We have seen that in the software industry, software architecture is considered to be important, but there is no widely accepted definition of what it is, or which elements comprise an architecture. The aspects of architecture that people agree on are that it is associated with the structure of the system, it is considered to be very important in establishing the big "ilities" of the system, and that there are many questions about the details of what a software architecture really is. The approach to architecture taken here is based on the idea that there is only one physical system being built. No matter how many views people have found in the literature and practice, there is only one elephant.

From the many suggestions of what constitutes a software system architecture, I have selected a set of elements that makes the definition of software architecture analogous with the definition of architecture of hard products. The definition is that the architecture consists of the subsystems that populate the system, the boundary that encloses the system, and the channels that connect the subsystems and cross the boundary. These subsystems are implemented in existing hardware and software implementation components. Like hard products, the elements of the architecture in this definition are the fixed, static structure of the product, and only a single level of subsystem is shown in any one diagram.

We can treat software like houses and computer hardware.

This definition satisfies many of the goals set for a software system architecture. It facilitates the design of emergent properties for the system because the structure of the entire system is visible. The fact that the elements of the architecture are static and have a physical component implementation makes the system visible and tangible to people other than those who write the code. Defining subsystems as enclosures with explicit communication channels provides a basis for standardizing interfaces and behavior allocation to enable systematic component reuse across multiple systems.

Designing emergent properties into a system imposes a constraint on the process of developing the design. There are two reasons for this. One reason is that decisions about system structure that support extensibility must be made at the big-picture level of the system, that is, at the level of the system architecture. The other is that decisions about architectural structure impact everything that follows. The constraint is that the system architecture should be developed before any detailed development work is done. In other words, know how tall the building will be before you start designing elevators.

The system architecture is the final output of the system engineering process. This chapter has described a representation of that architecture and some of the requirements that can be addressed at the system-architecture level. There are other views of the system that address other requirements and the output of that work is needed as input to the architecture design. The essential tasks needed to get from a statement of those requirements to the system architecture are the subject of the next chapter.

CHAPTER 2

Essential Tasks in the Development Process

CONTENTS

2.1 Introduction   25
2.2 Basic Principles of Evaluation   26
2.3 Essential Tasks   29
2.4 Essential Tasks in the Larger Process   31
2.5 Current Development Processes   31
2.6 A Proposal for a Software Development Process   34
2.7 Defining Essential Tasks   38
2.8 The Architecture Task Chunk   43
2.9 Summary   44

2.1 INTRODUCTION

Software is an industry. Education is available for the skills needed to develop and use software, people have software jobs that pay salaries, companies and departments exist solely to develop software systems, investments are made in software activities, and returns on those investments (ROIs) are calculated and anticipated. When the properties of the products do not match the expectations and needs of the stakeholders, or when the economics do not provide the anticipated ROI, people often look to process changes to improve things. In this broad outline, the software industry looks just like an industry that makes hard products like airplanes, cars, chemical plants, or computer hardware.

Unlike the hard industries, the software industry has not shown the kinds of improvements that process supervisors expected. Product quality on average has remained variable, if not low. Development productivity has risen, but not at the rate one might expect in an industry whose main products are used to automate most other industries. The needs of the industry have been accurately recognized and articulated in the advertisements for software development products for a long time; higher quality software, shorter time to market, and easier maintenance. Those same ads promise that if you just buy this box, your problems will be over, whether the box holds a language compiler, a debugger, a development environment, a CASE tool, a configuration manager, or a project manager.

There has been a succession of tools and techniques that each have enjoyed a brief time as the current hot solution. When it becomes apparent that the current hot solution is not delivering on the promises, a new solution is selected to replace it. The succession began with programming languages, from assembly through object-oriented languages, then came design methodologies presented in books and, one hopes, supported by CASE tools. All of these solutions in boxes have proved to be insufficient by themselves. As I write this, the search for the next solution is turning toward something that does not come in a box: process and organization discipline. It is an open question, whether given the current practices in software development, improvements in process and discipline alone will be sufficient.

Software development is a big place, here's a map.

The problem is that without measures, no amount of process discipline can deliver the desired results. As I discussed in the Introduction, the first attempts at developing "reusable" parts for guns failed for 50 years because there were no gauges to make measurements of the parts as they were machined. Manufacturing a hard product like guns to have reusable parts requires gauges to measure the product to see if it meets its requirements. Of course, the presence of gauges without the process discipline cannot deliver the results, either. So, to get off to a good start, this discussion of development processes and the Essential Tasks will open with a description of the Basic Principles of Evaluation. These principles serve to define the gauges for software design documents.

2.2 BASIC PRINCIPLES OF EVALUATION

The tasks and work products used in engineering a software system must explicitly account for every property of the system, build-time and run-time, that we wish to have expressed in the final product. Brad Cox's observation on measurement tools seemed to indicate that it was important to measure for those properties in the design documents. Looking for ways to do those measurements led to the formulation of these principles. They have proven to be useful in guiding my practice of software design. In fact, they are so useful that I have given them a name and their own section in the book: The Basic Principles of Evaluation. I will describe each of them here with a brief rationale. I will refer to them throughout the descriptions of the Essential Tasks.

Principle 1: *Document what the external goals are for each activity, and measure the output of the activity against those goals.*

Activity, here, refers to any goal-directed behavior, in particular to behaviors in software system development that deliver some design document work product. Doing diagrams just because they are called for in the methodology is like cutting boards without a plan.

Know where you are trying to go.

Principle 2: *Evaluate all engineering decisions against the goals those decisions are supposed to address.*

Evaluating engineering decisions against goals is very important for current software development practice, where system design is often labeled, "modeling the real world" or "modeling the requirements." Modeling or building a model of something, is very different from engineering that something. The thing that meets the requirements is different from the requirements. There are always millions of ways to design anything. Even if there is a detailed cookbook for carrying out the design, it is always possible that an error could be made. Developing a software system to meet some requirements is truly an engineering activity, with even more room for variation than in processes for developing other hard products. It is critical, then, that decisions made by the engineer be identified as engineering decisions and that they be evaluated to demonstrate that they did, in fact, effectively address the requirement.

Make sure each step is moving toward the destination.

Principle 3: *Always evaluate the results of any engineering decision before those results are used in another decision.*

We should demonstrate that each decision was good before committing the rest of the system to use the results. We do this because there are strong dependencies between design decisions. For example, the decision to have four wheels on a car impacts many other aspects of the design, such as power train and steering, the maximum size of the vehicle and how passengers and subsystems will be placed. A corresponding decision in the structured analysis methodology is decomposing the context diagram into the first set of 7 ± 2 functions. That decision has important implications for the modularity and extensibility of the system. It also places important constraints on all the subsequent decomposition decisions. The quality of that first decomposition decision limits modularity that can be designed into the system in subsequent decisions. If the decision was good, then the modularity potential of the system will be high. Later decisions can only maintain the potential or diminish it. If the decision was not good, the potential for modularity will be low. Later decisions cannot improve the modularity beyond the limits established by the earlier

Make sure the turn was in the right direction before taking the new course.

decisions. Unfortunately, in structured analysis, the first evaluations occur only after many decomposition decisions have been made.

Another example of a chain of unevaluated decisions occurs in object-oriented analysis. Objects are identified in the object model, their attributes and relationships are assigned, and sometimes behavior is identified and allocated to the objects. These are very important decisions that affect the ability of the system to deliver the required run-time behavior and constrain the build-time extensibility and maintainability of the system. The object-identity decisions are then used as input to another important structural decision, that of how to arrange the objects in a class inheritance hierarchy. If the first decisions about the structure of the objects were good, then decisions about inheritance can maintain the extensibility potential established in the first allocation. If the initial decisions about the structure of the objects implemented spaghetti, no amount of tinkering with inheritance will turn it into ravioli.

This principle was designed to make the quality of these engineering decisions visible at a time when they can be easily changed, which would be a worthwhile result in itself. In addition, Principle 3 can have a larger impact. That impact is to constrain any single application of the software design process to a range of only two levels of implementation components on the parts hierarchy: the target component and one level of subsystem. The reason is that the evaluation for the emergent properties of the system can only take place when the whole system is visible, that is, in the architecture diagrams (see Principle 5). As we will see when the Essential Tasks are described, the architecture is at the end of the information dependencies. Many of the earlier decisions can affect the emergent properties. If we follow Principle 3, we would make all of the decisions needed to describe the architecture of a system with a single level of subsystem. Only then could those decisions be fully evaluated for their impact on the emergent properties. Further decomposition would take place after we have satisfied ourselves that the emergent properties are still intact. If the design is carried out at a single level, it is a small step to do the implementation at that single level. With that small step we will have arrived at the same process and product structure that electronic hardware uses. An amazing result!

Principle 4: *Use run-time, or user requirements to evaluate presence and sufficiency of behavior and information. Use build-time or development-sponsor requirements to evaluate allocation of that behavior, the structures, and architecture of the system.*

Only plumbers and electricians appreciate a regular internal structure.

This principle grew out of the observation that the run-time functional requirements impose almost no constraints on the structure of the system. The run-time requirements constrain only the presence and sufficiency of function and state in the system. This is very important. The reason the system is being built is to satisfy the run-time requirements. However, almost any level of modularity, from spaghetti to ravioli, designed with a CASE tool or translated directly to code from the

ESSENTIAL TASKS IN THE DEVELOPMENT PROCESS | CHAPTER 2

requirements by the programmer, can provide a given set of run-time requirements. It is only at build-time, when a change made in one place results in bugs appearing in five other places, that the structure and allocation become important. If alternative structures are to be objectively evaluated, then it is important to have explicit build-time requirements, which I will call change cases in the next section, to evaluate relative merits of the two structures.

Principle 5: *All items that are to be evaluated together must be visible at the same time in the design documentation.*

The most economical time to catch errors and to design in emergent properties of a system is when the design is still on paper or its digital equivalent. The first four Basic Principles stressed the need for evaluation of design *decisions*. The fifth principle provides a way to evaluate design *notations*. Notations are sufficient if they fully enable the evaluations called for in the first four Basic Principles. For example, in the previous chapter, two architecture notations were mentioned: boxes-inside-boxes and boxes-and-channels. The boxes-inside-boxes notation does not show the channels, which are important for the evaluation of modularity. So, Principle 5 could be invoked to use the boxes-and-channels notation for architecture diagrams. The benefit of making good engineering decisions is reduced if the results of those decisions are not visible to reviewers of the design.

These principles, when combined with the tasks described next, provide the structure for the task descriptions and instructions in the following chapters.

2.3 ESSENTIAL TASKS

Think about the set of attributes and properties that we wish to see in any software system. They are the same for all types of software. A representative list of properties of a running system includes utility, usability, correctness, reliability, safety, and performance. The desirable properties of the system during build-time and its development process include the properties of incremental development, ease of extension, testability, visibility, tangibility, predictability, and manageability. All of these properties manifest themselves to some degree in every software system regardless of how its design is documented or what language it is written in. There are some basic truths about the properties of any large system, hard or soft, that should guide our actions. They are:

The Essential Tasks are the foundation of software development processes.

1 Properties that are not explicit design goals will not manifest themselves in the system.

2 The later in the development life a problem is discovered the more expensive it is to fix.

3 Emergent properties, those that depend on the entire system for their manifestation, cannot be "added in" to a system that does not manifest them.

The observation that all software systems have the same set of desirable properties implies that if we associate the activities in a development practice to the properties being addressed by the activities, then all practices and methodologies should have the same set of activities. There may be hope for unifying methodologies. This hope is diminished when we recognize that developing real systems is a complicated affair. It will always involve iterations, rework, phases, and increments. If methodologies describe a project or practice, then they should include something of the iterations and increments, which will make it harder to unify them.

The three "basic truths" about system development lead to an imperative to design in the properties and requirements while the structure of the entire system is still fluid. Both hard systems and software systems are fluid only while they are they are on paper. As soon as any significant part of the system is implemented in code or metal, the emergent properties of the system are fixed. They cannot be changed or improved without changing the basic structure of the system, and thus redoing most of the implementation work.

Cut and try on paper is vastly cheaper than cut and try in code.

Two results flow from this observation. The first is that we should have an explicit place, or places, in the design documents where each of the properties and requirements are addressed. The second is that any development practices that implement a part of the system structure without accounting for all of desired system properties should be avoided. I am not suggesting that the dreaded waterfall process be used, or that everything must be completely designed before any coding can begin. I am suggesting that the large-scale structure of the system and the emergent properties should get more attention at the beginning of each phase or iteration than is commonly the case.

The engineering issues are the same for all software systems.

The preceding discussion suggests that common and essential activities must be concerned with addressing the requirements and properties a system is to display and that they cannot address process and sequence of application. How a system will meet its requirements and manifest the properties should be visible in the design documents. The Essential Tasks, then, are those that produce those design documents.

Since there are many ways to document a given decision, the Essential Tasks are associated with categories of documents, rather than a specific notation. Each category addresses a specific set of concerns and properties. In each category, several styles of notation may be appropriate. Within a specific style of notation, there should be variations in formality of the notations available. Informal, back-of-the-envelope notations are just as important to the success of a system as the formal, verifiable notations used for documenting safety critical aspects of production systems.

2.4 ESSENTIAL TASKS IN THE LARGER PROCESS

I would like to describe a process universe for software products to provide a context for the Essential Tasks. It is important to provide this context here so that no one will leave with the impression that the Essential Tasks are all that is needed to deliver successful software products. I also want to offer some positive suggestions about what is needed to deliver those wonderful software products. To accomplish these ends, I will look briefly at current practices in both software and the electronic hardware industries, and then describe a hierarchy of processes for developing software products. At the bottom of that hierarchy are groups of tasks that engineer a software system. The collective purpose of these tasks, taken together, is to "design in" the properties and behaviors that the system is required to provide. These are the Essential Tasks.

The Essential Tasks are the foundation of software development processes.

2.5 CURRENT DEVELOPMENT PROCESSES

In the previous chapter, I described a hierarchy of software system architecture components that were enclosed in boundaries provided by hardware and software implementation components, Figures 1.3 and 1.4. The components at each level differ in many ways from each other and could reasonably be designed and developed by separate processes. It is interesting to compare the processes used to produce hard products, like electronic hardware, with the processes used to produce software.

2.5.1 Current Software Development Processes

If we look at the practices that populate the development processes in many software organizations, we see a wide spectrum in the formality, effectiveness, and maturity. These practices range from the rigor and formality of software development at NASA to the "leave the spec on my voice mail and I'll code it tomorrow" style of development. In a survey of development process maturities [HUM89], 85% of the organizations in the USA were found to be at level 1 of their process maturity index. This means that the vast majority of software development organizations use practices that are clustered at the informal end of the spectrum. Without effective design documentation, the first time an organization can "see" the system to evaluate it is when there is executable code.

When we look at the product and subproduct structure of the software industry, we see only two levels of products. One is tools and utilities, such as operating systems, compilers, and databases. The other is applications or systems. Members of the latter group are often very large, such as the air-traffic control system, or the baggage-handling system at the Denver airport. Having only two levels of the system,

The map should show the road you want to take.

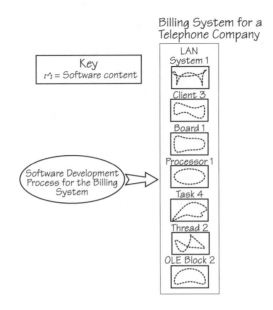

with one level having very large members is a contributor to many of the well-publicized problems with software development, particularly the perception that software is "intrinsically" more complex than hard products, see Figure 2.1. The people who conduct the application development process usually deal with components from the programming language level (functions and objects) up to collections of computers (as in client/server systems). Other problems aggravated by including many levels in a single process include low and variable quality, difficulty of reuse, low productivity growth, high expense of maintaining existing systems, and long times to market.

Single software projects address many levels of subsystem.

How can we make it better? There are two things we can do to improve the situation. The first is to develop the measurement tools, gauges, to measure how well a workproduct meets its goals. The Basic Principles of Evaluation were formulated to encourage effective evaluation of software design work products. The second is to separate software products into more levels and provide a separate process for each level. A model for this sort of process and product structure is available in the electronic hardware industry.

2.5.2 Current Hardware Development Processes

On the hardware side, the relationship between levels of component and development processes is different: each component has its own process. The result is that a single product, or system, is developed using just one level of subcomponent. In the process that develops the product, the needs for the system are determined, a system is designed to meet those needs utilizing whatever components are available from

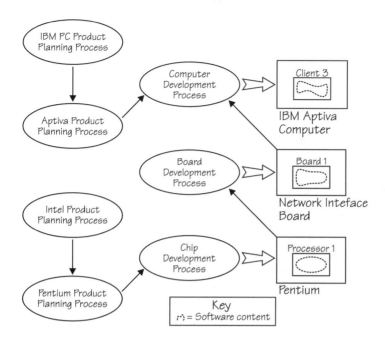

Figure 2.2
A software development process and the implementation enclosures it handles

the next lower level, and lastly, the system is built. If components are not available, a requirement for the needed component is developed and the process to produce the component is invoked. It works the other way, too. If the lower level processes come up with a hot new product, the designers that use that product as a component will alter their designs to take advantage of it. The obvious example is new chip development. There is, therefore, a contained-in hierarchy of processes that matches the contained-in hierarchy of product components.

The statement in the previous paragraph about lower level process coming up with a hot new chip has some process implications. In addition to processes for developing specific chips or boards, someone in a chip development organization is looking across multiple board products to determine what kinds of chips would be most useful—are *reusable* in software terms—to board developers. Designs of entire product lines of chips are coordinated to ensure that the chips work together and that they meet the needs of many developers of board-level products. Reuse in the hardware industry does not happen by accident. It is the result of conscientious and consistent design decisions that are applied across many individual chip and board products.

Another interesting aspect of hardware development processes is that the life cycle of individual products is well planned. When a new version of a chip is released, the next version is already in sampling and the following version is in prototyping. Someone in the organization is planning the product life cycle very carefully. Figure 2.2 shows some aspects of the hardware development processes.

The term *system* is quite relative. The chip developer's system is the board designer's subsystem. Each process and the people who conduct the process, have to deal only with two levels of components. Having to deal with only two levels of components at a time contributes to the manageability of electronic hardware development. This restriction of scope also allows the summed complexity of all the subsystems in a system to exceed that which any single process could handle.

What would software look like if it was developed using a similar process model and a similar product structure?

2.6 A PROPOSAL FOR A SOFTWARE DEVELOPMENT PROCESS

The same features that have helped the hardware industry address the issues of rapidly changing technology, growing complexity, and demands for high quality can be used in the software industry. While this book is about techniques useful near the bottom of the process hierarchy, I would like to sketch out what the whole hierarchy might look like. I will describe the process from the top down. When I get to the bottom, I will introduce the Essential Tasks.

A naming problem.
In talking about how the Essential Tasks fit into the hierarchy of processes, I have some difficulty is selecting words that will have a predictable meaning to readers of this book. The words *project, task, activity, phase,* and *technique* are commonly used to describe elements of software processes. The words are commonly arranged in some hierarchy, as in, a *project* is a sequence of *activities* that use one or more *techniques*. The difficulty is that how the words are arranged in the hierarchy varies widely among individuals. To facilitate this discussion, I would like to introduce a generic term for any goal-directed activity: *chunk*. A process at any level will be described in terms of its chunks. The content of the chunks at each level will be described.

We will begin our overview of a process for hard software products at the top and work our way down.

2.6.1 Cross Product Processes

Reuse is not an accident.
If reuse, interoperation between products, or consistency across products are serious goals in a software development organization, then a process should be implemented to deliver those goals. That is the cross-product level. Here, the requirements and architectures of multiple products are examined. Common features, structures, and architectures are developed, perhaps tried out and then introduced into the individual products. At this level, the chunks are the design studies carried out to define common architectures and the product life cycles of the individual products (Figure 2.3).

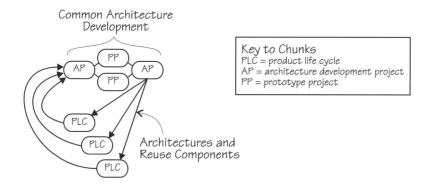

Figure 2.3

Cross
product
development
process
chunks

Common Architecture
Development

Key to Chunks
PLC = product life cycle
AP = architecture development project
PP = prototype project

Architectures and
Reuse Components

2.6.2 Product Life Cycle Processes

An individual product is propelled through its life cycle by a series of projects. Each project introduces some change to the product. A normal product life cycle might begin with a bright idea, be examined with a design study project and a few prototype projects, and then move to its first release with an informal development project. The product might grow with subsequent enhancement projects, and then be rewritten in a more formal project. New additions to the product are developed with their own development cycles. The chunks of the product level process are projects. This sequence of projects should be planned and designed as carefully as any individual project. Figure 2.4 shows a product life cycle consisting of project chunks.

Products have a life defined by projects.

Evaluations at the Product Level

The Basic Principles of Evaluation will be applied to each of the Essential Tasks in the engineering process. The justification for this was that measuring for specific, desired properties in the intermediate work products was the best way to ensure that the desired properties could be manifest in the final work product: the system running in the field. I used the word *could* because having a property designed in a design document is not the same as having it in the actual system.

Measurements of the products are important.

The Basic Principles of Evaluation can also be applied to the entire development process. The work product being evaluated is the software system, itself. Measuring the quality of the product and using the results to improve the process is the basis of the continuous improvement process in manufacturing. It is also the defining

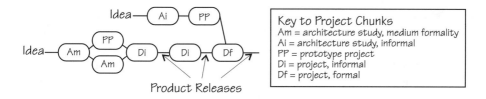

Figure 2.4

Cross product
development
process
chunks

Key to Project Chunks
Am = architecture study, medium formality
Ai = architecture study, informal
PP = prototype project
Di = project, informal
Df = project, formal

Product Releases

characteristic of a level 5 software process in the Software Engineering Institute's process maturity index. The importance of measuring quality and using the results to improve the product is well known. It is not quite so clear just how some of the system properties should be measured.

But the measurements are not well defined…yet.

We have seen that there are both run-time and build-time properties that a system should express. Quality measurements of errors, crashes, and other run-time properties of the system have been well described [KAN95]. Measurements of the build-time properties, such as extensibility, are not so well developed. Extensibility is a measure of effort expended per unit of system extension. Ease of development is a measure of development effort per unit of system development. The effort part—hours, people, and dollars spent on the work—is easy to measure. The problem is with the units of development and extension. It is still difficult to quantify software products. Lines of code and function points have been used. Lines of code has been discredited because it is like measuring the work of a carpenter by how many nails are used. Function points are units of requirements rather than units of software, although they have been empirically correlated with development effort.

Large-scale measures have been used successfully to measure productivity, that is, ease of development. By *large scale* I mean dollars in the annual development department budget divided by the number of new systems delivered to the field. I do not have any answers for questions about quantifying single software systems. That difficulty does not reduce the importance of measuring the properties of systems. If the organization cannot see the results of the improvements to the development process then those of us in the design business may as well be selling clothes to the emperor. When measurements are taken, I believe that they will show that explicit design for all system properties, combined with careful checking to see that the properties are preserved at all stages of the development cycle, are necessary ingredients in the production end of software development processes. This means that the decision about which of the Essential Tasks to include in a given project will have a quantifiable impact on the product quality.

2.6.3 Project Processes

Many kinds of projects are needed.

A *project*, for the purpose of this discussion, is a single commitment of time and money that is expected to deliver a piece of working software or a design specification for a system at a specified time. It is necessary to define *project* in scheduling terms because the work content of a project is quite relative. One person's project is someone else's task. In any case, a project will consist of some set of task chunks. A formal development project, the DF chunk at the product life cycle level, should have the risks eliminated in previous projects. If the scope was large, it might be divided into parallel development threads. The task chunk structure might look like that in Figure 2.5.

In this project, the system architecture is established first. The resulting subsystem specifications are used as input to the design and development sequences

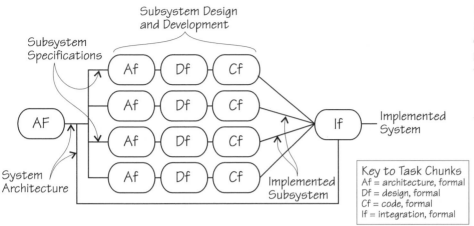

Figure 2.5

Formal development project task chunks

that design and build the subsystems. The entire system is then assembled and tested according to the system-architecture specification.

The task chunks for an informal prototype project, PP at the product level, might look like the following project (Figure 2.6). In this project, an informal design is developed, several iterations of coding are carried out, the design is revised, and a final prototype is developed.

Of course, one person's project can be another's task and vice versa. A production project that begins with more uncertainty than the formal development project described above, might use prototyping and architecture chunks to resolve the risks discovered in the first pass through the architecture chunk, as shown below. Less formal chunks can be used, subject to the quality and economic standards of the organization (Figure 2.7).

Phased, incremental delivery is a prudent approach to structuring projects. The increments should be defined from a well-established architecture, as shown in Figure 2.7.

I have not seen the process hierarchy just described implemented in very many of the software development organizations I have visited. There seems to be a wide-spread recognition that such a process hierarchy is necessary to achieve significant consistency and reuse across multiple products, but it appears to be difficult to

Changes in culture come slowly.

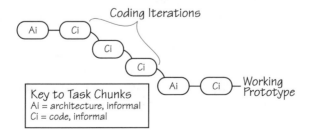

Figure 2.6

Prototype project task chunks

Figure 2.7

Informal development project task chunks

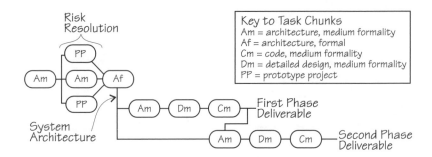

move away from the current view that a project and the resulting product is independent of all other projects. The difficulty appears to be cultural. Having someone like an architect *impose* structure on individual developers within a project is not a popular idea. Having someone outside the current project, like the product line architect, impose a structure on the entire project is an even larger change from the current practice. The best we can do to improve the situation is to identify our goals and begin taking the many small steps needed to reach them.

We have reached the bottom of the process hierarchy. The chunks at the next level down are associated with individual documents and executable components. This is the domain of the Essential Tasks. In particular, the Essential Tasks are the chunks of the architecture task chunk in the project level process. So, before I describe the content of the architecture task chunk, I would like to describe the Essential Tasks.

2.7 DEFINING ESSENTIAL TASKS

The Essential Tasks are defined by the properties and requirements to be satisfied, not the process of developing a system. The life cycle of a software system may begin with someone's blue-sky idea, proceed through some feasibility studies, some prototypes, development of the initial release, and then a long series of improvements, expansions, reconfigurations, and rewrites. Each of the events in that life cycle should involve one or more applications of the Essential Tasks at some appropriate level of detail.

The Essential Tasks look like a tool box for the software engineer. When a piece of software must be engineered, the appropriate tools are taken out of the box and are used in the appropriate order for the job at hand. In a cabinet maker's tool box there is no sequence of usage embedded in the saws, squares, and planes. There is some sequence imposed by dependencies between tasks. Thus, a board has to be cut to length with a saw before the ends can be trued up with the square and plane. There are some information dependencies between the work products, but the tools and the operation of the tools do not impose or even define a process of applying

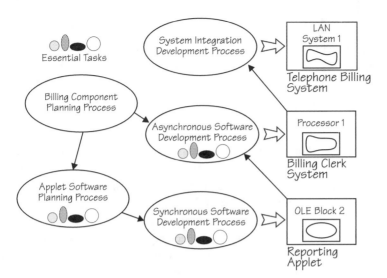

Figure 2.8
A proposed process structure for software development with essential tasks

them. Sequences, appropriate tool choices, and appropriate levels of formality are all important topics that are much easier to discuss if they are decoupled from the issue of how to do the basic woodworking operations. Descriptions of those sequences and processes are methodologies or practice guides. Using the Essential Tasks to evaluate and unify methodologies will be discussed in the Appendix.

In software terms, the Essential Tasks correspond to the basic woodworking operations. They describe how to do the basic engineering tasks needed to design a software system. The tasks and work products I will describe here will produce a design that corresponds to the output of a building architect. The size and shape of the system is determined, and the functionality and interface of all the internal subsystems are specified. Only one or two levels of subsystem are described, but at those levels, the design specifies all of the subsystems needed to make the system. The design is specified in its documents to the point that it can be used to demonstrate how all of the requirements and properties desired in the system will be met. The system design can serve as input to all detailed design of lower level components. The Essential Tasks are the tools for building such a design.

Essential Tasks are the saws and squares.

The Essential Tasks provide tools to design a single level of software component. The processes to design parts at different levels of the hierarchy may need different kinds of design tools, that is, they may use different sets of Essential Tasks. On the parts hierarchy, the Essential Tasks described here can be applied to one or two of the lower levels of software parts hierarchy, as shown below. Once the parts get bigger than computers on a LAN, different essential tasks from the Essential Tasks that work for lower-level components are needed. Every software system will not use all the levels of components. Figure 2.8 shows where the Essential Tasks fit in the software development process.

2.7.1 The Essential Tasks

Here are the basic engineering tools.

The work product categories and the associated tasks that I would like to nominate for inclusion in the list of Essential Tasks are the following: 1) run-time requirements, 2) build-time requirements, 3) state that the system maintains, 4) behavior identification and allocation, 5) system architecture, and 6) behavior description. Following Principle 1, the tasks can be divided into two groups: documenting the external requirements and addressing external requirements.

In this brief introduction to the tasks, and in the detailed descriptions later, I will recommend specific notations. Any notation can be used as long as it satisfies two criteria. The first is provided by Principle 5: the notation should facilitate the evaluations of the decisions that the notation documents. The second is that the notation should have a form and content that facilitates the use of the decisions by the downstream tasks. For example, in the run-time requirements task, use cases will be recommended for documenting functional requirements, but the traditional, voluminous functional requirements document will not be recommended. The reason is that use cases can be used directly in the behavior identification and allocation task, while the traditional functional requirements statement is very difficult to use in the downstream tasks.

In this section I will describe the requirements and properties addressed by each task. Later chapters will cover how to produce the work product.

2.7.2 Document External Requirements

Requirements impact a system twice.

If we look at the collection of Essential Tasks as a single activity, we can apply the Basic Principles to them. The result is the need to have a statement of the goals and requirements the system must meet that is independent of how that goal is reached. Having the requirements separate from the design decisions made to meet those requirements is the only way we can measure the effectiveness of the design decisions. I mention this here because of the common practice in software development of building "requirements models" using notations that embody many decisions about the content and structure of the system. Examples include using dataflow diagrams and object models to "model the requirements." The notations and instructions for documenting the requirements described here carefully avoid making decisions about the structure of the system.

Task 1: *Run-time Requirements*

While it is running

Users, whether human, machine, or other systems are concerned with what the system does when it is running. They are the source of the run-time requirements. The user requirements should document all aspects and properties of the system that are needed when the system is running. Run-time requirements have many components, including functional requirements, interfaces to support, information flows received and produced, and rules and algorithms to implement. They should also document, in quantified form, all properties that the running system is to exhibit, such as safety, reliability, performance, and effectiveness. These requirements drive the content of the system. They are the source of the evaluation criteria for the presence and sufficiency of information and behavior in the system.

Techniques and notations for documenting run-time requirements include use cases for functional requirements, data, record, and table formats for data interfaces, prototypes for human user interfaces, protocols, and state models for other control interfaces, and rules and text for describing algorithms.

Task 2: *Build-time Requirements*

Build-time requirements describe the properties and "behavior" the system should exhibit when it is not running. These build-time requirements consist, primarily, of changes that will be made to the system while it is "under construction." The source of these requirements is the person paying for making those construction time changes: the development sponsor.

While it is being worked on by developers

The ability of a system to gracefully support these build-time changes is determined primarily by the structure and allocation of information and behavior in it. Therefore, the build-time requirements are used to drive and evaluate decisions about how the content of the system is allocated and structured.

The build-time requirements consist of the instances of change that the system is expected to support when it is not executing. I have called these instances *change cases*, to place them as peers with the run-time use case requirements. The build-time requirements have been neglected. Perhaps a catchy name will increase their visibility.

2.7.3 Addressing the External Requirements

Task 3: *System State*

All software systems can be described as maintaining some kind of state. That state can include several things, depending on the nature of the system. Examples of the states that systems maintain include calls and connections in a telephone switch, customers and accounts in a bank system, the status of a claim in a claims processing system, and workflow and the status of documents in a collaborative engineering system. Providing a system with sufficient state information is a necessary prerequisite for the system to meet its run-time functional requirements and to maintain the required levels of integrity and consistency of the state. If there is insufficient state information in the system, no amount of function and behavior can make the system make up for the omission.

What does the system need to keep track of?

Representative techniques for documenting the system state include entity-relationship diagrams, object models, and object lists. Once documented, the system state should be evaluated against its ability to support the required functionality and to gracefully accommodate the state changes that will result from the change cases.

Task 4: *Identifying and Allocating Behavior*

What behavior potential should the system have, and how should it be structured?

The behavior identification and allocation task does two things: it accounts for the names of behaviors needed in the system to provide the required functionality; and it allocates those behaviors to components of the system. The state model provides some of the components of the system, and additional components may be nominated during this task.

Two important properties of the final system are being addressed here. One is the potential of the system to provide the services and functionality required of it by its users. The other is the ability of the system to be easily extended and maintained. How the behavior is allocated in the system, bounds the extensibility of the system. I have made allocation a separate task so that the behavior allocation can be evaluated before that decision is used by the behavior description, as suggested in Principle 3.

Representative techniques for documenting behavior allocation include dataflow diagrams (identification only, no allocation), collaboration-responsibility modeling (CRC cards), interaction diagrams, and event traces. The behaviors need to be complete and sufficient, so the identification decisions should be evaluated against the user requirements. How behavior is allocated is the main determinant of the modularity of the system, so the allocation decisions should be evaluated against the build-time requirements. Since most of the build-time properties are emergent properties, the evaluation must take place in the architecture diagram.

Task 5: *Software System Architecture*

What is the structure of the entire system?

Architecture describes the form and structure of the entire system as it runs. Since the architecture describes the entire system, it is the place, or the starting place, to address most of the emergent properties of the system, both run-time and build-time. Run-time emergent properties include performance, reliability, and security. Build-time emergent properties include extensibility, maintainability, reuse, configurability, and testability. In addition to designing in the emergent properties, the whole system, as expressed by its architecture, should also provide all of the system state and behavior developed in the earlier tasks. Thus, we should be able to evaluate the architecture for its ability to provide all the required user functionality. Because the architecture is the structure of the system, the primary evaluation criteria will be provided by the build-time requirements. The evaluation that I recommend of the behavior allocation decisions made in the behavior identification and allocation task, is to populate the architecture subsystems with the behavior model components and then evaluate the architecture and the behavior allocation decisions against the build-time requirements.

Representative techniques for describing the system architecture are not common in published design methods. Notations that can be used to address the system architecture include Mascot, subsystems in Wirfs-Brock, and subsystems and service packages in Objectory, and ROOM diagrams.

Task 6: *Behavior Description*

Behavior description accounts for the logic needed to actually carry out the behaviors named in the identification and allocation activity. The requirements being addressed here are those for run-time functionality and implementation of rules and algorithms. The behavior description supplies the content of the behavior potential allocated in the allocation task.

How should the behavior potential be expressed?

Representative techniques for behavior description include state transition charts, pseudo code, flowcharts, Structured English, and programming languages. Behavior descriptions should be evaluated against the functional requirements, rules, and algorithms described in the external run-time requirements.

I have already invoked the Basic Principles to justify keeping the external requirements really external to the system being designed. The Basic Principles can be invoked again to structure each of the individual tasks. That structure consists of the following three subtasks:

Use the Basic Principles of Evaluation.

1. Extract the goals, test cases or evaluation criteria that are relevant to the task from the external requirements: Principle 1.

2. Perform the task to produce the work products: notation selected by Principle 5.

3. Apply the test cases to the work products; that is, evaluate the decisions documented in the task: Principles 2, 3, and 4.

Those are the Essential Tasks. I trust most of the work products will be familiar to most readers of software methodology books. Things that are different compared to software methodology books are the connection of the tasks to the properties and requirements they address, and the emphasis on explicit evaluation of the work products against the external requirements. I believe that these two ideas are a good basis for unifying both the widely varying practices used in software development and the apparently widely divergent software methodologies.

We can now return to the process hierarchy and fill in the content of the architecture task chunk.

2.8 THE ARCHITECTURE TASK CHUNK

One pass through the Essential Tasks, from requirements to architecture, is a cohesive unit of activity with a very useful output—a plan for a software system. The Essential Tasks are the chunks of Architecture Task Chunk. "Architecture" indicates that the final output is the description of the system.

Table 2.1
Task content
of the
architecture
chunks

Essential task	AI: informal	AM: medium	AF: formal
User requirements	Use case names	Use cases, some descriptions, rules and algorithms	Use case names and descriptions, formal rules and algorithms, data definitions, constraints
Development sponsor requirements	Major change case names	Change cases	Change cases, constraints, product plan, reuse plan
System state	Categories of state components	State component names	Static object model
Behavior identification and allocation	Service names	Collaboration-responsibility model	Interaction diagram
Architecture	Subsystem names	Subsystem names and collaborations	Subsystems with detailed channel specifications
Behavior description	Not used	Not used	State transition models, formal logic

This is where the Essential Tasks live.

The architecture chunk can be applied in many situations. Some situations will call for more formality and detail than others. Therefore, the notations used in each situation should be dependent on the needs of the situation. The variable factor is how much time is devoted to each task. A useful range of formalities is three, which I will label informal, medium, and formal. These three chunks are sufficient to build a wide variety of projects. In Table 2.1 I have listed the techniques for each task for each of three levels of detail. The techniques are described in the chapters on the individual Essential Tasks.

The Essential Tasks are analogous to the engineering calculations needed to design (in the engineering sense) a product or system. When they are completed, the resulting design documents should show how all the requirements on the system will be addressed, to the level of detail appropriate for the type of project.

Most projects will use some other task chunks. A useful collection includes detailed design, coding and unit testing, integration and testing. Each of these chunks can be carried out at three levels of formality. Since these chunks are outside the scope of this book, I will leave them as black boxes in this discussion.

2.9 SUMMARY

The purpose of this chapter was to introduce the Essential Tasks and the Basic Principles of Evaluation and to place them in the universe of software development practice. The actual practice of software development is a variable affair. Organizations that depend on the quality and economics of software product development for some or all of their income would like to have the quality high and improving and the economics good and getting better. To help out, development methodologies are being invoked to improve the process and the practice.

In the form in which they are commonly applied, methodologies appear to be too big and too rigid to meet the needs of most real development organizations. They also appear to be mutually exclusive. Committing to use one methodology "forever" isolates the organization in the camp of the chosen method.

If methodology is supposed to provide guidance to developers of software systems, then we can overcome the problems pinned on methodologies by breaking them into two parts. The first part is the box of tools and the second is the hierarchies of instructions on how to apply the tools in appropriate sequences for various situations. The Essential Tasks are the tools in the engineer's tool box. The hierarchies of instructions are descriptions for the cross product, product, and project level processes. This book is devoted to describing how to use the tools. The hierarchies of processes described in this chapter give a context for the use of the Essential Tasks. *Methodologies are mostly task descriptions.*

Adding external requirements that document both the build-time and run-time requirements for a system make it possible to provide explicit goals for each of the tasks to address. Just following instructions for a task is not sufficient to ensure that a desired result is achieved. The Basic Principles of Evaluation provide suggestions on how to measure the output of each task to ensure that the intended design goals have been effectively addressed. These principles shape the application of the Essential Tasks. For me, they have served to eliminate the requirement that a methodology be a *Joy of Cooking* guide for software cooks. Having effective evaluations at each step means that errors can be caught and fixed while they are still paper errors and before they contaminate other decisions. *Essential Tasks and the Basic Principles*

Processes, consisting of sequences of the Essential Tasks, can be described with more flexibility if they do not have to convey instructions for the tasks at the same time. A hierarchy of processes, each consisting of chunks of subprocesses, is needed for each product to address the hierarchy of concerns. Those concerns include delivering the desired properties in the current version of the product, effectively shepherding a product through its lifecycle of projects, and effectively implementing consistency and reuse across several products. *Wheels inside wheels*

With this background, we are ready to examine the Essential Tasks and how their work products are evaluated in detail.

CHAPTER 3

The External Requirements Tasks

CONTENTS

3.1 Introduction   47
3.2 What are the Requirements?   51
3.3 Evaluating the External Requirements   52
3.4 Documenting the External Requirements   53
3.5 Requirements Task Summary   68

3.1 INTRODUCTION

The purposes of the external requirements task are to establish the complete set of design targets for the product and to provide a set of criteria to use in evaluating the design documents and the finished product. It is an often repeated truth that unstated goals are unlikely to show up in a product. Unstated goals also make very poor product-evaluation criteria.

The meaning of the term *external* needs some discussion. When a software system is placed in service, the users, who are external to it, might say, "This is much better than the old system," or they might say, "This is awful, I could do this in half the time it takes with the new system." The manger of the department that is using the system, and who authorized its purchase, might say, "Our productivity is up by 20% since we installed the new system," or she might say, "I can't see any benefit from installing the new system." The development department manager might say,

"The new customer service system needs only half the maintenance staff that we needed on the previous customer service system."

These are all reactions by stakeholders in a software system. The reactions are based on the properties of the system and are completely independent of which processes, methodology, prototypes, programming languages, databases, or development environments were used to develop the system. If we could write down the needs and expectations that the stakeholders have when they interact with the system, we would have the external requirements for the system. This is difficult to do, of course, but the idea is important. There are needs and criteria that stakeholders have that are independent of anything that is "inside" the system. Put another way, the external requirements on the system are separate from the system that meets the requirements.

The process that takes the external requirements as input and produces the system that is supposed to meet those requirements is the development process, which includes the design of the system. A million different systems could be designed and constructed to meet the same set of requirements. To effectively evaluate whether a particular design is meeting the requirements, the statement of the requirements must be separate from the design documents.

Know where you are trying to go before you start deciding how to get there. The requirements that will be documented in this task are external to the system being designed. They will be captured in a form that does not involve any decisions about the form and content of the system. I have belabored this separation of requirements and system to counter the practice recommended in some software methodologies of using notations like dataflow diagrams or object models to capture requirements for a system. Those diagrams usually find their way into the *later* stages of engineering process. Thus, work being done early, under the guise of documenting the requirements for the system, was really making engineering decisions about the system itself. The problem is not that the decisions are being made, the problem is that they are not treated as engineering decisions to be evaluated, but taken as givens for the system.

Now, having made the point that the expectations and requirements that stakeholders have for a system should be kept separate from the system and its design, I need to qualify that by saying that the requirements and the system are not independent. The stakeholders' expectations of properties and performance of systems can be higher or lower than what is feasible for systems to deliver. Expectations can also be changed by what systems do deliver. For example, customer support clerks in an insurance company who have had to access five mainframe systems on three different terminals to find out the status of Mrs. Smith's last claim are not likely to expect a system that will show them the claim and the related policies in a screen metaphor that looks like the paper documents. On the other hand, after they see some prototypes, they may become quite sophisticated in their expectations about what kind of information they would like to see when they call up Mrs. Smith's policy. At another extreme, users of CASE tools seem to have very high expectations about the capability of CASE tools to enforce consistency, provide design help, generate code, reverse engineer design documents from source code, and interoperate with other CASE tools and all the schedulers, builders, and configuration management systems in their tool chain. Meanwhile, real CASE tools are struggling with doing consistency checking on single diagrams and sharing single diagram types with other products.

Requirements and the things that meet the requirements are not independent, but they should be documented separately. Having the requirements separate from the design decisions on how to meet the requirements is essential to having independent measures of the design work.

The importance of the stakeholders' expectations about the system was introduced in the discussion above. There are two categories of stakeholders that have very different kinds of expectations about the system.

3.1.1 Who has the Requirements?

A software system may be in one of two different states: running or under construction. Actually, there are more states that a system may occupy, such as starting up, but for purposes of this discussion, two states are enough. By the definition of stakeholders, they are the people, or things, that have requirements and expectations about a system. Stakeholders can be classified according to the state of the system in which they are most interested. Those interested in the running system are the users, those interested in the construction are the developers. They each have a different view of the system and different kinds of requirements.

There is more to the life of a software system than CPU cycles.

3.1.2 The Run-Time View

The stakeholders who are concerned with the run-time properties of a system include the users who interact with the system, people who depend on the system but do not directly interact with it, and people who invest in the purchase and installation of the system in the hopes of achieving some return on the investment in the form of increased productivity or job quality. This last group of stakeholders I call the *user sponsors*. I have found it helpful to include them in the list of stakeholders having requirements on the system because they provide a larger and longer term view than that of the immediate users of the system.

Users of the system may be humans, machines, or other systems, depending on the kind of system being designed.

The requirements that run-time stakeholders have can be divided into two groups: services provided now and services to be provided in the future. The current services are the well-known user requirements. They include all of the run-time services and properties that the system should display. The future services include things which cannot be included in the current version for reasons of time, money, or technology constraints. All of the user run-time requirements are concerned with the performance of the system in the domain of the target user. This distinction between current and future requirements will be important when we look at the build-time requirements.

3.1.3 The Build-Time View

Stakeholders concerned with the build-time performance of the system include the developers paid to create, maintain, and enhance the system and the development sponsor. The development sponsor is the person who invests in the creation and enhancement of the system in the hopes of earning some return on the investment through sales of the system to users. In some organizations the development sponsor and the user sponsor may be the same person, in which case, the return on the development investment is the improved quality and productivity of run-time users. Including the person having an interest in the financial aspects of development provides a broader view of the requirements than would be available if we considered only the developers.

The development and maintenance costs are incurred when the system is not running.

The view of the developers, in particular of the development sponsor, is quite different from the user stakeholders. The development sponsor is concerned with the cost and efficiency of delivering the required functionality and run-time properties to the target users. He is also concerned with the cost and efficiency of modifying and extending the system to provide the future services to the target users. Most development organizations have more than one target user and they have more than one system under development or maintenance. The development sponsor is concerned with leveraging the work done on one system, for one user, to benefit the work being done on other systems for other users. The development sponsor's view of the world includes more systems and more users than that of the users of any one system.

Requirements are traditionally named for the people who have them. Hence, the name, *user requirements*. Actually, *user sponsor requirements* might provide a better vantage point to view the run-time requirements, but *user* is the traditional name. Following that tradition, I would name the other kind of requirements the *developer requirements*, or better, the *development sponsor requirements*. These names will probably present some problems for readers, particularly when some of the development sponsor requirements are drawn from needs of the users and their sponsors. I can suggest alternative names for the requirements that would present fewer problems with the content: *run-time requirements* and *build-time requirements*. The term *user requirements* is well established, but calling the other kind of requirements the *development sponsor requirements* is awkward. I have used the term *development sponsor* for several years, and it seems to need an undue amount of defending. For this book, I will use the terms run-time and build-time to describe the two categories of requirements that a system must meet.

3.2 WHAT ARE THE REQUIREMENTS?

The external requirements for a system should include all services, attributes, and properties that the stakeholders expect in the system. The requirements should also include all of the information about the environment and context of the system which the developers will need to carry out its design and implementation. That information includes anything that is in the environment of the system but is outside the scope of the system design.

All of the system properties should be documented in the requirements.

We have divided the stakeholders and their requirements into two camps: run-time and build-time. The kinds of information that constitute the run-time requirements include the role the system is expected to play in the user organization, the identities of the users (human and system) that interact with the system, the usages or services they expect of the system, the kinds of interfaces the system is expected to provide to its users, the information elements that flow across the system boundary, algorithms that the system is to implement, properties and attributes that the system should display, and nonfunctional constraints on the run-time system.

The kinds of information that constitute the build-time requirements include the instances of growth, change and reconfiguration anticipated for the system, constraints on the development process, and the role the system will play in the development organization.

The kinds of information just listed imply that the boundary and scope of the system are defined before the requirements are gathered. This is necessarily the case for any pass through the design tasks. The question of how to arrive at a specific scope for a system is one that should be addressed at one or two levels up the process hierarchy from the Essential Task level. For purposes of describing the requirements tasks, we can assume that the scope has been established.

The content of the external requirements called for here was developed by observing the development process and noting when a piece of information was needed. If that information was not produced by the development process, it was added to the requirements bucket. On comparing the content of the bucket with the requirements content of several methodologies, it appears that the information is the union of requirements called for in the individual methodologies.

3.3 EVALUATING THE EXTERNAL REQUIREMENTS

The goal of the requirements task is to document the information needed in such a form that 1) it can be understood and verified by people with knowledge of the system environment, and 2) it can be used as a gauge throughout the development process to determine if the product is meeting the requirements.

There are two kinds of evaluation that may be carried out for the requirements. One is reviews, which may be done as part of the requirements task. Reviews should be carried out with sources of the requirements and with the developers. The other kind of evaluation may only take place after the product is placed in service, which is to see if the product does, in fact, meet the users' needs. If it does not, the problem may be that the requirements were not an accurate statement of the needs, or it may be that the development activities did not correctly meet the stated requirements.

3.3.1 Semantics

Apples and oranges are OK, but don't mix fruit with tractors.

Analysis of the meanings of words and names will be used in the requirements task and in other tasks, to evaluate the work. The analysis of word meaning is called *semantics,* and I would like to talk about semantics before using the concept. In software development, the words we are concerned with are the names given to objects, messages, functions, data elements, and parameters.

I will use the phrase *semantic level* often in evaluating the work in the various tasks. Semantic level is a measure of the cohesion of a set of words. For example, the words *video cassette tape, customer, rental transaction, return a tape,* and *add a title* all come from the domain of a video rental store. The words *disk drive, file, cylinder, disk directory,* and *write a file* all come from the domain of a computer operating system. The words in each of these groups are from different semantic levels.

The words in the group *video cassette tape, customer, rental transaction, disk drive, file,* and *cylinder* mix two different semantic levels.

The value of using semantic levels to determine what is appropriate to include at any level of design is that it makes the design task simpler. Mixing two levels of concerns in one design task increases the complexity geometrically. Consider, for example, attempting to handle customers and disk drives in the same requirements document. If there were three kinds of customer and three types of disk drive we might be tempted to describe how each type of customer is stored on each type of drive, for a total of 9 combinations.

The semantic level of the words being used will be invoked as an evaluation tool in the requirements tasks and in all of the subsequent Essential Task descriptions.

3.4 DOCUMENTING THE EXTERNAL REQUIREMENTS

This section describes the content of the external requirements. The run-time and build-time requirements are described separately.

An introductory overview of the product and the current project should be written. This overview should describe the scope and goals for the project, and the functionality of the product. A brief summary of the products' (or components') role in their respective organizations might also be in order.

3.4.1 Run-Time Requirements

As with all the task descriptions in this book, the steps will be covered in a single sequence, primarily because books are a one dimensional space. Actual sequences, iterations and level of detail will depend on the needs of the particular project the task is being used in.

Contents

1 System Scope
2 Goals and expectations for the product in the user organization
3 Actors and their roles
4 Functional requirements
   - Use case names for each actor and role
   - Use case descriptions
5 Control interfaces with the outside world
6 Information interfaces with the outside world
7 Rules and algorithms the system is expected to implement or enforce
8 Non-use-related constraints

1. System Scope   Documenting the requirements for a system implies that the boundary between the context of the system and the system is known. The system can be briefly described in terms of the services it provides to its users. The context of the system can be described with a general description of the users.

2. Goals and Expectations for the Product in the User Organization   It is very helpful to know what general expectations the user sponsor has of the product. If the product is a utility to speed up a minor operation it might be treated differently than if it is automating the core business process of the user. Is the product a

There are lots of things that are determined by the system context.

standalone system or will it have to be integrated with other systems and applications? See the samples for an example of a product role description.

The actors are the sources of functional requirements.

3. Actors and Their Roles   The active part of the system environment can be described in terms of actors. An actor is any entity that is external to the system and interacts with the system at the top semantic level of the system. Examples that might be external actors include human users of a system, telephone lines, a machine tool, a remote database, a billing system, a keyboard and a disk drive.

I will use the term *nominate* when referring to the act of identifying elements of the system, because the nomination is subject to evaluation and confirmation. Not all nominees survive the evaluation process.

Nominees for actor must meet several criteria. They must be a source or sink of events or information for the system. The semantic level of dialogue and the information passed between the actor and the system must be at the application level.

For example, consider a system to manage a video rental store. Actor nominees might include the sales clerks, the store manager, stocking clerk, the accountant, the local database system, and the keyboard. Which of these nominees should be confirmed? We can make that evaluation by looking at the semantic level of the interactions between the actors and the system.

The sales clerk will be adding new members, checking out rentals, checking in returns, and looking up the status of "Gone With The Wind." All of these words are from the domain of a video store. The sales clerk is also, obviously, a source of events to which the system must respond. The sales clerk meets the criteria for being an actor, and we can confidently confirm the nomination.

What about the keyboard? The keyboard is clearly a source of events that the system responds to. But, what is the semantic level? The events from the keyboard are "here is a key code." Because key codes are not words in the video store domain, we conclude that the keyboard is not at the same semantic level as the video store system and should not be confirmed as an actor.

The database may be harder to confirm. It is a sink of information from the system and a responder to requests, but it is not a source of events. The dialogue between the database and the system may be in the form of SQL statements: "select 'title' from tapes where star = 'John Wayne'." Because the semantic level of the dialogue, while higher than the keyboard, is at the row, column, and table level, we could say that it is at a lower level than the application. For that reason I would treat a database as a peripheral to the system but not as an actor.

It is convenient to think of people actors as being physical people. But what happens when the afternoon shift manager also checks out rentals? When one person interacts with the system in two very different ways, such as being a normal user and an administrator, the idea of roles may be used. A role is cohesive set of dialogues between an actor and the system. Several actors may take on the same role. In our video store example, manager and sales clerk would be roles which could be distributed among the users of the system.

Once roles are introduced, they become the primary focus of the requirements documentation. The actors are then used to organize the roles for review by the domain authorities.

Roles and actors should be described with a name and description for each role or actor. The description should include the kinds of activities that actor carries out when working with the system. In order to facilitate the evaluation of the documentation, it is important that the words used for actor names and descriptions be taken exclusively from the domain of the actor. Put another way, the words used should be all of the same semantic level, and that level should be the application domain.

The CORE method has a good suggestion for evaluating requirements. In CORE the term corresponding to *Actor* is *View Point.* They suggest designating a View Point Authority to be responsible for evaluating the correctness of all descriptions of View Points. In the terms we are using here, it would be an Actor Authority for each actor. This person could be someone from the actor domain, or a person within the development organization who is knowledgeable about the domain and its actors. Any questions about how an actor works can be referred to the appropriate authority and the answers can be recorded.

4. Functional Requirements   There are a number of techniques for documenting user functional requirements. The functional requirements notation should meet two criteria: it should be easy for the sources and reviewers of the requirements to understand; it should not involve any decisions about the form and content of the system. A technique and notation that meets these criteria is the use case.

Of many possible techniques, use cases do the best job of capturing functional requirements in a useful form.

Use case is a term from Objectory used to describe a single usage of the system by an actor, or an actor playing a particular role. Another way to describe a use case is as a dialogue between an actor or role and the system.

A use case is a dialogue between an external actor, or actor in a role, and the system. The key question is how "big" should the use cases be? To be meaningful to the actor authority, it should be big enough to be named and described using only words at the semantic level of the actor's domain. To be useful to the developers, it should be of such a size that it can be described as a single thread of activities without major branches. These two requirements place upper and lower bounds on the size of a use case.

Consider three nominees for use case: "Administer Inventory," "Add a tape to inventory," and "double click on an icon." "Administer Inventory" is almost certainly too big to be described as a single thread, but the words are solidly in the application domain. It is too big because administering inventory will include activities like adding a new tape, removing a tape, asking for activity reports, and the

Getting the "size" of the use cases is tricky.

like. Each one of those activities is a sequence of steps that is different from the others. "Add a tape to inventory" uses words of the appropriate level, and it sounds like it can be described as a single thread of actions and reactions. A single-thread description would sound like, "User requests 'add tape,' system presents new tape display, user enters information, system confirms whether the title exists, assigns unique ID, and prints the bar code label." "Double click on an icon" is certainly small enough to be described in a single sequence, but the words *double click* and *icon* are not from the video-store domain. They are from the lower-level domain of user interfaces.

The mechanism of nominating use cases is to put on the hat of each actor and each role. With the hat on, nominate all the things that the actor can do to/with the system. For each nominee, consider the size and semantic guidelines suggested above. The result should be a list of use case names for each actor. I have found it useful to document all the use case names for all of the actors before proceeding to writing the use case descriptions. The appropriateness of the granularity and the completeness of the coverage can be judged by looking at the list of use case names. See the example for a representative list of use cases for our video store system.

A use case defined as a dialogue between the actor and the system is most useful when the actors are human. When the actors are not human, as is common in embedded systems, or when the "system" being designed is a subsystem in another application, the dialogue idea does not fit the interaction. In that situation, events provide a better approach to describing the requirements. The use case might be called an event case, or more commonly, an event list.

The dialogue between the actor and the system should be described. This collection of descriptive texts is the bulk of the user requirements. Both the content and style are important to the overall success of the design.

The descriptions provide the bridge between the users and the developers.

The description should describe the interactions between the actor and the system, as in, "The clerk requests monthly reports, the system responds with a list of available reports. The clerk selects the desired report. The system gathers the information specified for the report, formats it, and prints it on the default printer."

If the actor is a telephone line, the description might look like, "When the line goes off hook, the system establishes a call for that line. The system reads the destination address, looks up the appropriate trunk for that destination, and connects the call to that trunk. While the call is active, the dialogue is specified by Bellcore TTY 234 D call state diagram. When the incoming line goes on-hook, the line connections are broken, the call is logged and removed."

The use case description is a good place to describe any performance, response time, safety, or reliability requirements that apply specifically to the use case interaction. How often the use case is invoked is another useful piece of information that could be recorded here. Examples include things like, "the initial response must be less than one second," or "the resulting transaction must be atomic." Requirements that apply to more than one use case, or to the system as a whole, should be recorded in the problem description or in the constraints section. Examples of items in this category would include an annual down-time limit and system safety requirements.

These examples demonstrate the content and style needed to address the needs of the people involved with use cases. To be understood by the actor authorities, all of the words in the descriptions should be taken from the application domain. The technique I use to prevent from slipping down to the semantic level of the application innards is to only use one word or phrase when referring to anything that happens on the system side. In the examples above, I used *the system*. Everything the system does is described as *the system* does.... rather than referring to any internal part of the system, such as the database or the report engine. The functionality described in a use case should be limited to the algorithms needed to carry out the dialogue, rather than behavior descriptions that imply an internal allocation of behavior in the system.

The needs on the developer side are met by keeping the description to a single thread of events (splits, branches, and exceptions are described later), using complete sentences, carefully stating how the use case begins and how it ends. If there are preconditions or post conditions that must be met in the use case, they should be stated as part of the use case description. Performance and integrity constraints on the use case should also be documented. Examples of constraints are that the initial response time must be one second, or that entering a new member must be an atomic transaction.

Meeting the needs of diverse stakeholders imposes content and structural constraints on use case descriptions.

The run-time requirements need to state all of the rules and algorithms that the users expect the system to implement. Some of those algorithms can be stated as part of the use case description. For algorithms that are longer than can be conveniently associated with a single use case, the rules and algorithms category has been provided.

The need to limit a use case to a single sequence of events is dictated by how the use case will be used in the design process. That does not mean that there can be no branches or exceptions in the product. It does mean that each branch or exception must be given its own use case. The question is then, when is a separate use case required? A new use case is required when the branch or exception involves more than "a few" steps in the behavior model. A *few* is a small number, like five.

Additional use cases will be discovered during the process of describing those that were nominated originally. For example, in describing the "rent a video" use case, you discover the situation where the customer is not a member. When that happens, the clerk has to go through the process of signing the customer up as a member. There may be several steps in that process, so it would be appropriate to make "sign up a new member" a separate use case. It could be referred to in the "rent a video" use case, but the steps and interactions would not have to be described.

Some use cases, like "log in" and "sign up a new member" may be used in several other use cases. The Objectory Method suggests a formal name for that kind of relationship: a *uses* relationship. Any sequence of dialogue that appears in multiple places in a system should be named, described in its own use case and then "used" wherever it is needed.

Connections between simple use cases handle complex situations.

Use cases often mention error conditions that may occur during the normal sequence of events. If handling that error condition requires more than a few steps, that error condition should become its own use case. Again, Objectory has a name for this kind of relationship; it is called an *extends* relationship in Objectory. For example, in the "return a video" use case it may happen that a video entered in to the system as being returned is not a title in the inventory. The desired behavior when that happens might be to have the system check for similar sounding names, check to see if the title was recently removed from inventory, and prepare a little report for the clerk. That sequence of behavior is not part of the normal "return a video" behavior. It should be given a name, described and referred to in the normal sequence of events as extending the normal use case.

Some user interactions with the system involve repetitions of the same set of interactions and conditions for determining when to start and stop the repetitions. The logic can be described in the use case description. It should not appear in the behavior identification and allocation documents, but it will appear in the behavior description documents. (See Chapter 8 on behavior modeling.)

To summarize, any set of interactions that can be described in a single thread can be nominated as a use case. Looping logic can be included in the description. Branches and conditionals that result in big branches should be given their own use cases. Keeping the words in the use case titles and descriptions strictly at the application-level semantics will help prevent explosions in the numbers of use cases. The use cases should be bigger than the individual branches of the flowchart for the application. The temptation to make a use case from each branch in the flowchart should be avoided.

Humans are not the only actors that get interfaces.

5. Control Interfaces with the Outside World   I use the term *control* to refer to the interface between the system and all of its actors. For human actors, the idea of a user interface is well known, but what of the nonhuman actors? Any source of events in the outside world will require an interface with the system to recognize and receive those events. Control interface is a collective name for all interfaces with actors. Examples of nonhuman actor interfaces include a telephone line interface and the interface to a robot, when telephone lines and robots are actors in the system's context.

The details of the interface such as whether it is character or graphics based, which style of menus are used, and whether named lists or radio buttons are used, are all from a different semantic level than the application words. The details of the interface should not impact what the actor does with the system. That is, use case descriptions should be independent of the interface that connects the actor with the system. Whether a given interface is sufficient and satisfactory is determined by the actor. Therefore, the need for interfaces between the system and specific actors should be documented as part of the run-time requirements.

If the details of the interfaces are known, they can be documented and described during the requirements documentation task. They should, however, be handled separately from the use case descriptions. If the control interface is not known, a separate project should be initiated to determine what the user interface should be.

The issue of whether the interface with a given actor is known gives rise to an important question about system scope, particularly for nonhuman actors. If the behavior and interface of the external actor are not known, developers may be tempted to specify what they are. If this is done, then the actor is actually under the control of the development organization, and the actor is not really an actor. The actor should be moved into the scope of the current project and designed along with the rest of the system. For example, in our video store project when multiple stores must be handled, a central inventory and customer management system may be proposed. Such a system could be nominated as an actor for the system in an individual store. When the team attempts to describe the interface between the store and central systems, it may become apparent that no one knows what the interface is. It would be appropriate then to reject the nomination of the central system as an actor, and to add to the scope of the current design project the responsibility for managing central inventory and customer information. The central system actor should be replaced with the corporate managers and other stores that would use the central system services.

Interfaces define the scope of the system.

6. Information Interfaces with the Outside World   Another kind of requirement concerns the details of the information provided to and received from the world outside the system. Examples of this information include the content and format of reports, information users enter in the system, files received and produced by the system, and the content of messages sent to other systems. If these pieces of information are named and documented, they can be referred to in the use case descriptions. I suggest that the details of the data definitions not be included in the text of the use cases, but be documented separately. For example, if a system is to produce 55 reports, it would be very redundant to describe 55 use cases whose only difference is the content of the report. The report form and contents, should be listed in this category. See the example requirements documents.

Write down
all the rules,
policies and
algorithms the
system is
supposed to
implement.

7. Rules and Algorithms the System Is Expected to Implement or Enforce   The use case descriptions provide a place to record, explicitly or implicitly, the algorithms the system will implement. Often however, the rules, algorithms, and policies a system is to implement are so long that they are difficult to fit in a framework that nominally describes an actor's interaction with the system. Some of the rules and policies are not readily visible in the interactions with a single actor, such as those that apply to the organization as a whole, or to things internal to the organization. An example is the credit limit rules in banks. There are rules about how much of a bank's assets can be invested in any one area, such as Eurodollars or derivative instruments. Use case descriptions would be an awkward place to try to record those rules. Therefore, I suggest that another bucket be created, the rules-and-algorithms bucket, to hold all those rules and algorithms that do not fit conveniently into use cases.

8. Non-Use-Related Constraints   There may be user requirements that are not directly associated with individual usage. These requirements should be documented separately from the use cases. Constraints might include safety, performance, and reliability properties. They might also include platform requirements. Examples might include an uptime specification, such as 98% availability six days per week with a maximum outage duration of 30 minutes, or the system must run on the existing desktop hardware, which are 386, non-Windows computers each with one megabyte of memory.

3.4.2 Evaluate the Nominated Actors, Roles, Use cases, Interfaces, and Constraints

The process of describing actors, use cases, interfaces and constraints is usually very enlightening to all parties. After writing down the requirements, however, the work is not complete. It should be evaluated.

No magic here.
Developer
and user
authorities
must be clear
about what is
being
developed.

The actor authority should review the documents to ensure that the actors and roles accurately and sufficiently represent the domain. The usages should be consistent with actors' real activities and with the scope of the product. All of the words used in the descriptions should be from the user domain. The descriptions should accurately reflect the interactions between the actors and the system.

The development sponsor authority should review the descriptions to ensure that there is a clear beginning and end, that there are no logical or data "gaps," that the events follow a single thread, that implied branches, exceptions and shared sequences are described, and that clear, complete sentences are used.

It should be kept in mind that just because a requirement is written down does not mean that it must or can be delivered. The technical and economic feasibility of providing any run-time requirement should be resolved through a series of design studies conducted, one hopes, early in the product's life cycle. This cycle was mentioned in the process description. Here at the individual task level, the requirements will be treated as given. At the next level up the process hierarchy, they are subject to negotiation.

The examples sections gives some evaluations of the sample use cases descriptions and the changes needed to fix the problems.

With the user view of the system documented and evaluated, we can turn our attention to the build-time side.

3.4.3 Documenting the Build-Time Requirements

The build-time requirements describe the build-time changes that the system will be expected to support with grace and minimum disruption to the system as a whole. Many of the advertising claims for software development technologies, such as CASE tools, development environments, and programming languages, are aimed at the build-time needs of the development organization. Those advertising claims include ease of development, robustness in the face of change, and reuse of software components. If we do not have explicit instances of those changes, it will be very difficult to design a system to gracefully support the changes. It will also be impossible to demonstrate during the design process that the desired "ilities" have been designed into the system.

The first installment on the promises made by the technology vendors.

Contents

1 Project scope and goals
2 Role the product will play in the development organization
3 Instances of growth and change
4 Development sponsor constraints

1. Project Scope and Goals   Each development project is undertaken to meet some explicit objective. Meeting the objective is the justification for investing time and money in the project. That goal should be clearly stated at the beginning of the project. The goals can be stated as the questions that the project is supposed to resolve. Some projects, the production projects, will have as their goal to deliver a working product or to install an enhancement in an existing product. I hope that many projects will have other goal statements. Examples of other kinds of goals include the following:

The big picture from the development point of view.

- Determine the size, complexity, and potential areas of risk in a new software product.
- Demonstrate that the required throughput can be achieved with a given software mechanism.

- Propose several alternative mechanisms for providing insurance policy rules that can be administered at run-time.

- Specify the architecture of a system in terms of its subsystems and their interfaces with enough rigor so that separate subsystem development assignments can be made.

- Develop a subsystem given its external interface and a specification of its functional and information content.

2. Role the Product Will Play in the Development Organization   Most in-house development organizations work on a number of related product types. The development group in a bank, insurance company, brokerage, or manufacturing company will work exclusively on applications to support their business. Even a contract development organization will usually have regular clients they support or will have experience and expertise in a small number of system types. For example, a group that does embedded system development is unlikely to be called on to do MIS work on a mainframe.

How this product fits with other products

Because of this natural specialization, work carried out in one project can be used to enhance and improve other projects. The chances of realizing that improvement are maximized if the cross-project exchanges are explicitly planned for, which brings us to the reason for documenting the role a particular product and project will play in the development organization. If a goal is, for example, to develop reusable software components, then other projects will have to be altered to achieve that goal.

Most development organizations support more than one application and one set of users. The target users for the subject system are important, of course. Depending on the kind of development organization, in house, contract, or commercial developers, there will probably be other users or potential users who could also use functionality similar to that being designed for the subject system. These other users and their needs should be considered when describing the role of the target system in the larger development organization. If there are similar potential users, their needs may show up as alternative configurations the system should support.

The corresponding situation for commercial developers occurs when a line of related products is being developed or when the same product will be sold in different industries. It is important that these goals be documented.

Of course, some user sponsors are also concerned about cross-product issues. Some sample roles products and projects that might play in a development organization are shown in the examples.

Quantify what "ease of extension" really means.

3. Instance of Growth and Change   Any successful product, including software, will change and grow over its life. One of the more consistent claims made by vendors of software technology is that using their compiler-CASE tool-development environment will make your product robust and easy to maintain and enhance. The fact is that a product will only be easy to extend in these ways if it is designed to be easy to extend. It will be easier to design a product to be easy to extend if the engineer has some idea of what extensions must be handled. For that reason it is very important that the likely extensions be documented as part of the requirements for the system.

Each cohesive change made to the system at build-time is a change case for the system. I coined this term to make the build-time requirements look like peers of the run-time use cases. They play the same role for the build-time requirements that use cases play in the run-time requirements.

"But, you can't predict all the changes to a system over its entire life," is a common expression when the subject is extensions to software products. While that may be true, a great many of the extensions that a product will face are always known at the time the product is being developed. The real choice that I see organizations making is not between being able to predict *some* changes and being able to predict *all* changes. The choice is between predicting something and predicting nothing. If there is no requirement to consider extensions and no documentation of those extensions, it is highly unlikely that the product will be easy to extend.

The changes described above have the same content as the product plan. In hard products, like microprocessor chips, those future enhancements that are unpredictable in software are already under development when the current product is being released. The same thing can be done for software products.

The various kinds of change cases that the designer must consider when documenting build-time requirements include the following:

- Ports and changes in peripherals, platforms, and hardware configurations
- New actors the system must support
- Functional additions and configurations the system will support
- Changes in the application domain

The following paragraphs describe each of these change cases in turn, providing examples and discussion.

Computer hardware, peripherals, and auxiliary systems change much faster than the applications that run on them. Successful products and useful in-house systems are part of the business of the organization, and the business does not change when Intel introduces a new chip. However, the need to port a system does arise because Intel has introduced a new chip. The need to port a system comes about exactly because the hardware and peripherals change more quickly than the applications. So it is likely that most systems will have to be ported from one platform to another during their life. If a system is supposed to be easy to port, it must be designed to be portable. To design for portability, we need to know what will change in the ports.

Common changes in platform and peripherals include operating systems, hardware platforms, presentation systems, databases, printing, and network communications. Some places to look for these changes include technology trends, technology trends in the user organization, the role the product is to play in the user organization, and other markets or users the system will support.

Because of the widespread changes in both computer technology and user organizations, assume that all aspects of the platform, peripherals, and even the actors will change over the life of the system. Under that assumption, the task of identifying likely ports becomes a task of making a list of all the platform and peripheral interfaces the system must support.

Count on hardware and peripherals always changing.

Users may need to implement the system, or parts of it, on different hardware configurations. Each change in configuration can be described as a change case. (Unless, of course, the requirement is that the same software startup on different configurations and configure itself at startup. Then it is closer to a use case, or a "start-up case.")

For documentation purposes, it is sufficient to list the likely ports. The port to each new platform or peripheral is a change case for the system.

Some examples follow:

- The target users may wish to implement their client/server system on standalone PCs for field operation. There could also be other markets, besides the target market, for a software product that requires a standalone hardware configuration. Each hardware configuration is a change case for the original client/server system.

- The target system will be implemented on UNIX servers and UNIX clients. The target customer plans to move to NT servers and PC clients in the near future. That port is a change case. The same change case results if the development sponsor wants to sell the same system to other clients who use NT and PC client/server platforms.

- The target user, or other users, expect to change from Informix to Oracle database systems. Changing the database is a change case.

- A management information and reporting system was designed to produce reports. Users expect output from the system in a form that they can pick up in spreadsheets. The addition of spreadsheet output would be a change in the information interface the system must support and can be documented as a change case.

The people or systems that use a software product can change over time. Sources of these changes include growth and change in the target user environment, applying the product in a new environment, and the need to integrate the target application with other software systems. The addition of each new kind of user or actor can be documented as a change case. Some examples follow:

- An insurance policy pricing system originally used in the home office may be made available to the field sales staff. The sales people need a different sequence of operations than the home office user. Adding sales users is a change case.

- The trend is to give more people direct access to the software. A package tracking system was originally used only by company employees. In the near future, the user wants to make the tracking service available to customers through dial-up and on-line connections. The customer users need a different presentation and permissions environment than employees. Adding customer users is a change case.

- Future functional configurations that the system should support might include producing a standalone version of a client/server system to be used by sales people on their portable PCs, or the desire to produce a self-contained training and demonstration configuration for the system. Each change is a change case for the target system.

- An inventory control system was originally developed as a standalone system. The target users expect to integrate the inventory system with the accounting system within a year. The accounting system may appear to the inventory system as a new actor it must support. The change in actors is a change case.

Changes to the services that a system offers to its users come from two sources: 1) the target environment and, 2) the environments of the related systems that will feed off the target system.

Most new versions are defined by the new services added.

In the target environment, service extensions can come from a number of sources:

- Use cases that are deemed to be outside the scope of the current project
- Migration plans that require the target system to grow to replace existing systems
- Process and automation changes planned for the future of the target organization
- Anticipated changes to the products and services offered by the target organization
- Changes anticipated in the business or regulatory environment of the target organization and from new users of the system

If the system being designed is a replacement for an existing system, the kinds of change requests implemented in the past on the existing system are a good indication of the kinds of changes that can be anticipated for the new system.

If there is a product plan for the target system that defines the enhancements expected in the future, then that plan should be copied directly into the build-time requirements document. If there is no product plan, then the list of functional change cases developed here should be copied directly into the text of the project plan.

Some examples of these kinds of change cases follow:

- In a sales support system, business process reengineering efforts may result in having the sales support people also provide after-sale support. This would result in a change case to integrate the functionality of the service support system into the sales support system.

- Users have asked for the ability to define new reports on-line, but it was decided not to include it in the current scope. Adding on-line report definition could be a change case for the system.

- If the new pricing system is successful, there will be a need to introduce versions for sales people to use and a version for trainers and demonstrators. Each functional configuration can be described as a change case.

- If the development sponsor is hoping to leverage work done on the target system to help the development of other systems, then many aspects of those other systems can become change cases for the target system. For example, the development sponsor may wish to use the text editing function of a desktop publishing system in other applications, such as spreadsheets and presentation graphics systems. Being able to remove the editing "service" is a change case for the desktop publishing system.

Software systems make it easy to handle changing business conditions.

Changes in the domain of the application, that is to the things that the system manipulates, can come about because of changes in the target user environment or because the application is being "ported" to a different domain. Each of these domain changes can be recorded as a change case. Some examples follow.

- The target users are in the United States, but other users in Japan could use the same kind of functionality. The policy rules in Japan are different. The change case is to port the system to the Japanese policies.

- The target system is a customer service representative support system for an insurance company. The related product is a customer service system for a bank. The change case for the target system would then be to replace the insurance policies with bank accounts.

- In a policy-tracking system in an insurance company, anticipated regulatory changes will require changes in the kinds of policies offered, and thus, changes to the kind of policies that the system must handle. The change case is to introduce new kinds of policies.

4. Development Sponsor Constraints   The development sponsor may have requirements to place on the development project that are not change cases. The purpose of the "constraints bucket" is to provide a place to document those requirements. Examples of development sponsor constraints include standards and practices to be used in the project, tools to be used, the level of quality required in the product, and degree of rigor to be applied in the project.

Variations between project types include the types of documents produced, the level of detail required, the number of reviews, and the kinds of controls used. Until these differences are well known in an organization, it would be a good idea to describe the steps, documents, and reviews to be used on the current project. See the examples.

Evaluating Build-Time Requirements

Requirements of any kind may be evaluated for internal consistency and they may be reviewed by the people who are the sources of the requirements. In the case of build-time requirements, those people are likely to be the development sponsors. The primary evaluation technique is to have those people review the documents. See the example review comments in the sample.

Evaluation is review by knowledgeable people.

Example Techniques   For each of the content items mentioned in the external requirements discussion, I have listed techniques that are sufficient to document the item. *Sufficient* means they allow the requirements to be evaluated by the source of the requirements and provide the information needed by the engineers designing the system. Since my second major concern about techniques for documenting requirements, after sufficiency of content, is to not mix engineering decisions with the requirements, I will offer cautions on that topic as needed. Simple text is used for many of these items.

3.4.4 Requirements Notations

Notations for Run-Time Requirements:

1 Scope of the system. Simple text describing the functional and physical boundary of the system.

2 Goals and expectations for the product in the user organization. Simple text describing how the system will function in its environment now and in the future.

3 Actors and their roles. Simple text structure by actor or by role. Each has a name and brief description. Actors should be carefully limited to people and machines that exist only outside the boundary described in item 1.

4 Functional requirements. Use cases for each actor and role, text for use case descriptions. Text description of the dialogue and algorithmic responses of the system. Descriptions should not mention internal divisions of the system or refer to specific components or peripherals.

5 Control interfaces with the outside world. For human user interfaces, diagrams, screen shots or a working interface prototype are effective. Interface prototypes should be carefully limited to interface execution and avoid coding beyond the

interface layer. Prototypes of internal aspects of the system are one of phases at the next level up the process hierarchy. Nonhuman interfaces may consist of functions, event lists, or, as in the case of telecommunication interfaces, state transition models of the interface dialogue.

6 Information interfaces with the outside world. Descriptions of the physical form and content of information that crosses the system boundary (see item 1) in either direction. The entity-relationship diagrams and object models often used here have a way of showing up as output of the system state task. Those notation methods make system decisions under the guise of documenting external requirements, which should be avoided. I recommend that only individual, physical data elements such as the form and content of reports and file formats be described here.

7 Rules and algorithms the system is expected to implement or enforce. Simple text descriptions of sequences of operations and logical branches to formal logic statements, depending on the rigor required in the design. Rules and algorithms should not refer to any internal aspects of the system, such as "update the database before issuing the check."

8 Non-use-related constraints. Simple text description, structure by category of constraint. Emergent properties of the system, such as reliability and performance should be quantified.

Notations for Build-time Requirements:

1 Project scope and goals. Simple text.

2 Role the product will play in the development organization. Simple text.

3 Instances of growth and change. Simple text. Each change case named and described.

4 Development sponsor constraints. Simple text.

3.5 REQUIREMENTS TASK SUMMARY

Run-time requirements are different from build-time requirements.

We have seen that the requirements for a product or subsystem can be divided into two parts: requirements of the users and user sponsors concerned with the run-time performance of the system, on one hand, and the requirements of the development sponsor concerned with the build-time performance of the system, on the other. For the user requirements, all the external aspects of the system should be described: the user sponsor's goals and expectations for the product in its run-time environment (the return on the user sponsor's investment), the control interfaces the system must provide, the information flows (interfaces) that cross the system boundary, the rules and algorithms the system should implement or enforce, how its users, human and machine, use the system, and any other nonfunctional requirements and constraints the users need. A precondition for writing requirements in this form is that the system scope and boundary have already been defined. That boundary also defines where external requirements (should) stop and internal engineering begins. The user requirements are concerned with the run-time behavior of the system.

Partitioning the description of the run-time functional requirements by individual usage, is critical in making the requirements useful in the design process. For that reason, the only technique for documenting user functional requirements described here was the use case technique. In the other tasks, several techniques are mentioned, some working better than others (according to Basic Principle 5 about making notation support evaluations). Here, however, techniques for documenting user functional requirements that do not partition the documents by individual usages have difficulty being effectively used in the development process.

The questions about the scope of a system and the relative costs and advantages of alternative scopes can be addressed with design-study projects of the alternative scopes. That leads us to the next level up the process hierarchy, which I will not cover in this book.

From the user requirements we can determine what behavior and information the system must have if it is to satisfy those requirements. The user, or run-time, requirements impose no constraints on the allocation of that behavior. To find those constraints we need to look to the build-time requirements.

The development sponsor is the person taking a risk by investing in the development and enhancement of software systems. That person is concerned with the cost and effectiveness of operations carried out on the system at build-time. The key element that determines how hard or easy build-time operations are is how the behavior is allocated in the system. Development sponsor, or build-time, requirements document the kinds of changes the system is expected to undergo during its life. Those changes are made at build-time.

Build-time requirements constrain structure.

The development sponsor has a different view of the world than the users and their sponsors. Users are concerned with their own job or business, but most development sponsors are responsible for more than one product, often in more than one business, and always for more than one set of users. Some of the changes that the system must support will come from the target users. Others, however, will come from other products and contexts that the developer-sponsor expects the system to support. Each cohesive operation carried out on the system is called a change case.

The development sponsor requirements include the goals and expectations the development sponsor has on the product in its build-time environment, the change cases the system must support and any other constraints the sponsor needs to place on the build-time environment of the system. These requirements will be used primarily to impose constraints on the behavior and information allocation in the system. The change cases are used to determine the structure of the system.

If all we had were goals and measures, we could grow the process.

Recently, there has been a movement in the object-oriented methodology world to add a step to document user functional requirements with use cases. This is very encouraging. I hope that calls for more complete requirements documentation will become more common. A very effective "methodology" could be fashioned out of documenting external run-time and build-time requirements and describing how to measure design workproducts against them.

CHAPTER 4

External Requirements Example

CONTENTS

4.1 Run-Time Requirements   71
4.2 Build-Time Requirements   80

In this chapter the requirements documents for a small system have been annotated to illustrate the points made in the requirements task description sections. Comments are enclosed in square brackets [ ], and comments are placed immediately after the items to which they refer.

4.1 RUN-TIME REQUIREMENTS

4.1.1 Scope of the System

ACME Video Store is a large, growing concern. They rent videos to retail customers. The rental period and amount of the rental varies with the time of week and the kind of video. They also rent VCRs and game cartridges. They are considering moving into CD disk and player rental, with DATs another possibility. The store also sells a variety of general merchandise such as candy, popcorn, audio tapes, party favors, merchandise related to popular movies, and the like.

A general description is always a good idea.

The store keeps information on its members (customers) and uses the list for its quarterly newsletter. When videos are overdue, they try to call the customer, and if they cannot reach him or her, they send a letter. Late fees are charged for overdue items.

Management can set limits on member activities, such as the maximum number of tapes that may be held by one member, the maximum number of tapes in a single transaction, and the maximum number of overdue items held by one member.

The store has a running bonus policy, such as every 12th tape rental is free, or the second tape rented each month is free. These policies may be created and changed by management.

The system should manage inventory and be able to check actual inventory against system inventory. Items are added to the inventory. Rental items are removed from inventory when they become worn and they may be sold at any time for a value determined by the number of times they have been rented. Multiple copies of titles should be tracked individually.

The system should also manage the cash drawers, or tills, on each point of sale terminal.

The company would like to be able to track daily income, video returns, and overdue videos, at minimum. They would like to be able to track inventory of videos and other items. In the future, they would like the system to manage the creation of time sheets for the employees.

When the company expands to multiple stores, management will want to be able to dial in to any store and perform all the normal management activities: request reports, check activity for any view or period, etc., and exchange messages with the local store manager.

4.1.2 Goals and Expectations

The user's expectations.

- Provide improved data on which videos are moving.
- Provide better financial information.
- Automate inventory management.
- Provide real-time financial and inventory information.
- Provide flexibility in quickly implementing pricing plans and promotions.
- Support company growth to multiple stores.

4.1.3 Actors and Their Roles

- Sales clerk. The sales clerks answer customer questions and check out the videos and other items the customers are renting. They are also responsible for making calls about overdue videos.
- Stocking clerk. The stocking clerks are responsible for maintaining the inventory of rental items, videos, sale items, etc. They place new arrivals in inventory and remove items that are no longer being rented.

- Bookkeeper. The bookkeeper is responsible for keeping daily activity totals of the money taken in and the videos rented. This information is entered into the accounting system used by the store.
- Manager. The manager is responsible for tracking the performance of the store and the inventory of rental items. The manager makes the decisions about which items to add to the store, which to remove, and how to price and promote those items. The manager sets the various pricing policies used in the store.

The actors define the dynamic environment of the system.

4.1.4 Use Case Names and Descriptions

- Query inventory for a title (actor or director). Clerk requests "Find" and fills in one or more of the following fields: title, actor, director. The system searches the inventory for a match. The list of matching items is displayed with an indication of how many copies the store has, whether any are in stock, and whether they are reserved.

- Open membership. Person requests membership. The person completes an application, indicating name, address, phone number, and whether he or she wants credit, whether he or she wants an annual or lifetime membership. Store clerk receives the application. Clerk verifies credit and gives the customer a card. Customer pays for membership.

  [This use case describes the dialogue between the clerk and a customer. No mention is made of what the system does or what requests the user makes of the system. In this form it could be used as part of a business model, but it is not helpful in designing a system. Additional text needed to make the description useful for system design might read as follows: "Clerk requests new member and enters the information into the system. The system verifies that the person is not a current or canceled member. It also checks to see if anyone else at the member's address is a current or canceled member. The clerk enters credit verification information. The system prints a membership card. The system creates an account for the new member."]

Appropriate content and structure of the description is dictated by how the use case will be used.

- Rent a tape in person, or other item. The clerk presses the "Rent" button and scans, or enters the item ID (by scanning the bar code or entering the bar code number) into the screen.

  [Phrases like "presses Rent button" or "selects from a menu" should not be included in use case descriptions. That information is appropriate in the control interface section. The presentation details, like the fact that there is a rent button, are too volatile to merit inclusion in the basic interaction between the system and its actors.]

  The system verifies that the item is on hand. If present, the system prompts for the customer's name. The name is verified as being a member and as not having exceeded any of the limits (maximum videos out, money owed, number of overdue items, etc.). If the name is not in the member list, the system prompts for "New Member" information: name, address, phone, and driver's license or credit card ID. The system determines the due date. Acceptable responses include a number of days or a date. The amount is shown for that item.

If the item is not present, the system indicates that the item is loaned out (and when it is due back), or that it is not carried.

As each item is entered, the system checks to see if a special applies. If it does, the modified price is shown and a message indicating which special was used is shown. There is a prompt for another item. Other items may be entered or "Total" pressed. The price and tax are shown. Clerk enters cash tendered, or credit card, and the system shows the required change. Two copies of a receipt are printed and the transaction is recorded by the system. When the clerk enters "Done," the inventory and cash drawer are updated.

- Return a tape. Members return items to the desk, or for CDs and videos, may drop them off in the return box outside the store. The clerk enters the "Return" mode. He scans the bar code on the item. As soon as it finds a match, the complete item identification and member identity are presented.

  The item is marked returned and is returned to the storage shelf. The system updates inventory and the customer's activity status.

  If the tape is late, a late charge is calculated and displayed. The clerk may ask the customer for the late fee and receive payment. The clerk selects payment, enters cash tendered. System shows change and updates the cash drawer content. If the customer is not there, the clerk indicates "Not Paid" and the system adds the late fee to the member's account.

- Rent a tape over the phone. The two methods of renting a video are renting in person and making a phone reservation and arranging for delivery. When the customer makes a selection, the clerk checks availability, validates membership, and records the rental.

  The clerk gives the video to the driver for delivery. If it is a delivery, the driver takes the tape, drives to the customer's house, and hands the tape to the customer; the customer signs the receipt. The driver returns the receipt to the clerk.

  [This description suffers from not including the system behavior.]

- Sell an item. A customer brings the item to the clerk. The customer need not be a member for a sale. The clerk selects "Sale" and scans the bar code, or manually enters the ID number. The system shows the price. If the clerk enters a quantity, the system calculates the total price. The clerk may continue to scan items to be purchased. Clerk enters "Total" and the system calculates and displays the total price, including sales tax. Clerk enters cash tendered and the system calculates and displays the change returned. When the clerk enters "Done" the system updates the inventory and the cash drawer totals (credit card sales are also supported). If the clerk requests a printed receipt, the receipt will be printed. The transaction is recorded.

- Verify membership. The clerk asks to verify a membership. The clerk enters the customer's name. The system checks to see if the name is a current member. If one or more members with the entered name are found, the systems presents the names and addresses to the clerk. The clerk may select one of the presented customers as the current customer.

If the customer has any outstanding rentals, overdue items, or money owed (from fines), the system will indicate the number and maximum past due time on the verification presentation.

- Request list of overdue items. At least once per week, a clerk will request a list of overdue items. The list consists of the name, address, and phone of the member, the overdue items, and when they were due. The list may be printed out, or the clerk may select customers and the system will write a reminder letter for each customer selected, including the items due and when they were to be returned.

- Request a list of all items out on rental. At any time, commonly at the end of the day, a clerk may request a list of all items out on rental. The system prepares the list and the user may have it printed or just displayed.

- Add new titles, copies to inventory. When new items are received by a store, the inventory clerk logs them into the system. The system tracks the name, artist, director (if applicable), date the item was produced, and number of items received. A bar code is assigned to the item and, if necessary, bar code labels are printed. If the title is already in the system (adding another copy) no additional entry is required.

  Sale items that already have a UPC bar code on them are scanned, and a quantity is entered. After logging an item into the system, it will be available for rental, sale, user queries, and inclusion in inventory and activity reports.

- Remove old titles. Items may be removed from inventory because the manager has decided they have been inactive for too long, they are worn out, or too many people have complained about them. The stock clerk removes the item and then logs the removal into the system by scanning the item's bar code and selecting "Remove."

  When the last copy of a title is removed, the system prompts for confirmation to remove the title.

- Check actual inventory against system inventory. In the inventory verification mode, clerks scan the bar codes on all items on the shelves. For nonrental items, like posters or candy bars, an item may be scanned and then a number may be entered, which indicates the quantity of that item present. When the clerks have checked all items in the store, they enter "Done" to the inventory mode. The system prepares a report of all the discrepancies discovered: items on the shelves, but not in the system and items in the system, but not on the shelves. For rental items, the system will report discrepancies between the number owned and the combination of items on the shelf and out on rental.

- Request reports. The accountant or manager may log in with report permission. The user requests reports and then selects from the list of report types. If an activity report is selected, the current date, another date, or a range of dates may be specified. If a range of dates is selected, a report is prepared for each day in the range. After selecting the date, the items in the report may be selected. The items may be a single item, items specified by name,artist, director, type of item, or all items at the store. The report consists of the total number of transactions for the selected items and the total income collected.

The user may select activity summaries. These reports give dollar income and number of rentals for each of the items selected for the specified time period. The user may specify items by name, director, artist, type of item, or all items. Member activity may be requested by individual member or by time period. Time periods may be specified as a single date, range of dates, week beginning, range of weeks, month, or range of months. When a range of periods is specified, the report gives values for each period in the range. The report may be selected as summary or detailed. Summary gives a single value for each type of item selected. A detailed report gives values for all items included in the query.

Branches have to be handled carefully.

[The number of *ifs* and *mays* in this description indicate that it could be either separated into multiple use cases or described in a more generic way. If each of the branches were larger, several sentences or more, then making separate use cases would be appropriate. Since they are relatively small, I would suggest removing the branches by saying that, "the user enters selection criteria for the report." The details of what gets entered for the different reports could be handled in the data interface section. There, each of the reports could be described along with the selection criteria for each.]

- Request daily activity summary. The accountant or manager may log in with report permission. The user requests reports and then selects from the list of report types. If an activity report is selected, the current date, another date, or a range of dates may be specified. If a range of dates is selected, a report is prepared for each day in the range. After selecting the date, the items in the report may be selected. The items may be a single item, items specified by name, artist, director, type of item, or all items at the store. The report consists of the total number of transactions for the selected items and the total income collected.

- Request inventory listings. Any clerk may request an inventory report. When the report is selected, the clerk may specify which items the report should include and the time of the report. The default is *now*, but future times may be specified to check availability of items that have been reserved. Choices include a single item, items specified by name, by artist, director, type of item, or all items. The report lists each of items selected and the following information: number owned, number in stock, number reserved, and number overdue.

- Request daily, weekly, monthly yearly activity summaries. An operator with administrative permission may request activity summaries. These reports give the dollar income and number of rentals for each of the items selected for the specified time period. The user may specify items by name, director, artist, type of item, or all items. Member activity may be requested by individual member or by time period. Time periods may be specified as a single date, range of dates, week beginning, range of weeks, month, range of months. When a range of periods is specified, the report gives values for each period in the range. The report may be selected as summary or detailed. Summary gives a single value for each type of item selected. A detailed report gives values for all items included in the query.

[Three of the last four use cases are redundant.]

- Administer users. Users with administrative clearance may administer users. Users have names, addresses, phone, password, and clearance assignments. The system displays a list of users. The administrator may select one for editing or select "add a user." The system displays the selected user's information. The administrator may make changes. When the administrator selects "done," the system records the changes.

- Administer members. Clerk requests "Members." Clerk is prompted for member's name. Clerk enters name and is presented with a list of members with that name, showing name, address, and family members. Clerk may select one of the names. System presents detail of member information, including tapes out, overdue, money owed. Clerk may change any personal information: address, family members that may rent, phone, or credit card info. (Only a manager may alter the account information). Clerk may select "New," in which case the system presents a blank member data screen. Clerk fills information and saves it. That member may immediately check out videos.

- Administer member rental limits. A manager requests "Rental Rules." The system presents the current rules and limits. The rules have the form of setting a limit on the value of variables. The variables include the number of items rented, number of overdue items held, the longest overdue period, money owed, and the maximum items in a single rental. If no values are provided, the limit is not applied.

- Request member activity. A user with administrative permission may request reports at any time. The system presents a list of available reports. The user selects "Member Activity." The system prompts for member name or ID and the time period. For the indicated member the system retrieves and presents information on the member, the number of rentals made in the last month, the number of videos currently held, the number overdue, the longest overdue period, and the rental fees paid in the last month and since he or she became a member.

- Edit inventory item. A manager may request "Edit Inventory." Manager is prompted for type, name, or ID. The manager enters name or ID and is presented with current information about the item. Data that may be changed include prices, late fees, and the formula for calculating the selling price. Manager may request that the changes be saved. The changes are updated in the inventory.

- Edit types and categories. A manager may request "Edit Types." A list of current types and categories is displayed. Manager may select one, in which case the system presents current information about the type or category. If a name change is entered (or a new name is entered), the system checks to see that it does not duplicate an existing name.

Manager may remove types and categories (select "Remove") only if there are no items in the inventory under that type or category.

- Administer specials. A manager may select "Edit Specials." The system presents a list of the names of current specials. User may select one to edit, remove, or create a new one. Each special has a name and a rule for calculating whether it applies. Specials are defined as calculations and relationships between a number of predefined variables. Those variables include the day of the week, the base price, the number of items being rented, and the number of items rented in the current month by the customer.

- Close and reconcile cash drawer. The clerk selects "Close." The system prompts for the cash count of the money in the drawer. The system prints a report showing activity since opening, the amount that should be in the drawer and the actual amount counted. The user may enter corrections to the cash drawer.

- Start the cash drawer. After logging in, the clerk selects "Start Cash Drawer." The system prompts for the amount of cash to be added to the drawer and enters normal operating mode.

4.1.5 Control Interfaces

User Interfaces (Samples)

- User interfaces. Figure 4.1 shows sample user interface specifications.
- Nonhuman interfaces. There are no machine interfaces at the application level in this application.

Figure 4.1
User interfaces for the Select Reports Dialogue and the Specify Report Dialogue

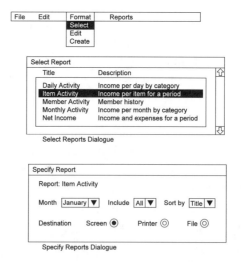

EXTERNAL REQUIREMENTS EXAMPLE I CHAPTER 4

4.1.6 Information Interfaces

Table 4.1 shows a sample file format and two sample reports.

Table 4.1

Accounting system file records and sample reports

Record Name	Separator	Fields: Name/ Type/Size				
Sale	tab	Member Text 30	Amount Dollar 7	Type Char 2	Date Date 10	
Bill	tab	Vendor Text 30	Amount Dollar 7	Due Date 10	Description Text 80	
Invoice	tab	Customer Text 30	Amount Dollar 7	Date Data 10	Number Number 15	Description Text 80

Report Content Overdue Report			
Name	**Titles Held**	**Overdue, days**	**Fine due**
Smith, James	Horse Feathers	3	3.00
123 Maple Any Town, NY 10234	New York Stories	8	8.00
		Total	11.00

Member History Report					
Name	**Join Date**	**Total Rentals**	**Total Sales**	**Fines Paid**	**Fines Outstanding**
Smith, J	3/4/92	$123	$10	$4	0

4.1.7 Rules and Algorithms

- Rentals will only be made to people who have provided adequate identity and credit information.
- Rentals will be denied to anyone with an outstanding balance of $20 or more.
- In any discrepancy between system inventory and real inventory, the real inventory will be taken as the true value.
- An audit trail will be maintained of all inventory discrepancies and the corrections made to inventory.

4.1.8 User Constraints

- Using the system must be at least as fast as manual checkouts.
- Point of sale unit hardware must be DOS or small Mac.

4.2 BUILD-TIME REQUIREMENTS

The development organization and sponsor of the development is Rough and Ready Systems. R&R is a small software development company that hopes to grow substantially by leveraging the work done on past systems to benefit present and future systems. R&R has a contract with ACME Video to develop a system for ACME stores. It is R&R's first venture in rental store support systems.

4.2.1 Project Scope and Goals

The project will deliver a working system to the customer, beginning from a statement of need provided by the customer. The customer has not been receptive to the suggestion of having multiple stages, each separately budgeted.

> ["Big Bang" projects run a greater risk of being late due to unanticipated problems than projects that take a more incremental approach. This is not an issue here at the level of individual documentation techniques, but it is important at the level of project sequences.]

4.2.2 Role the Product Will Play in the Development Organization

The development organization has different goals from the user organization.

- We wish to enter the market for rental store support systems.
- Video rental is the first product. Others might include furniture and contractor's equipment, home owner's equipment, and party supplies.
- We will define the role this product will play in meeting those goals.
- The initial system should be readily configurable to suit other video stores.
  – At minimum, the architecture structure should be applicable to other products.
  – It is desirable to be able to reuse components in other systems.

4.2.3 Instances of Growth and Change

The change cases for this system are listed below:

1. Add new rental and sale items, media, and equipment.
2. Support school and corporate customers.
3. Manage time sheets for employees.

4 Support growth to multiple stores.

5 Integrate with accounting system.

6 Add custom report definition capability.

7 Integrate with corporate inventory database.

8 Configure for another customer on a different platform, different look and feel, single workstation system.

Ports

9 Change computer platforms.

10 Change presentation implementation package.

11 Change Database.

Future Configurations

12 Equipment rental system.

13 Retail and party goods rental system.

> [Change cases 1–7 could be viewed as coming from the target customer. Change cases 8–13 were derived from the development sponsor's goals for the product]

4.2.4 Development-Sponsor Constraints

Because this is a production project, all product features and product "ilities" must be demonstrated to be present in design documentation before proceeding with final implementation.

CHAPTER 5

The System State Task

CONTENTS

5.1 Introduction   83
5.2 Notations   87
5.3 System State   88
5.4 Evaluation   90
5.5 Carrying out the Evaluations   91
5.6 Summary   93

5.1 INTRODUCTION

5.1.1 Which Properties Are Being Designed?

The name of this task is somewhat unusual. Most readers, on looking ahead a few pages will say, "Oh, this is the _____." In the blank they will say, data model, entity model, information model, or object model, depending on where they are from. Outside of the function-centered practices, this is one of the most widely practiced tasks using the most consistent notation in the industry. In spite of that, I have had a great deal of trouble finding a name for this task that does not offend one camp or the other. The object people are loathe to have it called anything that smacks of data, but many of the names used by this camp imply something quite different from what we need here. The terms *business object model* and *domain object model* imply something that is not related to a specific software system. Static object model, or just object model, is usually interpreted to mean that a complete system is

We have a slight naming problem here.

Figure 5.1

**Subtasks
and work
products in
the system
state task**

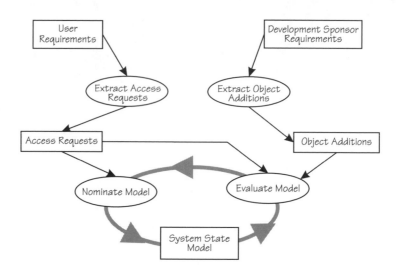

being described. If any of the object words are used, then the non-object people feel
that we are talking about something different from what they do. The structured
and information engineering people interpret this task as modeling the essential
business or as designing the database tables. So, what is needed and why did I call it
system state?

Every system keeps track of something to help it carry out its job. In "database
applications" that something is viewed as the content of the database tables (whose
design occupied the majority of the engineering time). In switching systems, it is
viewed as the state of the calls and connections in the switch. The set of values in
that something at any given time will often be used to determine how the system
will respond to events in the outside world. (In the switching system, the design of
those responses to events probably occupied the majority of the engineering time.)
Systems usually devote considerable CPU cycles to acquiring, maintaining, and
using that something. I believe that a name which accurately describes "that something" in all types of systems is *system state.*

The system state, however it is represented, is a component of the system. The
content of the state must be designed by the engineers of the system to enable the
system to meet its run-time requirements. The structure of the state elements must
be designed so that when the state needs to be changed at build-time, the changes
can be made without redoing most of the state-design task.

*Here's what
it is, pick a
name that
suits you.*
We can further define the system state by comparing it to the way it is treated in
different methodology camps. Because the system state is an internal component of
the system, it is not the same as a model of the environment outside the system,
although such a model might be a useful input to the process of designing the state.
Nor is it the file or database tables that may be used to store the information content of the system state. How the state is stored should not have any direct

relationship to the content and structure of the system state. A given system needs the same state regardless of whether the state information is stored in cyberspace or on papyrus. Nor is the system state the complete system. A complete system must also include the machinery to interact with the outside world, to manipulate and maintain its state, and to use its state in providing the required services. Those aspects of the system will be addressed in other Essential Tasks.

I chose the term *system state* to describe the output of this task to indicate that we are talking about something that is very much a part of the system, is not something outside the system, but is not the entire system. *System state* also indicates something that should be essential for the system to operate. Unfortunately, the notation that I have found to be satisfactory to describe the system state is the same notation that the object people have been using both to describe the domain outside the system, the "real world," and the complete system. It is the same notation that the structured and information engineering people have been using to describe the business outside the system, and the data content and structure of tables in databases.

I hope this discussion will serve to define what the system state is and how it is different from some related ideas that are, unfortunately, expressed in the same notation. The system state must be designed to meet the build-time and run-time requirements of the specific system that is being engineered. State-like designs developed to meet other needs, like modeling the business or designing databases, are not designs of components of a software system.

The specific property of the system being addressed in this task is the need for sufficient internal state to allow the system to meet its run-time requirements.

5.1.2 Evaluations

Two kinds of evaluation should be made. The first is that the state provided is, in fact, sufficient to meet the run-time requirements for functionality and information. The second is that the structure of the state is flexible enough to gracefully handle the changes to the state that will result from carrying out the change cases on the system. Because the system state is not the entire system, the external requirements do not bear directly on the system state. Therefore, some work must be done to extract evaluation criteria from the external requirements that are appropriate for use on the system state model. The evaluation criteria extracted from the run-time requirements will be called *access requests,* and those extracted from the build-time requirements will be called *system state change cases.*

System state can be evaluated against build-time and run-time goals.

5.1.3 Notations

A notation that is found to be sufficient is the static-object notation, or the very closely related entity-relationship diagrams. This type of notation provides enough information to enable demonstrations that test if the access requests and system state changes are supported by the design. When less formality is needed, two other notations are useful. One is a list of categories of state elements, and the other is a list of the names of state elements, with descriptions, but with no structure or attributes shown.

5.1.4 Develop Evaluation Criteria

All aspects of a design should be evaluated against requirements the users and the development sponsors place on the system. These requirements are documented in the external requirements, but they are not in a form that can easily be applied to the system state model. This is because the requirements are intended to apply to the entire system, but we are dealing here with a subset of the system, namely, the system state model. For that reason, we have to do some work to get the requirements into a form that is relevant to the system state model.

If we look ahead to the system architecture, (Figure 9.6) we can see that the system state components are passive servers to the other system components. The conversation between the system state components and the other system components takes place at a different semantic level from the level of the conversations between the external actors and the system. We have to translate, or extract, the access requests that the system components will send to the domain model components.

Access requests come from use-cases.

Each use case and information output will contain a number of explicit and implicit access requests that the system state model will have to support. These requests will include requests for information, and requests to add to or change the system state model. For example, every piece of information presented on the screen or contained in a report will have to be obtained from the model with an access request. Every time a new element is added to the model, or an existing element is changed, such as a customer or a video, the request will be carried to the model in an access request. I am not suggesting that one access request be generated for every field in all the outputs. Some grouping and selection are required.

If the model must support these access requests, then the list of those requests is a good source of evaluation criteria for the system state. The example section describes the process of extracting access requests from the use case descriptions and from the information outputs.

The use case descriptions and the information outputs contain the user requirements. The access requests extracted from them contain the user requirements as they apply to the system state model. We can say then, that if the system state model can support all the access requests, it will meet the user requirements.

The development sponsor requirements, in particular the likely extensions, impose another set of requirements on the system state model. Some of the extensions will require changes and additions to the system state model. We should extract—guess at, really—the changes and additions we think will result from the descriptions of likely extensions. These changes will constitute the evaluation criteria for determining if the system state model can support the development sponsor requirements. The example section shows how likely changes in the system state model are identified in the development sponsor requirements description.

Build-time changes are the source of evaluation criteria for the structure.

There are an infinite number of different model state configurations for any system. The great majority of them are inadequate to support the system, but there are a great many that are sufficient. The sufficient models may be distributed along a continuous spectrum from an attribute-rich model to an object-rich model. It is essential then that there be some objective way to evaluate a nominated model to determine, first if it is sufficient, and second if its position on the spectrum is satisfactory. I suggest that the access requests and extensions to the system state model developed here provide the means of making those evaluations. The actual process of making the evaluations is described in the evaluation section of this chapter.

Designing the system state doesn't have to sound like counting angels on pinheads.

5.2 NOTATIONS

The complete output of the system state modeling task consists of one or more diagrams showing the system states and their static relationships. Each unique element in the model should be specified with a name, description, list of attributes, and a list of relationships the element must support. A sample set of specifications are shown in the design documents. The descriptions are separate from the graphic elements.

State element modeling is the core of many OO methods, where it is called object modeling, and many data modeling methods, where it is called entity modeling. There is a rich set of notations available.

The notation is widely known.

Figure 5.2 shows a generic system-state notation. The main variations between individual notations are the shape of the box and how the cardinality of the relationships is indicated. The solid circle indicating one-to-many is from Rumbaugh.

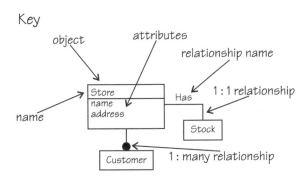

Figure 5.2

Key to system state notation

Figure 5.3
Objectory
entity object
notation

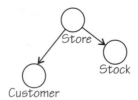

The needs of the specific project should dictate the degree of rigor and completeness of the system state model output. The minimum system state model output consists, simply, of a list of the main categories of system state elements. The increments of completeness might have the following sequence: state element names and descriptions, relationships, attribute names, attribute types, relationship specifications. Samples of each output variation are shown in the examples section.

In evaluating alternative notations, the most important criteria is whether the notations support the required evaluations. If, after doing the work to produce a system state model, we cannot evaluate the work against the requirements, we have no way of knowing whether we have achieved our goals.

A notation that does not support the evaluations is not worth using.

An example of a notation that is not sufficient is the Objectory entity object notation. While the Objectory tool records all of the required information about attributes, attribute types, relationships, and their cardinality, only the object name and the existence of the relationships is indicated in the diagram. An example is shown in Figure 5.3.

5.3 SYSTEM STATE

I am going to use the word *state element* in this section, in place of the words, *object* and *entity*. *Object* and *entity* are the words usually applied to the little box with the attributes and relationship lines connected to it. It sounds a little awkward, but I think that the value of not using words that often refer to things outside the system design justifies the awkwardness.

The system being designed is different from its environment.

There is a common expectation about building system state models that is not very realistic, which is that it is a process of "modeling the real world." This expectation is at the base of the motives for using object technology: systems will be better if they contain the same "things" that their domains contain, and that it is easy to "discover" what those things are. Grady Booch made it sound very simple in his book *Software Engineering with Ada.* There he described the process of discovering objects as underlining the nouns in the functional requirements document. As I hope will be obvious, this is never sufficient, but it is a good way to find an initial list of state element nominations.

The completeness of the initial list can be improved by using use case descriptions instead of a single functional requirements document. Use case descriptions tend to have more detail than global functional requirements documents. The reason the suggestion was made in the user requirements section about using complete sentences with all subjects and grammatical objects carefully identified is that the use cases are used as a source of system state element nominations.

The examples section shows an initial list of nominated state elements derived from the use case descriptions. Some of the nouns will seem to be "naturally" attributes of other state elements, such as the address of a customer. An initial evaluation that can be applied to state element nominations is the following. If you can think of a situation where the state element will be accessed in its own right, then make it an state element. If it will only be accessed in association with another state element, nominate it as an attribute of that state element.

Some state element candidates are indicated by nouns in the functional requirements and algorithms.

Even carefully worded use cases may not be complete. Another source of state element nominations is conversations about the domain of the system, whether among domain experts or developers. By listening carefully, you can often discover additional nouns to nominate as state elements. I have often found words that occur with great regularity in conversation that do not appear on the initial list of state element nominations. I have worked on three call-processing systems where the developers refused to have a call-state element.

Nominating the state elements is not a mechanical operation.

An early evaluation that can be used during the nominating process is the semantic level. All of the state element names for a given domain should come from that domain. In our example, the words *video, VCR, tape, member,* and *customer* are all from the video store domain. Words like *database* and *printer* are from a different domain, or put another way, are from a different semantic level. A word like *transaction* may be marginally in the video store domain, but *rental transaction* would be better. Mixing state elements from multiple domains, or semantic levels, makes the discussion of behavior modeling very much more complex than it needs to be.

The names of the state element nominees should be carefully chosen to have an unambiguous meaning among domain authorities. I am often surprised at how much controversy a name like *policy* can evoke in an insurance company application. A two- or three-sentence description is often helpful in clarifying what the state element represents. The name and description of a state element nominee also have a strong influence on what attributes and behaviors people allocate to it. The example section shows the initial list of state element nominations.

If the possibilities for variation in naming state elements are large, the possibilities in nominating attributes and relationships are vast. The reason is that the relationships people nominate come from the sentences they use to describe the domain. If one person says, "members rent video tapes," he or she may nominate *member* and *tapes* as state elements with *rents* as the relationship. Another person may say, "the store has video tapes which are either in stock or a rented." He or she

Patterns of speech and word sequence are sources of state model structure.

would nominate the state elements *store* and *video tape*, with an attribute of status (rented or in stock) to describe the same aspect of the domain.

Because there is a great variation possible in nominated relationships, I suggest that a very iterative process of nominate-evaluate-change be used. The evaluation step is described in the next section. A first cut at a system state model is shown in the example section. This will be heavily modified in subsequent evaluation and change cycles.

There is nothing concrete about objects, attributes, and relationships. This interchangeability between state elements, attributes, and relationships leads to a simplified definition of the three. State elements are the names of boxes in the diagram, attributes are anything whose name is written below the state element name inside the box. Relationships connect boxes. While this may seem irreverent in view of all that has been written about object and entity modeling, there is really nothing intrinsic in the words that identifies them as attributes or as objects.

It is not necessary, or even desirable, to have all elements related to one another. Some elements may be connected only through process or control components, which are introduced in the behavior model and architecture tasks. Because we have other opportunities to connect all state elements into a unified system, we do not have to connect everything here in the system state model.

5.4 EVALUATION

Perhaps because of the OO myth that domain objects and relationships simply model the real world, I have found that people are quite vehement in the defense of the objects and relationships that they nominate. To avoid such long arguments, it is very important to have a way to evaluate the model nominations. There are four kinds of criteria we can use.

The first criteria, discussed above, is the semantic level of the state element names.

The second criteria is whether the model is sufficient to support the user requirements. The gauge for this evaluation is the access requests that were derived from the use cases and information outputs. With this measure, we can determine if the model is in the spectrum of sufficient models. That spectrum runs from state element-rich models on one end to attribute-rich models on the other. Examples from each end of the spectrum are shown in the examples sections.

The third criteria, applied after we have determined that the model is sufficient, is whether the model is efficient. This criteria is based on the fact that responding to access requests by traversing state elements and relationships is faster than by searching attributes. We clearly cannot optimize for all access requests, so some ranking of requests is needed. Before introducing the fourth criteria, I would like to offer a digression on introducing such a low-level concern as efficiency so early in the process.

Why introduce efficiency into what is nominally an analysis activity? The conventional wisdom in software is that there are two parts of the development process; analysis and design. Analysis is not supposed to be concerned with any implementation concerns, like representation in a language, efficiency, or hardware distribution. I fully agree with the exclusion of programming language concerns, but I think there is a problem with separating activities that result in changing the form of the model, like how well the model supports the user requirements. If we derive a model that is only sufficient early in the process and wait until later to evaluate its efficiency, we may compromise its sufficiency in trying to make it efficient. Any change to a model should be evaluated against all of the requirements the model must support. The net effect of always evaluating changes against all requirements is that we consider all sources of change at the same time. For that reason, I recommend looking at sufficiency and efficiency at the same time.

An architect always designs with the final product in mind.

The fourth criteria comes from the development sponsor requirements: Can the model gracefully handle the likely changes and extensions that we have identified for the system? The result of applying each of these criteria to the model nominations is usually one or more changes to the system state model. We cycle through evaluation and change until the designers are comfortable with model. The trade-off being made is between the simple and slow access of an attribute-rich model on one hand, and the speed and complexity of a state element-rich model on the other.

5.5 CARRYING OUT THE EVALUATIONS

5.5.1 Semantic Level

Look over the list of state element names and brief descriptions. All of the names and words in the descriptions should come from the application domain. In most cases, the computer hardware and subsystems, like the disk, printer, and database, are not part of the application domain. State elements that are not of the appropriate level should either be removed from the model, or moved to a separate model that addresses that semantic level.

A common example of the latter situation occurs when there is an administration function in the system. The words used to describe administration of the system are different from the words used to describe what the system does. The state elements and relationships that describe the administration should be in a separate model from the state elements that describe the domain of the application.

5.5.2 Sufficiency of the Models

The connection between the user requirements and the system state model is made with the access requests derived from the user requirements. To determine if the nominated models are sufficient, we should walk through each of the access requests on the model and satisfy ourselves that each request can be handled.

Sufficiency of the model is necessary but not sufficient.

The steps involve finding an entry point that matches the given information, finding whether and where in the model the desired end point is, and then determining if the end point can be reached from the entry point. If the access request is a change or update, any necessary changes to dependent state elements should be possible. When traversing the model, it is helpful to note whether the decisions about where to go next are made by moving across a relationship or by searching for an attribute value in a collection of state elements. This information is useful in the next stage of the evaluation. Chapter 6 describes each of these steps.

When an access request cannot be satisfied, the model should be modified. The kinds of modifications possible include changing state elements, attributes and relationships. My observation is that the most common source of problems is a lack of state elements, so my first suggestion for fixing problems is to add more state elements and relationships. Some alternative ways of fixing a problem are shown in the examples discussion.

The end result of these walk-through-and-modify cycles is a system state model that can be shown to satisfy all of the requirements placed on it by the users of the system. This does not mean, of course, that there is any guarantee that the model will, in fact, be sufficient. It just means that we have documented and reviewed our best attempt to make a sufficient model. While not a guarantee, it does wonders for improving the chances that the model will be sufficient.

The fact that a model is sufficient means that it is in the set of sufficient models that populate the spectrum between state element-rich and attribute-rich models. Our next step is to determine if we are comfortable with the position along the spectrum.

5.5.3 Efficiency

Efficiency affects the structure: it cannot be addressed separately.

The trade-off being evaluated here is between greater speed and state-element model structural complexity on one hand and less speed and structural simplicity, on the other. In general, the most frequently used access requests, or those with the tightest response-time requirements should be supported with the most efficient structures. Those requests that are less frequently used or that have slow response time requirements can be supported with less efficient attribute searches. This kind of evaluation implies that the access requests have their frequency of use and response time requirements noted, which implies that the use cases record how often they would be invoked.

The evaluation process involves examining the path that is followed in responding to each access request. If the access request is a high priority request, the path should be direct, as short as possible and have few attribute search steps. Low priority requests can be longer and involve more attribute look-ups.

Chapter 6 walks through several efficiency evaluations.

5.5.4 Extensions and Additions

We have evaluated the model nominations against the user requirements, but we
have not yet addressed the development sponsor requirements. For that we will use
the change and extension scenarios developed earlier. The approach is to treat the
addition of each build-time change to the system state as a scenario. The scenario
may be applied to the system state model being evaluated. If the new state element
can be added without changing many existing state elements and relationships, the
model is sufficient. If many changes are needed, the model should be changed to
accommodate the change.

*Design the
state for ease
of extension.*

Chapter 6 walks through several change scenarios and demonstrates some kinds
of changes that can be made to the model.

5.6 SUMMARY

The term *system state* is a generic term that represents whatever it is that the system
keeps track of. Providing for adequate system state in a system is an essential prerequisite for being able to meet the run-time functional and information requirements.
The system state task designs the form and content of the system state elements.

The technique of doing the design and the notation used are very similar to the
techniques used in object and entity modeling. Contrary to much published advice,
the structure of the system state model is not simply a reflection of the "real world."
The system state model is created by engineers to meet the needs of a specific software system. The state elements, attributes, and relationships that any individual
nominates depends on how they think and talk about the system. Therefore, evaluating the nominations against the access requests and state element change cases is
critical to obtaining a model that will, in fact, adequately support the systems that
use it.

The set of sufficient models occupy a spectrum that ranges from element-rich to
attribute-rich. Efficiency in responding to the high priority access requests can be
used as a criteria for selecting which point on the spectrum is best.

No behavior issues were addressed in the system state task. Those will be covered
in the behavior tasks.

CHAPTER 6   

System State Modeling Examples

CONTENTS

6.1 Derive the Criteria   95
6.2 Derive State Elements   99
6.3 Evaluate the Nominations   103
6.4 Evaluating Three Versions of the Model   107
6.5 Fixes   116
6.6 Completing the System State Model   119
6.7 Summary of the Example   120

6.1 DERIVE THE CRITERIA

Before beginning the task of building a system state model, it is important to derive criteria to use for its evaluation. Those criteria, of course, should be based on the external requirements for the system. In some tasks, the external requirements can be used directly in evaluating a design document. In other cases, such as the system state model, the criteria need to be derived from the external requirements. The form needed here is not the same as that needed for the requirements. A useful set of criteria for the system state model consist of access requests, derived from the use cases, and new state elements that must be added to the system, derived from the change cases. Each of these will be derived here.

6.1.1 Extract Access Requests

Sample Use Case

Consider the following fragment of a use case description for the case "rent a tape:"

Derive the impact of the use case on the state model.

The clerk presses the "Rent" button and scans, or enters the item ID (by scanning the bar code or entering the bar code number) into the screen.

1 The system verifies that the item is on hand. If present, the system prompts for the customer's name.

2 The name is verified as being a member and as not having exceeded any of the limits (maximum videos out, money owed, number of overdue items, etc.).

3 If the name is not in the member list, the system prompts for "New Member" information: name, address, phone, and driver's license or credit card ID. The due date is requested. Acceptable responses include a number of days or a date. The amount is shown for that item.

4 If the item is not present, the system indicates whether the item is loaned out (and when it is due back), or whether it is not carried.

5 As each item is entered, the system checks to see if a special applies. If it does, the modified price is shown and a message indicating which special was used is shown. There is a prompt for another item. Other items may be entered or "Total" pressed. The price and tax are shown. Clerk enters cash tendered, or credit card, and the system shows the required change.

6 Two copies of a receipt are printed and the transaction is recorded by the system.

7 When the clerk enters "Done," the inventory is updated.

Discussion of Sample Use Case

Sentences (1) and (2) imply that queries have been made: given an item number, get its status; and given a customer name, get his or her membership status.

Sentence (3) does not contain enough detail, but it appears that a new member is created and added to the system. The access request might be stated as: given membership information, create a new member and add the member to the member list.

Sentence (4) suggests that, either the status returned in the query at (2) includes information about its return time, or a separate query is needed such as: given an item number, return rental information about the item.

Sentence (5) is another example of a requirement that is missing some information. We don't know what the nature of the specials are. We could formulate a very general query, like: given a customer name, date, and number of items on this rental, and current item, return the price of the current item and the special applied, if any.

Sentence (6) implies a great deal more than is stated. From other use cases we know that we can find out which member has rented which items. This implies that during check out, the system must record which items the member is renting. This is a case where more detail in the use case description would be very helpful. We could formulate an update access request as follows: given a member and an item, record the rental of the item by the member. Looking ahead to the next access request, we can see that we should not save the transaction until the rental transaction is done. Perhaps we should describe two operations, record and save, with the understanding that *save* means change inventory, while *record* means it can be easily changed.

Sentence (7) implies the following access: given a member, a set of rental items and prices, save the rental transaction for the member and update the inventory with the items rented.

Use cases are only a hint about what the system must do.

Extracted Access Requests from the Use Cases

The access requests I extracted from the use cases are listed below:

1 Find an item. Given any type of item, title, artist, or director, return a list of all items matching the specification: number owned and number available.

2 Find a member. Given the member's last name, find all members with that name. Return a list of all members with the specified name.

3 Request overdue list by item. Given the current time and date, return a list of all items that are more than 4 hours past due. Show the item, member name, and due date.

4 Request overdue list by customer. Given a customer name, current time, and date, find all overdue items checked out by the customer.

5 Find an item being returned. Given the name of the item and its type (video, CD, VCR, etc.) find the outstanding rental receipt or receipts for that item. Return a list of all the customers who have checked out that title. If the customer's name is also supplied, return the transaction (rental receipt).

6 Find copies of a title currently loaned out. Given the name of a title, return how many copies are out on rental and who has them.

7 Get activity summary. Given an inventory item and a time period, find all the rentals that occurred on that item for the period.

8 Remove an item from inventory. Given an item name and a flag to indicate a specific copy or all copies, remove the item from inventory. Determine if any copies of the item are currently out on rental.

9 Add an item to inventory. Given the name, type, and unique ID of an item, add the item to inventory. Update all relevant counts and inventory data.

10 Add a new pricing special. Given a name, type, and rules; add a new pricing special to the system.

11 Get current inventory list. Given the request, collect a list of all items in inventory, showing name, type, number of copies owned, and number out on rental.

12 Mark an item as rented. Given the ID of a rental item, find the item and mark it as rented an update the item's activity summary.

13 Remove a category. Given a category name, remove the category from the system.

14 Add a category. Given a name and type of a new category, add the category to the system.

15 Get member activity summary. Given a member ID, get the last five items rented, dates of rental, total expenditure since becoming a member, money due, and overdue rentals.

16 Access paths from information outputs. From the member history report: given a member name or ID, get the total rentals, sales, and fines paid. Given a member name or ID, get the member's outstanding fines.

6.1.2 Extract System State Change Cases

Model extensions from development sponsor requirements.

Change Cases

The change cases that were developed for this design are shown below:

1 Add new rental and sale items, media and equipment.
2 Support school and corporate customers.
3 Manage time sheets for employees.
4 Support growth to multiple stores.
5 Integrate with accounting system.
6 Add custom report definition capability.
7 Integrate with corporate inventory database.

System State Change Cases

From item (1) we can anticipate that new kinds of rental items will be needed. They will probably need their own grouping by type of item and category. The new items may have attributes similar to the present items.

School and corporate customers called for in item (2) will be very different from the retail members that the store handles now. The corporate customers would have very different rules and limits. For example, the retail specials and rental limits would probably not apply. The billing and payment practices will be quite different.

Item (3) calls for employees and time sheets. The semantics will be quite different from the semantics of renting videos.

The growth to multiple stores may require a point of view that is not present in a single store system. Views of inventory may have to account for the presence of multiple stores.

From this brief tour through the change cases, we have the following new state elements that the model may have to accommodate:

- Multiple stores
- Employees
- Time sheets
- School members
- Corporate members
- New rental rules and limits
- Categories
- Types
- Rental items

With some evaluation criteria in hand, we can begin the process of designing a system state model for our system.

6.2 DERIVE STATE ELEMENTS

Although the practice is never sufficient, a convenient place to start looking for state elements is the use case descriptions. The list below is a simple extraction of nouns from the use cases and from the problem description.

Nouns Extracted from the Problem Description

Video tape, VCR, game cartridge, CD (future), CD player, DAT, candy, popcorn, audio tape, party favor, merchandise, member, letter, rental limit, bonus, policy, cash drawer, inventory, rental item, copy of a title, title, time sheet (future), store, activity report, period, messages

Nouns extracted from the Actors List

Actors should only be nominated as state elements if the system must maintain information about them. Just because they exist in the domain does not mean that they should automatically be included in the system state model. In this case, the system will probably have to track the users of the system for login, and in the future, for time sheets. Another reason the system may need to keep track of actors is for log-in and access privileges. I will include the following actors as nominations: Sales Clerk, Stock Clerk, Bookkeeper, and Manager.

Nouns Extracted from the Use Case Descriptions

I will try not to write down duplicates:

- Query inventory. Name, address, phone number, membership, application, current member, cancelled member, address, member account.
- Rent a tape. Item ID, member list, due date, special, price, cash tendered.
- Return a tape. Bar code, activity status, late charge, payment.
- Sell an item. Sale, quantity, sales tax, receipt, transaction.
- Verify membership. Fine.
- Request list of overdue items. Overdue item, overdue list.
- Add new titles. Artist, director, production date.
- Remove old titles.
- Check actual inventory against system inventory. Posters, quantity, discrepancies.
- Request reports. Report permission, report, date range, type of item, income (from rentals), time period, member activity, summary report, detailed report.
- Request inventory listings. Inventory report, number owned, number in stock, number reserved, number overdue.
- Request activity summaries. Administration permission, activity report.
- Administer users. Administration clearance, password (for users), clearance assignments.
- Administer members.
- Administer member rental limits. Rental rules, variables.
- Request member activity. Member ID.
- Edit inventory item. Late fee, formula for selling price.
- Edit types and categories. Type (of rental item), category (of rental item).
- Administer specials. Special, rule (for a special).
- Close and reconcile cash drawer. Cash, cash drawer, cash drawer report.
- Start cash drawer.

There seem to be many kinds of reports, so it may be useful to group all the reports together. The words *permissions* and *clearance* mean the same thing, and there are several types of each that can be grouped. Making these groupings and sorting the list alphabetically results in the following:

- activity status
- address (member)
- application for membership
- artist
- bar code
- cancelled member
- cash
- cash drawer
- cash tendered
- category (of rental item)
- clearance assignments
- clearances
  - administration clearance
  - administration permission
  - report permission
- current member
- date range
- director
- discrepancies
- due date
- fine
- formula for selling price
- income (from rentals)
- item ID
- late charge
- late fee
- member account
- member activity
- member ID
- member list
- membership
- name (customer)
- number in stock
- number overdue
- number owned
- number reserved
- overdue item
- overdue list
- password (for users)
- payment
- phone number
- posters
- price
- production date
- quantity (of a sale item)
- receipt
- rental rules
- reports
  - activity report
  - cash-drawer report
  - detailed report
  - inventory report
  - report
  - summary report
- rule (for a special)
- sale
- sales tax
- special
- special (rental pricing)
- time period
- transaction
- type (of rental item)
- type of item
- variables (in rules)

The task is now to organize these words into state elements, attributes, and relationships. How much detail is required depends on the needs of the project. Just listing the state elements, as above, may be sufficient for a quick feasibility study. Showing the "main" state elements and their relationships may be sufficient for a design study used for estimating. Accounting for everything in the model may be required for a formal implementation project. (See Chapter 2.) In this example, I will take the middle road. The "main" state elements, attributes, and relationships will be shown. The details of report structures and the inner workings of members will be ignored.

6.2.1 Nominate State Elements, Attributes, and Relationships

System state structure hard codes the queries.

Where to begin? The model is being built to support the access requests, so the access requests are a good place to look for guidance. If the access requests have not been written down, then it is helpful to think about how the system will use the model. Many of the requests seem to involve looking up tapes (and other rental items) in inventory, so a reasonable start would be to nominate an inventory state element that holds the things in inventory (Figure 6.1).

Figure 6.1
Inventory with many items

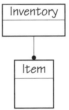

Looking at the access requests, I can see that there are some things I need to know about an item in inventory, such as what kind of thing it is—video tape, game cartridge, etc.—what its name is, who made it, and the like. As a first cut, I will make all those things attributes of the items in inventory. This nomination is subject to confirmation (Figure 6.2).

Figure 6.2
Attributes of the items

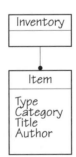

Looking further, I notice that customers seem to figure prominently in the access requests, again with many requests involving looking up a customer given a name. So I will nominate a similar structure for customers: something to hold all the customers (Figure 6.3).

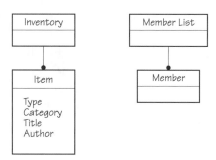

Figure 6.3
Inventory and member list with many members

Once again, there are things about customers I need to know, such as names, addresses, phone numbers, how many items they have out on rental, and how much money they owe the store. I will make most of these things attributes of the customer, except the items out on rental. Since I already have items in inventory, I can show a relationship between a customer and an inventory item (Figure 6.4).

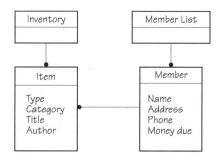

6.3 EVALUATE THE NOMINATIONS

Just as this simple model seems to address a big fraction of the access requests, so it might be appropriate to pause here and evaluate our early nominations against the access requests to see how we are doing. The access requests provide evaluation criteria: for each request, find an entry point on the model, and traverse the model until the desired information is located.

Evaluations are useful during design.

6.3.1 Using an Access Request for Evaluation

The first access request in our list was: given any type of item, title, artist, director, return a list of all items matching the specification, the number owned, and the number available. The Inventory is connected to all the items in inventory, so it makes a good entry point. Starting at Inventory, we can take our input parameters, type, title, and author, for example, and ask each item if it matches the parameters. We can traverse the model to get to the desired information. Can we return the required information? The access request states that the number owned and the number available are needed. These values were not included in our attributes, so our model, as it stands, is lacking some information. Our brief evaluation exercise helped us discover a problem, which we can now fix by adding the attributes of the number owned and the number rented to the Item. (See Figure 6.5.)

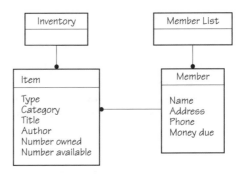

Figure 6.5

Fixing a problem by adding attributes to an item

6.3.2 Elevating an Attribute to a State Element

Rich structure supports efficient access.

This model is now sufficient to support the first access request. Can we do better? As it stands, the model is attribute-rich. That is, it uses lots of attributes and relatively few relationships. Like all attribute-rich models, traversing the model involves many lookups. In the traversal just described, we would have to query every item in inventory to determine, for example, how many John Wayne videos the store has. It seems likely that at the source of most of the access requests the type of item will be known. That is, a person asking for a John Wayne movie will always specify that they are looking for a video tape, as opposed to a game cartridge. We could make the model more responsive to the access requests by elevating the type attribute to a state element. (See Figure 6.6.) This addition of structure to the model will save looking at all the game cartridges when we just want a video. Both versions are sufficient, but this new one is more efficient. Efficiency, here, means application-level efficiency, not execution efficiency in a database query.

The model does not include very many of the nouns that were extracted from the use cases, so it is certainly incomplete. But I can use the access requests as a guide in

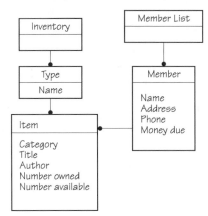

Figure 6.6
**Promoting an
attribute,
type, to be a
state element**

building the rest of the model. If the model is built by following the access requests, then I can be more confident that when I evaluate the model against them, it will be sufficient. This practice also helps emphasize the importance of evaluating the model against the external user requirements.

6.3.3 Adding New State Elements

If I look at the access requests named, "request overdue list by item" and "request overdue list by customer," I can see a problem. The current model will not support them because there is no due date. The fix might be to add a due date to something. The question is, to what? If I add a due date attribute to the customer, then there will be a problem handling multiple due dates. If I add a due date to the Item being rented, there is a problem with the number owned and the number available attributes. The owned and available attributes imply that there is one Item "state element" for all the actual items that have the same title. Having a due date attribute that can be set when someone rents the actual item implies that there is one item state element for each physical item in inventory. In addition, there was a statement in the original description about tracking each physical item separately. So, we might conclude that there is a problem in the present model.

I propose two additions to address this problem. The first addresses the problem of having multiple copies of the same title: make the title, author, actor, etc. a separate state element, called *title*, and make a separate state element for each physical copy of that title called *copy*. Note that this reflects one common way of talking about tapes in inventory: "We have 130 copies of *Fatal Attraction*." Each Customer would rent a specific Copy, so we could put a due date in each Copy, and perhaps, a status to indicate whether it is rented, overdue, or available. Our model now looks like Figure 6.7.

A good state model never looks like its first version.

This addition makes the model sufficient to handle the two access requests concerned with overdue items. It is not, however, very convenient to look up the

Figure 6.7
Replacing
item with
title and
copy
elements

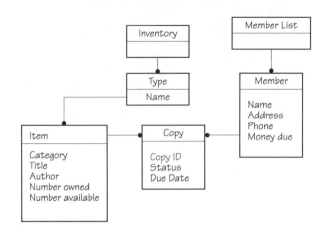

overdue items. We would have to check every item in inventory, or every member to find which are overdue. However, if we look at some of the other access requests, such as those concerned with how much money a member or tape has made, we see that there is still a problem.

The model can be further improved by adding a Transaction state element to carry the information about each transaction. A transaction is an arbitrary combination of items from inventory and a member. The term *transaction* is on the list of nouns. That it should have this particular definition was my idea. There is nothing in the domain that compels me to associate a particular definition with a particular word; it was an engineering decision on my part. Capturing that combination in a separate state element makes it easier to get to the information, and it makes it easier to capture historical information. Doing so is the primary justification for inventing that definition. We can provide an Active Transactions entry point in the model and save the transaction in a Past Transactions bucket for historical reference. The model now looks like Figure 6.8.

Figure 6.8
Adding
active and
past rental
transactions
to the state
model

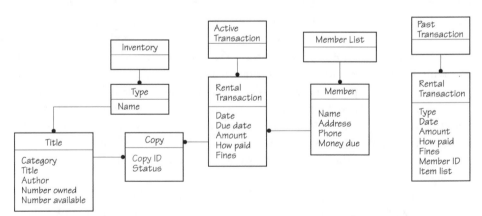

I did not nominate any relationships between the Past Transactions and the rest of the model because I envision that there will be a separate process that will decide when a transaction has been completed and that will process the Active Transaction into the Past Transactions.

Now we can check to see if the new model is still sufficient for the access requests. I can still satisfy the requests about overdue items by going to the Active Transactions, pulling out the ones that are overdue and then asking for their (the transaction's) copies or members.

This model would be sufficient, but not very elegant, if we had to support the request of a member asking which videos he had out. To support that request, we could add a relationship to state that a Member has a Rental Transaction.

6.4 EVALUATING THREE VERSIONS OF THE MODEL

The discussion above indicates the complicated thought processes involved in developing a state element model for the first time. There are two other points that I think are very important. One is that there are at least a million ways to model any given system. The other is that evaluating any model against all the external requirements is the key to delivering models that are both sufficient and efficient.

There are objective evaluations for system state models.

To demonstrate these points, I have three different system state models for the video store system. I offer them here to demonstrate the point that there are many ways to design the system state. Figure 6.9 was my first attempt at a static design. The second, Figure 6.10, was done by a student in a design course that used the video store as the class exercise. The third, Figure 6.11, is my revision of my first attempt. I will evaluate each against the external requirements to demonstrate the evaluation process.

First Cut Model

A comment about modeling styles and conventions: there are at least two ways to represent one-to-many relationships. One way is to draw a one-to-many relationship line and label it with the name of the group. In Figure 6.9, for example, the Store has many Users. This is shown with a solid circle line from Store to User. I could label that relationship "Users." Another way to draw the same sort of relationship is shown on the other side of Store. The Store has Inventory. Inventory is shown as a separate state element that holds the many items in inventory. There is a one-to-one relationship between Store and Inventory. If I were labeling relationships, I would label it simply as "has." In general, the more state elements that are shown in the diagram, the simpler the relationship names will be. My usual practice is to show many state elements. The result is that my relationship names are quite simple, which is why I usually do not label my relationship lines.

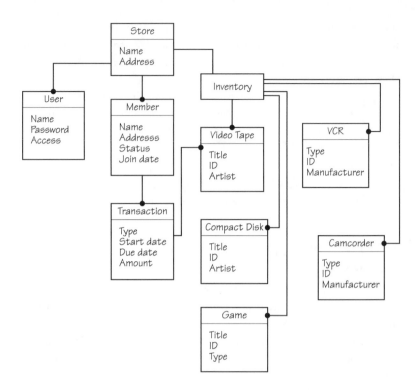

Figure 6.9
A first cut at a system state model for the video store system

First Cut Evaluation

How to evaluate designs is a major theme of this book and for that reason, I want to provide ample demonstrations of the techniques. But in the interest of brevity I do not want to take up too much space. So to satisfy both goals, the following design evaluations are presented in a very terse form in Tables 6.1 through 6.3.

Table 6.1   First cut evaluation

Access Request	Entry Point	Traversal	Information Available	Result
1. Find an item	Store or Inventory	Inventory, Type, match parameters on Items, but Director not available	Number owned by counting matches, number rented only available by traversing all Members and all Transactions	Mostly sufficient, but missing Director. Efficiency on number owned and available very poor.
2. Find a member	Store	Match parameters on all Members	Members with name matches available	Sufficient and acceptably efficient
3. Request overdue list by item	Store	Through all Members to all Transactions	Items overdue available from Transactions, but unless "Date" includes time, the 4-hour past due cannot be determined	Indirect entry point, inefficient traversal, and time stamp missing

Table 6.1   First cut evaluation (continued)

Access Request	Entry Point	Traversal	Information Available	Result
4. Request overdue list by customer	Store	Through all Members to all Transactions	Members with overdue Items available, Items overdue available from Transactions, but unless "Date" includes time, the 4-hour past due cannot be determined	Indirect entry point, inefficient traversal, and time stamp missing
5. Find an item being returned	Store	Through all Members, all Transactions to each Item in each transaction to find matches	Member and rented Items are available, but a way to record that the Item was returned is not available, there is no place to record the history of the Transaction	Very inefficient traversal, ability to handle transaction closure not present. This access request will be very frequently exercised. Response time will be important.
6. Find copies of a title currently loaned out	Store	Through all Members and Transactions (no path is available from an Item in inventory to the customer who has it out)	Which Members have which Items is available	Traversal is very inefficient. This may not be a time critical access request.
7. Get activity summary	Inventory or Store	Inventory to Inventory Item or Store to Member to Transaction	There is no information available on historical Transactions. If the present Transactions were saved, it would be possible to search them for the date range and the specified item.	Information not available
8. Remove an item from inventory	Inventory and Store	Inventory through Type to Item and Store to every Member to every Transaction to every Item (to determine if any are out on rental)	All required information is available.	The access is very inefficient, which may not be a problem for this access request.
9. Add an item to inventory	Inventory	To Type	None needed, but the model is probably deficient	If rest of the model is sufficient, this access request can be supported.
10. Add a new pricing special	None available	Not supported	Not supported	Pricing special is missing from the model
11. Get current inventory list	Store and Inventory	Through Type to each Item, Through each Member, through each Transaction.	Inventory items and their rental status are available	Very inefficient traversal

Table 6.1   First cut evaluation (continued)

Access Request	Entry Point	Traversal	Information Available	Result
12. Mark an item as rented	Inventory	Through Type to Item (look up item ID)	Activity summary and rental status not available	Information missing
13. Remove a category	Inventory	No target point	Category missing from the model	Access request not supported
14. Add a category				Not supported, see 13
15. Get member activity summary	Store	Lookup Member ID	Unless historical Transactions are available, this request cannot be supported. Expenditure since becoming a Member is missing (could be calculated if all Member Transactions were available).	Access request not well supported

Conclusions of the Evaluation Against Access Requests

The model in its present form is less than successful at supporting the access requests. The result of this evaluation should be that the model is revised to address the problems discovered during this evaluation. Because so many things are missing, evaluating the model for extensibility would not be fruitful. That evaluation will be done on the third system state model.

Student System State Model

This model was developed by a student in a design course (Figure 6.10). It is not a very successful model, but it is representative of the kinds of models and problems that are often produced. I present it here to demonstrate how problem models can be dealt with objectively.

Watch for creeping features. The first thing to notice about this model is that there are several things in the model that do not appear in the problem description or in the Use cases. Examples include the Distributor-Bill-Purchase Order section and Reservations. Software designs often wander far from their original goals. A key role that evaluation can play is to identify the wandering before it gets translated into code.

Student System State Model Evaluation

I will only do enough evaluation of this model to point out some of the major problems (Table 6.2). When problems of this type are identified, the next action should be to completely redo the model.

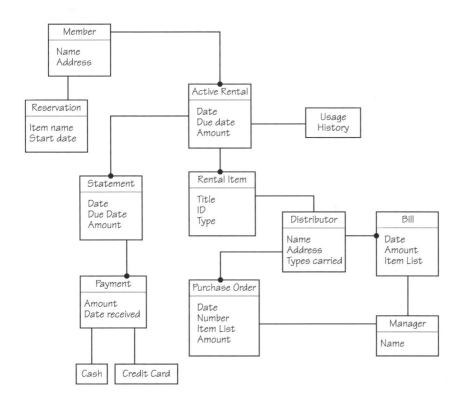

Figure 6.10

A student's cut at a system state model for the video store system

Table 6.2 Student model evaluation

Access Request	Entry Point	Traversal	Information Available	Result
1. Find an item	There are no entry points associated with Items in Inventory (nor are there entry points associated with anything else)	Rental Item is only associated with Active Rental, so no traversal is possible		Access request is not supported
8, 9, 10. Remove and add items to inventory, get inventory items	None available		Whether an Item is in inventory is not available	Access request is not supported

The Distributor-Purchase Order state elements are not called for in any of the access requests. That section should be examined to determine if the state elements represent requirements that were missed or if they represent requirements expansion on the part of the engineer. Even bad models can be quite enlightening.

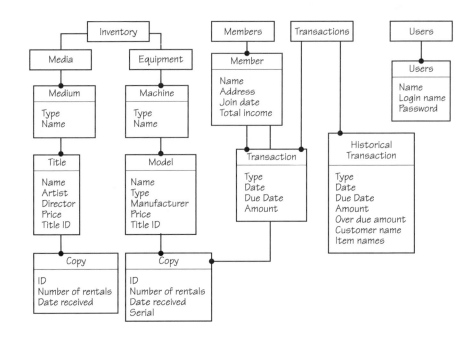

Figure 6.11
A second cut at a system state model for the video store system

Final Model

This system state model (Figure 6.11) is a revision of the first model. It corrects some, but not all, of the problems. Some of the problems have been left as exercises for the interested student.

Designs get better with experience. By way of general overview, the model has more entry points than the previous models. The Title-Copy separation has been made. The Transactions entry point provides access to both current and historical transactions. The evaluation of this design follows in Table 6.3.

Table 6.3   Final model evaluation

Access Request	Entry Point	Traversal	Information Available	Result
1. Find an item	Inventory	Inventory, Type, match parameters on Titles	Number owned by counting copies, number rented only available by traversing all Transactions. Could be fixed by giving copies a status or a relationship with their active transactions.	Sufficient. Efficiency on number available very poor.
2. Find a member	Members	Match parameters on all Members	Members with name matches available	Sufficient and acceptably efficient

Table 6.3   Final model evaluation (continued)

Access Request	Entry Point	Traversal	Information Available	Result
3. Request over-due list by item	Transactions	Through all Trans-actions to overdue Items	Items overdue available from Transaction, but unless "Date" includes time, the 4 hour past due cannot be determined	Good entry point, time stamp missing
4. Request overdue list by customer	Transactions	Through all Trans-actions to Members with overdue Items	Members with overdue items available, Items overdue avail-able from Transactions, but unless "Date" includes time, the 4 hour past due cannot be determined	Good entry point, time stamp missing
5. Find an item being returned	Transactions	Through all Trans-actions to each Item in each Transaction to find matches	Member and rented items are directly available, but a way to record that the item was returned is not available. A sta-tus on Copy would help.	Satisfactory traversal, ability to handle transaction closure not present. This access request will be very frequently exercised. Response time will be important
6. Find copies of a title currently loaned out	Inventory	Through Medium, to Title, to Copies, then through Trans-actions to copies loaned out. This could be improved by adding a status to Copy.	Which members have which items is available	Traversal for copies loaned out is very inefficient. This may not be a time critical access request
7. Get activity summary	Transactions	Transactions to all current Transac-tions or to all Historical Transactions	Information is available	Information is available and the traversal is sufficient for this, non-time critical access
8. Remove an item from inventory	Inventory and Transactions	Inventory through Type to Title and Copy. Transactions to every Transac-tion to Copy (to determine if any are out on rental). Sta-tus on each copy would be helpful here.	All required information is available	The access is very inefficient, which may not be a problem for this access request
9. Add an item to inventory	Inventory	Through Type to Title	None needed	This access request can be sup-ported
10. Add a new pricing special	None available	Not supported	Not supported	Pricing special is missing from the model

Table 6.3 Final model evaluation (continued)

Access Request	Entry Point	Traversal	Information Available	Result
11. Get current inventory list	Inventory and Transactions	Through Type to each Item, Through each Transaction to Copy for rental status	Inventory items and their rental status are available	Inefficient traversal
12. Mark an item as rented	Inventory	Through Type to Item (look up item ID)	Activity summary and rental status no available	Information missing
13. Remove a category	Inventory	No target point	Category missing from the model	Access request not supported
14. Add a category			Not supported, see previous item	
15. Get member activity summary	Member, Transactions	Lookup Member ID, look up Transactions for the Member	All requested information is available	Access request supported

Overall, this model is an improvement over both of the previous models: more of the access requests are supported. There are still some missing items, including rental status on Copies, pricing rules, and Categories. The interested reader may wish to make further modifications to the design.

6.4.1 Evaluation Against Likely Extensions

The new state elements to be added to the model are listed below, with a discussion of the ease or difficulty of making the addition.

Multiple Stores

Adding Stores to the model offers a chance to demonstrate the interchangeability of state elements and attributes. One possibility is to add Store as an attribute of Copy. That would provide a view of the "corporate" inventory that made it look like one big inventory. The problem is that many of the traversals would have to change to account for the new parameter.

Another possibility is to add Store as a new state element above Inventory, and perhaps to add Store Name as an attribute to Inventory. This approach has the advantage that traversals at the lower levels of the model would be unchanged. If this approach were used, the model could be judged to gracefully support the extension to multiple stores. This approach is described in the Fixes section.

Employees, Time Sheets

In this extension, Users would become Employees. Time sheets and payroll compose a semantic domain that is separate from the semantic domain of rentals and inventory. In the present model Users are completely separate from the rest of the model, so this new domain could simply replace the present Users "island." The model can, therefore, support the change.

School Members, Corporate Members

If these new kinds of members have the same kinds of relationships as retail members (members have transactions) and their behavior interface is the same (interfaces have not been developed, yet), then the new members can be handled easily in the present model structure. The big variation will be in rental and billing relationships for the new members. As these items are not included in the present model, it is hard to judge how well the model will handle the change.

New Rental Rules and Limits

These things do not appear in the current model, so changing them is moot. Some approaches to adding and changing Rental Rules will be discussed in the following, Fixes section.

Categories

Categories did not appear in the current model. They were shown as an attribute of Title in Figure 6.7. Consider the changeability of Categories if category were an attribute of Title. Changing Categories was described as an online, administrative activity. If Category were an attribute, adding and changing Categories would involve changing all the instances of Title, or all the Titles, that have the changed Category. We should still have a master list somewhere of what the currently defined categories are. This is missing from the model. I would judge a model having Categories as attributes of titles to be sufficient but not very elegant or efficient in its support of this change.

Another approach is to make Category a state element. This would make editing and changing Categories easier. This approach is shown in the Fixes section.

Types, Rental Items

New Types can be handled by adding new Medium or Machine state elements. The new type could carry its own analogues of Title and Copy. As long as the interface to the new Medium, Title, and Category adhered to the existing protocol for those components, the model should be able to handle the additions as simple additions.

6.5 FIXES

This is the good part.

This system state model does a fair job of supporting the external requirements, as stated in the access requests and state element additions. There were a number of problems that turned up in the evaluation. To complete at least one cycle, I would like to look at fixing some of the problems.

1   Missing rental status in copy. Adding a Status attribute to Copy to indicate whether a copy is rented would avoid the need for several laborious lookups. The price for such convenience is that when we put behavior in the system we will have to ensure that both the status in Copy and the appropriate things in Transaction get updated.

2   Categories as state elements. Defining Category as a constituent of Medium that holds Titles would facilitate the editing of Categories as well as some of the lookups (when the question is, "Which comedies was Jackie Gleason in?"). The relevant fragment of the model is shown in Figure 6.12.

Figure 6.12
Adding category elements to better support the access requests

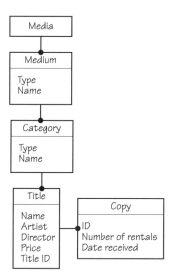

This arrangement might hinder lookups that do not involve the Category. We could provide two paths to a title: one though the normal inventory route and one through Categories. Again, this increase in structural complexity makes the model more supportive of the access requests, but requires more sophisticated maintenance behavior. In this case, when a new Title is added to the system it will have to be added to both the Medium and the appropriate Category. This approach is shown in Figure 6.13.

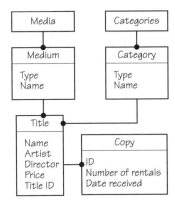

Figure 6.13
Making categories their own entry point to the model

3 Multiple stores. Growing the model to multiple stores without upsetting the present, single store model can be achieved by adding the multiple store view on the "top" of the model, as shown in Figure 6.14.

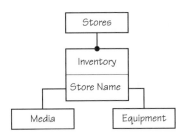

Figure 6.14
Changing the model to accommodate multiple stores

4 Rental specials. The rules and limits have been neglected up to this point. It is not uncommon to have several aspects of a system be neglected. Since we have discovered the neglect early through our evaluations, now would be a good time to fix it. I will outline my ideas for adding rules to the model to demonstrate the process of identifying and allocating relationships in system state modeling.

The rules may be invoked in any transaction and they may be edited online by the manager. This last requirement implies that the rules and specials must be defined separately from the machinery that executes them. The first question is, what are the rules connected to? To answer that, we should look at the dependencies. A limit on how many tapes a member may have checked out at one time depends on the member and the tapes on all of the active transactions for that member. A limit on checking out anything after a certain amount is outstanding depends on the member and the member's current account. A special of getting every fifth rental free depends on the member's recent activity and when the special was last invoked.

Putting rules in the state model makes them easy to change.

From this description, it appears that the many of the rules depend on the combination of the member and the member's recent rental activity, and what is being checked out in the current transaction. The thing that connects the member and the rental is the transaction, so the transaction might be a reasonable place to connect the rules and limits.

This example is a middle-level detail model, so that showing the rules and limits connected to a Transaction is included, but we can exclude the interesting task of developing the actual form of the rules. We should note that in the above description of the rules, several variables were mentioned, such as the outstanding amount, recent rental history, and when a special was most recently applied for a member. These variables should be shown in the appropriate state elements in the model.

When a change is made to a rule or limit, we need a way to start using the rule. New rules, limits, and specials will not apply to any transactions before the effective date of the new rule. We could provide for this by adding a Transaction Server to the model. The text (or whatever it is) of the rules would reside here, where it can be edited. When a new transaction is needed, it would be requested from the Transaction Server (that will be covered in the behavior model). The transaction provided would have the current versions of all appropriate rules and limits. All of this is a nomination, subject to confirmation and with many alternatives possible.

The revised fragment of the model is shown in Figure 6.15.

Figure 6.15
Introducing transaction elements and rules

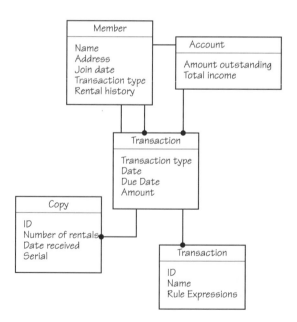

5 Adding corporate and school members. With the rental rules accounted for, we can now address the issue of adding different kinds of members. Assume for the moment that the new kinds of members are just like the old kinds of members, but with different rules, pricing schedules and policies. We have provided a Transaction Server as a place to get Transactions and to hold the "source" for the rules and limits. Perhaps we could provide a second server for transactions for commercial members. Then do we end up with a separate server for each kind of member? That does not sound very elegant.

Future additions can have a big impact on model structure.

Another possibility is to add an attribute to Transaction, and a matching attribute to member to indicate the "type" of transaction that is allowable (with the associated rules and limits). If that were done, then selecting a transaction would require specifying the kind of member requesting the transaction. The member types would be editable at the same time the rules and limits are edited. The bottom line is that to handle the addition of new kinds members we will provide a "transaction type" parameter that will be used to select the appropriate kind of transactions for that kind of member. The end result of this round of fixes is shown in Figure 6.16.

6.6 COMPLETING THE SYSTEM STATE MODEL

Once the model passes the evaluations, it should be documented. Things that should be recorded include the name and a brief description of each state element,

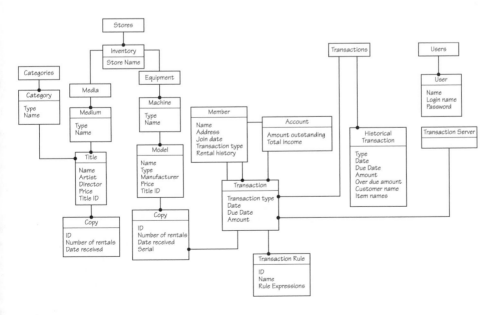

Figure 6.16
Revised final version of the system state model for the video store system

the name and distribution of each attribute, and the relationships the state element has in the model.

6.7 SUMMARY OF THE EXAMPLE

The state model is more than nouns in the real world.

This example covered most of the main activities in developing a system state model for a system design. These activities include the following: extracting the evaluation criteria from the use cases and change cases; nominating an initial list of things from the use case descriptions; organizing the things into state elements, attributes, and relationships; using the evaluation criteria to guide the restructuring of the initial model; evaluating the entire structure against the criteria; and revising the model to address the problems discovered in the evaluation. An example of nominating attributes and relationships based on dependency considerations was given.

However the system state model is developed, the key factor determining its suitability is whether it satisfies the external goals for the product. In the case of the system state model, the form of the goals in the external requirements is not directly useful, so some work must be done to put it in a compatible form, namely access requests and state element additions.

Of all the diagrams and decisions described here, the advice offered, is that one element is more important than all the others. That is the explicit evaluation of the decisions against criteria directly derived from the external requirements. With evaluations in place, the wrong diagram can be used, poor decisions can be made in developing the diagram, but those problems can be detected in the evaluations. Without evaluations, any decision, good or bad, can be carried into the final product.

CHAPTER 7   ✧   ✧   ✧   ✧   ✧

Behavior Identification and Allocation Task

CONTENTS

7.1 Introduction   121
7.2 General Approach   128
7.3 Techniques   133
7.4 Collaboration-Responsibility Model   147
7.5 Service Modeling   152
7.6 Summary   159

7.1 INTRODUCTION

7.1.1 What Properties Are Being Designed?

In the behavior identification and allocation task, the behavior content of the system is defined and the gross structure of the behavior is determined. The behavior content determines whether the system will have the potential of providing the functionality and information called for in the run-time requirements. The gross structure of the behavior places an upper limit on many of the build-time, emergent properties of the system, such as extensibility and ease of maintenance.

The difference between spaghetti and modularity is in the allocation.

In this chapter, first the process of identifying, allocating, and evaluating behavior will be described in general, and then three different techniques will be described in detail. The examples section works through each of the three techniques.

121

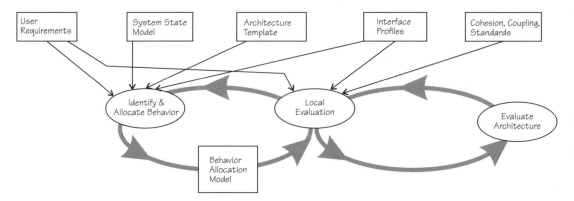

Figure 7.1 Subtasks and work products in the behavior identification and allocation task

The nature of the behavior allocation decisions and the kinds of components we have (to which to allocate the behavior) deserve some discussion before we look at the mechanics of making those decisions. In this discussion, I will use system architecture diagrams to talk about the components that are available, so I invite the reader to look ahead to Chapter 9 for a description of those diagrams before proceeding here.

7.1.2 Kinds of Components

Allocating behavior implies that there are components to which to allocate. I am using the word *component* rather than *object*, to avoid limiting the discussion to programming language instances of classes. These components can include client and server computers on a network, heavyweight tasks in an operating system, lightweight threads, instances of classes in a programming language, and families of functions.

We need the right components before we can allocate behavior to them.

How many kinds of components are "enough?" The answer is, if we can meet the user and development sponsor requirements, we have enough. Since user requirements can be met with any number of component types, from one to a thousand, I will use the development sponsor requirements to evaluate how many kinds of components are enough. Bear in mind that having enough kinds of components is only a part of the battle. The other parts of the battle include making appropriate behavior allocation decisions and assigning effective interfaces to the components (Figure 7.1).

In the architecture chapter I go to some length to demonstrate why we should use six different kinds of subsystems to assemble our systems (device, virtual device, presentation, dialogue, service, and model). The need for these six subsystems was derived from looking at the kinds of changes that systems need to support. The question here is, how many kinds of components are required in the behavior model if we are to address the user needs and end up with components that we can allocate to subsystems in the architecture? My answer is three: process, control, and information. In their responsibilities, these behavior model components correspond to the service, dialogue, and model subsystems in the architecture. Information components are responsible for maintaining the state and internal consistency of those things that the application manipulates. Process components are responsible for providing the user-level services which require manipulation of multiple information components. The control components are responsible for deciding when services get invoked, in what sequence, and under which circumstances. The following discussion presents a rationale for why these three are enough.

We need enough component types in the behavior model to effectively populate the architecture subsystems. A one-to-one relationship could be used, with one model component for each architecture subsystem type. The problem is that in the behavior modeling task, the boundaries are not visible, so there is no explicit place to hang a lot of interface machinery, like presentation components. Instead, the behavior modeling task, being nominally part of analysis, focuses on the application domain. The process, control, and model components should be described exclusively in application terms, without much reference to boundaries. Extensibility analysis described in Chapter 9 demonstrate the importance of separating information, service, and control. These three should be enough to describe the application-level activities of any application (except for getting things across the boundary of the application).

"Right components" is defined by the architecture we will be populating.

I am further encouraged that these three are sufficient because they correspond approximately, to the three biases common among software cultures. The biases are process, information, and interface. People who hold each bias believe that an entire system can be described in terms of their bias. Information people focus on the entity-relationship diagram, the table definitions, or the system state model, and relegate the other two aspects to afterthoughts. Process people focus on the functional breakdown of the system, and relegate information and interface to the details. Interface people paint the screens and leave the rest for later. In fact, all three are important and deserve their own section in the system. These three sections are most obvious in the architecture diagrams. The information section may, of course, have its own behaviors.

We can see a correspondence between these ideas and the ideas in Jacobson's *Objectory* model. Jacobson in the *Objectory Method* [JAC92] pioneered the idea of multiple kinds of objects by suggesting that three kinds of objects are needed: entity, control, and interface. The correspondence with the discussion here is that the Objectory's entity matches the model, control includes service and dialogue, and interface includes presentation subsystems (in the architecture). I have left the lower-level interface functions to the architecture sections where we can see the actual, physical boundaries. I think the separation of dialogue from function or service can be justified by examining the common change cases, as described in Chapter 9.

There may be other kinds of components that would be useful. I suspect that the total useful number of different kinds of components is relatively small (less than ten). In any case, I suggest that the only criteria for *enough* is whether the system can gracefully handle the change cases and adequately provide the use cases.

Interfaces need more attention than they now receive.

These three kinds of components have been described here and in the Objectory method, by the kinds of responsibilities they have. This is a helpful (conceptual) starting point, but I have not found it to be sufficient when I design these components. All components should be encapsulated by a message interface. Because the message interface is the only thing visible to users of the component, that interface should characterize the component. Now, we define a message as a request for some operation which consists of a control part, the message name, and optional information flows that may be associated with the control signal, i.e., parameters and returns. Following my model, we should be able to distinguish one type of component from another by looking only at the messages in the interface of the component.

Describing a component in this way, by its operations, is not a new concept. The abstract data type of Computer Science 101 is a data structure defined by the operations on the structure. Dave Parnas [PAR79] proposed information clusters, which consist of data and the functions that manipulate the data. Object-oriented programming languages have provided language support for these older concepts.

Unfortunately, there are a number of problems with the way interfaces are described in OO programming languages, and in most OO design notations. The common practice is to describe only the massages received by an object and only those that are implemented or overridden in the class being described. It is also common to ignore the information flow aspects of the message. And finally, it is not a common practice to characterize an object by the messages that make up its interface. Objects are usually characterized by their class name and attributes. The result is that in the behavior allocation task there is no way to identify the kinds of objects to which one is allocating. During evaluation, the results of many behavior allocation decisions are simply not visible.

Give the interface its own notation.

To address this problem, I propose a new notation, the only new notation proposed in this book. The notation is an interface view of a component that describes all of the messages received by a component (an instance of a class at the lowest level of component) and all the messages sent by the component to components outside itself. Each message is described by its control signal (message name), information flows that accompany the signal (arguments), and information that is returned as a result of the message (return types). To help in evaluating modularity (described later), the diagram should also show the names or kinds of components that receive the messages sent by the component. Figure 7.2 shows an example.

When viewing a complete interface specification, it is important to be able to see both control and information flows. To make the two more distinctly visible, I like to put a box around the information flows.

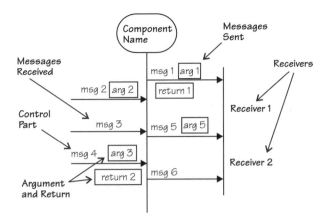

Figure 7.2
**Key to inter-
face view
diagram**

I have never seen anything like this diagram in any of the object-oriented literature I have read. A diagram like this should play the same essential role in reusing
software components that the pinout diagram plays in reusing integrated circuits.
The lack of this kind of diagram in the OO literature is a major contributor to the
slow progress in reusing software components.

Now we have a way to visually describe a component only in terms of its interface. We can now address the question raised earlier, "How can we distinguish
between the different kinds of components by looking at their external interfaces?"
The answer is that their interface views have different profiles. Figure 7.3 compares
the three kinds of profiles for the three kinds of components.

*The interface
profile type is
related to, but
different from,
the com-
ponent type.*

Control Interface Profile

A control profile is concerned with receiving events, or requests for actions, and
invoking the appropriate sequence of behaviors in other components. It is concerned with what and when, but not with how. The message names are of the form
"do this," "do that," "start," or "stop." Components with control profiles should not
be doing a lot of processing, so the information flows (status and acknowledgments)
should be small. If a control profile must handle larger information flows (like text
or graphics to be displayed), it should just pass them through without changing
them. Control profiles may communicate with many other components of any
type, other controls, processors, and servers. Control coupling is not as damaging to
the modularity as use coupling. (More on coupling in the behavior model evaluation section.)

Process Profile

Components with a process profile have the job of transforming one kind of information (component or object) into other kinds of information or components. The
information flows can be large. Process profiles usually receive some sort of control

Figure 7.3

**Definitions of
interface
profile types**

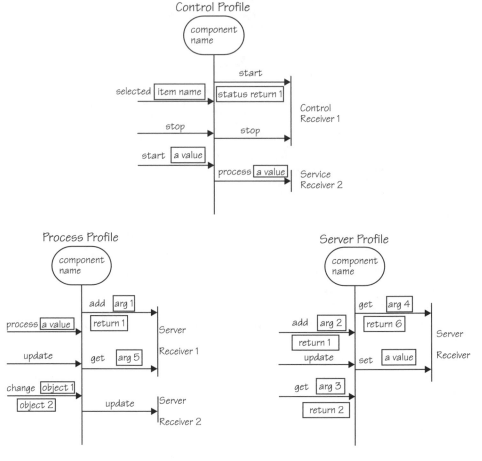

signals (start, stop, do this, etc.), and they may communicate with components having server profiles. To minimize use coupling, they should not communicate with components having process profiles, and in particular, there should be no information flows between components with process profiles.

Server Profile

Components with server profiles should be primarily receivers of requests. They are often sources and sinks of information, so the information flows may be large. They will often send messages to other server profile components in the system state model, but usually not to service or control components.

The purpose of this rather long digression was to introduce the use of multiple kinds of components. Now that we have them, the next concern is allocating behavior to all those different kinds of components and evaluating the allocation. The interface profiles can provide guidance in making our behavior allocation decisions.

7.1.3 Evaluation

Because we have two kinds of requirements, build-time and run-time, we need two kinds of evaluations. This need was the inspiration for Basic Principle 4: evaluate behavior and information identity against run-time requirements and evaluate structure and behavior allocation against build-time requirements. The user requirements will be addressed directly in the way the behavior is identified (by walking through the use cases). The evaluation against use cases is intrinsic to the behavior modeling techniques that are described in this chapter. Explicit evaluation consists of comparing each allocation diagram with the use case used to build the diagram.

The build-time properties of extensibility and ease of maintenance are emergent properties of the system, and need to be evaluated with the entire system visible. Because the behavior allocation decisions made during this task have a direct impact on those properties, the final evaluation of the allocation decisions should be made as a part of the process of evaluating the architecture on its ability to provide the emergent properties called for in the build-time requirements.

Final evaluation of the allocation must be done in the architecture.

The desire not to propagate bad decisions through a design was the basis for Basic Principle 3: Do not use the results of a engineering decision until the results have been evaluated. The effect of adhering to that principle in this process is to postpone the behavior description task until after the architecture has been developed and evaluated. Only then, after we are satisfied that our decisions have been good, should we look at investing the time and energy to describe the details of the behavior logic.

Having said that the final evaluation of behavior allocation must wait until the architecture evaluation, I should also say that several local evaluations can be made that will contribute to the modularity of the system. I call them *local* because they are not tied directly to any outside requirement, but we can make our job of meeting external change case requirements easier if we evaluate our behavior allocation for local modularity. This local evaluation is based on the component types and interface profiles described above, and coupling and cohesion concerns at the single component level.

7.1.4 Variations

There are three different ways to address the properties that are handled in this task, each of which represents a level of detail. Each uses a different notation: interaction modeling using interaction diagrams, collaboration-responsibility modeling using class-responsibility-collaboration cards, and service modeling using text descriptions of the services. The task will be described in general and then each of the three variations will be described.

There are three ways to record allocation decisions.

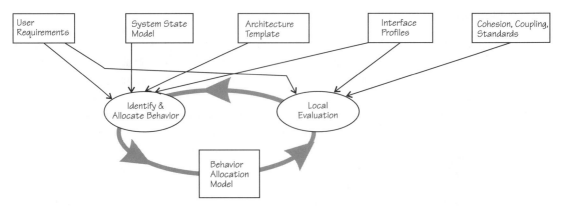

Figure 7.4 **Subtasks and work products in the behavior identification and allocation task**

7.2 GENERAL APPROACH

The behavior identification and allocation task populates the entire system with behavior, so that the external requirements will bear directly on the task. The evaluation criteria are the portions of the run-time requirements that identify behavior. Those requirements are the functional requirements (use cases), algorithms, information interfaces, and control interfaces. These requirements should be used as the evaluation criteria. From the build-time requirements, the change cases form the relevant criteria. The change cases can only be meaningfully applied to the system architecture, so the evaluation of the behavior allocation decisions will be carried out at the same time the architecture is evaluated for its ability to support the change cases.

If the project is informal, the size of the design and evaluation task can be reduced by choosing a subset of the use cases and change cases to use for design and evaluation. The cases chosen should be selected so that they will exercise all the major parts of the system.

Partition the documents by use case. Briefly, the steps in the behavior identification and allocation task are as follows. To support the evaluation against the user requirements, the allocation documents should be partitioned by use case. For each use case, you should nominate components that will participate in the response (inventing new ones if necessary). Nominate the behaviors needed in the components to provide the response. Next, allocate the behaviors to the nominated components. When all the use cases have been described, evaluate each individual response model to see that it will really provide the required response, and evaluate the complete behavior allocated to each component for cohesion, coupling, and modularity. Finally, the model components should be allocated to the architecture subsystems and the architecture evaluated for its ability to support the change cases (Figure 7.4). The evaluation of the architecture is described in Chapter 9.

7.2.1 Nominating Components

As Jacobson has pointed out, any single usage of the system can result in ripples of behavior that may extend completely through the system. There cannot be a one-to-one correspondence between an external usage, a use case, and a single component inside the system. There must be several components that will participate in the response to each use case. The question is, how do we decide what kinds of components are appropriate? The guidelines offered here are based on the discussion at the beginning of this chapter on the kinds of components and on the kinds of subsystems in the architecture.

A use case response can ripple throughout the entire system.

System State Components

Very often, the use case will involve the things the system maintains: the elements of the system state. A use case to rent a video will involve the inventory and a tape in the inventory. A use case to validate a customer will involve the customers. A use case to sell a stock will involve the stock and the portfolio. If a system state model for the system is available, system state elements to nominate for participation the use case response can be found by looking at the underlined nouns in the use case and finding the components in the system state model that have that information.

Most use cases will need to use or change the system state.

If a system state model is not available, the underlined nouns in the use case description can be used directly as nominees for participation in the use case response.

I should mention that it is possible to stop with just system state elements and allocate all behavior to the "noun" components. This approach can be made to work, but the results will be a brittle and hard to extend system, so I do not recommend it.

Finding system state elements to nominate is relatively straightforward. Finding other kinds of components is less straightforward. Some kind of structural framework is needed to guide the nomination of other components. The form for this can be as formal as an architecture diagram, or it can be as informal as the idea that "I want to use two (or three or four) kinds of subsystems." Architecture frameworks are discussed in Chapter 9. The informal thinking is given in the first part of this chapter on kinds of components.

I have found that having an architecture template in mind can provide very useful guidance in the process of nominating components to participate in the response to a use case. The template developed in Chapter 9 will be used here to help with component nomination. If we are going to populate the architecture subsystems with components from the behavior model, we will need at least one component for each kind of subsystem in the template. The template is shown in Figure 7.5.

Use the architecture to guide component nominations.

Figure 7.5
A generic system archi-tecture template

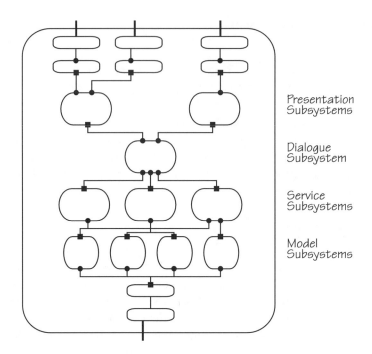

Presentation
Subsystems

Dialogue
Subsystem

Service
Subsystems

Model
Subsystems

The question of how to get an architecture template when we haven't "gotten to" the architecture yet can be addressed in two ways. First, the template was derived from considering a set of change cases that are quite generic across many software systems, so that templates can exist independent of any application. Second (and this is a reference to the sequence of projects in a product's life cycle, which is nom-inally beyond the scope of this book), a feasibility study can be carried out that does not require a detailed behavior model, but does yield a preliminary architecture. That preliminary architecture can be used as the template for the behavior model-ing activity being discussed here.

With a template in mind, we can now proceed to nominate components, in addition to the system state components already mentioned, to participate in the response to a use case.

Interface Components

All use cases should involve some dialogue with external actors. So a good starting point is to nominate one interface component for each kind of actor, or role, that participates in the use case dialogue. This information should be available in the user requirements documentation. If you wish to stop here, with just interface and system state components, you will be building a two layer system, which, while quite common, is still very brittle in the face of change and growth. If the goal is to build systems that are not brittle, then additional kinds of components are needed, and we should proceed to nominate other components to populate the architecture template shown in Figure 7.5.

Dialogue/Control Components

A use case is a dialogue between external actors and the system. It often involves a sequence of requests, actions, and responses. Some users will actually have that dialogue with the system. It is a good idea to nominate at least one component to manage the sequence of the dialogue. On evaluation, it will probably turn out that several of the controllers are so similar that they can be readily combined into one, but one controller per use case is a good place to start.

Service Components

Service components are the most difficult (for me) to identify and nominate. If the work has already been done, that is, if an architecture has been defined, then for each service component in the architecture that looks like it might participate in the use case being modeled, there should be at least one service component in the behavior model.

If this is the first time through and there is no architecture defined, a service component is needed whenever some behavior is identified that is dependent on two or more system state elements. This activity is easiest to do during the next step, identifying and allocating behavior. If no service components leap out at you while you are nominating participants in the use case, the need for them may become apparent later.

As a result of this activity, we now have a list of components (the ones suggested above) plus the system state components, nominated to participate in the response to the use case. The assertion is that this set of components is sufficient to provide the use case to the system's external actors and that behavior can be allocated to these components so that the system will not be spaghetti. Whether this happens will be determined in the evaluations.

Having the right components is half the battle.

I am assuming that these are all "new" components, that is, they have not existed before and have no behavior allocated to them. This is the most common situation at the time of this writing. Hopefully, it will not remain the most common. If there are preexisting components available, then the nominating process would involve looking at the list of available components in addition to scratching your head for new ones.

7.2.2 Identifying and Allocating Behavior

The behavior in a system should be exactly that which is required to provide the use case to the system's users. In order to evaluate whether that use case was, in fact, provided, the documentation of the behavior identification and allocation work should show what behavior was allocated to which components for each use case.

The other half is allocating behavior to them.

The basic technique is to lay out the components that have been nominated as participants in the response to the use case. The designer walks through (reads) the use case. For each action described or implied in the use case description, one or more behaviors are nominated (invented, really) and allocated to the components. *Components* is plural because there are always two components involved in each behavior: one to recognize the need and invoke the behavior, and another to carry out the behavior. Usually, each action described in the use case will require several behaviors in the system. The behaviors are identified as message names, responsibilities, or function names, depending on the particular technique being used.

Examples of doing behavior modeling will be given in the technique sections. For now, I want to emphasize that two separate and very important engineering decisions are being made for each behavior. First is identifying the behavior. This is a decomposition of the larger behavior described in the external use case. The granularity of the decomposition, how big each of the behaviors are, is a key element of the decision. The semantic level of the words used can serve as guide, but experience on the part of the engineer is the main prerequisite.

The behavior-allocation decision has the biggest impact on the system.

Having identified and nominated a behavior, the next engineering decision is where to allocate it. This involves deciding which component should know to ask for the behavior and which component should provide the behavior. The choices include allocating the request to the components that have already been nominated and nominating a new component just to hold the behavior. The quality of these decisions determines whether the system will look like a rational assemblage of discrete components or a bowl of spaghetti.

How those decisions are made also determines the level of logical complexity and volume of code that will be required. When inappropriate behaviors are allocated to a single component, the number of logic statements, and code volume, required to make them all work together grows large. It is very important then, that the behavior allocation decisions be very carefully evaluated before the results are used in further decisions. The nature of the evaluation depends on the behavior modeling technique being used, and is covered in the sections that follow each technique.

7.2.3 Evaluation

The evaluation against the run-time requirements consists of reviewing each one of the diagrams to see that it provides the behavior implied in the use case description or the algorithm description. The close connection between the run-time requirements stated in a use case and the diagram demonstrating how the system will provide the use case justifies the form of both the use case and the use case response diagram. The evaluation against the build-time requirements is covered in the architecture chapter.

7.3 TECHNIQUES

There are three behavior modeling techniques that I have found useful in designing systems. I call them detailed interaction modeling, collaboration-responsibility modeling, and service modeling. These are techniques for identification and allocation of behavior. The first is due to Jacobson [JAC92]. This notation is the interaction diagram, which in turn is based on telecommunication diagrams for describing communication between nodes in a network. The second is based on the Beck and Cunningham article [BEC89] on the Class, Responsibility, and Collaboration (CRC) card technique, and was expanded by Wirfs-Brock [WIR90]. The third technique, service modeling, is not usually identified as a kind of behavior modeling, but I have found that in certain kinds of projects if fills the role of a behavior model. It is also a necessary part of nominating service components. It is an activity that is implied in the Objectory method by the need to identify service packages. I have simply elevated it to the status of a behavior identification and allocation technique.

Three techniques are available.

The following sections describe each of the techniques and give examples of their application.

7.3.1 Interaction Model

The interaction diagraming technique was developed by Jacobson, but the idea of modeling scenarios has been widespread. I have added two enhancements to the Jacobson notation to better document the behavior allocation decisions and make evaluation easier.

The interaction diagraming technique is the most formal of the behavior modeling techniques we will look at. It also captures the greatest amount of information of any of the three techniques. Its advantage is that it can produce complete component interfaces. Its disadvantage is that to use it you have to think through everything. The technique can, of course, be used at lower levels of detail. It requires some practice to become proficient, and first cuts at using the technique often result in very bad behavior allocation. When clients are considering writing production code without doing interaction diagrams, I like to remind them that they will probably make the same decisions in their code that they made in their first cut at the interaction diagrams: the behavior allocation is likely to be very bad. And once coded, or course, the organization is condemned to live with and pay for maintaining spaghetti until it is rewritten. The cost of some up front paper and pencil work is subatomic by comparison.

Interaction diagrams are worth the effort.

Notation

The notation is shown in Figure 7.6. There is a minimum of one diagram per use case:

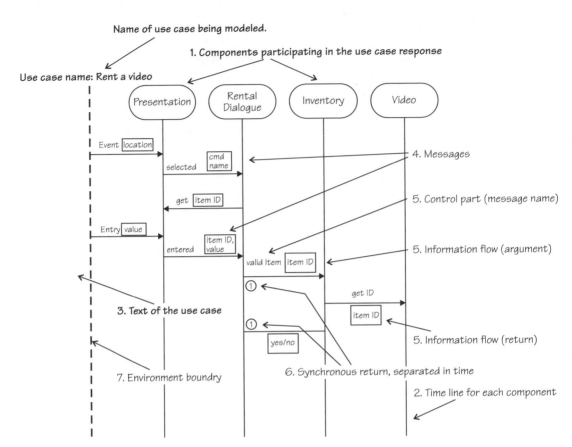

Figure 7.6   Key to interaction diagram notation

1   Each diagram shows the components that participate in the use case. The assumed type of profile for each component should be indicated in the diagram to serve as a guide for behavior allocation.

2   Each participating component gets a named time line.

3   The text of the use case description can be shown in the left margin.

4   The communication between components needed to provide the use case response are shown as arrows between the time lines. The sequence of messages down the time line represents the real sequence of message in that particular use case. Arrows can represent synchronous, send-wait, or asynchronous, send-no wait, messages. If the message are asynchronous, there will be no return information flows. (See the next item.)

5 Each message can be shown as a control signal or message name, information that accompanies the message, arguments, and information that is synchronously returned by the message. Because I like to be able to visually distinguish control and information flows, I put a box around the information flows. Arguments follow the message name on top of line, returns are shown below the line. Information flows are not necessarily dumb data. They can be objects or other components. Showing the "dataflows" with the messages is an addition to the Objectory technique.

6 When a component must send other messages in order to provide a synchronous response to a message it has received, I can show that sequence with the numbered lines. The line with no arrow and an information flow under it is the synchronous return to the message arrow with the corresponding number. Asynchronous responses can be shown with another message line.

7 A line for the environment boundary indicates where the modeling stops. It represents the component having the lowest semantic level to be shown in the diagram.

This notation is sufficient to document all aspects of the behavior identification and allocation task, and it does a good job supporting the evaluations that follow. It is certainly not the only notation able to do that, nor is it the optimum notation. But it is sufficient for our purposes.

The basic steps of the task are, for each use case, to nominate participating components, identify behavior, and allocate behavior. After all the use cases are modeled, all allocations to each component should be evaluated against local modularity, coupling, cohesion, and interface profile criteria.

7.3.2 Develop an Interaction Diagram

Nominating Components

Two kinds of concerns arise when you nominate components to participate in the response to a use case. One concern is what kinds of components to nominate; the other is the semantic level of the component names. As was the case in the system state modeling task, it is important to restrict each design activity to a single semantic level. This avoids the problem of having to deal with geometric combinations of unrelated items. In the behavior modeling task, the effect of using only one semantic level is to require that the words used for component names, messages, and information flows all come from the level, or domain of the use case.

Looking at the architecture template, or the preliminary architecture diagram, select components to populate each of the subsystems that might be involved in responding to the use case, as described above.

This modeling technique can be applied directly to components in the architecture. In that case, all the nominated components would be selected from subsystems in the architecture diagram. If we are modeling components before the architecture, then all the nominated components should be smaller than architecture components. The example section shows both approaches.

The good architect always looks ahead to the final product.

I have found that there is value in doing detailed behavior allocation on analysis components that are small, rather than on architecture subsystems. Carrying out and evaluating behavior allocation is a large task. I prefer to do it only once. If I can pick the granularity of my analysis components correctly, then they should remain intact regardless of how I change the architecture. Changing the behavior allocation to one or more components, as in splitting one component into two, requires revisiting the use case interaction diagrams in which the original component appeared and revising them to reflect the new component identities and behavior allocations. This is necessary to ensure that the new allocations will still be able to provide the required response to the use case.

If, on the other hand, I can pick analysis components that are small enough to be atomic under all architectures, then I only have to do the detailed behavior model once. I can allocate my analysis components intact to any architecture. The process of allocating analysis components to architecture components will be described in the architecture section.

Always do a feasibility first.

My bottom line suggestion is to do enough feasibility design study projects to arrive at an architecture before undertaking a detailed behavior model. Then the architecture components can be used as guides for selecting behavior model components of the appropriate granularity.

By whatever means we choose, we now have a list of components nominated to participate in the system's response to the use case. The next step is to identify and allocate behavior.

Behavior Identification and Allocation

This description assumes that all of the components we are dealing with are being built for the first time. This is the most common situation today. If some of these components were being reused, then, instead of scratching our heads for the identities of behaviors, we would look through the behaviors (messages) in the component's interface and pick the ones that did what we wanted.

The basic process is to put all of the components nominated for this use case in an interaction diagram and write the text of the use case description in the left margin. Then read through the use case description, and invent and allocate behaviors as messages between the components. The examples section demonstrates the actual steps in building an interaction model.

I strongly recommend (and this is a difference with the recommendations in Objectory) that each message be described with a message name (the control part) and include any information elements that accompany or are returned by the control signals.

To the cries of "too much work," and "too much detail," I have two replies. One is that ideas about what information is needed by each message are in your head when you are thinking through how the components will communicate to provide the use case response, so they may as well be captured while they are fresh. If it is done later, then the process of nominating the information flows will have to be repeated. The other reply is that putting the information flows in the diagram as it is built keeps you very honest. It is very easy to see when information needed to carry out a behavior implied by the message name is missing. It can be fixed on the spot. It is more difficult to see these problems when information flows are being added to a message name as a separate activity.

You should put the information flows in the diagram.

There are several guidelines I can offer to help with the process of nominating message and information flows. The first concerns the semantic level of the words chosen for messages, arguments, and returns. The words should all come from the same domain, that of the application, and should have the same semantic level. If the application domain is a video store, an insurance company, or a telephone switch, then words like database, file, disk, shared memory, table, row, and column, and operations on those kinds of things should not appear in the behavior model for use cases on that system. This restriction prevents coupling the top level of an application to details of the platform and peripherals.

If we look at the architecture picture again, the application domain words should be used for all interfaces of all components from dialogues through models. Beginning with the side of the presentation components that face the system boundary, words from other domains may be used. This means that the presentation type components should form the edges of our interaction model. The semantic level of the message interfaces is the key to effectively hiding and encapsulating modules of the system.

Another guideline concerns what work is really being done. The behavior model is described as identifying and allocating behavior. While that is true, the basic mechanism of how the system will work internally is also being specified. It is important that the designer be aware of this fact. The first interaction diagrams undertaken in a behavior modeling activity are often very difficult to do. There seem to be so many possibilities, and indeed, there are. Basic mechanisms that must be selected include how generic to make the presentation, where to do the translation between system-state elements from the model and forms that are more readily displayed, how to get changes made by the user back to the model, and many more. All of these things will be decided by the time the system is running. My suggestion is that they be decided in the behavior model, that the decisions be made consciously, applied consistently throughout the system and that the decisions be carefully evaluated before being cast in code. The example describes making some of those decisions.

Guidelines for the allocation decisions.

A third guide to allocating behavior is to bear in mind the kind of interface profile each of the nominated components should have. Restricting the interface profiles of each component to one of the three types described earlier, control, process, or server helps prevent allocating inconsistent behaviors to a component. Dialogue components have control profiles, service components have process profiles, and interface and model components have server profiles. I have found that having some indication on the diagram of what kind of profile each component is supposed to have keeps me from making inappropriate allocation decisions. In the evaluation activity we can catch and correct bad decisions, but it is much more efficient to make them correctly the first time.

Message names are critical.

Message naming practices deserve some comment. Message names in software systems play the same role that pinouts and bus definitions play in electronic hardware systems: they encapsulate and isolate components, and their standardization is the basis for all reuse. The names form a vocabulary that should be adequate for elegant and efficient expression of system designs. Once again, there is a wide spectrum of possible naming practices. At one end of the spectrum, only one message name is needed, something like, *message*, or *send*. Everything else, including the name of operation being requested, is carried as parameters to the one message. This is not a recommended practice.

At the other end of the spectrum, message names have the name of the operation, but operations are called by different names depending on what component is receiving the message. The message name also carries information about the types and categories of its arguments. The result is that message names look like the previous sentence and there are thousands of unique messages in a system. Examples include messages like, *openAccountWithMinimumAmount "name", "amount"*, and *newAccount "name", "amount"*.

Between these two extremes is a vocabulary of message names that is rich enough to express the operations and concise enough to support consistency and reuse. I have no guidelines to offer except to be aware of the goals and the trade-offs available to reach them.

More use cases appear during the process.

Even though you spend considerable effort in making sure that each use case consists only of a single thread of activity, it is quite common to discover branches during the detailed modeling activity. The branches can arise because some internal event is discovered, such as at midnight we automatically generate summary reports, or because of an error condition that requires considerable processing. If the branch can be handled with just a few messages, then it can be handled in the current interaction diagram. If it requires more than a few, it should be given its own use case and its own interaction diagram.

A word is in order about logic and state modeling. The interaction diagrams described here do not provide for showing branches, iterations or states. Iterations and short branches can be described in the text of the use case description, but they cannot, and should not, be shown in the diagram itself. One reason for this restriction is that the logic and state live inside the components. The view in the interaction diagram is like that of a wiring diagram of integrated circuits on a board.

Only the connections are visible. The specification of logic is a behavior description activity. It is an important activity that should be done only after the behavior identification and allocation decisions have been made and evaluated.

This restriction on behavior description activities supports basic principle number 3: Always evaluate the results of any engineering decision before those results are used in another decision. The engineering decision being made here is what behavior to allocate to which component. The decision that depends on the allocation decision is to describe what logic and state are needed to allow each component to correctly provide all of its allocated behaviors. As we will see in the evaluation section, many of our initial behavior allocation decisions will be changed, which will upset any internal logic or state descriptions based on the original allocation. My strong recommendation is to not do any state or logic modeling until after the behavior allocation is complete and fully evaluated. In other words, defer behavior description until the identification and allocation decisions have been fully evaluated. That evaluation will not be complete until after the architecture is evaluated, which means that the behavior description should be put off until after that time.

Putting off behavior description until later saves a lot of rework.

The technique is best explained by the example, so I refer the reader to the example section. When each interaction diagram is completed, we are asserting that we have completely described how the system will provide the subject use case. We are also asserting that we have allocated the behaviors in such a way that our components are well modularized and are not pathologically coupled to one another. When all the use cases have been described in interaction diagrams, we are asserting that we have completely accounted for all of the user required behavior.

Even a brief glance at the example description should indicate that there is much more to behavior modeling than just making it work. The concerns about coupling and modularity should be addressed in parallel and concurrently with concerns about whether we're putting in enough behavior.

7.3.3 Evaluation

Two kinds of evaluation are possible here: evaluation of the interaction diagrams for completeness and feasibility, and evaluation of the behavior allocation decisions on a per-component basis.

Of the interaction diagrams we can ask, "Have all the use cases been diagrammed? Does each diagram cover all the behavior described in the use case description? Have we added features or requirements to the use case that are not appropriate, or are not part of the scope of the system?"

A complete set of interaction diagrams for the example is shown in the appendix. The components with their behaviors represent a single level of decomposition, with the size of the decomposition guided by the size of the architecture components. It is common in traditional software methods to immediately decompose these components to a lower level with no further work. As this would use the results of the decomposition and allocation decisions without evaluation (Basic Rule 3), I do not recommend it.

As an aside to users of object-oriented programming languages, I should point out that casting these components into inheritance trees is another engineering decision that uses the results of allocation decisions made in the behavior model. For the same reason given above, casting inheritance should be put off until the evaluations are complete.

Instead of proceeding with any further engineering decisions, I suggest that the behavior identification and allocation decisions just made be evaluated. We will look at a local evaluation in this chapter. The complete evaluation of the allocation decisions requires the system architecture. The bottom line is that the next decomposition should not occur until after the architecture has been defined and evaluated. In other words, only finished, implementation components get decomposed, just like in the design of hard products.

The interface view provides the basis for many local evaluations. The evaluation we can carry out here involves looking at all the behavior allocated to each component, as expressed in its complete interface. The complete interface includes all the messages received by the component and all the messages sent by the component to other components. This information is directly and immediately available from the interaction diagrams. For each unique component, it is simply the aggregation of all the message arrows that end on that component's time line and all of the message arrows that originate on the component's time line. A sample interface view is shown in Figure 7.7.

The process of collecting this view is quite mechanical. Pick a component name, place it on an interface view diagram. Look at each interaction diagram. If the current component appears in the interaction diagram, check off the component, copy all the message names (with arguments and returns) that are received by the component to the left side of the interface view, and the messages sent by the component to the right side of the interface view. Also note on the interface view the name of the receiver of the messages sent by the component. The reason for doing this will be described shortly. This algorithm can be carried out by people or computers.

If we repeat the collection algorithm until all components are checked off on all the interaction diagrams, we will have a one-interface view for each component with a unique name. A sample interface view is shown below. Each interface view will show us the complete interface profile and all dependencies on external components. We can now ask a number of questions about each component to determine if it is sufficiently robust and modular to confirm its nomination as a component of our system.

All of the interface views should be scanned first, because some of the questions will concern comparing different components. The questions we can ask of each component and what to do when problems are found are described below. The order of their listing is approximately the order I ask them. The example section shows the evaluation on real interface views.

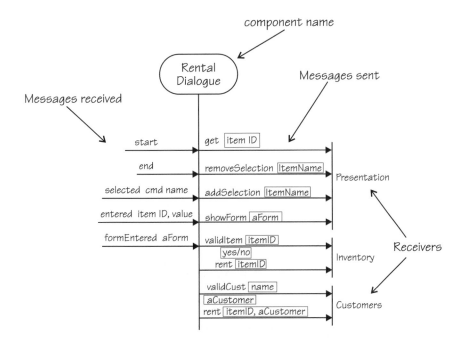

Figure 7.7
Example of the interface view for a component

Is the semantic level appropriate?   We should look at the names of compo- *Semantic level, again!*
nents, messages, parameters and returns. If we are working at the top level of an
application, say a video store or call processing, then component names like *file,*
database, table, ordered collection, and *shared memory,* are from a lower semantic level
and are not appropriate components. Those components should be removed from
the diagrams. Applications should talk only about tapes, customers, calls, and subscribers. How, or whether, they are stored somewhere is the concern of a different
semantic level.

Message names like *show dialogue box* or *read file* suffer from the same problem:
their semantic level is below the application level words. Message names can simply
be changed to use higher level semantics, like *selectFrom "list"*, or *getAccountNamed*
"Joe Smith".

Are the component and message names similar to other components?   There are *Naming*
many interaction diagrams in a system model. It is difficult to be absolutely consis- *consistency is*
tent in all the diagrams, even when only one person is doing the work. As a result, it *difficult but*
is common to find message names and components that are very similar to one *important.*
another. In the interest of arriving at an elegant and concise vocabulary of message
names, similarities should be merged and inconsistencies resolved.

Introducing consistency in message names is necessarily a tedious, time-consum-
ing and entirely manual task (computers are notoriously ineffective at
understanding the meaning of words). It is a task that not everyone is able to do.
How many times have you heard, "It doesn't make any difference, they're just

Figure 7.8
**Example of
an incomplete
interface
(no "put"
operations)**

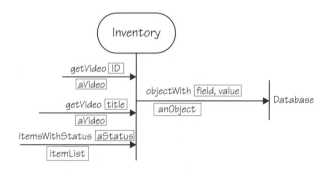

words"? However, if this task is not done, or is done badly, the initial system will be more complex than it need be, change and enhancement will take more time than they should and reuse will be very difficult.

Once again, the system architecture can serve as a guide for where consistency of vocabulary is needed. The example section describes the process.

*Completeness
checks turn up
missing use
cases.*

Is the behavior complete?   There is a fairly common piece of advice in many OO design methods that behavior allocation should be done by "writing down the operations on each object." Since there is no input from the required use of the component, this is entirely inadequate as a technique for making behavior allocation decisions. It is, however, a good approach to evaluate the completeness and symmetry of the behavior that was allocated to a component. If a component has messages asking for information, but none is put in, something is missing (Figure 7.8).

Incomplete behavior in a component indicates either that some of the interaction diagrams missed some behavior, or that there are missing use cases. The fix is to reexamine the use cases and the interaction diagrams to find the missing behavior.

Is the behavior cohesive?   *Cohesive* is a very fuzzy term. Nonetheless, it helps to look at the interface profile, particularly the messages received, to see if they sound like they are all closely related. Are they consistent with the behavior implied by the name of the component? Are the output messages related to, and consistent with, the input messages?

Is the interface profile all one type (server, process or control)?   I believe that modularity and simplicity are increased when components have profiles that are "purely" one of the three types. This is most important in the control and service, or process, type components. Control-type behavior changes at different times from processing and service behavior. Service behavior, and service components, are often configured in different ways in different systems. Therefore, it is important to keep the two kinds of behavior in separate components. The example in Figure 7.9 shows a component with mixed-message types.

Is the behavior too dependent on one external component?   The value of showing the receivers of messages sent by a component in an interface view is that dependen-

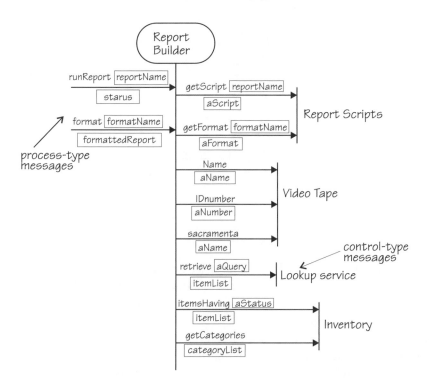

Figure 7.9
Interface view showing mixed process and control profiles

cies and couplings are immediately visible (Figure 7.10). *Too dependent* is a relative phrase, but we can start with an extreme example. If all the messages a component sends go to the same receiver, we can ask if the component deserves to exist. Perhaps it should be merged with the receiver of its messages. Lesser degrees of dependency may still merit fixing. If five out of nine messages sent by a component go to the

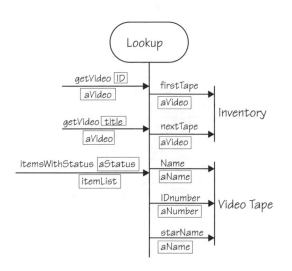

Figure 7.10
Interface view showing exposure of search behavior

Figure 7.11

Interface
view showing
reallocation
of behavior
to hide the
search
behavior

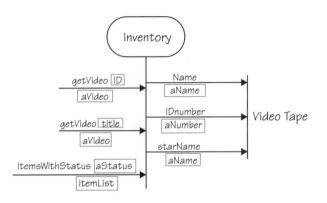

same receiver, we can try to find a higher level message to replace the five messages, and thus reduce the dependency (Figure 7.12).

Another kind of excessive dependency occurs when one component knows about things that should be private in another component. In the example below, lookup knows how to search inventory for a tape. Inventory could do its own search, as shown in the reallocation.

Is the behavior use-coupled to an inappropriate component?   Dave Parnas [PAR79] defined use-coupling by saying that *A* is use-coupled to *B* if *B* must be present and operating in order for *A* to do its job. An extreme and common example of use-coupling occurs in systems where everything must work in order for anything to work. Use-coupling is indicated by a return information flow to a message. If *A* sends a message to *B* and does not care whether *B* responds or not, that is a control relationship, and *A* does not require *B* (Figures 7.12 and 7.13).

Figure 7.12

An interface
view showing
use-coupling

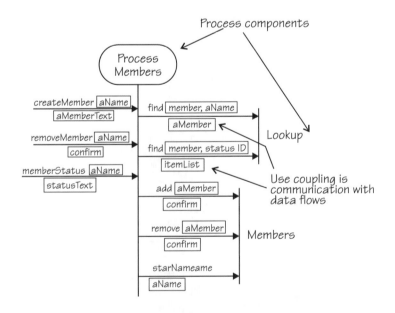

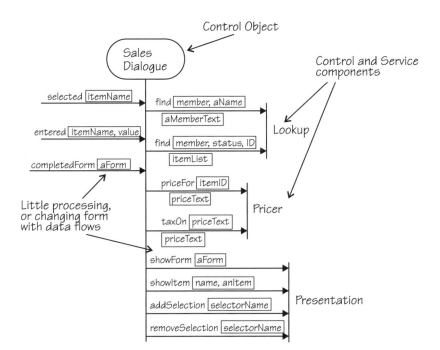

Figure 7.13

An interface view showing control-coupling

Some use-coupling is necessary, but too much hurts the modularity of the system. It is most damaging when two components that we wish to use separately are use-coupled. Service components, or components with service profiles, are the most likely to be used separately. Control components should only be able to engage in control-coupling, which is less damaging because there should be no significant data flows involved. Any message between components with server profiles that has a return information flow should be changed. Information flows between service components should be passed through server components, and control coordination between them should be handled with a control component. The problem and the fix are shown in Figure 7.14.

Use-coupling is an especially dangerous form of coupling.

The fixes to almost all the problems involve the same thing: changing the behavior allocation. I have said that the interaction diagrams contain a statement of how the system will meet the user requirements. Moving behavior from one component to another could cause one or more interaction diagrams to "break;" that is, the components could no longer collaborate to provide the required response to the use case. Therefore, when we want to change a behavior allocation, we should think up a new allocation scheme and redo the affected interaction diagrams using the new allocation scheme. This will ensure that our system will still provide the required behavior to its users.

When I first read that idea, redoing interaction diagrams when we move behavior, in one of Jacobson's OOPSLA papers [JAC87], my immediate reaction was that it was too much work. After all, those diagrams are hard enough to do the first time

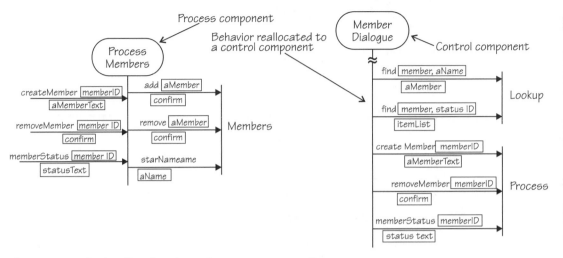

Figure 7.14 Behavior allocation changed to remove use-coupling

without going back and redoing them. But after trying it I found that redoing interation diagrams turns out to be a fairly comfortable and natural process. The examples section demonstrates some reworks of interaction diagrams.

The fastest way to do something is to do it right the first time.

The most efficient approach to doing the modeling is to do it right the first time and avoid the problem of redoing anything. One technique for encouraging appropriate behavior allocation decisions the first time is to have some indication in the interaction diagram of what kind of interface profile is expected for each component. I have found it helpful to put each profile type on a different level in the interaction diagram, as shown in Figure 7.15.

This visual guide makes it easy to keep profiles consistent, and to avoid introducing inappropriate use-coupling. (Service components should not talk to one another.) Another possibility is to use different icons for components having different kinds of interface profile.

Even if it takes extra work, it is very important from an engineering design point of view to be able to assert that this system will meet all the stated user requirements. It is not good engineering practice to say, "This set of diagrams demonstrates how the system will meet most of the user requirements; but some I'm not sure of."

At the completion of these behavior modeling and evaluation activities the engineer should be able to assert and demonstrate that the system can provide all of the required responses to every use case and that the set of components, when taken together, can provide all of the required behavior. The first assertion is important in evaluating the completeness of the design. And the second assertion is important when we allocate behavior to the architecture components (see Chapter 8).

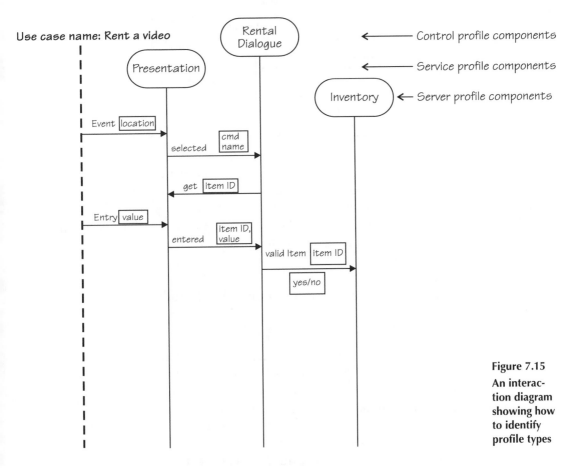

Figure 7.15

An interaction diagram showing how to identify profile types

7.4 COLLABORATION-RESPONSIBILITY MODEL

Collaboration-responsibility modeling, or C-R modeling for short, covers the same ground as interaction modeling and uses about the same sequence of steps. In fact, it could be described as a variation of the interaction modeling technique, except that it has its own history and published methods to support it.

7.4.1 Notation

The notation consists of recording each component's name, description, responsibilities and collaborations. The first notation was the Class, Responsibility, Collaboration card, or CRC card shown in Figure 7.16 [BEC89].

Figure 7.16
Key to class-responsibility-collaboration card notation

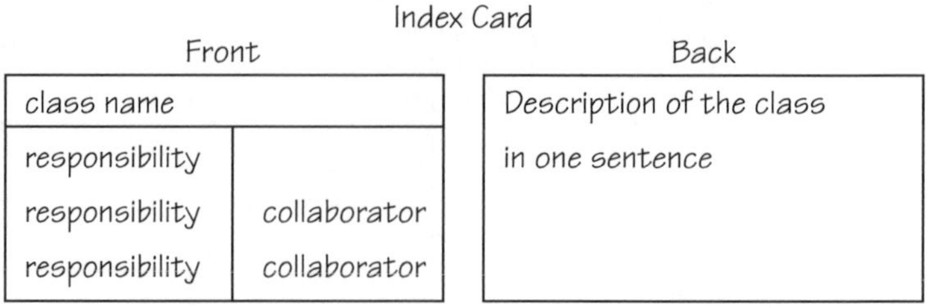

Index Card

| Front | | Back |

class name		Description of the class
responsibility		in one sentence
responsibility	collaborator	
responsibility	collaborator	

CRCs are informal interaction diagrams.

The same information can be captured in component dictionary of a CASE tool. A key difference between this technique and the interaction modeling technique is that all of the documentation is done on a per-component, or per-class, basis rather than the per-use-case basis as in the interaction modeling technique. This practice results in a significant reduction in the amount of information that is captured by using the technique.

7.4.2 Develop a Collaboration-Responsibility Model

Identify and Allocate Behavior

The algorithm for the technique is as follows. For each use case, nominate participating components, walk through the scenario of the use case, identify behaviors as responsibilities, and allocate them to components. For each responsibility, nominate collaborations with other components needed to carry out the responsibility. Evaluation is carried out by collecting all the components in a single diagram with all collaborations indicated.

Each of these activities will be described in the following sections.

Nominate Participating Components

This activity is identical to the corresponding activity under the interaction modeling technique. All of the options and variations apply here.

Behavior Identification and Allocation

Responsibility is behavior with no names to invoke it.

In the previous section on interaction modeling, behaviors were identified and allocated in terms of the messages that invoked them. Here they will be identified and allocated as responsibilities. A responsibility is a service or group of services that a component offers to its users. A responsibility is "bigger" than messages. The relationship is nicely demonstrated in the Responsibility Driven Design Method [WIR90]. In that method, behaviors are allocated as responsibilities. Then, late in the process, one or more messages are assigned to each responsibility to allow users of the component to invoke them.

A collaboration indicates that one component must communicate with another in order to carry out its responsibility. In C-R modeling only the need to communicate and the identity of the collaborator is recorded.

An informal technique like CRC notation does not support a full evaluation.

The process of identifying and allocating responsibilities is the same as identifying and allocating messages, described in the previous section. A responsibility represents a decomposition of the total system behavior. The size or granularity of the decomposed piece is critical. The allocation issues are identical to those described in the previous section. The examples section walks through a collaboration-responsibility modeling session.

There are two major differences between the technique used here and that used in the interaction modeling. One is that the need for communication between components is recorded as a collaboration rather than as explicit message sends, and the other is that no information flows are recorded.

Not recording information flows delays some of the work that must be done and it also limits the value of the results. There is no reduction in the total amount of work that must be done, because all of the decisions about message names and information flows must be made before the system can be implemented.

7.4.3 Evaluation

Behavior modeling primarily addresses the user requirements, so it is important that the results of collaboration-responsibility modeling be evaluated against the user requirements. Unfortunately, there is usually not enough information captured in the C-R modeling documentation to evaluate whether the use cases have been adequately modeled after the initial walk through is completed. Because only the results of the allocation decisions are recorded, there is no documentation of how the components were assembled to provide each use case. Because of the inability to explicitly evaluate how the user requirements were met, I recommend that this technique be used only to verify preliminary architectures. This usage will be described in Chapter 10.

A collaboration graph is a bottom-up architecture.

If, in spite of this recommendation, the technique is used as the major behavior modeling vehicle, then some evaluation is required. The things that can be evaluated are all local issues. They include cohesion of responsibilities, relative distribution of responsibilities, and connectedness of the collaborations.

Cohesion of Responsibilities

Each component is documented with the list of responsibilities that have been allocated to it. Looking down the list, a judgment can be made as to whether the responsibilities are sufficiently similar to one another to justify keeping them in the same component (Figure 7.17).

Cohesive

Report Dialog	
Responsibility	Collaboration
Maintain report forms	
Request display of report form	Presentation
Request script	Report List
Request script execution	Lookup Service
Request format	Report Formatter
Request print of report	Presentation

Noncohesive

Report Dialog	
Responsibility	Collaboration
Maintain report forms	
Display of report form	Screen
Request script	Report List
Request script execution	Lookup Service
Request format	Report Formatter
Execute script	Inventory
Maintain video status	
Print of report	Printer

Figure 7.17 CRC cards showing cohesive and noncohesive responsibility allocations

When you discover a problem, the fix is to move the offending responsibilities to another component or to invent a new component to carry them. As was the case in the interaction modeling technique, moving behaviors may cause one or more of the use case responses to break, so we should revisit the use case response models. If there are no documents showing what components are involved in the response to each use case and what responsibilities were used or allocated, then it is very difficult to revisit and revise the response model. Of course, one can just move the responsibilities and not worry about the response to the use cases. That can be fixed when the problem shows up, say, in testing, or when some hapless users find that their favorite use of the system doesn't work.

Relative Distribution of Responsibilities

The problem being addressed here is allocating too much responsibility to a single component. *Too much* is defined in relative terms. If most of the components have five to ten responsibilities, but one has 20 and another has 28, there may be a problem. The problem could be that there really was too much responsibility allocated to those components. It could also be that the behavior was decomposed to a lower level for the 20 and 28 responsibility components than for the others.

Fixes include moving responsibilities and renaming them. The caution about moving responsibilities and breaking use case responses, discussed above, also applies here.

Connectedness of the Collaborations

It is entirely possible to allocate the CRC cards to architecture subsystems, derive subsystem collaborations, and evaluate the resulting system architecture against the change cases, but a local evaluation can be done without touching the architecture. The technique is to draw a collaboration graph, as suggested in Wirfs-Brock. The

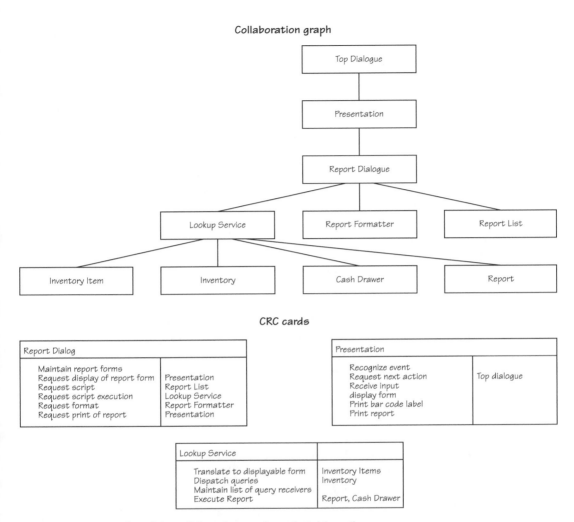

Figure 7.18 CRC cards and the collaboration graph produced from them

graph is constructed by placing all of the components on a diagram and drawing a line from each component to each of its collaborators, as shown in Figure 7.18.

The basic evaluation question to ask of the collaboration graph is, "Is this spaghetti?" If the graph looks like everything is connected to everything else, it is.

The fix, as always, is to reallocate the responsibilities. The examples section contains an illustration of the process. The problems of how the components provide the use cases remain the same here as elsewhere. This problem is associated with moving behaviors without an audit trail.

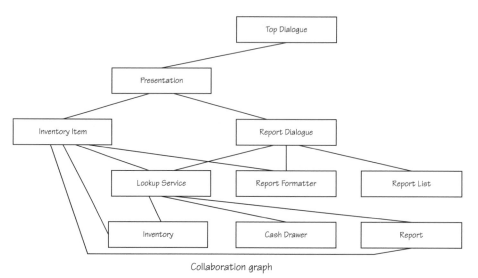

Figure 7.19
Collaboration
graph
showing all
collabora-
tions with
inventory
item

Collaboration graph

The collaboration graph shows all of the components in the entire system in a single diagram. Unfortunately this practice may lead to spaghetti-like collaboration graphs: components that are passed around between many of the components will have collaborations with many components, like Inventory Item in the Figure 7.19.

7.5 SERVICE MODELING

Service components enable functional enhancements by showing clean additions.

A *service* is a very well-defined concept in the telephone industry. A service is something that is offered to subscribers, that subscribers may use and pay for. In the software industry, outside telephone companies, service is not so well defined. It sounds suspiciously like *function*. In function-centered design, everything is a function or a service. In domain object-centered design, the only services, or functions, are methods on the real world objects, and there is no such thing as a service component. Between these two extremes lies a place where service components can coexist with other kinds of components.

Service modeling is the nomination and evaluation of components whose role is to provide discrete units of functionality. The complete, high level functionality of a system should be provided by the complete collection of all the service components contained in a system.

The idea of having services contained in physical components derives from Jacobson's service packages in the Objectory method [JAC92]. There it is described as a grouping of smaller components into packages that may be used to configure a system to provide specific functionality, or services, to its users.

I propose that service modeling is a useful, standalone way to account for the behavior of a system, independent of the other behavior modeling techniques described previously. I find service modeling useful when doing a quick feasibility study, and in conjunction with interaction modeling to help nominate process components. In the feasibility study project, it serves as the complete behavior model for the system. For that reason, I have elevated service modeling to the status of a complete behavior modeling technique.

Service modeling is different from and should be elevated above a functional description of the system in that the services identified are to be packaged up in their own components. Functions in a functional description are not necessarily associated with just one component.

The goal of service modeling is to nominate a set of components that support the functional growth and configuration of the system. These service components should be able to be reconfigured to provide variations in system functionality to meet the needs of different kinds of users. When it is time to expand the functionality the system offers to its users, that expansion should take place largely by adding more service components.

Having well-defined service components is an essential prerequisite for having an extensible, configurable system, so it is important to do a good job nominating service components. I have also found that nominating service components is one of the more difficult tasks in designing systems. Because of the great value of having a good set of service components, I feel it is worth the trouble of trying to nominate them.

7.5.1 What Are Service Components?

The idea of service components is based on Jacobson's service packages [JAC92]. Jacobson defines services as a unit of functionality that the user may want. The key part of the definition is that the service is atomic. That is, the user either wants all of the service or none of it. If we look at the architecture of a system that contains service components we can see some other characteristics of service components (Figure 7.20).

Service components are units of growth.

If services are different from other kinds of components, such as models and controllers, then the question is, what behaviors do they have? Service components exist solely to facilitate growth, change, and configuration of system functionality, so there is nothing in the user's domain that offers any guidance as to what a service should be. To nominate behavior allocations to service components we must know something else—what the growth, change, and configuration steps are.

That last paragraph contains a somewhat circular statement. If we knew what the growth, change, and configuration steps were, we would have the service definitions. So one of the key techniques for nominating service components is to define the increments of implementation, growth, and configuration the system should

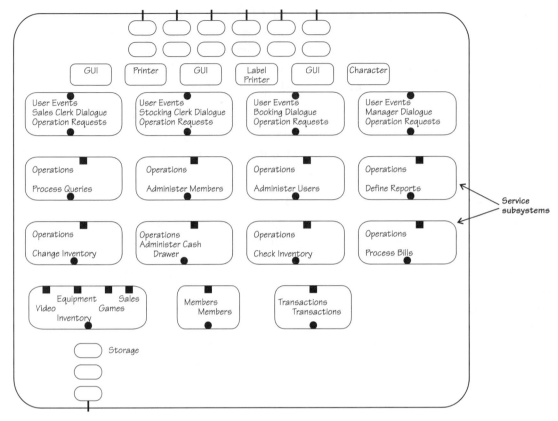

Figure 7.20   Architecture diagram showing service subsystems

support. This definition is best done while looking at an architecture diagram. It is demonstrated in the example in Chapter 9.

Looking again at the architecture diagram we see that services are separate from the models that they manipulate and from the controls and presentations that invoke them. Behaviors in service components are responsible for knowing "how to do things" and "what to do them to," but they are not responsible for knowing all the things that can be done nor when to invoke them.

Service components should be separate from the models because there are often other services that also manipulate the models. Behaviors in service components must be atomic: either we want all of the behaviors in a service component, or we want none. Behaviors should not be replicated anywhere else, so there will be no requirement to add or change behavior in more than one place. Both of these requirements concern only behaviors at the level of the application.

Finally, service components must be completely independent of one another. Effectively, this means that there can be no direct communication between service components. This requirement comes entirely from the role assigned to service components: we should be able to mix and match services freely to supply the different increments and configurations of the system. If service *A* must talk to service *B*, then we cannot build a system that has service *A* but not service *B*. Moreover, any coordination between service components should be done by controllers, and any sharing of results should be done through model components.

Service components cannot be use-coupled to each other.

The preceding paragraphs describe service components. I want to emphasize, again, that service components exist solely to meet the development sponsor requirements for a flexible, configurable, easy-to-grow system. So, the criteria we will use to select and evaluate service components involve the build-time requirements, in addition to making the system "work."

7.5.2 Nominating Service Components

I can suggest two starting points for nominating services components. The first is use cases and behavior dependency considerations, and the second is the increments of implementation, growth, and configuration. The second is also the source of criteria that should be used to evaluate the service component nominations.

Nominating services takes several cycles.

7.5.3 Service Components from Use Cases

Each use case represents a "service" that the system offers to its users. Therefore, one starting point is to nominate one service component for each use case, naming them with the use case name. While very simple, some thought about the functionality contained in these service component nominations will indicate that they may have much in common. The use cases are intended to describe how users, external to the system, use the system. But external users have no concern for whether the services are atomic, redundant, or anything else. The result is that the service components nominated from use case names are never atomic. So, the next step is to sort out the redundancies to try to arrive at a set of atomic service components.

Service components are not always directly useful to users.

The process of eliminating redundancies from services nominated from use cases can be described as a process of decomposing the use case into a sequence of responsibilities and then selecting only those responsibilities that do not "belong" to either the presentation and control components or the model components. I understand that this sounds like doing a complete responsibility behavior model, but not if you do away with a degree of formalism. Scratching your head for a few seconds while looking at the use case description constitutes the least formal approach. Carrying out and documenting a complete behavior model constitutes the most formal approach. The examples section provides a fairly informal approach to service modeling.

I emphasized the word *belong* in the previous paragraph to remind the reader that whether a behavior belongs to a particular component is entirely in the mind of the designer. A more cumbersome, but more accurate, way to say the same thing is, "...selecting only those responsibilities which the designer feels should be allocated to either the presentation and control components, or to the model components."

The words I used to describe the process of decomposition to responsibilities makes it sound like the responsibilities are sitting there, just waiting to be picked up. This is not the case. Nominating responsibilities that are of the appropriate granularity with appropriate names requires knowledge of the domain, the system implementation and architecture, and experience with the technique. The same can be said for all design techniques, but I want to reemphasize the requirement here.

If this process of selecting responsibilities that don't belong to the front end or back end were repeated for all of the use cases, we would have a list of responsibilities to consider for inclusion in the service components. Assuming some sort of consistency in naming responsibilities, the designer should be able to look over the list and nominate groups of cohesive responsibilities as service components. See the next chapter for an example.

7.5.4 Service Components from Increments

Service components are very close to increments.

Incremental implementation is a powerful technique for enforcing modularity. Dave Parnas [PAR79] and Ivar Jacobson [JAC87] have argued eloquently that building a system in small increments is a very effective way to enforce modularity in a system development. The basic suggestion is that after the complete system is designed, a small piece of the total system is implemented, executed, and tested by itself. Then another piece of the system is implemented, added to the first, and tested. This process is repeated until the initial release of the system has been assembled.

The advantage of this approach is that the increments, once added and tested, can be considered to be "complete." If, however, in adding subsequent increments, you have to go back and alter existing increments, then they have to be tested again and we cannot call them complete.

The advantages of this approach are many. It enforces modularity, discourages pathological coupling, and gives sponsors a warm, fuzzy feeling that progress is being made. Increments also make wonderfully concrete scheduling milestones.

After its initial development, a product is always enhanced by increments of functionality. The definition of "easy to extend" is the same as the definition of incremental development given here. Extensions are implemented by adding or replacing components, rather than by changing code in many existing components. Doing the initial development by adding components goes a long way toward ensuring that the future enhancement will also be carried out by adding components. (There are no guarantees, of course.)

There is a price to be paid for building a system in increments. It is that the system must be designed to be built in increments. The increments must be specified before they are implemented. I have already suggested that the increments that occur after the initial release of the system (the extensions) be documented as part of the external requirements. The suggestion being made here is that the increments to be used during the initial development be nominated and evaluated as part of the design process.

In the past, I have tried to nominate services as part of the requirements gathering activity, but I have always found it to be very difficult to do early in the process. A more detailed knowledge of the system internals is needed than is available during the requirements activity. That knowledge becomes available only in the behavior modeling and architecture activities.

As defined, the increments of development are the finished components of the system implementation, which is exactly the definition of the architecture components (see the architecture chapter). We have the makings of a chicken and egg situation here. To do the architecture, we need the service components, to do the service components, we need the architecture. That is the nature of engineering design and explains why engineering is a separate discipline from science, on one hand, and construction on the other. So, in this section I will describe the process of nominating implementation increments using the knowledge available in the behavior modeling activity. In the architecture chapter, I will describe defining increments using knowledge available during the architecture activity.

Increments become change cases for the architecture evaluation.

Part of the bottom line of "all this increment talk" is that some of the increments will be our service components, which is what we started off looking for. The other part of the bottom line is that our increments of development and enhancement will be the primary criteria we need to evaluate whether the architecture we nominate is sufficient.

7.5.5 Nominating Increments of Development and Enhancement

In "Designing Systems for Ease of Extension and Contraction," Dave Parnas [PAR79] suggested that the first increment be the minimal subset of the system functionality. A minimal subset is functionality that, while not directly useful to the system's users, is still meaningful in the user's context.

The first approach is to begin from a port on the boundary of the system and add increments to grow toward the other ports. In a human user driven system a minimal subset might be the ability to receive and display keyboard input. If the dialogue control is a separate component from the presentation, then the minimum subset would not have to change menus. If the output of the project is a deliverable product, then this minimum subset is not the same as a user interface prototype. It is supposed to be the final, deliverable presentation component in the system. The prototypes were done in earlier projects.

A second approach is to begin with one of the system state models and grow outward from that. This approach has the disadvantage that there is no user interface available early, but in systems that have a complex system state model, it is valuable to get the model up and running. It also means that some temporary machinery will have to be constructed to exercise the model. That machinery could be the test machinery, if separate test systems are being used.

A third approach is to look at the interaction diagrams, or whatever technique was used to document the behavior identification and allocation decisions. The increments can be defined in terms of the set of components that implement part of the thread of a use case. An advantage of this approach is that it is directly tied to behaviors that are meaningful to the user. The examples section nominates increments from the interaction diagrams.

After the minimal subset is defined, the increments that follow should grow outward, toward the final deliverable for the project. The example section shows one set of increments for our sample system. The suggestion that increments should be strict additions to the previous increments means that the size of the increments is dependent on the size of the architectural components used in the system.

Having made a cut at a list of increments for the system, we should look to see if any sound like likely candidates for nomination as services.

The development increment list should smoothly merge into the increments that constitute the future growth of the system. The example shows the list of likely extensions appended to the list of development increments. This combined list of development increments and extensions constitutes the primary criteria that will be used to evaluate system architecture nominations. Keep this list handy.

7.5.6 Evaluation

There is a circle here: service component–increment–service subsystem.

Since the service model does not contain a great deal of information, the evaluations are necessarily qualitative. The list of services is not very informative by itself, so I recommend that a system architecture be developed using the services as the service subsystems. This would be a very preliminary architecture. The run-time requirements can then be evaluated by walking through some representative use cases on the architecture diagram. The service list is sufficient, if it looks like the use case can be provided by invoking a reasonable combination of the subsystems.

Service components exist to enable the system to be implemented, enhanced, and reconfigured by adding and removing discrete components rather than by altering the innards of many existing components. Therefore, the appropriate way to evaluate the nominated service components against the build-time requirements is to try to assemble all expected increments, configurations, and enhancements for the system from the subsystems in the preliminary architecture diagram. If the services required in each of the increments and configurations can be provided by selecting from the list of service subsystems, then the service model is sufficient. If not, then new services should be nominated. The examples section walks through the process. See Chapter 9 for a discussion of developing architecture diagrams.

7.6 SUMMARY

Behavior identification and allocation is an important step in software system design. Regardless of the particular techniques used, several features should always be present. The identification of behaviors and information should be tied directly to the user requirements, allocation of behavior to components in the system should be an explicit engineering decision, and the allocation decisions should be evaluated against external requirements for changes and extensions. These "shoulds" are here because they constitute the minimum set needed to give the system a chance of meeting its external requirements.

The three techniques described here, collaboration-responsibility modeling, interaction modeling, and service modeling may be mixed and matched in many ways depending on the needs of the project. They represent the best techniques I have found for documenting the identification and allocation of behavior in software systems.

The output of this task is a collection of components with behaviors allocated to them. Those behaviors are allocated in the form of message names or responsibilities. The assertion we should be able to make is that taken together these components will provide all of the run-time requirements. We should be able to demonstrate this fact by assembling the components to provide any of the run-time requirements. The demonstration that the emergent, run-time properties, reliability, performance, etc., have provided will have to wait until the behavior components have been allocated to a system architecture.

The collection of interface views should name and structure all the behavior in the system.

CHAPTER 8

Behavior Allocation Examples

CONTENTS

8.1 Interaction Model   161
8.2 Collaboration-Responsibility Model   189
8.3 Service Model   201

8.1 INTERACTION MODEL

The use case being modeled is to add new titles or copies to inventory. When a new item is received by a store, the inventory clerk logs the item into the system. The system tracks the name, artist, director (if applicable), date the item was produced, and the number of items received. A bar code is assigned to the item and if necessary, bar code labels are printed. If the title is already in the system (adding another copy) no additional entry is required.

Sale items that already have a UPC bar code on them are scanned and a quantity is entered. After logging an item into the system, it will be available for rental, sale, user queries, and inclusion in inventory and activity reports.

8.1.1 Nominating Components from Scratch

If no system state model is available, we might nominate *inventory, item* (with name, artist, director, and date), and *sale item*. If we looked at a system-state model, we might select *inventory, category, title, rental item,* or *sale item.* If I were a very naive designer, I might stop there, thinking that only system state elements will

Use cases are neutral on which components we use.

participate in the response to the use case. While it is entirely possible to design and build a system like that, it would fail almost all the tests for modularity, extensibility, and portability.

I prefer to keep my actor presentations separate from my control, so I always nominate a presentation, Stocking Presentation, and a separate sequence controller, Stocking Dialogue Controller, for starters. Thinking ahead, if I name a different presentation for each use case, I will end up with very tight coupling between my presentations and my controllers. I can justify the differences between the controllers, but do I have to have different presentation components for every different kind of interaction? I should be able to make a more generic presentation, through appropriate behavior allocation, so I will change the name to *Clerk Presentation*. Now I will have a different presentation for each kind of actor that the system supports. This is a considerable reduction in presentations from having one per use case.

The names we pick for components have a subtle yet profound effect on the behavior we end up allocating to them. Something called a Stocking Presentation is likely to have its screen appearance, fields, and locations, allocated to the presentation. If we know from its name, Clerk Presentation, that it is going to handle all of the clerk interaction, we might be less eager to allocate information or behaviors specific to any one use case to the component.

If I have no other framework for reference, I will stop here with my nominations. As I go through the behavior allocation process, I will watch for opportunities to nominate other components.

8.1.2 Nominating Components Using an Architecture Diagram

An architecture diagram is a good guide for nominating components.

If we have an architecture diagram available, or a template in mind, we can use it as a guide for nominating components to participate in the use case. As an example of an architecture diagram, see Figure 8.1. The architecture template I have chosen suggests that there should be components to populate the following subsystem types: presentation, dialogue, service, and model.

Looking at the architecture, read through the use case description and see which architecture components might be involved. (See the section on collaboration-responsibility modeling.) This use case begins with a supply clerk operating the user terminal. The GUI Presentation subsystem will receive input and display output. The flow after that looks like it should through the Stocking Clerk Dialogue and Change Inventory to Inventory.

With that framework in mind, I would nominate *Clerk Presentation, Stocking Dialogue Controller,* something from *Change Inventory, Inventory,* and of course, *items in inventory.* In other words, I should have at least one behavior model component for each architecture subsystem that I think will be involved in responding to

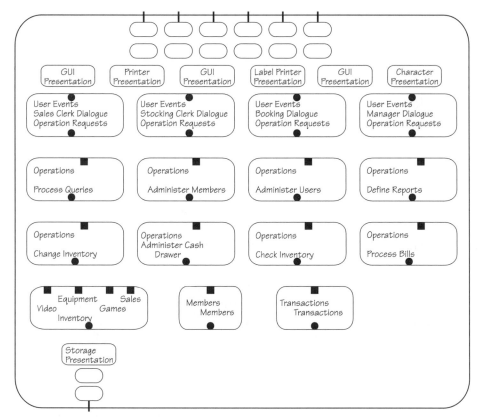

Figure 8.1
The architecture diagram used as a template for identifying components to participate in the use case response

the use case. The components nominated for the behavior model should always be smaller than the architecture subsystems.

I said *something from Change Inventory,* because at this point in the process I cannot see what kind of behavior I need as a service. It will depend on which mechanisms I select for this system.

8.1.3 Building an Interaction Diagram

Put the nominated components in an interaction diagram as shown in Figure 8.2.

The order of the components across the top has no modeling significance. I sometimes put interface and control components on the left side, and service and model components on the right. If I know there will be many messages between two components, I will try to not put them close together. That will leave room on the message arrows for message names and arguments.

The text of the use case should be copied down the left margin. I had been doing interaction diagrams for several years before the Objectory method was available to me. I always kept the use case description on a separate sheet of paper, but putting it on the diagram is more convenient.

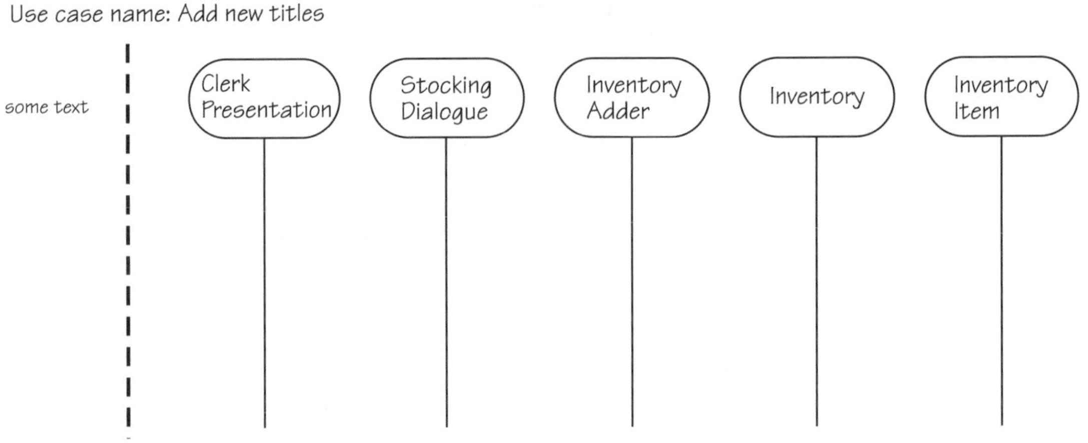

Use case name: Add new titles

Figure 8.2   An interaction diagram populated with components that participate in the response to a use case

The environment boundary can represent anything you want. I suggest that it be the first component that has an application-level interface. In most systems, depending on the basic mechanisms selected, that would be a presentation-type component. How the inputs and outputs get through the system boundary is the concern of another level of domain.

Expanding the Text of the Use Case

Now, we are set to begin. Read the first sentence of the use case description. One hopes that it describes a clean start to the dialogue, like, "user requests inventory stocking." If it begins with "user enters name of item being added," then we do not know how we got to the point of being ready to receive the new-item name. This example describes the start of the use case from the point of view of the organization, but not from the point of view of the system. It needs to be fixed. There are two choices: go back to the external model and make the change there, or make the change here. For now, I will make the change here. That means we will have two versions of the use case description in the design documents.

Developing a behavior model often uncovers problems in the requirements statement.

The expanded text describing the start might look like this: When new items are received by a store, the inventory clerk logs the item into the system. The clerk logs into the system and requests "add inventory." If the clerk selects "new," the system requests new title information, including name, artist, director (if applicable), date the item was produced and number of items received. If the clerk selects "add," the system requests the title. The clerk enters the title, and the system verifies that it is a current title and requests the number of items being added. A bar code is assigned to the item and, if necessary, bar code labels are printed. If the title is already in the system (adding another copy) no additional entry is required.

Use case name: Add new titles

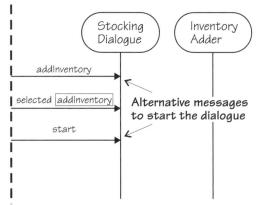

When a new item is received by a store, the inventory clerk logs the item into the system.

The clerk logs into the system and requests "add inventory." If the clerk selects "new," the system requests new title information, including name, artist, director (if applicable), the date the item was produced, and the number of items received. If the clerk selects "add," the system requests the title. The clerk enters the title, and the system verifies that it is a current title and requests the number of items being added. A bar code is assigned to the item and, if necessary, bar code labels are printed. If the title is already in the system (adding another copy) no additional entry is required.

Figure 8.3   Interaction diagram showing three alternative messages to recognize the event

Addressing Message Questions

After replacing the text in the margin, we are again ready to start. Logging in to the system should be a separate use case, so I will ignore it here. We assume that "add inventory" is an option available from the top level of the display. The action in the diagram starts when the user requests "add inventory." There is some keyboard or mouse activity that we will not show because the semantics are below the application. The first question is: What behavior is needed? The user did something, so some behavior to recognize the request by the user might be appropriate. The event will come from the environment boundary. Remember that we chose to have the presentation components serve as the environment boundary to keep the semantics at the application level.

The next two questions are: Who should receive the message coming from the presentation, and what should the message be? Looking at our nominated components, the Stocking Dialogue Controller looks like a good choice because its responsibilities include interpreting user requests. Three possibilities for messages come to mind. One is "addInventory," another is "selected 'add Inventory'," and the third is "start." The diagram would look like Figure 8.3.

Many important decisions are being documented with these lines and names.

Addressing Mechanism Questions

Having proposed three alternatives, we come to mechanism questions. The first is, does the presentation "tell" the controllers that input has been received, or do the controllers poll the presentation for input? I have chosen arbitrarily to have the presentation tell the controllers. These lines and arrows do not represent "how it is;" they represent arbitrary design decisions that I have made.

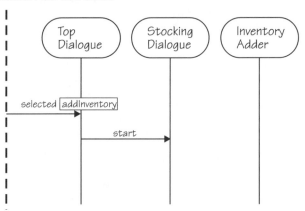

Use case name: Add new titles

When a new item is received by a store, the inventory clerk logs the item into the system.

The clerk logs into the system and requests "add inventory." If the clerk selects "new," the system requests new title information, including name, artist, director (if applicable), the date the item was produced, and the number of items received. If the clerk selects "add," the system requests the title. The clerk enters the title, and the system verifies that it is a current title and requests the number of items being added. A bar code is assigned to the item, and if necessary, bar code labels are printed. If the title is already in the system (adding another copy) no additional entry is required.

Figure 8.4   Adding a top dialogue to the participating components

Establish mechanisms early. The second mechanism question is: How much routing responsibility do we want our presentation components to have? There will be many dialogue components, one for each major activity. As shown in Figure 8.3, the presentation "knows" which of those many dialogues should receive the message. This implies that knowledge of which dialogues are present is embedded in the presentation component. While this is a perfectly respectable allocation decision, it does couple presentation processing concerns with control concerns.

Adding a Top Dialogue Component

We could decouple those concerns by introducing another control component, which I usually call the *Top Dialogue*. This component is responsible for receiving all user control input and directing it to the appropriate activity dialogue. It is also a handy place to catch global commands like "quit" and requests to change activities. The Top Dialogue is responsible for knowing which activity dialogues are present. By introducing this new component and reallocating some behavior, we can remove the control behaviors from the presentation. Our diagram now looks like Figure 8.4.

Adding Behaviors to the Stocking Dialogue

We can allocate the responsibility for modifying the selections available to the clerk, to the Stocking Dialogue, by asking the presentation to display choices, and giving it the list of choices (Figure 8.5).

This message represents another mechanism decision. The presentation is not responsible for knowing what the menus are. It is told what to display. When it is told what to display, it should also be told who is asking—hence the "name" and

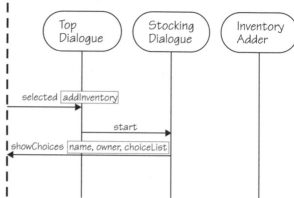

Use case name: Add new titles

When a new item is received by a store, the inventory clerk logs the item into the system.

The clerk logs into the system and requests "add inventory." If the clerk selects "new," the system requests new title information, including name, artist, director (if applicable), the date the item was produced, and the number of items received. If the clerk selects "add," the system requests the title. The clerk enters the title, and the system verifies that it is a current title and requests the number of items being added. A bar code is assigned to the item and, if necessary, bar code labels are printed. If the title is already in the system (adding another copy) no additional entry is required.

Figure 8.5   Identifying behavior and allocating it to the stocking dialogue component

"owner" arguments. This way, when the user makes a selection, the request can be routed to the appropriate dialogue controller. This is one of several possible mechanisms for managing menus. It also demonstrates the value of putting both control and information flows (arguments) in the same diagram.

I have encountered widespread resistance to including information flows in interaction diagrams, usually because it represents "too much work." I submit that it is not, because the decisions about which information flows accompany the control flows must be made some time. In fact, there are two advantages to making the decisions here, the first being that I am thinking about it. If I specify the information flows later, I have to regenerate my thoughts.

But a more important reason for documenting information flows during the detailed behavior modeling activity is that it keeps me very honest. Why did I include the argument "owner" when the dialogue asked to have the menu displayed? Because I knew that there is a separate routing component, and that to do its job, it must have some way of knowing to whom to route the selections.

Another comment about choice of message names: I have said that the semantic level of the messages is key to effectively hiding sites of change. If I want my presentation components to hide the details of what kind of presentation is actually being displayed, the messages I send need to provide that hiding. For that reason, I chose the message, *showChoices* rather than *showMenu*. By avoiding message names that come from the semantic level of a particular presentation style, like *button, popUpmenu,* or *listBox,* I make it easy to change presentations without changing the users of the presentation. The semantic level of the words is the key to effective hiding of sites of change.

Names and semantic level are still important.

The next sentence of the use case description reads, "If the clerk selects 'new,' the system requests new title information, including name, artist, director, the date the item was produced and the number of items received." This represents an exchange between the clerk and the system that I might design as shown in Figure 8.5.

I propose that the presentation knows how to handle something called a "field list." A field is a self-defining entity that carries information like names, default values, or allowable entry values. This allows the presentation to display the field, receive input, and do local validation without having to have any knowledge of the field's contents. The field should carry enough identity information so that when it is returned to its controller, the controller knows what each field is. This kind of information should be documented in a component dictionary. The use of field components may or may not be a great idea, but for now it is the proposal for a mechanism to keep the presentation from having application-specific knowledge. I have documented it so it can be reviewed and compared with alternative proposals.

Getting Information from the User

It is important to apply the mechanisms consistently.

The next sentences read, "If the clerk selects 'add,' the system requests the title. The clerk enters title and the system verifies that it is a current title and requests the number of items being added." I will talk about the branch later, but for now I have a choice about how much detail to show. The selection and the system's response with a request for more information are similar to the messages used earlier. If both the users' selections and system's responses are described by parameterized messages, I could say that this piece of the interaction between the system and clerk has already been described. I could also add more detail in the diagram to show this interaction. My suggestion is that you add details until you have convinced yourself that the patterns really are the same (Figure 8.6).

The second exchange of menu selection and information entry does indeed look just like the first one, so I will stop duplicating the entries within diagrams (Figure 8.7).

Verifying the Title

The statement that the system should "verify the presence of a title" is a new kind of behavior. It seems quite reasonable to expect that the Stocking Dialogue will know that the title must be verified now. We have recognized the need for a piece of behavior, to verify a title in inventory, and we have already allocated the responsibility for invoking the behavior to the Stocking Dialogue. The next question is who should implement the behavior?

Looking over our list of participating components, it looks like Inventory is a likely place to find information about what titles are in inventory. So I will have the dialogue ask the inventory to verify the title. The message might be "verifyTitle 'title name'." What should the return be? Choices include a yes/no or the title component itself, if present. This introduces another mechanism issue. How do we handle

Use case name: Add new titles

When a new item is received by a store, the inventory clerk logs the item into the system.

The clerk logs into the system and requests "add inventory."

If the clerk selects "new," the system requests new title information, including name, artist, director (if applicable), date the item was produced, and the number of items received.

If the clerk selects "add," the system requests the title. The clerk enters the title, and the system verifies that it is a current title and requests the number of items being added. A bar code is assigned to the item and, if necessary, bar code labels are printed. If the title is already in the system (adding another copy) no additional entry is required.

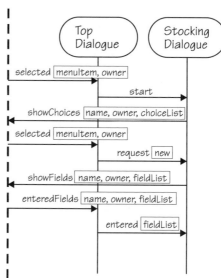

Figure 8.6
Behavior allocation for a mechanism to get information from the user

verify and retrieve? Should verify requests just result in verify and a return of yes/no, or do we always want the thing being verified, so that verify requests should always return the component if it is present? Or, should we do our verifications by asking to retrieve the item being verified?

These are important questions because they influence how many messages we end up with and how consistent our interfaces are. As a first cut, I will propose a mechanism that separates verify and retrieve operations. That decision will result in the messages shown in Figure 8.8.

Use case name: Add new titles

The clerk logs into the system and requests "add inventory"...

If the clerk selects "add," the system requests the title. The clerk enters the title...

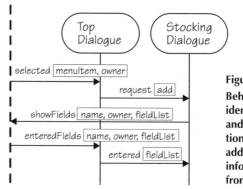

Figure 8.7
Behavior identification and allocation to get additional information from the user

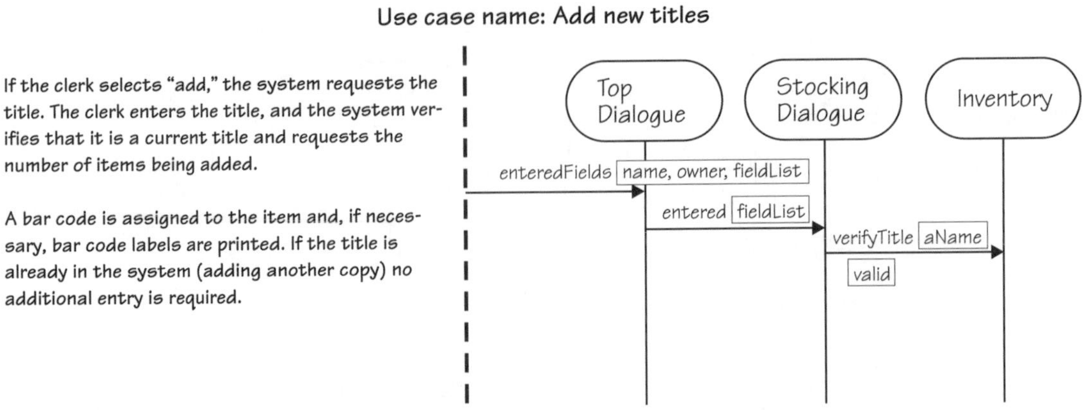

If the clerk selects "add," the system requests the title. The clerk enters the title, and the system verifies that it is a current title and requests the number of items being added.

A bar code is assigned to the item and, if necessary, bar code labels are printed. If the title is already in the system (adding another copy) no additional entry is required.

Figure 8.8 Behavior allocation to verify that a title is in inventory

A word about the branch in the use case description. The text said, "If the clerk selects 'new'..." and, "If the clerk selects 'add'... ." These are branches. I chose to handle them in a single diagram because each branch is very small. If the branches had contained a larger number of different steps, I would have nominated each branch as its own use case. We could still choose to make two use cases here: one to add a copy of a title already in inventory and one to add a new title and at least one copy.

We need to see information flows to decide when to start the process.

Since we are showing only one use case in this example, I will proceed with describing both situations in this diagram. At this point in the action, the Stocking Dialogue has accumulated all the information needed to add new titles or copies. The use case description then says, "A bar code is assigned to the item, and if necessary, bar code labels are printed. If the title is already in the system (adding another copy) no additional entry is required." At the time the use case description was written this may have seemed like a sufficient explanation. From our present point of view, inside the system, we can now see that some additional work is needed. In particular, we have to create new title or copy components and to assign new item ID numbers before we can print bar code labels. Again, we need to expand the use case description with the greater detail now available to us. The new text might read as follows:

When a new item is received by a store, the inventory clerk logs the item into the system. The clerk logs into the system and requests "add inventory." If the clerk selects "new," the system requests new title information, including name, artist, director (if applicable), the date the item was produced and the number of items received. If the clerk selects "add," the system requests the title. The clerk enters the title, and the system verifies that it is a current title and requests the number of items being added.

Creating New Titles

The system creates new titles for the new copies and assigns unique ID numbers to the title and copies. A bar code is assigned to the item, and if necessary, bar code labels are printed. If the title is already in the system (adding another copy) no additional entry is required.

In adding the new text, we have identified a new behavior: making new title and copy components.

The second question is: Where should we allocate it? It seems that the Stocking Dialogue component is now aware of the need to create new components, so we could allocate the responsibility for asking to that component. Which component should actually create the new components? There are several choices. Smalltalk programmers might answer, "the appropriate class objects" but class objects, while important, were not among the components nominated to participate in the use case response so I would not recommend adding them. Class objects come from the programming language domain and should not appear in a behavior model at the application domain level.

Allocation is not a straight-forward decision.

Looking over the list of components nominated to participate in the use case response, I see four possibilities: Stocking Dialogue Controller, Inventory Adder, Inventory, and items in inventory. In doing interaction diagrams, people often ask a video component, for example, to make a new video component. If we do that, how do we get the first one?

Two of the other possibilities share a common problem. If we allocate the creation responsibility to either the dialogue or the Inventory Adder component, then there will be some avoidable coupling between the system state model and either of these components. We will have to change the component creation behavior in the dialogue or Inventory Adder component whenever we add new kinds of items to the inventory. That is quite doable, but we can avoid the coupling by allocating the responsibility for making new inventory components to the Inventory component itself. My nomination for behavior allocation goes to having the Inventory create new inventory components. That might look like Figure 8.9 in an interaction diagram.

Look ahead to coupling evaluation when allocating behaviors.

The return values from the requests for new title and copy raise another mechanism question and demonstrate the value of showing both control and information flow in the same diagram. The question is, who is responsible for populating the new components with the raw information? Do we pass the raw information to the Inventory with the request for a new title and copy, do we return the empty title and copy components and let the dialogue populate the information, or do we have some intermediate component, like Inventory Adder, populate the information? If there are no arguments with the request for the new components, then the requestor must be populating the components because Inventory does not have the information. If we want Inventory to populate the components, we must show

See? Information flows are a good idea.

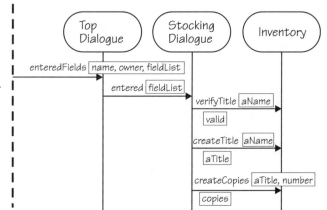

Use case name: Add new titles

When a new item is received by a store, the inventory clerk logs the item into the system.

If the clerk selects "add," the system requests the title. The clerk enters the title, and the system verifies that it is a current title and requests the number of items being added. A bar code is assigned to the item, and if necessary, bar code labels are printed. If the title is already in the system (adding another copy) no additional entry is required.

Figure 8.9   Behavior allocation to create new titles

arguments to provide the information. As you can see, this is a coupling and modularity issue, not a "does it work?" issue.

This question would not even have to be brought up now if we were only showing message names in the diagram. That does not mean the question would not be resolved, but it does mean that it would probably be resolved by the programmer in a manner that may or may not improve the modularity of the system, and may or may not be consistent with how similar questions are resolved in other areas of the system.

For now, I will opt to have Inventory populate the new components, so I will pass the necessary information as arguments with the request for new components. That means, again reading the information flows, that there must be enough information to allow the Inventory to know what kind of components are being requested. The resulting diagram might look like Figure 8.10.

8.1.4 Issues about Allocation Decisions

Modularity is not a free lunch. It comes from careful behavior allocation.

Writing out all the questions and issues that come up during detailed behavior modeling is very tedious. It is also tedious to read. But there is a very important point here. The coupling, cohesion, and modularity of the system are determined entirely by how the behavior and information allocation decisions are made. Most published design methods do not describe behavior allocation as something that even requires a decision. One simply writes down what the operations are—like looking at a car and writing down how many wheels it has. Obviously, a car has four wheels, what's to decide? That most cars have four wheels was an arbitrary design decision, now reduced to a standard by long repetition and successful experience.

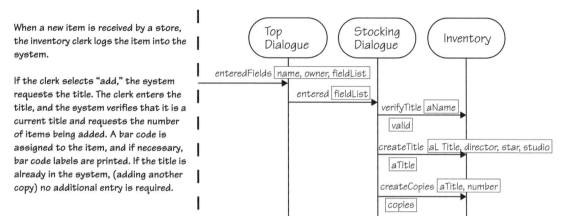

Use case name: Add new titles

When a new item is received by a store, the inventory clerk logs the item into the system.

If the clerk selects "add," the system requests the title. The clerk enters the title, and the system verifies that it is a current title and requests the number of items being added. A bar code is assigned to the item, and if necessary, bar code labels are printed. If the title is already in the system, (adding another copy) no additional entry is required.

Figure 8.10 Behavior allocation to create and initialize new titles

The decision has been made other ways, as in three- and six-wheeled cars, or moon cars with legs.

All these allocation decisions get made one way or another. My point is that unless they are made consciously and early in the process, with an eye toward modularity and consistency, they will probably be made badly. The modularity, and thus maintainability and extensibility of the resulting system will be less than it could be. This means that allocating behavior to software components should be a very conscious decision-making process in which many trade-offs between competing alternatives are made. In other words, behavior allocation is an important engineering design decision. Those decisions cannot be made by CASE tools or other development environments.

I will turn now from the detailed description of the process to present a draft of a completed interaction diagram for this use case and two others: Return a Tape and Rent a Video (Figures 8.11–8.13).

I can offer one mechanism comment that will resolve the problem of which behavior to allocate to the "something from Change Inventory." I have chosen to allocate the responsibility for translating between system state elements and forms that can be displayed to a component that is separate from the system state model and the display machinery. That component is the Translator in the interaction diagram. I would expect to allocate it (see the Architecture Chapter) to the Change Inventory architecture subsystem. Translation from one form to another, necessarily, has multiple dependencies—the source, on one hand, and the destination, on the other. This way I can isolate that multiple dependency in a separate component.

In working through the diagram, I realized that there "should" be a verification of the entered information. I added the appropriate text to the use case description

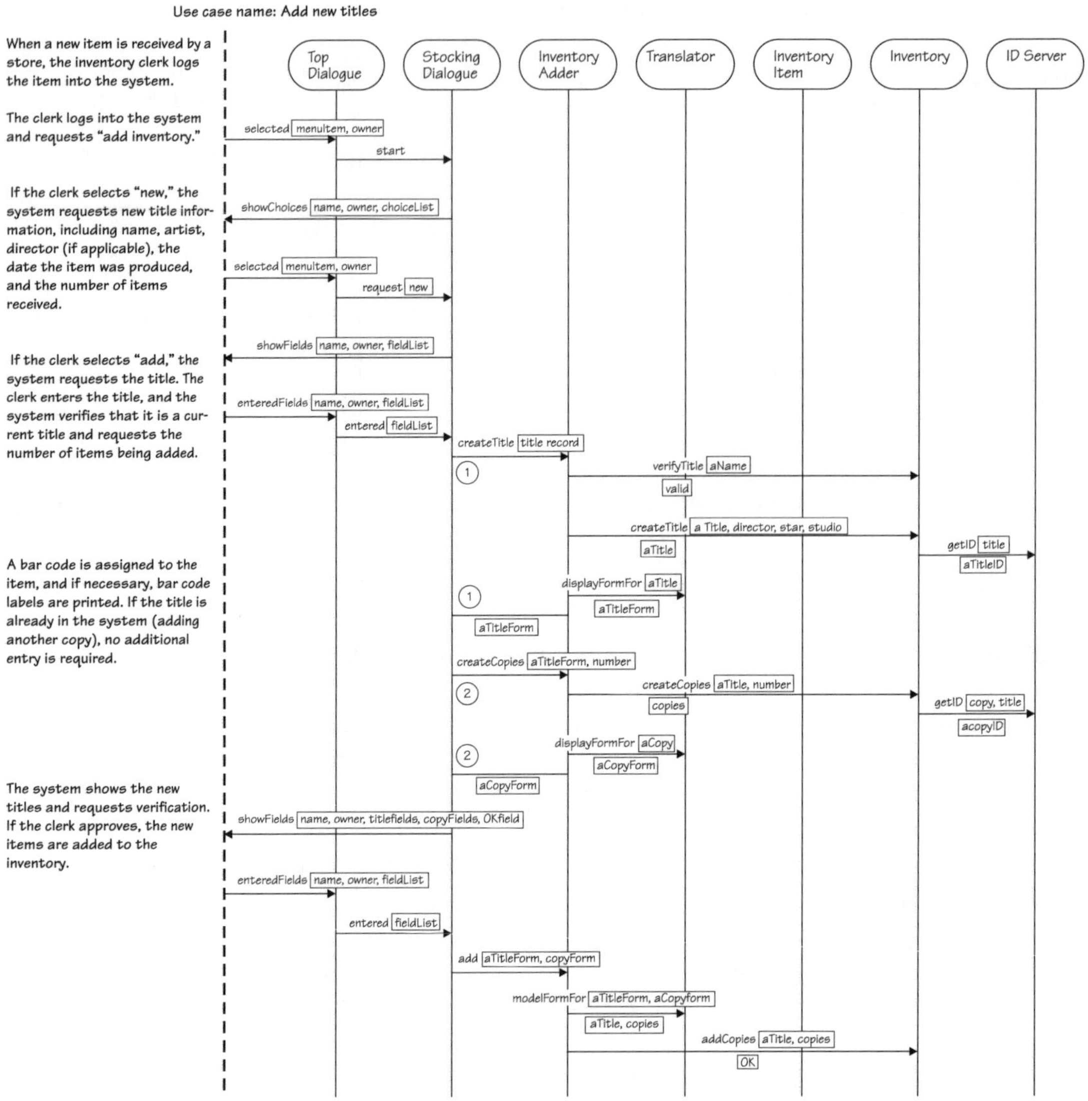
Use case name: Add new titles
When a new item is received by a store, the inventory clerk logs the item into the system.
The clerk logs into the system and requests "add inventory."
If the clerk selects "new," the system requests new title information, including name, artist, director (if applicable), the date the item was produced, and the number of items received.
If the clerk selects "add," the system requests the title. The clerk enters the title, and the system verifies that it is a current title and requests the number of items being added.
A bar code is assigned to the item, and if necessary, bar code labels are printed. If the title is already in the system (adding another copy), no additional entry is required.
The system shows the new titles and requests verification. If the clerk approves, the new items are added to the inventory.
Top Dialogue
Stocking Dialogue
Inventory Adder
Translator
Inventory Item
Inventory
ID Server
selected menuItem, owner
start
showChoices name, owner, choiceList
selected menuItem, owner
request new
showFields name, owner, fieldList
enteredFields name, owner, fieldList
entered fieldList
createTitle title record
1
verifyTitle aName
valid
createTitle a Title, director, star, studio
aTitle
getID title
aTitleID
displayFormFor aTitle
1
aTitleForm
aTitleForm
createCopies aTitleForm, number
2
createCopies aTitle, number
copies
getID copy, title
acopyID
displayFormFor aCopy
2
aCopyForm
aCopyForm
showFields name, owner, titlefields, copyFields, OKfield
enteredFields name, owner, fieldList
entered fieldList
add aTitleForm, copyForm
modelFormFor aTitleForm, aCopyform
aTitle, copies
addCopies aTitle, copies
OK

Figure 8.11 A completed interaction diagram for the use case Add new titles

and provided the verify behavior in the diagram. Additions to the use case descriptions should be reviewed and approved by the use case authorities.

This completes the nomination phase of a detailed behavior model for a single use case. Interaction diagrams for the other use cases are shown in the examples section.

The last step in developing an external behavior description is to collect the results of the message identification and allocation decisions in interface views.

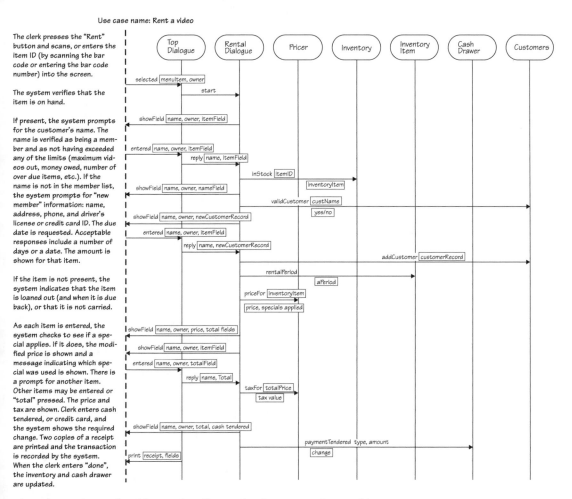

Use case name: Rent a video

The clerk presses the "Rent" button and scans, or enters the item ID (by scanning the bar code or entering the bar code number) into the screen.

The system verifies that the item is on hand.

If present, the system prompts for the customer's name. The name is verified as being a member and as not having exceeded any of the limits (maximum videos out, money owed, number of over due items, etc.). If the name is not in the member list, the system prompts for "new member" information: name, address, phone, and driver's license or credit card ID. The due date is requested. Acceptable responses include a number of days or a date. The amount is shown for that item.

If the item is not present, the system indicates that the item is loaned out (and when it is due back), or that it is not carried.

As each item is entered, the system checks to see if a special applies. If it does, the modified price is shown and a message indicating which special was used is shown. There is a prompt for another item. Other items may be entered or "total" pressed. The price and tax are shown. Clerk enters cash tendered, or credit card, and the system shows the required change. Two copies of a receipt are printed and the transaction is recorded by the system. When the clerk enters "done", the inventory and cash drawer are updated.

Figure 8.12 A completed interaction diagram for the use case Rent a video

These interface views are the primary output of the external behavior description. They are also the input to an important phase of the evaluation which I will describe next.

8.1.5 Evaluating the Results

A behavior model expressed as interaction diagrams can be evaluated directly against the user requirements. As is the case in the collaboration-responsibility modeling, the evaluation against development-sponsor requirements will have to wait for the architecture phase. For now, the behavior allocation decisions can be evaluated against local completeness, cohesion, coupling, and interface-profile type.

Use case name: **Return a tape**

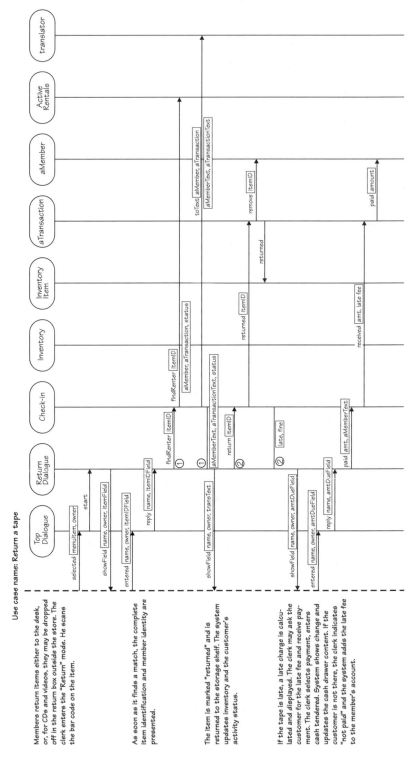

Members return items either to the desk, or, for CDs and videos, they may be dropped off in the return box outside the store. The clerk enters the "Return" mode. He scans the bar code on the item.

As soon as it finds a match, the complete item identification and member identity are presented.

The item is marked "returned" and is returned to the storage shelf. The system updates inventory and the customer's activity status.

If the tape is late, a late charge is calculated and displayed. The clerk may ask the customer for the late fee and receive payment. The clerk selects payment, enters cash tendered. System shows change and updates the cash drawer content. If the customer is not there, the clerk indicates "not paid" and the system adds the late fee to the member's account.

Figure 8.13   A completed interaction diagram for the use case Return a tape

Evaluating Against User Requirements

Each interaction diagram contains the user requirement, in the form of the use case text, and the explicit statement of how the system will provide that use case. Evaluation of the behavior identification and allocation against the user requirements consists, simply, of revisiting each of the diagrams and determining if all of the use cases have been modeled and whether the messages in the diagram look like they are doing everything implied in the use case.

First, confirm that the diagram matches the use case text.

Looking at the diagram in Figure 8.11, for example, the correlation between the use case text and the behaviors looks pretty good. There is, however one exception. The text calls for printing bar code labels for the new tapes, and that is not shown in the diagram. That omission should be remedied.

Interface Views

Examples of interface views are shown in Figure 8.14. These interface views were developed from the messages allocated in the three use cases shown in Figures 8.14–8.16.

Completeness

Local completeness can be evaluated by looking at the symmetry of the messages in the interface. For example, the Presentation component appears complete in that there are requests to display choices, individual and multiple fields, and ways to return entries or selections of those things.

Compare that interface with those of Inventory Item, Transaction, and Member. Inventory Item shows only messages for requesting rental period and returning videos. Transaction shows only messages related to returning a rented item. Something is missing: if the item can be returned, it must be rented too. We can see the source of the problem if we compare the interaction diagrams for the "Rent a video" and "Return a tape" use cases. The behaviors to create and record the transaction were left off the diagram. Another difference between the two interaction diagrams is that the return model used a Check-in component, while the rent model did not. These problems will be addressed in the revision.

Coupling and Cohesion

Inventory Adder seems to have two kinds of responsibilities: get things in and out of Inventory and arrange for the translation of inventory things between model and text forms. It seems that translation is not very tightly cohesive with getting things out of Inventory. The messages received by the Inventory Adder have almost the same names as the messages sent by the component. That means Inventory Adder is not doing very much work that relates to adding things to Inventory. At the very least the name is not appropriate for what it does. The fixes might include changing the name and changing the behavior allocated to the component. We could take the

Doing local evaluations should help architecture evaluation.

Figure 8.14   Interface views for the control components in the video store system

behavior about deciding when to create new titles out of the Stocking Dialogue and allocate it to Inventory Adder.

The Presentation component presents an example of coupling. All the messages it sends go to Top Dialogue. We could merge the two components, leaving a Presentation that knows where to route the requests. In this case, I would argue that the value of explicitly separating the control and routing aspects of the system from the presentation behaviors justifies the excessive coupling between the two components. Presentation components have high potential for reuse if they are adequately

Figure 8.15 Interface views for the service components in the video store system

independent of specific applications. That would justify keeping Top Dialogue out of Presentation. If they were merged, then we would have to ensure that the interface for registering dialogues and routing events is the same in all applications where we want to (re)use Presentation.

Interface Profile Types

The interface views in the figures have been grouped by the kind of role they play, control, service, or server. We can ask if the message profiles are consistent with

Figure 8.16
Interface
views for the
model compo-
nents in the
video store
system

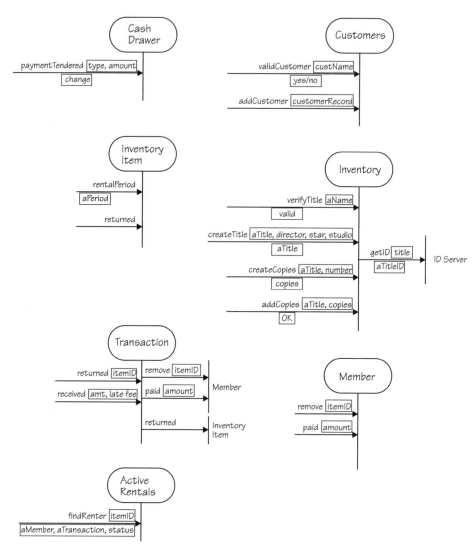

those roles. The control components (Figure 8.16) should have control profiles. The interface profile of Top Dialogue is a very clean control profile. There are no data flows being returned from the messages it sends. Rental Dialogue, however, has several information returns. This make the interface less of a pure control profile. While this may work well, it does mean that the changes to control aspects may involve accounting for more processing behavior than is necessary. I will leave this one as it is.

Among the service components, Check-out demonstrates the kind of dependencies that justify having a separate service component. Check-out communicates with three different kinds of system state elements. It isolates the dependencies in one place.

Inventory Adder does not look like a very good service component. It communicates with only one system state element. It also communicates with an obvious service component, Translator, and receives a return data flow. Inventory Adder is use-coupled to Translator. The same use-coupling is shown in Check-in. This represents a mechanism problem that should be resolved in the next revision. Earlier I suggested that Inventory adder could be given responsibility for deciding when to create new titles. I will make that change by having the dialogue just say "addCopies." The Inventory adder will be responsible for checking to see if the item is already in inventory or if it is a new title.

The system state elements should have server interface profiles. For the most part, they do, although the interfaces are obviously incomplete. They receive messages and send very few. Transaction communicates only with other system state elements. For the three use cases modeled in this example, the interface profiles of the system state elements are adequate server profiles.

Revisions

All of the changes mentioned above should be made by returning to the interaction diagrams affected and revising the behavior identification and allocation decisions using the ideas developed during the evaluation. The revised interaction diagrams are shown in Figures 8.17–8.19 and the resulting interface views are shown in Figures 8.20–8.22.

In the "Return a tape" diagram (Figure 8.13), the responsibilities for looking up the member and requesting the return of the tape were moved to the Check-in component. The communication with the Transactions was changed to have it explicitly return the status and late fine, if any, when the item was returned. The revised interface views for Transaction and Active Transactions show the creation of a new transaction, but there seems to be no removal of the transaction when all the items are returned. That was not covered in the interaction diagram for the use case.

This is where we make the design better.

In the "Rent a video" diagram (Figure 8.12), a Check-out component was added. I envisioned this as a service-type component, so I chose to avoid giving it any state associated with a particular customer's checkout activity. Because of that, I allocated the responsibility for getting a new transaction to the Check-out component, but I gave the transaction back to the Rental Dialogue. Now, adding the items to the Transaction is the responsibility of the Rental Dialogue. This keeps the state related to the dialogue out of the service component, but it is inconsistent with the mechanism used in the Return diagram of having the dialogue handle only the "text" versions of the model components. I also added the behaviors needed to record the transaction after the customer has paid for the rental.

This example illustrates a very detailed model. It is the kind of work that would be done to support production-quality coding. Any of the details may be omitted, such as information flows or showing the details by putting menu items up on the screen.

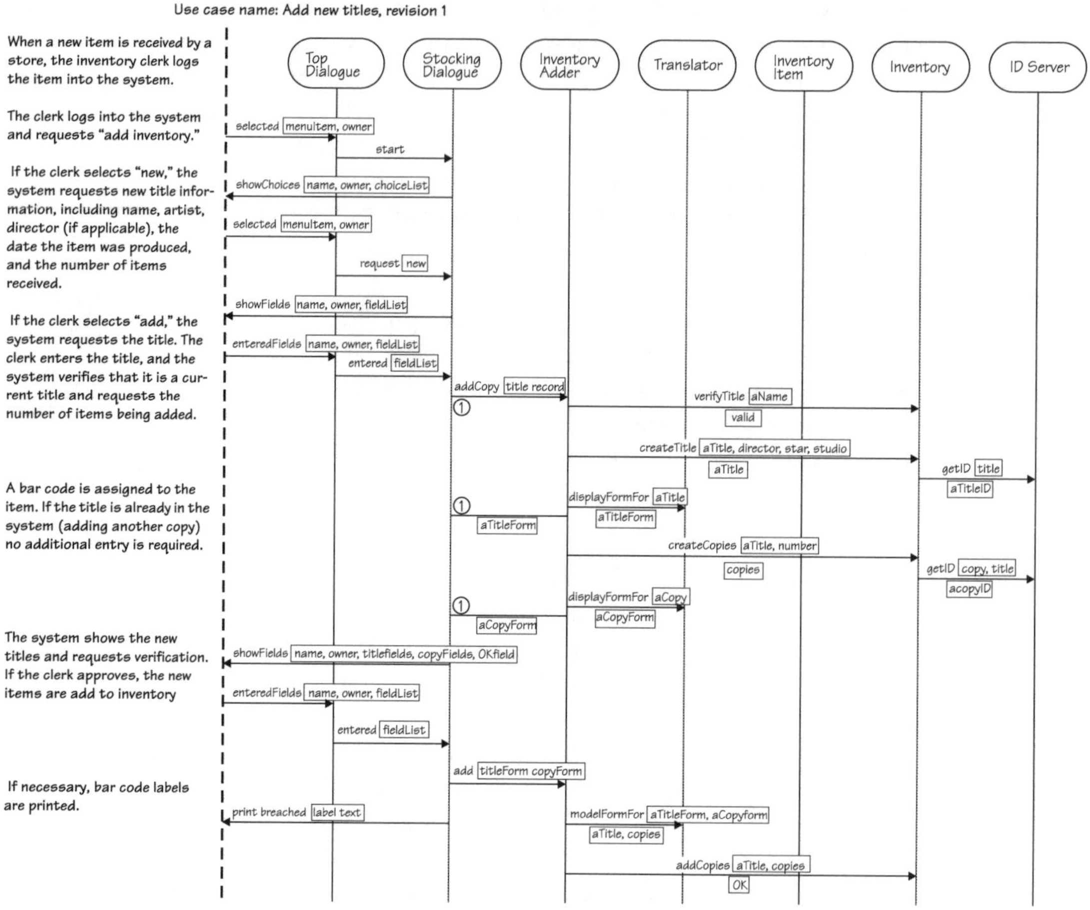

Use case name: Add new titles, revision 1
When a new item is received by a store, the inventory clerk logs the item into the system.
The clerk logs into the system and requests "add inventory."
If the clerk selects "new," the system requests new title information, including name, artist, director (if applicable), the date the item was produced, and the number of items received.
If the clerk selects "add," the system requests the title. The clerk enters the title, and the system verifies that it is a current title and requests the number of items being added.
A bar code is assigned to the item. If the title is already in the system (adding another copy) no additional entry is required.
The system shows the new titles and requests verification. If the clerk approves, the new items are add to inventory
If necessary, bar code labels are printed.
Top Dialogue
Stocking Dialogue
Inventory Adder
Translator
Inventory Item
Inventory
ID Server
selected menuItem, owner
start
showChoices name, owner, choiceList
selected menuItem, owner
request new
showFields name, owner, fieldList
enteredFields name, owner, fieldList
entered fieldList
addCopy title record
verifyTitle aName
valid
createTitle aTitle, director, star, studio
aTitle
getID title
aTitleID
displayFormFor aTitle
aTitleForm
aTitleForm
createCopies aTitle, number
copies
getID copy, title
acopyID
displayFormFor aCopy
aCopyForm
aCopyForm
showFields name, owner, titlefields, copyFields, OKfield
enteredFields name, owner, fieldList
entered fieldList
add titleForm copyForm
print breached label text
modelFormFor aTitleForm, aCopyform
aTitle, copies
addCopies aTitle, copies
OK

Figure 8.17 Revised interaction diagram for the use case Add new titles

Good design is worth the investment.

This example demonstrates the role of effective design documentation in the development of a system. Doing the diagrams does not, in any way, guarantee the success or quality of the results. They do, however, make problems and inconsistencies visible. If they are visible, it is possible to make changes to improve the situation. In particular, I have found that interaction diagrams and interface views, with the massive detail shown, are very effective in identifying problems.

8.1.6 Implementation Increments

This is just one of several places to look for increments.

The interaction diagrams are a convenient basis for selecting implementation increments. The increments will be defined as collections of components from our behavior model. The choices for increments may be revised when the architecture is available. Looking at the interaction diagrams in Figures 8.17–8.19, we could start

Use case name: Rent a video, revision 1

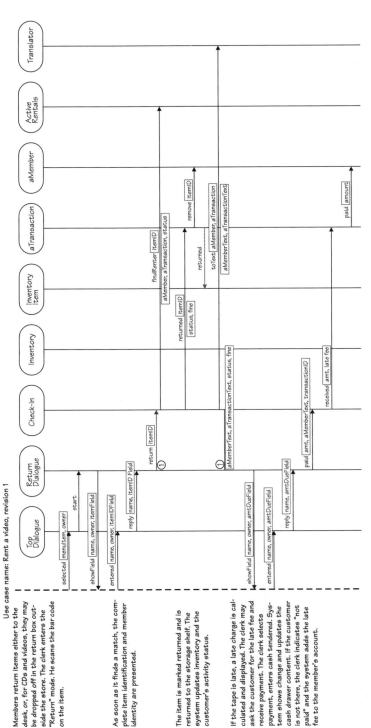

Members return items either to the desk, or, for CDs and videos, they may be dropped off in the return box outside the store. The clerk enters the "Return" mode. He scans the bar code on the item.

As soon as it finds a match, the complete item identification and member identity are presented.

The item is marked returned and is returned to the storage shelf. The system updates inventory and the customer's activity status.

If the tape is late, a late charge is calculated and displayed. The clerk may ask the customer for the late fee and receive payment. The clerk selects payment, enters cash tendered. System shows change and updates the cash drawer content. If the customer is not there, the clerk indicates "not paid" and the system adds the late fee to the member's account.

Figure 8.18 Revised interaction diagram for the use case, Return a tape

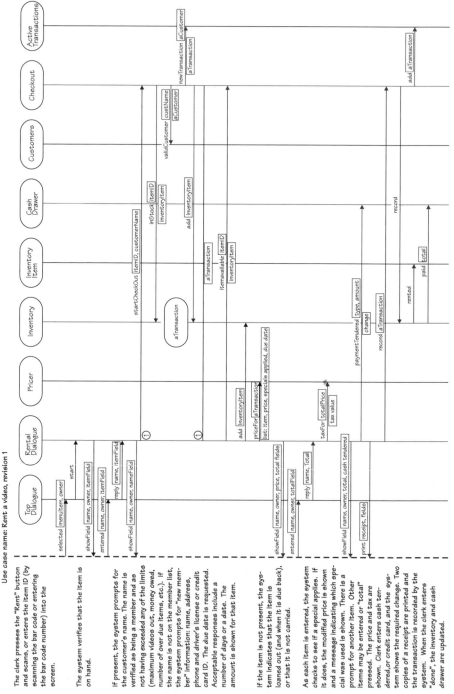

Figure 8.19 Revised interaction diagram for the use case, Rent a video

from the user side. The Presentation and Top Dialogue form a useful starting foundation, but that does not do anything. If we add one or more dialogue components, we

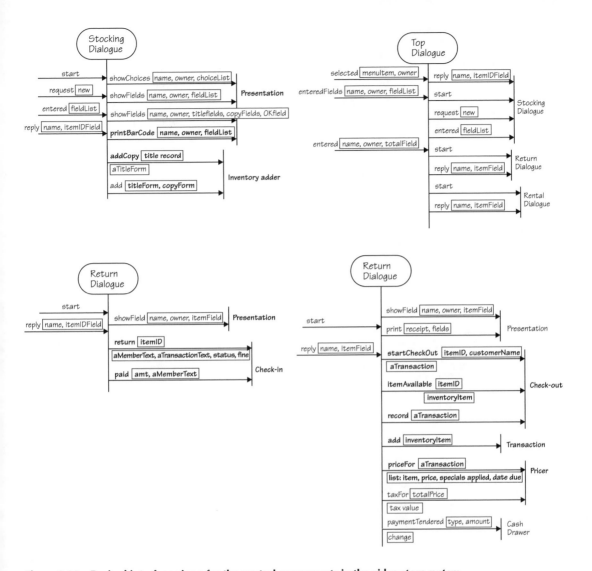

Figure 8.20   Revised interface views for the control components in the video store system

will have a fragment of the system that will exhibit behaviors that will be meaningful to users. A useful minimal subsystem could include Presentation, Top Dialogue, Rental Dialogue, and Return Dialogue. All of the remaining dialogue components would make easy increments to add to the minimal subset. Having an increment that includes the user interface is attractive for testing purposes and for making managers feel comfortable.

For the next increments, we have a choice. We could add service-type components. The problem is that without the underlying system state elements, the

Figure 8.21   Revised interface views for the service components in the video store system

services would add very little observable functionality to the system. The other choice is to make the system state elements the next increment. In this case, the question is how to exercise the system state model increment. If the dialogue components talked directly to system state elements, this would be a viable approach. There would be a problem if there was no direct connection to the system state elements (i.e., if dialogues communicated only with service components). In that case, separate machinery to exercise the model would have to be built. Of course, if test systems are planned for the system, then the system state model and its test systems

186   BEHAVIOR ALLOCATION EXAMPLES | CHAPTER 8

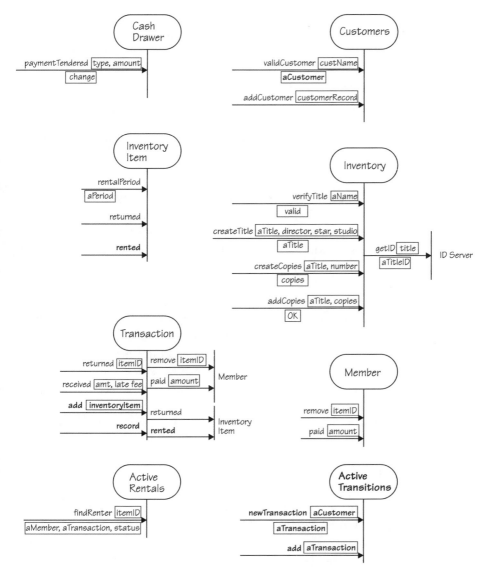

Figure 8.22
Revised interface views for the model components in the video store system

could be a very natural increment. I think that having the system state model up early is valuable, so I will prefer this approach. See Figure 8.23.

In order to implement the behaviors shown in the interaction diagrams, the system state model increment would include Inventory, Customers, Active Rentals (Transactions), Customer, Inventory Item, and Transaction. The complete list of system state elements is available in the system state model documentation.

It would be useful to build the entry-point components first. These include Inventory, Customers, and Active Rentals. These components should function even

Figure 8.23

**Implementa-
tion increments
shown on
components
in an interac-
tion diagram**

if they are empty. The individual system state components, Inventory Item, Customer, and Transaction, could be added as a separate increment.

The system state elements can be implemented with no connection to physical storage. That means they will have to be initialized with additional software, but disconnecting the model in the application from storage is a very useful separation to make.

The last increments, by process of elimination, are the service components that connect dialogues with the system state model. These would include Check-in, Check-out, Pricer, Translator, and Inventory Adder. We should be able to add them in one at a time and exercise them with the front end dialogues already in place. Any use coupling will be immediately obvious when the services are executed. For example, none of the main service components, Check-in, Check-out, etc., will work if Translator is not present and working.

The implementation increments nominated up to this point can be organized into three groups:

- Front-end increments: Presentation and Top Dialogue, one increment for each of the Dialogue components.
- Back-end increments: Entry-point components (Customers, Inventory and Active Rentals), all of the system state elements in a single increment.
- Middle increments: one increment per service-type component, Check-in, Check-out, Inventory Adder.

Since the front-end and back-end increments are not connected, they could proceed in parallel.

Of course, no implementation should be undertaken until the behavior allocations and interfaces for all the components have been established and evaluated.

8.2 COLLABORATION-RESPONSIBILITY MODEL

For comparison purposes, we will consider the same use case for collaboration-responsibility modeling, Add new titles, copies to inventory.

When a new item is received by a store, the inventory clerk logs the item into the system. The clerk logs into the system and requests "add inventory." If the clerk selects "new," the system requests new title information, including name, artist, director (if applicable), the date the item was produced, and the number of items received. If the clerk selects "add," the system requests the title. The clerk enters the title and the system verifies that it is a current title and requests the number of items being added. A bar code is assigned to the item and, if necessary, bar code labels are printed. If the title is already in the system (adding another copy) no additional entry is required.

Nominating Components

The use case and the component nominations are the same as in the interaction modeling example, so I will simply reproduce them here.

Nominated Components

- Clerk presentation
- Stocking dialogue controller
- Inventory adder
- Inventory
- Items in inventory

8.2.1 Nominating Responsibilities from Scratch and Allocating Them

We have a list of components that we have nominated as participants in the response to the use case. We now need some behaviors for those components. Since we are doing a collaboration-responsibility model, the behaviors will be identified as responsibilities, allocated to the component of our choice. Communication between components will be documented as collaborations, that is, the need to communicate, between components.

The normal process of carrying out a collaboration-responsibility model is the same as the process described in the interaction model section. The difference is that instead of documenting behaviors as messages between components, the behaviors are noted as responsibilities. Instead of ending up with one diagram for every use case and then having to collect the behaviors into the interface views, we have only the interface view with behaviors recorded as responsibilities.

Nomination and alloca-tion can be treated as separate decisions.

As I was developing this example, I thought it might be interesting to identify responsibilities all at once and then allocate them a separate operation. I found that having a set of detached responsibilities was useful for collaboration-responsibility modeling and service modeling. I don't know that I would recommend it as a general practice, but it provided a useful insight into the behavior of the system. In any case, I will use that approach in this section and the next. Remember that when the responsibility list was developed no specific components had been nominated. The responsibilities were grouped by the "type," or layer, of architecture components where they might be allocated. Those types, for the framework I chose, included presentation, dialogue, service, model, and model presentation.

Responsibilities of this Use Case

Returning to the task at hand, collaboration-responsibility modeling, we have a list of specific components to which we want to allocate behaviors. The responsibilities for this use case are listed below to aid the process of identifying and allocating responsibilities:

- Presentation:
  - Recognize event.
  - Request next action for "add inventory."
  - Display for "item type, name or ID."
  - Request next action for "item type, name or ID."
  - Display form "actor, director, date, type, category, quantity."

- Dialogue:
  - Display form "item type, name or ID."
  - Request item "name or ID."
  - Request display form "actor, director, date, type, category, quantity."
  - Request ID "title ID."
  - Request ID "new title."
  - Request print bar code "ID."
  - Request add to inventory "item, quantity."

- Service:
  - Return item ID.
  - Return title ID.
  - Return new title.
  - Return new copy.

- Model:
  - Return item "name or ID."
  - Create new title.

– Create new copy.

– Add "item, quantity."

- Model presentation.

In this example, I will take each sentence from the use case description in turn, choose components from the component list and responsibilities from the responsibilities list, allocate the responsibility, and nominate collaborations.

Allocating the Clerk Request

I will start with, "The clerk logs into the system and requests 'add inventory'." The login part is not relevant here, but it should be covered in its own use case. The responsibilities that address that action, from the List, are:

- Recognize event.

- Request next action for "add inventory."

The component most responsible for communication with the user is the Clerk Presentation, so I will allocate these first two responsibilities to that component. The Clerk Presentation now looks like Table 8.1.

Responsibility	Collaboration
Clerk Presentation	
Recognize event	
Request next action for "add/new inventory"	Stocking Dialogue Controller

Table 8.1
First allocation to the CRC card for Clerk Presentation

The next question is: Do we need any collaborations to execute those responsibilities? "Recognize event" may have to talk with some lower-level machinery to get the event up from the keyboard. I will ignore that here because the semantics will be below the application level. "Request next action" will need an external collaborator only if we allocate the responsibility for knowing about "next actions" to another component. So, we need to allocate the next behavior before we can determine the collaborators for this component.

My preference is to separate the behaviors of presentation from deciding what to present. I happen to think it is a good idea because it enhances the portability and extensibility, but there are many other ways that decision could be made. That decision was what caused me to put "display form 'item type'…" in the Dialogue category in the original responsibility list. If I remain consistent with that allocation approach, then I will allocate responsibility for deciding how to respond to the request for "next action" to the Stocking Dialogue Controller. With that allocation,

We still have to look ahead to the final product.

I can now say that the Clerk Presentation must collaborate with Stocking Dialogue Controller in order to carry out its responsibility to "request next action." The responsibility allocation to date is shown in Table 8.2.

Table 8.2
Allocation to
the Stocking
Dialgoue Con-
troller CRC

Responsibility	Collaboration
Clerk Presentation	
Recognize event	
Request next action for "add/new inventory"	Stocking Dialogue Controller
Stocking Dialogue Controller	
Request display form "item type, name or ID"	

Consistency across use cases is important.

Thinking ahead to other use cases, I would expect to use a similar mechanism for them: the Presentation recognizes events, and a Dialogue Controller decides what to present next. The way this is going, there will be many different controllers working off the same presentation. The question is, How does the presentation know which controller should receive the request? This is not a question we can resolve and document here because the collaboration-responsibility technique does not support recording information flows. We can keep the question in the back of our minds and bring it up again when we are using a more detailed technique than this one.

The ball is now in the Stocking Dialogue Controller's court. I have allocated to it the responsibility for knowing what to display next and asking that it be displayed. That means the controller will have to evaluate the requests from presentation in terms of the current state of the dialogue. I should add a responsibility to maintain the state of the dialogue. That responsibility requires no collaboration. After interpreting the request the controller will need to get the display changed appropriately. In doing so, it will have to collaborate with the Presentation to actually get something put on the screen.

The basic mechanism I have selected for this system is that the Presentation displays what it is requested to display, receives input on the displayed things, and then asks whatever made the display request what to do next. This was an engineering decision on my part. There are many other ways to accomplish the same thing but the designer should be aware of which mechanisms are being used (Table 8.3).

The ball is passed back to the Presentation's court when the controller asks for the input form to be displayed. Presentation should be responsible for displaying the form.

Responsibility	Collaboration
Clerk Presentation	
Recognize event	
Request next action for "add/new inventory"	Stocking Dialogue Controller
Display form	
Stocking Dialogue Controller	
Maintain dialogue state	
Interpret requests for "next action"	
Request display form "item type, name or ID"	Presentation

Table 8.3
Allocating the collaboration between Presentation and Dialogue

Allocating the Verification

The next part of the description is "the Clerk enters the title, and the system verifies that it is a current title and requests the number of items being added." This will involve some entry by the user into the form that was just displayed. The Presentation will receive the input. Since that sounds like a different kind of responsibility from the previously allocated responsibility of "recognize event," I will add a new responsibility, "receive input." This was not in the original responsibility list, but it seems like a good idea. Invoking my assumed mechanism, the Presentation will then return the filled-in form to its requestor and ask for the next action. I have already noted that responsibility, so I will not replicate it (Table 8.4).

Responsibility	Collaboration
Clerk Presentation	
Recognize event	
Request next action for "add/new inventory"	Stocking Dialogue Controller
display form	
receive input	
Stocking Dialogue Controller	
Request display form "item type, name or ID"	Presentation

Table 8.4
Adding responsibility for filling in forms to the CRC card

The description calls for the system to verify that the title is a current title in inventory. The question, now, is where to put the responsibilities. From the responsibility list, the responsibilities involved in carrying out the verification include "request ID 'title'," "return title ID," and "return item." In the initial list I distributed them over the dialogue, service, and model component types. There are a great many variations possible for distributing this behavior. The possibilities extend along spectrum from having the dialogue know everything about looking up titles in inventory to having the inventory understand what "verify" means. I prefer a middle position on the spectrum: keep the dialogue and inventory relatively simple and allocate all the processing to service components. In this case, that preference translates into having Inventory Adder be responsible for talking to Inventory and returning the information in a form that the Dialogue can use. The allocation of the responsibilities, with slight embellishments, is shown Table 8.5.

Table 8.5
CRC cards for a service and model components

Responsibility	Collaboration
Stocking Dialogue Controller	
Request display form "item type, name or ID"	Presentation
Request verify "title"	Inventory adder
Inventory Adder	
Request item	Inventory
Inventory	
Find "title"	Items
Retrieve "title"	Inventory presentation
Item	
Maintain "title"	

We have verified the presence of the title, and the control is back with the Dialogue Controller. The next step is to request the number of items being added. This sequence looks just like the previous sequence of displaying a form and receiving input, so I will not replicate it here.

My preferred behavior allocation is that the Dialogue Controller be responsible for knowing that enough information has been entered and that the required conditions have been met, e.g., that the title is valid, to request that the items be actually added to inventory. I prefer that any processing needed, to actually add the items, be carried out by the service and model components. That processing should include creating bar codes if necessary.

Note   I am being very careful to emphasize that these behavior allocations are decisions that I am making. They are not "natural" or "the way it is." There are many other ways those decisions could be made, but this is always the case, no matter how the process is described.

Engineering is different from modeling.

Allocating Assigning the Bar Code

The use case description calls for "A bar code is assigned to the item and, if necessary, bar code labels are printed." Looking at my responsibility list for this use case, I see bar codes mentioned in the controller category, but they do not appear anywhere else. That responsibility allocation implies that the dialogue is responsible for generating its own bar codes. Bar codes do not seem to be closely related to the user's dialogue with the system. They seem more related to the state of the inventory because they are determined by how many things have been added to inventory. Another symptom of being dependent on inventory is that if there were multiple users with multiple dialogue controllers, their use of bar codes would have to be coordinated. For all those reasons, I will change that allocation so that the Inventory Adder is responsible for keeping track of the bar codes.

Having thought through all of the above, it now looks like a good idea to have the dialogue know when something is ready to be added to the inventory, and to make the Inventory Adder responsible for deciding that bar codes are needed. After all that, I am ready to add some more responsibilities to my components (Table 8.6).

I believe that we have finished with the model of this use case: the new items have been successfully added to inventory. One might ask about some of the details that were overlooked in this model, such as the new versus existing title branch. The answer is, I ignored them. Collaboration-responsibility modeling is a fairly informal technique, particularly when practiced in the CRC card form. I do not think that leaving off some branches is any worse than not addressing message names or information flows. If more detail and completeness is desired, use the interaction diagram technique.

I described the thought processes I used in developing the model in considerable detail because I believe that they are an important part of developing a successful design. Designers should consider all of their decisions in the context of the other use cases and the external requirements for the system. These microevaluations that took so many words to describe are not a substitute for the separate evaluations carried out on all the behavior allocations, but they make the evaluations much easier.

It is faster to do it than to describe it.

The process described above should be repeated for all use cases.

Table 8.6
Respnsibility allocation for handling bar codes

Responsibility	Collaboration
Clerk Presentation	
Recognize event	
Request next action for "add/new inventory"	Stocking dialogue controller
Display form	
Receive input	
Print bar code labels	
Stocking Dialogue Controller	
Request display form "item type, name or ID"	Presentation
Request verify "title"	Inventory adder
Request add to inventory	Inventory adder
Request bar code printing	Presentation
Inventory Adder	
Request item	Inventory
Generate bar codes	
Assign to items	Items
Inform add requester of bar codes	Stocking dialogue controller
Inventory	
Find "title"	Items
Retrieve "title"	Inventory presentation
Add new items	
Item	
Maintain "title"	
Maintain bar code	

8.2.2 Evaluating the Collaboration-Responsibility Model

In collaboration-responsibility modeling there is no documented connection between the use cases and the behaviors allocated to the components. This makes the evaluation of completeness difficult. We can, however, evaluate the elegance and modularity of the allocations by drawing a collaboration graph. We draw the diagram by placing one symbol for each component on the diagram. Then, reading down the list of collaborations for each component, draw a line for each collaboration. The result for our example is shown in Figure 8.24.

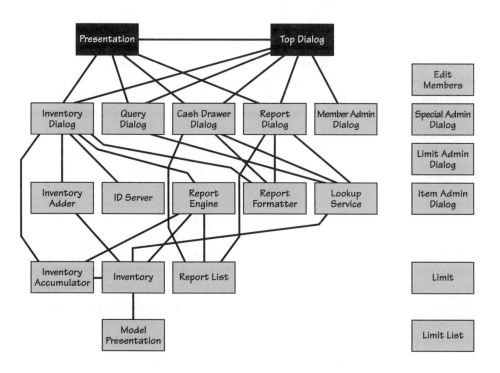

Figure 8.24
Collaboration graph for all components in the video store system

A collaboration graph is an architecture without the subsystems.

Because I think that the architecture is the basic organizing structure for the system, I have organized the collaboration graph to match my preferred way of drawing the architecture: presentation, dialogue, service, and model laid out from top to bottom. There is no requirement for arranging things this way, but I think it facilitates the evaluation process. Nor is there a one-to-one relationship between the kinds of component (presentation, dialogue, service, and model) used in the behavior model and the components in the architecture. It is entirely possible, for example, that some of the dialogue components could end up being allocated to service subsystems in the architecture. In spite of all that, I still like to arrange a "big view" of the systems from presentation to model.

Evaluating the Collaboration Graph

Two kinds of evaluation are easily carried out on a collaboration graph: local completeness and "webiness." There are two very important kinds of evaluations that cannot be done using collaboration-responsibility modeling. One is evaluations of extensibility, portability, and the like. That will have to wait for the architecture diagram. The other is direct traceability of the behavior model back to the user requirements. Put another way, with collaboration-responsibility models, the designer does not have a document that explicitly shows how the model provides each use case. That will have to wait for a more detailed behavior modeling technique, such as interaction diagrams.

Local Completeness

Local completeness is determined by looking at the local components, their responsibilities, and collaborations. It is evaluated by looking only at the collaboration graph and the responsibilities allocated to each component. This process is different from external completeness, which is determined by comparing behavior in the model with external user requirements.

Collaboration graph can catch missing use cases.

Looking at the graph, we see that some of the components have no collaborations or responsibilities. This could be because the mechanism assumed when the components were nominated was not the one used during the modeling. It could also be due to not modeling the use cases that used those components. In the present diagram, the latter cause is the reason for all the orphan components.

It would seem important that all the model components whose responsibilities include maintaining information about the state of the store, should have access to the Model Presentation for persistent storage. A quick scan of the model components shows that Cash Drawer, Transaction Log, Inventory Accumulator and Report List have no collaboration with the Model Presentation. It may be okay for the atomic model elements, like Item, Sale Item, Report, and Member to have no collaboration with the Model Presentation because it keeps them independent of how they are stored. If the Model Presentation is going to be responsible for creating the new components, then it does seem necessary for the Model Presentation to collaborate with those components during their translation between storage and application forms.

Given their responsibilities, it seems that ID Server and Report Formatter should collaborate with some source of information.

All of the above are problems with the current behavior model that became visible when viewed in a collaboration graph. These problems can be fixed in several ways. One is to patch up the individual components directly. For example, if I think the Model Presentation should collaborate with Item, I could just add a some responsibilities to Model Presentation and a collaboration with Item directly on the Model Presentation description. It is possible to make all corrections this way, but I would not recommend it.

To ensure that the behavior model continues to meet the user requirements after I have made the changes, that is, provided the use cases, any changes and additions done to the model should be done in the context of a response to the use cases. In this example, that means that to make any addition, I should repeat the walkthroughs of the uses cases that involve the components I wish to change. Unfortunately, the techniques for doing collaboration-responsibility modeling do not document the individual walkthroughs. They simply document the results of the walkthrough as responsibilities and collaborations allocated to each component. The best we can do here, after the collaboration graph is available, is to do the revisions by walking through the use cases on the collaboration graph.

Keep a tight connection between behaviors and the use cases.

Fixing a Model Presentation Problem

If I want to fix the problem with Model Presentation not collaborating with Item, I can pick a use case that involves the components of interest, such as renting a video. The relevant portion of the use case description is reproduced below.

Rent a tape, or other item   The clerk presses the "Rent" button and scans, or enters the item ID (by scanning the bar code or entering the bar code number) into the screen. The system verifies that the item is on hand. If present, the system prompts for the customer's name.

If the item is not present, the system indicates that the item is loaned out (and when it is due back) or that it is not carried.

When the clerk enters "done," the inventory and cash drawer are updated.

Recalling the walkthrough for this use case, the collaboration between Inventory and Model Presentation came about when the Inventory wanted an Item that had not been retrieved from storage. To get the Item, Inventory collaborated with Model Presentation to do the retrieval. Here is where I can identify and allocate the new responsibilities. My preference is to have the Model Presentation be responsible for all translation between storage forms and the application forms, so that Inventory will only have to deal with "pure" application components. For that reason, I will allocate the responsibility for creating and initializing the new Item to the

Model Presentation. It should, then, also be responsible for unpacking the Items when they have been modified and are being returned to storage.

Webiness

My first, subjective impression, when looking at the collaboration graph, is that it is not very elegant. The collaborations do not look very disciplined. Two areas attract my attention. First is the Presentation-Top Dialogue-Dialogues circle. The second is the rather messy looking collaborations between dialogues, services, and the model subsystems.

Recalling the behavior allocation from the walkthroughs, the inputs went through the Top Dialogue to the individual dialogues, but most of the outputs went directly from the individual dialogues to the Presentation. Normally, circular control flows are a problem because it is difficult to keep the individual components on the circle coordinated. If the Top Dialogue functions only as a filter to grab the high level commands, like "quit," the present allocations may be acceptable. In any case, the situation should be investigated to be sure that we have not distributed behaviors such that coordination becomes difficult.

Webbiness is an easy visual inspection.

The dialogue-service-model collaborations look quite messy. For example, the Rental and Sales Dialogues collaborate with both the Lookup Service and the Inventory. Some activities, such as Check-In, are provided by service components, while the dialogues go straight to the Inventory for others. I am also bothered by how many dialogues talk directly to Cash Drawer. Does Cash Drawer need a collaboration with Model Presentation to store its state and contents? My original goal in nominating the Lookup Service component was to provide a higher level functional interface to the model via the service components and to provide a place for translating between model forms and forms that are readily displayed. Having the dialogues all collaborate with both the services and the model, I believe, complicates the dialogue components and introduces additional dependencies. Those dependencies could be removed by reallocating those responsibilities that need the model components to the service components. That will probably result in the need for new service component nominations.

Perhaps "kinds of transactions" is a useful vehicle for identifying useful kinds of services. This is, after all, a transaction-centered system. With transactions in mind, I might nominate service components of Inventory Change, Rental Transaction Manager, Payment Transaction Manager, Reporting, and Administration. I will leave it as an exercise for the interested student to revisit the use case walkthroughs to identify and allocate responsibilities to these new components.

The above process, making one set of component nominations, identifying and allocating behaviors (as responsibilities in this case), evaluating the decisions, and making changes to those decisions, is the normal design process. Doing the first steps and stopping before the evaluating and taking change steps is not sufficient.

8.3 SERVICE MODEL

Service modeling is a technique used to identify nominations for service subsystems very early in the design process. It is important that the services be identified early because if they are not, the behaviors that would have been allocated to the service subsystems will get allocated to other components. The example that follows is described as if it were being carried out after the external requirements have been documented, but before almost all other analysis has been started.

This is a trip around the circle of service nominations.

8.3.1 Deriving Service Nominations from Various Sources

Because I find the process of nominating service components difficult, my approach is to make many nominations from several sources and then select the nominees that look like they have the best chance of supporting the increments and change cases. The sources I will use in this example are the main functions that the system provides: the use case names, change cases, and responsibility lists from each use case.

From the Main Functions

The brief, functional description developed as part of the user requirements is reproduced below.

ACME Video Store is a large, growing concern. It rents videos to retail customers. The rental period and amount of the rental varies with the time of week and the kind of video. It also rents VCRs and game cartridges and is considering moving into CD disk and player rental, with DATs as another possibility. Managers sometimes use specials to promote specific products. Specials include one free rental after two regular rentals in a month, or every eighth rental is free. The store also sells a variety of general merchandise such as candy, popcorn, audio tapes, party favors, merchandise related to popular movies, and the like.

The store keeps information on its members (customers, really) and uses the list for its quarterly newsletter. When videos are overdue, they try to call the customer and if they cannot reach the customer, they send a letter. Late fees are charged for overdue items. Rental activity is tracked and recorded for each rental item and for each customer.

Looking over this text, I might pick out the following services that the system provides to its users:

- Rent items.
- Sell items.
- Administer specials.
- Add and administer members.

- Report overdue items.
- Record and report rental activity.

These items are about all that are referred to directly in the description. There are obviously more that are needed. Using my domain knowledge, I can add some more:

- Add/remove items from inventory.
- Take inventory.
- Track cash drawer.
- Track employee hours and schedules.
- Respond to questions.
- Generate reports.
- Define reports.

Not all of these services may require a separate component in the architecture to implement, but they are a place to start.

From the Use Case Titles

This is a brute force approach. The use cases are supposed to describe all of the functionality required of the system by its users. The names of the use cases provide another view into the services that the system must deliver, but the trouble with the use cases is that there was no attempt to make their behaviors atomic. That is, there will be much overlap of functionality implied in each use case. Nonetheless, looking over the list of titles is a good technique for identifying more service nominations:

- List of use case titles
- Query inventory for a title
- Open membership
- Rent a tape, or other item
- Return a tape
- Sell an item
- Verify membership
- Request list of over due items
- Request a list of all items out on rent
- Add new titles, copies to inventory
- Remove old titles
- Check actual inventory against system inventory

- Request reports
- Request daily activity summary
- Request inventory listings
- Request daily, weekly, monthly yearly activity summaries
- Administer users
- Administer members
- Administer member rental limits
- Request member activity
- Edit inventory item
- Edit types and categories
- Administer specials
- Close and reconcile cash drawer
- Start the cash drawer

Looking down the list, it is clear that the functionality implied by each of these use cases is not unique to each, but the list provides a window on the complete system functionality. The question is: Can I formulate a list of service names, which, when taken together, will account for the functionality implied by the use cases? The services I nominate should be atomic. That is, they should not share any, high-level functionality. This requirement implies that a single use case may invoke several of these atomic services. They should represent the main units of functionality that will be added to the system as it grows and matures. Finally, they should be independent of how their results are used or presented.

I can group the use case names by obvious similarities, such as similar function or association with the same target:

- Questions of inventory:
  - Verify membership
  - Request list of overdue items
  - Request a list of all items out on rental
  - Query inventory for a title
- Request reports:
  - Request daily activity summary
  - Request inventory listings
  - Request daily, weekly, monthly, yearly activity summaries
  - Request member activity
- Change inventory:
  - Add new titles, copies to inventory
  - Remove old titles

- Rent a tape, or other item
- Return a tape
- Sell an item
- Edit inventory item
- Change users:
  - Administer users
- Check inventory (Could this be a combination of request and change inventory plus accumulating discrepancies?):
  - Check actual inventory against system inventory
- Change things:
  - Administer members
  - Open membership
  - Administer member rental limits
  - Edit types and categories
  - Administer specials
- Administer cash drawer:
  - Close and reconcile cash drawer
  - Start the cash drawer

The organizing ideas I used to make these groupings included what was being manipulated, as in change inventory and change users; and similarity of function, as in change things. I will take these function categories as my first nomination of services. They are listed below:

- Questions of inventory
- Request reports
- Change inventory
- Change users
- Check inventory
- Change things
- Administer cash drawer

I will continue to treat the list of use case names as a definitive list of responsibilities that the system has to its users.

Quick Evaluation of Nominations So Far

Having made the nominations, it would be appropriate to run through a quick evaluation to see if we are in the ball park. Three questions we can ask of the service subsystem nominations and the responsibilities allocated to them are:

1 Will the responsibilities allocated to each service always be used as a package?

2 Is there significant redundancy in functionality between the nominated services?

3 Are any of the responsibilities clearly dependent only on a single state element?

Let's look at the first two nominations with their use case responsibilities.

- Questions of inventory:
  – Verify membership
  – Request list of overdue items
  – Request a list of all items out on rental
  – Query inventory for a title
- Request reports:
  – Request daily activity summary
  – Request inventory listings
  – Request daily, weekly, monthly yearly activity summaries
  – Request member activity

Question 2 is the easiest to address for the first two groupings. The behavior is basically the same for all the responsibilities in both groups: extract some information from inventory. If we assume that the questions can be parameterized, then we can assume that they can all be "executed" by the same service. The responsibilities in both groups seem to be pretty basic to the operation of a video store, question 1, so we can group them together.

As for question 3, dependency on system state elements, all the queries involve searching over many rental items, customers, etc., so the behavior is not directly dependent on a single system state element. I expect the behavior to actually iterate over the inventory and that it should reside in the inventory subsystems. The behavior left for the service component will probably involve interpreting the higher level requests and perhaps translating the results into a generic, readily displayed form.

Revised Service Nomination

My revised service nomination is a query processor with the combined responsibilities of the first two original nominations, as shown below.

- Process queries:
  – Verify membership
  – Request list of overdue items
  – Request a list of all items out on rental
  – Query inventory for a title
  – Request daily activity summary

– Request inventory listings
– Request daily, weekly, monthly and yearly activity summaries
– Request member activity

There are three service nominations called "change something." If I assume that their behavior is concerned primarily with ensuring that the appropriate sequence of operations is carried out, I can justify saying there is little redundancy between them (question 2). As long as the actual operations on the inventory, retrieving something, or adding a new item, are carried out by the inventory, we can say that none of the behavior will be directly dependent on a single state element (question 3). The third service, Change Things, is poorly named and rather incohesive. It could be Administer Members if I moved the last two use case titles up to the Inventory service. The responsibilities in each would then be quite cohesive and unlikely to be used separately (question 1):

- Change inventory:
  – Add new titles, copies to inventory
  – Remove old titles
  – Rent a tape, or other item
  – Return a tape
  – Sell an item
  – Edit inventory item
  – Edit types and categories
  – Administer specials
- Change users:
  – Administer users
- Administer members:
  – Administer members
  – Open membership
  – Administer member rental limits

The last two service nominations, Check Inventory and Administer Cash Drawer, are good nominations because they appear to be likely units of configuration. That is, it seems likely that some systems would be configured without those services. That possibility, alone, is sufficient to justify their nomination as services.

- Check inventory:
  – Check actual inventory against system inventory
- Administer cash drawer:
  – Close and reconcile cash drawer
  – Start the cash drawer

Comparing the nominations from basic functions list, I see three services that do not explicitly appear in the previous list. They are Report Overdue Items, Record and Report Rental Activity, and Define Reports. The first can be handled by the Process Queries, as can the report part of Record and Report Rental Activity. I expect that the record part can be handled by (allocated to) the rental items, themselves. That leaves only Define Reports as a new service nomination, which is a good nomination because it corresponds to one of the change cases. We now have the following nominations:

- Process queries
- Change inventory
- Administer members
- Administer cash drawer
- Check inventory
- Change users
- Define reports

From the Change Cases

Because the change costs provide the final criteria for whether we have done a good job of nominating service components, they are a good place to look for nominations:

1 Add new rental and sale items, media and equipment
2 Support school and corporate customers
3 Manage time sheets for employees
4 Support growth to multiple stores
5 Integrate with accounting system
6 Add custom report definition capability
7 Integrate with corporate inventory database
8 Configure for another customer on a different platform, different look and feel, single workstation system

Ports

9 Change computer platforms
10 Change presentation
11 Change database

Future configurations

12 Equipment rental system
13 Retail and party goods rental system

In looking down the list, I see two change cases that might imply new services: Support school and corporate customers, and Add custom report definition capability. The custom reporting we already have. Supporting school and corporate customers may require a new billing approach. To isolate that behavior in a single component, I will add Process Bills as another service nomination.

Some of the change cases are concerned with adding new things to the model or supporting new externals, such as change cases 8 to 11. I do not know enough about those new domains to predict whether equipment and party goods rentals will require different services from those in a video store. (It would be appropriate to go conduct some quick feasibility studies in those domains to resolve that issue.)

The list of service nominations, up to this point is:

- Process queries
- Change inventory
- Administer members
- Administer cash drawer
- Check inventory
- Change users
- Define reports
- Process bills

I will close our discussion of the nominations now, and take up the next part of service modeling: confirmation.

8.3.2 Evaluating Service Nominations

Did we do any good? Service modeling, as I usually practice it, is an informal activity. It is usually done early in a project. For that reason, the evaluations also be informal. We should convince ourselves that the nominated services look like they can account for most of the high-level functionality offered to users: that they are atomic and that they will support the functional growth and configuration called for in the change cases.

Completeness

If I compare the service nominations with the use case titles, I can get an informal feel for whether the service list is sufficient. That comparison is shown in Figure 8.25. I have labeled the use cases with the numbers of the services which, I believe, will participate in them.

Since there is at least one service to associate with each use case, I will judge the service nominations to be complete.

Participatory Services	Use-Case Titles
①	Query inventory for a title
①③	Open membership
①②④	Rent a tape or other item
①②④	Return a tape
②④	Sell an item
①	Verify membership
①	Request list of overdue items
①	Request a list of rented items
①②	Add new titles, copies to inventory
①②	Remove old titles
①⑤	Check actual inventory against system
①	Request reports
①	Request daily activity summary
①	Request inventory listings
①	Rquest daily/weekly/monthly/yearly activity summaries
①⑥	Administer users
①③	Administer members
①②	Administer memer rental limits
①	Request member activity
①②	Edit inventory item
①②	Edit types and categories
①②	Administer specials
④	Close and reconcile cash drawer
④	Start the cash drawer

Service Nominations

- Process queries ①
- Change inventory ②
- Administer members ③
- Administer cash drawer ④
- Check inventory ⑤
- Change users ⑥
- Define reports ⑦
- Process bills ⑧

Figure 8.25

Use cases for the video store system showing which service components participate in the response to each use case

Atomicity

These service nominations are, for the most part, associated with the things they manipulate, such as members, inventory, and users. At the application level, they could be judged to be nonoverlapping. One exception is the Check Inventory and Process Queries services. I could see a way to implement Check Inventory in terms of Process Queries. If they are peers of each other, then they must duplicate much of each other's behavior. One fix might be to implement Check Inventory in terms of the other services rather than as a peer of the other services. It could be viewed as a dialogue component that maintains the state of the inventory checking process as it progresses. I will eliminate Check Inventory as a service, and redefine it as a dialogue component.

Figure 8.26
Change cases
for the video
store system
showing
which service
components
provide the
change case

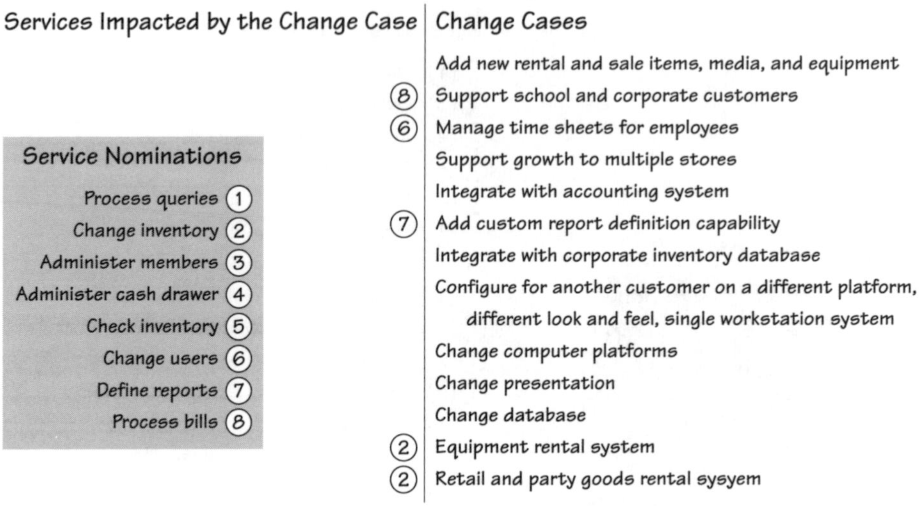

Services Impacted by the Change Case | Change Cases

Add new rental and sale items, media, and equipment
⑧ Support school and corporate customers
⑥ Manage time sheets for employees
Support growth to multiple stores
Integrate with accounting system
⑦ Add custom report definition capability
Integrate with corporate inventory database
Configure for another customer on a different platform,
      different look and feel, single workstation system
Change computer platforms
Change presentation
Change database
② Equipment rental system
② Retail and party goods rental sysyem

Service Nominations

Process queries ①
Change inventory ②
Administer members ③
Administer cash drawer ④
Check inventory ⑤
Change users ⑥
Define reports ⑦
Process bills ⑧

Change Cases

The services, at least by the time they get to architecture subsystems, are supposed
to directly support the change cases that require changes to the system functionality.
I can compare the service nominations with the change cases to see how well they
support the changes (Figure 8.26).

All of the change cases are not primarily functional changes. It appears that the
nominated services do a pretty good job of isolating the effects of the change cases.
Although my assertion, that the system can be changed from renting videos to renting equipment without changing the Process Queries service, implies a very generic
query-processing system.

For now, however, I will accept the nominations with the one change that Check
Inventory be removed as a service component.

CHAPTER 9　　　✧　✧　✧　✧　✧

The Software System Architecture Task

CONTENTS

9.1 Introduction　211
9.2 Architecture Templates　214
9.3 Develop a System Architecture　225
9.4 Allocating Behavior to Architecture Subsystems　237
9.5 Evaluate Architectures　246
9.6 Allocation across Hardware Boundaries　250
9.7 Architecture Summary　257

9.1 INTRODUCTION

This chapter picks up where Chapter 1 left off. In this chapter, we will use the definition of the software system architecture and the notation of choice introduced in Chapter 1. This chapter will discuss how to develop architectures for software systems. A separate section is devoted to developing a generic architecture template for systems by evaluating several alternative architecture structures.

This is where it all comes together.

9.1.1 What is Being Addressed?

The software architecture addresses the physical structure of the system (Figure 9.1). It describes the form and shape of the single "thing" that is the software system. This is the first of the Essential Tasks in which the entire system is visible. It is, therefore, the place where the emergent properties of the system can be designed in. In this chapter I will focus on the build-time emergent properties, such

Behavior allocation is also evaluated here.

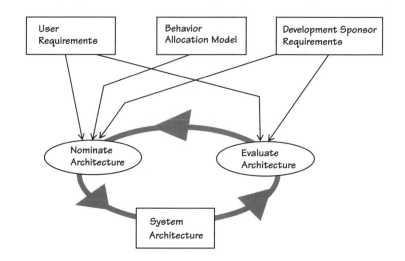

as extensibility and maintainability. The run-time emergent properties, such as reliability and throughput, require more information than we have developed in this set of Essential Tasks.

Evaluating the architecture for its ability to support the build-time requirements means also evaluating the behavior allocation decisions made back in the behavior identification and allocation task. The coupling between the subsystems is determined by how the behavior was allocated to components in the identification and allocation task, and how the components were allocated to the subsystems in the architecture diagram. The robustness of the encapsulation of the subsystems is determined by their interfaces, which in turn are determined by the interfaces of the behavior model components allocated to the subsystems.

9.1.2 How to Measure System Architecture

The "ilities" are designed in here. The system architecture represents the entire system, so it should meet all of the external requirements on the system and we should be able to demonstrate that fact. We have, however, already addressed the run-time requirements in the system state and behavior tasks. In those tasks, the user requirements were explicitly addressed and the results were evaluated to demonstrate that the requirements were, in fact, successfully addressed. All of the components developed in those other tasks will be allocated to subsystems of the architecture, so the system architecture should meet all of the requirements addressed in the other tasks. That leaves the build-time requirements and the emergent run-time properties. Since the engineering decisions made in this task primarily address the build-time emergent properties, the primary evaluation criteria will be the build-time requirements, specifically, the change cases.

9.1.3 Handling Variations

The architecture of a software system is a collection of physical subsystems. All representations of a system should show the same set of subsystems. Variations in the representation are found in the amount of detail shown in any individual diagram. At a minimum, the system boundary and the subsystems (with their names) should be shown. This is the preliminary architecture diagram that is used in feasibility studies. Increasing amounts of information about the architecture can be added to meet the needs of different situations. Increments of detail include the names of channels connecting subsystems, the control and information element content of the channels, and the physical media of the channels.

9.1.4 Developing Evaluation Criteria

The evaluation criteria for the system architecture are the build-time change cases. They can be used directly to walk through the changes on the architecture diagram to demonstrate that the architecture does, in fact, support the change cases. Formal evaluation of the architecture against the application level run-time requirements is not necessary if a full evaluation against the run-time requirements was carried out in the behavior identification and allocation task.

9.1.5 Notation

In order to talk about architecture, we need a picture. The best notation for software architecture that I know of is the Mascot notation. The Mascot notation [JACK88, SEL94] consists of subsystems with named ports and windows that are defined in terms of the channel type they provide or require. The enclosure of the subsystem is complete, both send and receive ends of the channels are part of the subsystem specification, and the channels themselves are named and typed separately as parts of the architecture specification. Every diagram should show an explicit boundary for the subject system or subsystem. Figure 9.2 shows a sample Mascot specification.

Figure 9.2
Key to the
architecture
diagram
notation

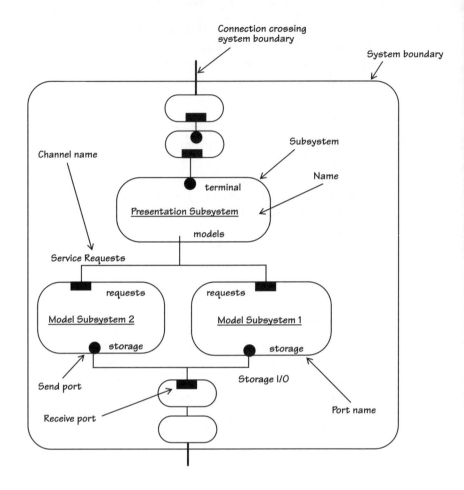

This kind of notation—a complete enclosure, channels named and typed separately from the subsystems that use them, and both send and receive ports in subsystems named—is essential to establishing any kind of true software component. With a notation in hand, we can proceed to build a software architecture.

9.2 ARCHITECTURE TEMPLATES

This justifies the architecture template I have been using.

Drawing an architecture diagram for a software system is analogous to drawing the first sketches of what a building will look like on a blank piece of paper. The building architect must resolve the many conflicting requirements the building must meet, in a single structure. The architect of a software system plays the same role. To be able to draw that first sketch, the architect must have some general ideas about system structures that will meet the requirements. So before I talk about how to nominate subsystems, I would like to describe several general architecture structures for software systems. Each structure will be evaluated against a representative set of change cases. At the end of the evaluation, we will be able to select the structure that does the best job of meeting the build-time requirements.

The structure of the architecture is shaped by the decisions we make about how to provide the change cases. If the change cases for different systems are similar, we might expect the shape of the systems designed to provide those change cases to be similar. In documenting change cases for a variety of systems, I have found that the change cases remain quite constant over a wide variety of systems. That being the case, it should be possible to develop an architecture structure that can serve as a template for specific systems. We will derive such a template in this section.

Common change cases lead to common architectures.

I have said that software architecture should be evaluated against the change cases, and so each of the architectures I describe will be evaluated against a set of change cases, listed below. I have also said that an architecture must meet its users' requirements for functionality. For the purpose of this discussion on architecture templates, I will provide a list of generic responsibilities to allocate to our generic architecture subsystems. These responsibilities will be used to represent the user requirements:

Generic Change Cases

1 Port to a different hardware platform and operating system
2 Change presentation package without changing the look and feel
3 Change look and feel of user presentation
4 Add a new actor who has a different pattern of using the system
5 Add new services to the system
6 A new kind of system state element is added to the domain that the system must handle
7 Change the physical storage system, i.e., the database
8 Configure multiple systems with different sets of functionalities
9 Change from a single user implementation to physically distributed, multiuser implementation

Generic Responsibilities

• Recognize user input
• Associate input with/screen elements
• Display control elements
• Display application elements
• Request display of control options
• Control available options

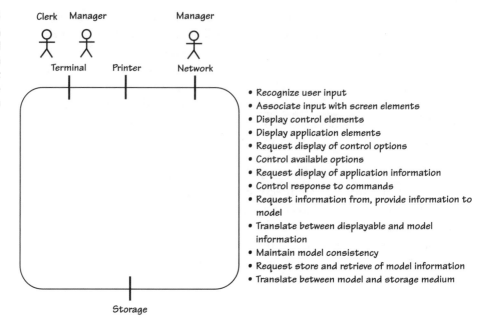

Clerk   Manager   Manager

Terminal   Printer   Network

- Recognize user input
- Associate input with screen elements
- Display control elements
- Display application elements
- Request display of control options
- Control available options
- Request display of application information
- Control response to commands
- Request information from, provide information to model
- Translate between displayable and model information
- Maintain model consistency
- Request store and retrieve of model information
- Translate between model and storage medium

Storage

- Request display of application information
- Control response to commands
- Request information from, provide information to model
- Translate between displayable and model information
- Maintain model consistency
- Request store and retrieve of model information
- Translate between model and storage medium

These responsibilities are common in many kinds of user-driven systems. I will use them to represent all the required behavior of our generic system.

The process will be described in detail later.

The process of describing and evaluating architectures used in this discussion is the same one I will suggest for all architecture development: draw the border and describe ports, nominate components, allocate behavior, and evaluate against the change cases. For this discussion, the boundary and ports will be the same for all cases. Since there is only one sequence of responsibilities for this system, I can list the responsibilities along one edge of the system boundary. See Figure 9.3. Each of the alternative architectures will provide the same set of behaviors to its users.

Keep in mind that we are working with a rather informal behavior model. The functionality for the entire system is stated as the short list of responsibilities. We can only guess at what collaborations and interfaces will be needed. Yet, even with these very crude descriptions of system architectures and behaviors, we can say some very useful things about the system structure (Figure 9.4).

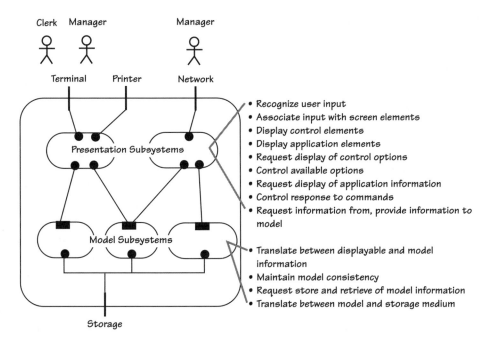

Figure 9.4
A two-layer
architecture
showing one
way to
allocate the
generic
responsibilities

Presentation Subsystems

- Recognize user input
- Associate input with screen elements
- Display control elements
- Display application elements
- Request display of control options
- Control available options
- Request display of application information
- Control response to commands
- Request information from, provide information to model

Model Subsystems

- Translate between displayable and model information
- Maintain model consistency
- Request store and retrieve of model information
- Translate between model and storage medium

9.2.1 Two-Layer Architecture

In nominating subsystems to make up the architecture the first question is: What kind of subsystems should be nominated? The answer can be stated in terms of how many layers and kinds of subsystems will be used in the structure. The first structure we will consider is the simplest and the most common structure in existing software systems: the two-layer architecture. There are two kinds of subsystems in this system—presentation type subsystems, and model subsystems. All the behavior and information in the system is allocated to one or the other kind of subsystem. Figure 9.4 shows a generic, two-layer architecture and one possible allocation of responsibilities between the kinds of subsystems.

This is the most common system architecture.

There are abundant examples of systems using this architecture. In forms-based applications, most 4GL systems and database systems, the presentation subsystems are the forms and screens. All of the application logic is allocated in the form, often associated with a field or menu item. In these kinds of systems, the model subsystems are viewed as relational tables with the interface to the tables being SQL.

In applications using object technology and this architecture template, the presentation subsystems are usually called windows, or views and controllers, and the model subsystems are domain-object models. Again, most of the presentation and application logic is allocated to the window subsystems. The main difference between the forms-based systems and OO systems is that in the OO systems, the object model has more behavior allocated to it than the table model. This object-style behavior allocation is the one shown in Figure 9.4.

Evaluating the Nomination

At this point we have nominated subsystems and allocated behavior to them. Next, we need to evaluate the nominations. In this example, the user requirements have been met by definition because all of the required behaviors (represented by the responsibility list) were allocated to the architecture subsystems.

Applications with this structure can work; that is, they can provide the functionality that their users want. In this example, the interesting question is: Can this architectural structure meet the build-time requirements? To answer this question, we need to walk through the change cases.

In doing so, we encounter another question: Does this diagram tell us anything that will help with the evaluation? The answer is, if it doesn't, then it should not have been drawn. If the diagram is going to facilitate this evaluation of the nomination, then we must assume that the boxes have some meaning and significance. The meaning we need is that the coupling between things inside a box must be tighter than between things that are in different boxes in the diagram. With this assumption in mind, we can evaluate how well the two-layer architecture handles our change cases.

The first four change cases can be considered together because they all affect responsibilities that are allocated to the window subsystems:

1 Port to a different hardware platform and operating system

2 Change presentation package without changing look or feel

3 Change look and feel of user presentation

4 Add a new actor who has a different pattern of using the system

Questions to ask in the evaluation

To evaluate the effect of each change case, I will ask two questions: Is the impact of the change limited to one subsystem? Does that subsystem contain behavior and information that is not affected by the change? (For a more detailed design evaluation, I recommend three other questions, described later.) If we consider Change Case 2 (changing the presentation package), the answer to the first question is that only the window subsystem will be affected. This is good. The answer to the second question is that there are many other kinds of behaviors in the window subsystems in addition to presentation behavior. This is not so good. It means that changing the presentation could also affect the control logic and application processing. I would conclude that this architecture, with the behavior allocation shown, does not support Change Case 2 as well as I would like.

The same rationale, with the same results, could be repeated for each of the four change cases being considered. The effects of each change can be limited to the windows subsystem, which is good; but there is too much other, unrelated behavior in that subsystem, which is bad.

Change Cases 5 and 8 can be considered together because they are both concerned with the services that the system offers to its users:

5 Add new services to the system

8 Configure multiple systems with different sets of functionalities

The service responsibilities are invoked by the dialogue responsibilities. The services in turn access the system state to carry out their operations. In a two-layer architecture the three allocation choices we have are to put all the service responsibilities in the window subsystems, to split the service responsibilities between the window and model subsystems, or to put all the service responsibilities in the model subsystems. The first choice is shown in Figure 9.4.

Change Cases 5 and 8 both involve changing service responsibilities. If we choose the first option, only one subsystem would be affected by the change, the window. But there is much unrelated behavior in that subsystem. The second choice, splitting the service responsibilities between window and model, means there are two subsystems to change, and both have unrelated behaviors. The third choice sounds just like the first, but applied to the model subsystem. We can conclude that this architecture has a serious problem handling change cases involving services.

Change Case 6 adds new system state elements to the system:

6 A new kind of system state element is added to the domain that the system must handle

Only one subsystem is affected (the model) by adding more system state elements. This will be true only if adding system state elements does not change the interface between the model subsystem and the other subsystems in the architecture. If the interface must be changed, then we will have to change the users of the model subsystem, which is not desirable. There appear to be few responsibilities not directly related to system state elements in the model subsystems. Conclusion: this architecture is sufficient to handle changes to the system state elements.

7 Change the physical storage system

I will assume for this analysis that most of what gets stored is in the model subsystems. If we also assume that there are no calls using the storage medium interface up in the window subsystem (not always a safe assumption) we can say that this change affects only one subsystem and that there is no unrelated behavior. This really is not true, and we will revisit this issue in the next architecture. For now we could conclude that this architecture can handle changes to the storage medium.

9 Change from a single user implementation to a physically distributed, multiuser implementation

This change case is more difficult to evaluate because we really need more information than we have about the design, but let's proceed with what we have. If the state of each user's dialogue with the system is contained in the window subsystem, and if we assume that we wish to provide each user with a consistent view of the model, we could handle this change case by replicating the window subsystem for each user and having them all share a common model subsystem. For this change to work, we would have to provide a way of queuing the requests from the multiple users as they try to share the single model. If that action could be handled by adding another subsystem, then this architecture could be judged to be sufficient to provide this change case.

So, what is the score? Of the nine change cases considered, the architecture could not handle seven. That is not very good. The two-layer architecture is implicit in most the methodologies and all of the technologies with which I am familiar. By technologies I mean windows and GUI development systems, 4GLs, database development packages, and windows based, object-oriented systems. We have just shown that the two-layer architecture is incapable of supporting a large majority of the change cases that it is likely to be asked to support. This is not to say that systems with two-layer architectures cannot be changed and expanded. What this analysis tells us is that the effort required to implement those changes and expansions is much greater than it needs to be. Are there better alternatives?

9.2.2 Four-Layer Architecture

The first architecture suffered from putting too many behaviors in one container. The fix is to make more containers. Consider Figure 9.5.

*This is close to
the three-layer
architecture
that is
becoming
popular.*

For this architecture I have taken some of the behaviors allocated to the window subsystem in the previous example and reallocated them into a presentation subsystem and an application subsystem. The presentation subsystems are now responsible only for screen I/O. The application subsystems are responsible for the logic and processing of the application. I added some interface machinery, which I have labeled device subsystems, between the storage port and the model subsystem and allocated to it responsibility for translating between the model forms and the forms used in storage.

Evaluating the Nomination

We can now briefly evaluate this architecture nomination for its ability to handle the change cases:

1 Port to a different hardware platform and operating system

If all platform and operating system calls are restricted to the device subsystems, and if the device interfaces do not change when we change the internals, then this

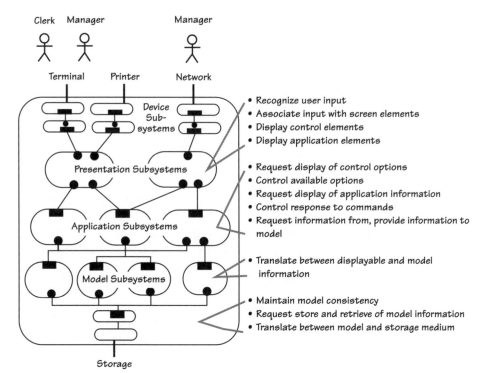

Clerk Manager   Manager

Terminal   Printer   Network

Device Sub-systems

- Recognize user input
- Associate input with screen elements
- Display control elements
- Display application elements

Presentation Subsystems

- Request display of control options
- Control available options
- Request display of application information
- Control response to commands
- Request information from, provide information to model

Application Subsystems

Model Subsystems

- Translate between displayable and model information

- Maintain model consistency
- Request store and retrieve of model information
- Translate between model and storage medium

Storage

change will affect only the device subsystems, and there should be little unrelated behavior in them. OK.

2 Change presentation package without changing the look and feel

3 Change look and feel of user presentation

These changes should be contained within the presentation subsystem, which contain little unrelated behavior. OK.

4 Add a new actor who has a different pattern of using the system

This change should be limited to the application subsystem, but there is behavior in the application subsystem that is not directly related to the sequence of operations being requested. Not OK.

5 Add new services to the system

We have the same problem with service additions in this architecture that we had in the two-layer architecture: it is difficult to restrict the effects of this change to one subsystem. Still not OK.

6 A new kind of system state element is added to the domain that the system must handle

If the system state elements live in the model subsystem, and if the external interface does not have to change when we add the new system state element, we can gracefully handle this change. OK.

7 Change the physical storage system

If all of the storage system dependencies are located in the storage presentation and the existing application side interface does not have to change, we can handle this change case. OK.

8 Configure multiple systems with different sets of functionalities

The basic functionality offered to users is contained in the application subsystem, so the unit of configuration might be the application subsystems. This is hindered in this architecture by the fact that the application subsystems have logic and sequence behaviors that must be maintained separately for each user. Not OK.

9 Change from a single user implementation to physically distributed, multi user implementation

The evaluation here is the same as it was in the two-layer architecture. The presentation and application subsystems would have to be replicated for each user. OK.

The "ilities" are better, but not great.

Out of nine change cases, this architecture can handle six, a considerable improvement. The remaining problems occur in adding new actors and services. If we make one more reallocation, the situation should get much better.

9.2.3 Five-Layer Architecture

A bit radical, but look at its "ilities."

In this architecture, the application processing responsibilities have been allocated to their own service subsystem, leaving the control and sequencing responsibilities in what I like to call a dialogue or dialogue-controller subsystem (Figure 9.6).

Evaluating the Nomination

Nothing else in the architecture has changed, so we only need to look at the three change cases that we could not provide in the previous architecture nomination.

4 Add a new actor who has a different pattern of using the system

If we assume that the new actor will need the same services that previous actors needed, then the effects of this change can be limited to the dialogue subsystem. Whether we have to change the presentation depends on whether we choose to hard code the menu items in the presentation or let the dialogue tell the presentation what to show. If we have to change the command options offered to the user very often, it would be better to not code them into the presentation subsystem. The dialogue subsystem is concerned only with sequences of commands, so there is little unrelated behavior in the dialogue. OK.

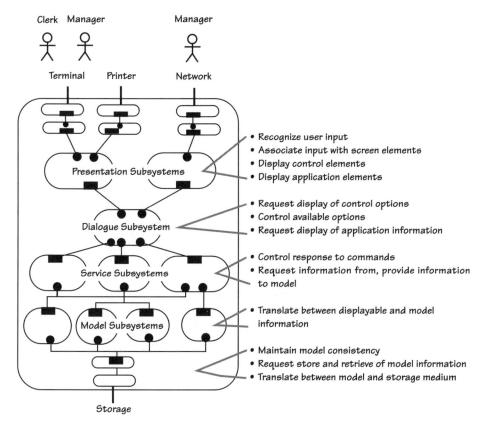

Clerk Manager   Manager

Terminal   Printer   Network

Presentation Subsystems

- Recognize user input
- Associate input with screen elements
- Display control elements
- Display application elements

Dialogue Subsystem

- Request display of control options
- Control available options
- Request display of application information

Service Subsystems

- Control response to commands
- Request information from, provide information to model

Model Subsystems

- Translate between displayable and model information

- Maintain model consistency
- Request store and retrieve of model information
- Translate between model and storage medium

Storage

5   Add new services to the system

We now have a subsystem whose role in life is to house services. By definition, adding a new service should consist only of adding or replacing a service subsystem. For this to actually work, the behavior allocation must be carefully arranged so that the behaviors that get added in the future can be cleanly contained in service subsystems. The other requirement, which we cannot address here, is that the interfaces between the service subsystems and the models on one side and between the services and the dialogues on the other, must be robust enough to handle the service additions without being changed. When the new service is added, we may have to inform the dialogue that the new service is available, but that should be a fairly small change. This change case is OK.

8   Configure multiple systems with different sets of functionalities

Having separated the user-specific dialogue from the service behavior, we can now make the service subsystem the unit of configuration for other systems in this domain. Again, dialogues may have to be changed for each configuration, but that should not be a big job. OK.

We now have nominated an architecture that can meet all of the run-time requirements, because all the required responsibilities have been allocated to the architecture subsystem, and it can meet the build-time requirements because we have demonstrated that it can handle all of the change cases. This architecture is at least, sufficient. It may not be optimum, but it will provide all of the use cases and all of the change cases. This is a very important assertion to be able to make.

The change cases are quite consistent from system to system and domain to domain. They do not vary nearly as much as use cases across applications and domains. Because the structure of this architecture was derived from the change cases, I submit that this particular structure can meet the build-time requirements for most systems. There may be other structures that will also meet all the requirements, but this one is a good place to start. Thus, this architecture can serve as a guide for the first strokes of the pen on an empty system boundary. While it can serve as a template for the system architecture, this architecture deserves some elaboration before we move on.

9.2.4 The Generic Architecture Template

A key aspect of any successful system architecture is that it has enough kinds of subsystems to gracefully support all of the anticipated changes. Another key aspect is that behaviors are allocated appropriately to the subsystems. A useful set of subsystems consists of the five types listed below:

1 Device driver and virtual devices are provided for each port that crosses the system boundary. These subsystems provide portability and isolation of the system from the local peripherals and platform. The semantic level of their names and interfaces is below that of the application level subsystems.

This is the generic architecture template. 2 Presentation subsystems are provided for each kind of display or view required by actors outside the system. They are responsible for translating between the forms used inside the system and the forms expected outside the system. Multiple presentations may be needed to serve a single port. The application-side protocol for the presentation subsystems must hide the specifics of the presentation from the other application subsystems. Presentation subsystems are needed for every connection that crosses the system boundary. Presentations for human users are well known, but presentations for hard copy peripherals, databases, and network channels are just as important.

3 Dialogue controller subsystems are provided for each kind of user, or each category of interaction with the system. The dialogue subsystems are responsible for managing the content and sequence of the dialogue between the system and its actors on the outside. The dialogue invokes system services to carry out requests received from the actors.

4   Service subsystems are provided for each unit of growth and change indicated in the change cases. Service subsystems exist solely to be the units of functional growth, change, and configuration. They should encapsulate functionality that may be added or removed from the system.

5   Model subsystems are provided as buckets for cohesive groups of whatever the application is maintaining (called the system state elements in this book).

Suggesting that a system have any fixed structure, and in particular suggesting that a system consist of multiple layers is a good way to provoke controversy among many current practitioners of the art of programming. Certainly, systems with fewer kinds of subsystems can be built and they can meet the run-time requirements, but they will have a very hard time meeting any reasonable set of build-time requirements. If the practice of evaluating the structure of a system against the change cases were more widespread, I believe everyone would be designing systems that look at least a little like the one in Figure 9.6.

Dividing the system structure up into six kinds of subsystems, and allocating behaviors to the subsystems appropriately, enables the system to gracefully handle a representative list of change cases. These change cases are common to many types of systems. Therefore, the six-subsystem structure should meet the needs of many types of system. The vertical structure of the architecture can be used as a template for developing architectures for many kind of specific system. The horizontal structure, that is, the names of the specific subsystems, is necessarily specific to every system.

9.3 DEVELOP A SYSTEM ARCHITECTURE

I will describe the creation of a system architecture at a level where the components are meaningful in the semantics of the application. In terms of the implementation levels just described, this usually corresponds to things at or below the level of operating system tasks. (Organizing the components upward to the next higher-level implementation units will be discussed later in this chapter.) I have found that a pure, top-down approach does not work very well. By *top-down*, I mean drawing the first architecture diagram at the computer and LAN level of subsystem. The reason is that at that level, the software architecture is completely dictated by the hardware architecture and allocating behaviors to computers, while possible, is not very satisfying. The semantic level of computers is far removed from the semantics of the application. I find that if I target subsystems at about the level of tasks, I have enough flexibility to develop an interesting design.

Now we return to the architecture process.

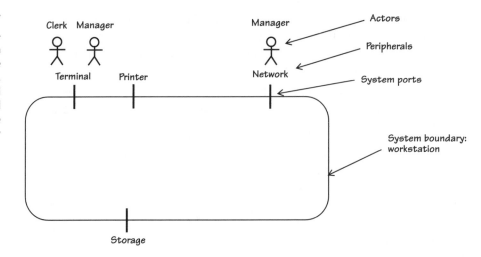

Figure 9.7
An architecture diagram showing the boundary, external actors, and ports on the boundary

Clerk Manager

Terminal   Printer

Manager

Network

Actors

Peripherals

System ports

System boundary: workstation

Storage

9.3.1 Draw the Boundary

The boundary is very important.

The first step in drawing a system architecture is to draw the boundary and specify its physical significance. Not having a boundary in architecture diagrams is a major contributor to the common problem of having I/O calls distributed unevenly throughout applications. If the architecture is being specified for a client-node computer, for example, then the boundary represents the physical boundary of the computer. If a UNIX process object is being designed, then the boundary represents edge of the memory space of the process.

If the system is being designed for the first time and the hardware allocation decisions have not been made, the easiest place to start is to have the boundary represent the system boundary. That is, the complete scope of the system is inside the boundary, while all actors and peripherals connected to any part of the system are outside the boundary. Since there are no hardware boxes in the architecture, I call it the boxless architecture. This is the situation I will describe next. Allocation across hardware components will be covered after the system architecture is developed (Figure 9.7).

9.3.2 Identify the Ports

Ports keep you honest.

The next step is to identify all of the connections to things outside the system boundary, that is, things that cross the boundary. If the boundary represents a computer, then the "ports" in the architecture should correspond to the physical ports on the computer. There would be one for the user terminal, one for the printer, one for the network connection, and one for local storage. If the boundary represents the system without the hardware, then the ports in the architecture diagram should represent the connections to each of the actors and peripherals with which the system must communicate.

Note the change in the scope of our concerns. During the requirements documentation task, we explicitly excluded "dumb" peripherals from consideration as actors because their semantics were below the level of the application semantics. Here in the architecture task, one of the key evaluations we want to make of the architecture is whether it is adequately portable across multiple platforms and peripherals. To answer that question, we must be able to see what the peripherals are, and how they are connected to the system.

9.3.3 Nominate Subsystems of the Architecture

The system boundary is the blank sheet of paper waiting for the stroke of the architect's pen to give shape and substance to the new system. This shaping task is easier if we have a template in mind to help guide the pen. We can use the template from the discussion above.

Use the template.

In order to be able to draw pictures for this discussion, I have to use a specific domain so that I can name the subsystems. I do not want to use the example from Chapter 10, because it is described at great length there. So, for this next discussion I have chosen the domain of accounting as the source for my subsystem names. The system being described here is an accounting system.

When we talk about nominating architecture subsystems for the application, I will recommend that all of the subsystem names, responsibilities, and interface names be drawn from the application semantics. Because of the importance of evaluating the portability of the system, I suggest that subsystems that connect the peripherals to the system and isolate the system from changes to those peripherals be shown in the architecture. These interface subsystems should have a lower semantic level than those subsystems that occupy the center of the architecture diagram. I believe that the imperative to be able to see all aspects of the system needed for evaluation outweighs the suggestion of maintaining a single semantic level in each design document.

A general guideline for selecting a size of subsystems comes from the earlier discussion about hardware boundaries. The process of allocating subsystems across hardware boundaries will be easier if we do not have to split any of the software subsystems we nominated in the boxless architecture. Put another way, if we make our initial choices of software subsystems small enough, they can remain intact through all the later allocation to hardware. This guideline can be applied with the same technique described for sizing subsystems in the behavior model: look ahead to the possible hardware architectures that must be supported. Select architecture subsystems that will not have to be broken in any of the anticipated kinds of allocations to hardware systems.

The architect always looks ahead.

Nominate Virtual Device Subsystems

The name *device driver* comes from the situation where the boundary of the software system corresponds to a hardware boundary and every physical port has a device driver to communicate with the wires on the other side of the port. The role of the device driver is to translate between the communication medium used inside the system and the communication medium used outside the system. Even though not all software systems have a connection to hardware, such as those bounded by tasks or threads, there is still a need for translation across the boundary. This is why I call the subsystems that are attached to the ports *virtual device* subsystems.

Device subsystems provide platform independence.

Nomination is straightforward: nominate one virtual-device subsystem for each port. The role of the virtual device is simply to provide a fixed interface to a generic device so that the actual device drivers, contained inside the subsystems, can be changed without affecting anything on the outside of the virtual device. These subsystems serve to isolate the rest of the system from the operating system, the peripherals, and any platform-specific features, and from any knowledge of the nature of the boundary.

The semantic level of the application-side interface for the virtual device will necessarily be higher than that of the device driver itself. I say necessarily because that is how the virtual device hides specific devices from the rest of the system. If the physical port in question requires specific status check function calls, the virtual device interface might have a simple status-request message that would return the results of the specific status-check calls made inside the virtual device subsystem.

To summarize, nominate at least one device-type subsystem for every port that crosses the system boundary. While it is not common today for developers to actually have to write device-type subsystems, I think it is valuable to put these subsystems in the architecture so that issues of portability can be addressed.

Nominate Presentation Subsystems

Presentation subsystems provide appearance independence.

Presentation subsystems are responsible for translating between the form of the things inside the application and the form the external actor, or peripheral, wants to use. This is a higher level activity than that of the device subsystems, which translate between the communication medium used inside the systems to the communication medium used outside the system. The presentation subsystems nominated depend on the actor (person or other system) or peripheral and on the presentation medium the actor is using.

If individual events in a dialogue with a user are related to one another, then the state of the presentation must be unique for each user of the presentation. We will need at least one presentation subsystem for each user. Whether these subsystems should be grouped in separate subsystems for each user is a separate decision, one that could rest on what scheduling machinery the designers want to use and what extensions the system must support.

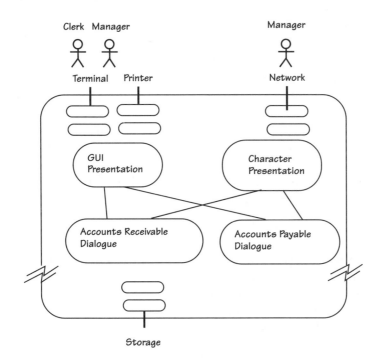

Figure 9.8
Adding device,
presentation
and dialogue
subsystems.
Dialogue
subsystems
are associ-
ated with the
services
being used

Presentation subsystems are not window objects in a class library; nor are they windows in a 4GL development package. The presentation subsystems may house one of these kinds of window objects, but the subsystems should not be implemented as any vendor-specific technology. This preserves the portability of the application across multiple window vendors' technologies.

We will need a separate presentation for each different form of presentation. For human users, for example, the presentation that supports a GUI terminal will be different than the presentation that supports a character-based terminal. In this example, shown in Figure 9.8, assume that we will support GUI and character presentations for users. See Chapter 10 for a discussion of mixing and matching presentation subsystems, users, and ports.

Human users are not the only ones that need a presentation. Any connection to a port that leaves the system is a candidate for a presentation subsystem. Databases and printers are prime examples. I should emphasize the importance of having a robust presentation for databases. The database view of the world, as rows and columns in tables, uses a much lower semantic level than applications. It is important that none of the database-level semantics appear anywhere in the top levels of the application. A database presentation subsystem can serve as an effective barrier between rows and tables on one side and customers, calls and bills on the other. I emphasize this because of the very common practice of coding SQL statements everywhere in the application.

Presentations are more than windows.

The question of whether to put all the presentation components inside one presentation subsystem, or to give each kind of presentation its own subsystem can be addressed by considering the change cases. If the system will be configured with one kind of presentation and not the other, they should be allocated to separate subsystems. If the two kinds of presentations will always appear together, then they can safely be allocated to the same subsystem.

To summarize, nominate at least one presentation subsystem for each different kind of external presentation, for example, one each for GUI and character presentations. A single port, such as a network or file system, can support multiple presentations. Presentation subsystems should be independent of the kind of actor and application that will be using them.

Nominate Dialogue Control Subsystems

Dialogue-control subsystems are responsible for managing the dialogue between external actors and the services and resources available inside the system. They make appropriate choices about services available to the users, interpret the user requests, and invoke services to carry out those requests.

Dialogue control subsystems are usually very control-oriented, and their behavior can be described in terms of state machines. The challenging question in nominating dialogue subsystems is what they should control. I would like to describe the process of deciding what kinds of dialogue subsystem to use.

Dialogues provide actor independence.

The two common choices for handling dialogue subsystems are to associate them with the external actors or with the services they invoke. For example, in our accounting system, we might nominate a dialogue subsystem for each of the major kinds of activities supported by the system: general ledger, accounts payable, accounts receivable, and so on. An alternative approach is to nominate dialogues for each kind of actor using the system: accounts receivable clerk, manager, and so on. A fragment of an architecture with service-based dialogues is shown in Figure 9.8.

The first question I would ask of this architecture nomination is: How do we decide which kind of activity will be carried out? That is, the user wants to do accounts receivable, where is the behavior that invokes the appropriate controller? The obvious place is the presentation, since it can "see" all the available controllers. But, now the presentation has application-specific control knowledge and would have to be touched whenever the controllers are changed. If that is not satisfactory, we could add another control dialogue whose job is to run the top level. The result is shown in Figure 9.9.

Design decisions are always trade-offs.

Having dialogues that correspond to the main activities is satisfactory as long as the activities represent the controlling state behavior. Another situation occurs when the controlling behavior is the user identity. This occurs when there are complex rules about which user role may access which services, or when the service

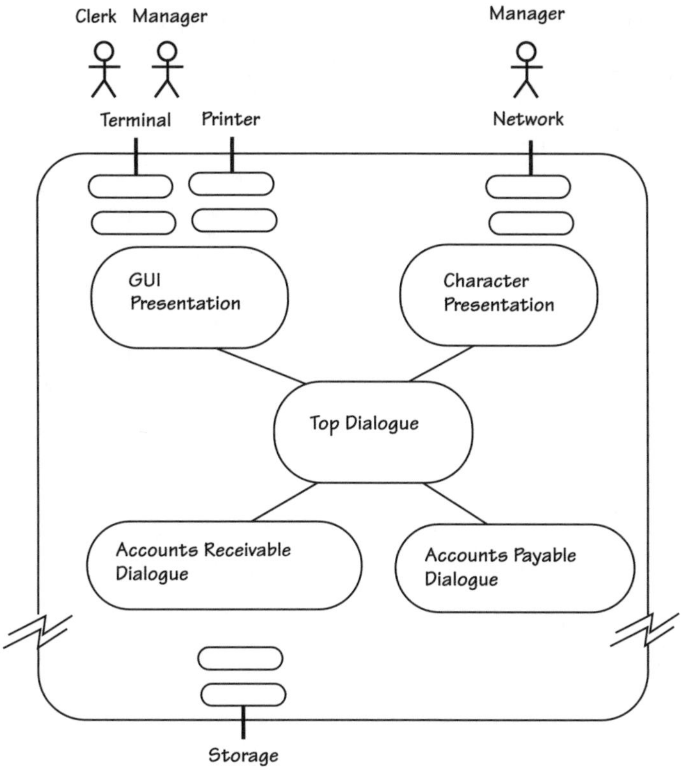

Figure 9.9
Adding a top dialogue subsystem

Figure 9.9 diagram labels: Clerk, Manager, Manager, Terminal, Printer, Network, GUI Presentation, Character Presentation, Top Dialogue, Accounts Receivable Dialogue, Accounts Payable Dialogue, Storage

subsystems in the system are smaller than the services the user is thinking about. In that situation, the top level dialogue controllers might be associated with user roles, as shown in Figure 9.10.

This configuration would work best in a situation where the services can be mixed in arbitrary ways for each user role. Multilevel control architectures are also possible for very complex systems.

The deciding factor, as it always is, in grouping behaviors into subsystems is what changes the system must support. If the user roles change more frequently than the services offered, then having subsystems for individual roles would do the best job of supporting the change cases. If there were change cases calling for reconfiguration based on services offered, then having the controllers correspond with the activities would be better.

To summarize, we can nominate control subsystems for each of the changeable units of control. These are usually associated with either, or both, the user roles or the activities the users engage in. Dialogue controllers will be easiest to change if they are restricted to control behaviors and do not engage in processing or changing the form of their inputs and outputs.

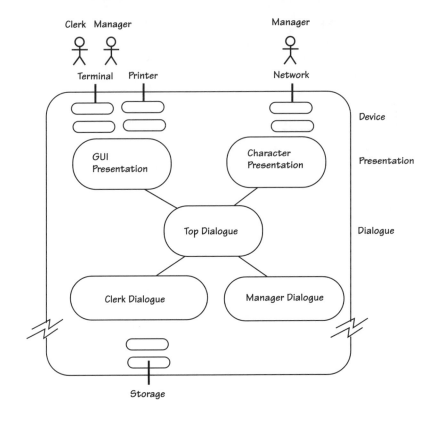

Figure 9.10
Adding device, presentation and dialogue subsystems. Dialogue subsystems are associated with the actors using the system

Clerk Manager

Manager

Terminal   Printer

Network

Device

GUI Presentation

Character Presentation

Presentation

Top Dialogue

Dialogue

Clerk Dialogue

Manager Dialogue

Storage

Nominate Service Subsystems

Services provide growth independence.

Service subsystems exist to be the units of functional growth and change for the system. Their behaviors are usually functional in nature; that is, they change the form of their inputs and outputs. Their behaviors are usually dependent on multiple kinds of system state elements. Since we have decided to separate control from processing, the service subsystems should not have control-type behaviors visible in their communications with other services and control subsystems. In fact, they should have no communication at all with other service subsystems. They should also be atomic. That is, there should be no duplication of application-level behavior in any of the service subsystems. All of these *should's* and *should-not's* are derived entirely from the role the service subsystems are to play in the system—that of a pluggable unit of functionality.

The designer's task is to identify and allocate behavior to service subsystems that meet all those *should's*. I have never found this to be an easy task. Some approaches were discussed with behavior modeling in Chapter 7. The best approach I can suggest is to write down the responsibility list for each use case, extract all the middle responsibilities, and group them to provide the functional increments from the change case list. The choice made in Figure 9.11 is to nominate one service

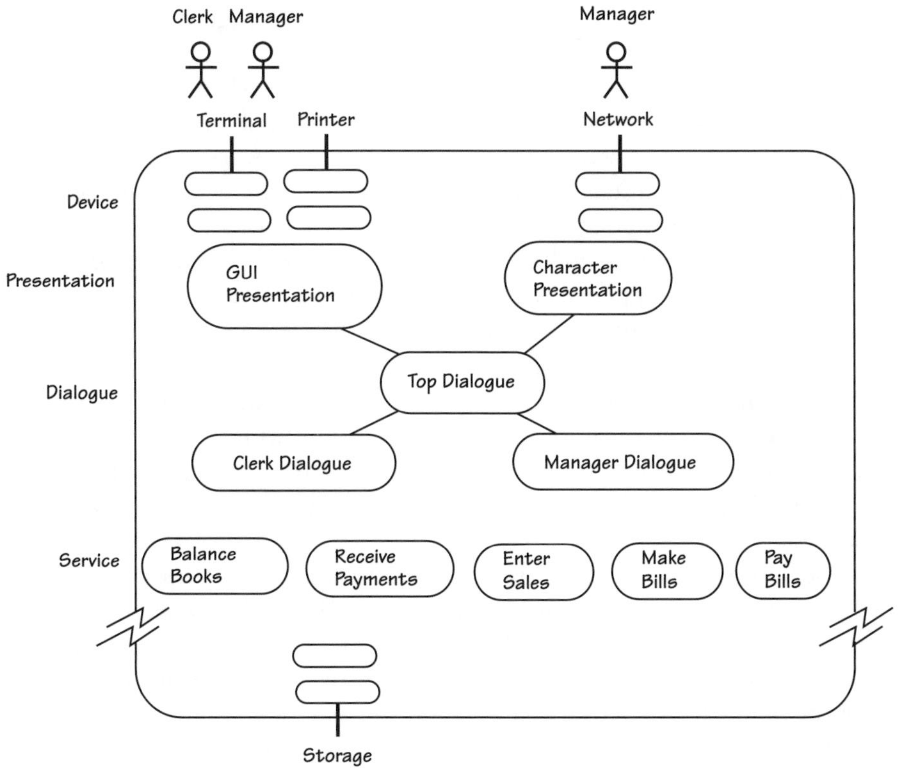

Figure 9.11

Adding
service
subsystems

subsystem for each user-recognizable activity, Balance Books, Enter Sales, and so on. This is a reasonable starting point, but it is unlikely to result in an architecture that supports the service related change cases. More cut-and-try cycles are needed. Chapter 10 shows some of those cycles.

If the dialogue subsystems were named for the services, then the service subsystems could offer slightly lower level behaviors, such as Query Accounts, Process Transactions, and Reporting. Chapter 10 shows the process and its difficulties. Figure 9.11 shows an architecture diagram with some service subsystem nominations.

To summarize the service subsystem nomination process, we are looking for functional subsystems that can be used to implement the functional growth and configuration increments called for in our change cases. The combination of dialogue and service subsystems provide the users with the behaviors they want.

Nominate Model Subsystems

Model subsystems provide a home for, and entry points to, the system state elements. The requirement that architecture subsystems be fixed means that most of the system state elements are not candidates for architecture subsystem nominations. I have found the idea of entry points to be a very helpful guide in nominating subsystems.

We should also examine some examples of the differences between fixed architecture subsystems and transient components. The main elements of our sample system state model in an accounting application, are books, accounts, journals, and customers. Individual instances of a book or account are transient because we could have a system with no books, accounts, journals, or customers, as when we turn the system on for the first time and no data have been loaded. If there is no data, what is there? The shelves to put the data on. Those shelves are the model subsystems. Thus, the accounts subsystem will exist whether there are any accounts in the system or not.

Model subsystems provide a home for the stable state models.
The system state components will have behaviors allocated to them that involve maintaining their own integrity and their relationships with their neighbors in the system state model. The subsystems on the other hand, can have behaviors that involve looking up, fetching, and storing the system state elements that the subsystem holds.

If we look over the names of the service subsystems and dialogue controllers, we can get an idea of what they will be manipulating. We might nominate one model subsystem for each of those things. Depending on how detailed our thinking is, this could be quite a few subsystems. At the other extreme, just one model subsystem might be nominated—Books, or The Company, in our accounting example. The problem with having a single model subsystem is that one subsystem would have to support a great many messages to allow the dialogue and service subsystems to retrieve what they need. There would also be some traversal in every request to get from the top of the model to the desired model component. Between the extremes of one and too many subsystems lies the just right number. The most frequent accesses should be given their own entry point. It is a also good idea to provide access to the top of the model (The Company in our example) to support the less frequent access and unanticipated requests.

The model subsystems are shown in Figure 9.12.

To summarize the guidelines for nominating model subsystems: they should provide a place for the other subsystems to gain access to the system state elements that they wish to manipulate. There should be one subsystem for the top level of each cohesive system state model and at least one entry point for each of the main access points, with *main* being determined by frequency of access. Whether each entry point needs its own subsystem should be determined by walking through the change cases. Chapter 10 describes the process of nominating subsystems for our example system.

Having looked at how to nominate subsystems for the architecture on the first pass, I would like to lay out an architecture and look for other subsystems that might be needed.

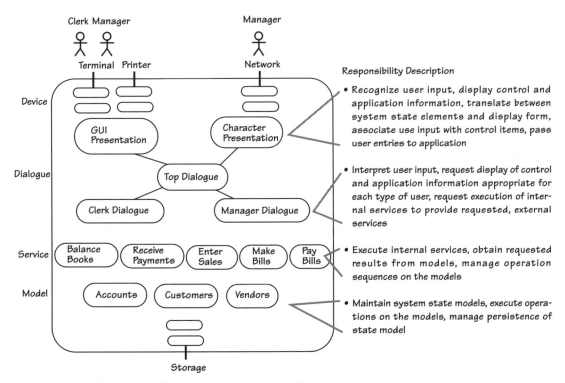

Figure 9.12 Adding model subsystems. Generic responsibilities allocated to each subsystem layer shown.

9.3.4 Refining an Architecture

If we look at the results of our initial subsystems nomination efforts (Figure 9.12), we can make some significant improvements in the system architecture, even at this early stage. This activity is an example of the application of modularity and extensibility concerns to system design. The basic issue being addressed here is behavior allocation. Modularity and other build-time requirements are addressed in the following pages.

In a user-driven system, much of what the system does is concerned with displaying various aspects of the system state elements to the user. The issue that determines whether the system is easy to extend is not whether we have to display system state elements, but how the behavior for translating for display is allocated. With the architecture in front of us, I would like to consider three alternatives for allocating the behavior to display things for the user.

The first alternative is to allocate all responsibility for display and translation to the presentation subsystems. To get something displayed, the requester would pass the thing to be displayed to the presentation subsystem. The presentation would know how talk to each system state element to extract the necessary information and display it on the screen. The advantage of this approach is that the system state

System architecture is a good place to address emergent properties.

elements are completely free of display dependencies. The disadvantage is that the presentation is intimately familiar with the protocol of each of the system state elements. Any change or addition to the system state elements will require a corresponding change in the presentations that handle them. But presentation systems are usually sufficiently complicated to warrant trying to avoid making those kinds of changes. So what else can we try?

An example of designing in modularity

The second alternative is to make the system state elements responsible for producing information that can be used directly by each of the kinds of display in the system. This alternative might be implemented as a set of display messages that all system state elements would respond to. We might still pass the system state elements to the presentation for display, but the common display protocol would avoid introducing system state element dependencies into the presentation. Now when we change and add system state elements, as long as they implement the display protocol, the presentation subsystems can handle them with no change, which is good. But the cost is that when we change or add to the display, we have to change some, perhaps many, of the system state elements. After carefully crafting the system state elements to faithfully embody the rules and constraints of our system, it seems unfortunate to have to change them just because the display in one application has changed. In fact, if the display-related behavior is peculiar to one application, we have reduced the potential for reusing the system state elements in other applications. This alternative is not entirely desirable either.

The first two variations, where the display translation behavior was allocated to the front end, the presentation, and to the back end, the system state elements, were unsatisfactory. As a third alternative, we could allocate the responsibility for translating between system state elements and the display to a new subsystem whose sole job is to do the translation and isolate the cross dependency from the rest of the subsystems. This subsystem might be called a Display Translator. Its job is to extract information from system state elements an put it in a form that can be easily used by the presentation. Why is this a better arrangement than the other two alternatives?

If we change the presentation, or add a new kind of presentation, we will have to change the presentation, and perhaps, the translator. The presentation change is unavoidable. Whether the translator must be changed depends on whether the presentation can make do with the existing translator output. If we have to change the translator, it has the advantage that it does not involve the system state elements. It is concerned only with the translation.

The same argument can be made for a change to the system state elements. We would probably also have to change the translator subsystem, but its scope of responsibility is limited. I believe that the modularity and ease of extension of the system is increased by isolating the necessarily messy cross dependencies in a single subsystem.

The next question is, where should we put the translator subsystem? Because the Display Translator is dependent on multiple system state elements, and because it changes the form of its inputs and outputs, it looks like a service subsystem. My only reservation is that its semantic level is not quite that of the application domain. It exists only because of the internal processing required to get information from the application to the screen. In spite of that, I suggest that we place the translator subsystem with the service subsystems.

Having recognized the need for a separate translator function by evaluating the changeability of the architecture, it is the responsibility of the behavior-modeling activity to determine exactly what behavior, components, and interfaces are needed to actually carry out the translation tasks.

The previous discussion is an example of the kind of effort needed to develop systems that can deliver on the advertising promises made for software development technologies. Systems will be modular, easy to extend, and robust in the face of change only when their designers explicitly evaluate alternative designs for modularity, ease of extension, and robustness against explicit requirements for growth and change. That evaluation must involve trying out the anticipated changes on each of the alternatives.

Significant issues can be addressed with an informal architecture diagram.

The previous discussion is also an example of the very useful work that can be done using a very preliminary version of the architecture diagram. By preliminary, I mean that we have defined the architecture subsystems only in terms of their general responsibilities. There has been no detailed behavior allocation and no interface specification. This fact is the basis for recommending that a feasibility study be done at this level of detail before the investment is made in any more detailed design, prototyping or production activities.

To summarize the initial refinement activity: as soon as a set of subsystems have been nominated and their responsibilities allocated, we can begin to walk through some of the anticipated changes and evaluate how gracefully the nominated structure will handle them. Often, additional subsystems will be identified which can be nominated to participate in the architecture. These additional subsystems will have implications for the behavior model, so it is a good idea to carry out at least a preliminary architecture development before a detailed behavior model effort is undertaken.

9.4 ALLOCATING BEHAVIOR TO ARCHITECTURE SUBSYSTEMS

Up to this point, we have nominated a set of subsystems to populate the architecture. We have described their behavior only in terms of broad responsibilities and we have made some informal evaluations as to the ability of our structure to support the change cases. In Chapter 8 three kinds of behavior modeling techniques were described: collaboration-responsibility, interaction, and service modeling. In the description of the process of developing a system architecture I have followed up to

The architecture needs behavior.

now, there has been a lot of talk about identifying services and describing subsystems in terms of their responsibilities. These are indeed behavior-modeling techniques. I have found that my main use of the collaboration-responsibility style of behavior modeling is in the development of system architectures. Being quick and informal, it is a good way to account for the required behavior without going to all the trouble of doing a detailed behavior model.

While an informal description of behavior is useful, a fuller specification of a system architecture needs more detail. In particular, it needs a more detailed specification of the behavior and the interfaces of the architecture subsystems.

There are two approaches to allocating behavior to the architecture. One is to identify the behaviors at the individual function or method level, and allocate them directly to the architecture subsystems one method at a time. The techniques for doing this kind of behavior modeling have been described in Chapter 8. In this approach, the components that are nominated to participate in the response to each use case will be architecture subsystems.

Allocating behaviors one at a time to subsystems leaves open the question of how to organize the behaviors inside each subsystem. It also blurs the distinction between components that address the user requirements and subsystems that address the development sponsor requirements, which is a very useful distinction. For these reasons, I do not recommend allocating behaviors directly to the architecture subsystems.

The second approach is to carry out the behavior-modeling activities on components that are smaller that the architecture subsystems and then allocate the components to the architecture subsystems. The end result is the same—architecture subsystems get explicit behaviors allocated to them—but the unit of allocation is a cluster of small behaviors and the local information they need to function. Those clusters of behaviors are relatively independent of the architecture subsystems to which they may be allocated.

Separating behavior allocation from architecture lets us do a better job at both tasks.

An important advantage of doing the behavior modeling on small components and allocating them separately to the relatively larger architecture subsystems is that the architecture structure and the component allocation to the subsystems can be changed without affecting the work done in the behavior modeling. This is important because carrying out a detailed behavior model is a substantial piece of work. If we can arrange things so that we only have to do it once, we save ourselves much work.

In order to have the behavior components retain their identity through all the various architectures and allocations we might try, the components must be small enough so that we will have no need to divide them in any allocation to architecture subsystems. How can we know what will be *small enough* when we are doing the behavior modeling if we can't see the architecture? The answer is that we can't. We have to have the architecture in mind when we do the behavior modeling. This allows us to pick a granularity, or size, of the components we invent for the behavior model that will be small enough so they will not cross the boundary of any architecture subsystem. This is yet another reason for carrying out a feasibility study to arrive at an architecture before any detailed behavior modeling is done.

I have tried to separate the description of the design tasks from sequence of applying the tasks. However, some concerns for the sequence of tasks in projects have crept into this discussion of individual tasks. To explain how an architecture is obtained before getting to the architecture task, I must look ahead to the sequence of projects in a product's life. The sequence I recommend is to do an informal architecture study and a feasibility study as the first project. This does not require a detailed behavior model, but does produce the first cut at the architecture. In the projects that follow, the preliminary architecture is available as a guide in developing the more detailed behavior models. This approach gets around the chicken and egg problem of having the architecture before the behavior model.

The discussion in this chapter up to this point has covered deriving the first cut architecture, as shown in Figure 9.12. I will now assume that a detailed behavior model has been developed and that we have available a complete set of components with their behavior and interfaces completely specified. A few of these are shown below.

Our current situation is that we have a set of components which, when taken together, have all of the behavior and information needed to provide all of the required run-time requirements. We also have a set of architecture subsystems with general responsibilities that will allow the system to provide the required change cases gracefully. If we can place all the components in the subsystems in such a way that we don't break the modularity, we will have a system which will provide all of the change cases and all of the use cases. We will have completed our assignment to design a good software system.

The process of allocating components to subsystems is one of matching responsibilities. Components that do presentation should be allocated to presentation subsystems, components that do the services, should be allocated to the service subsystems (assuming an architecture framework calling for service subsystems was chosen). All the system state elements should be initially allocated to the model subsystem that seem appropriate. Note that the control subsystems are absent from this list of straightforward allocations.

Another behavior allocation task

It is possible and may be appropriate to allocate control components to almost any subsystem in the architecture. In general, a control component should be able to see the things that it controls.

Consider control components Reporting Controller and Transaction Entry Controller, in our accounting example. Reporting Controller communicates with Execute Report Scripts and Report Formatter, both of which were allocated to the same subsystem, Reporting. Transaction Entry Controller communicates with Process Invoices and Process Payments, which are in different subsystems. My first allocation would be to put Reporting Controller in the service subsystem with its

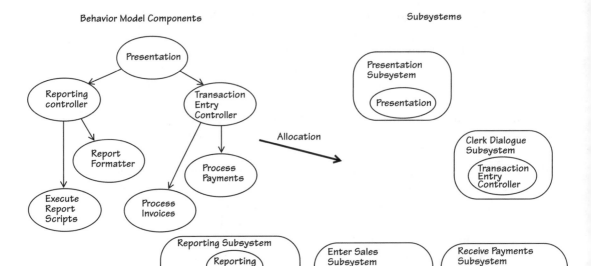

Figure 9.13 Allocation of behavior model components to architecture subsystems

controlees and to put Transaction Entry Controller in a dialogue subsystem that can see both. This allocation is shown in Figure 9.13. This results in having the presentation subsystem communicate directly with a service subsystem, which I prefer to avoid.

On the other hand, if Reporting Controller and Transaction Entry Controller were both invoked in the same way from the top dialogue, it might be more consistent to put both in a dialogue subsystem. That would eliminate the problem with presentation communication with a service subsystem. The appropriate choice might be indicated after the evaluations are completed. See Chapter 10 for a walkthrough of the process.

9.4.1 Deriving Subsystem Interfaces

Subsystem interfaces can come from the allocation model. We now have architecture subsystems populated with components that can provide their behavior and information. We have not yet determined what the interfaces of the subsystems actually are; nor have we determined the real connections between the subsystems.

In Chapter 7, I extolled the virtues of specifying components with an interface view and of noting the receivers of the messages sent by the component. The reason for recording the receivers of the messages will now become apparent. For each of the components in a subsystem, we can determine whether the receivers of its

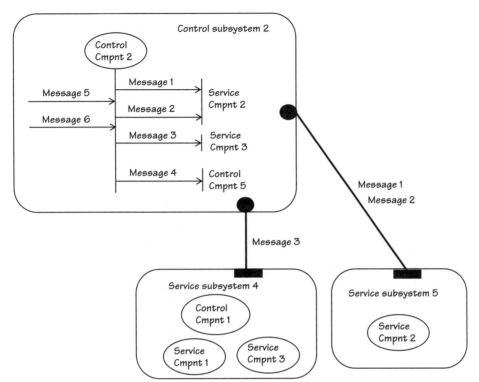

Figure 9.14
Deriving
subsystem
interfaces
from the
behavior
model
components
allocated
to each
subsystem

messages are in the same subsystem or if they were allocated to another subsystem. When a receiver is in another subsystem, the message sent becomes part of an external channel of the subsystem, Figure 9.14.

If we look for component receivers that are not in the same subsystem with the sender, we can identify all the messages that cross subsystem boundaries. The result will be an almost complete specification of the communication connections between subsystems and message interfaces of each subsystem.

If we allocate all the components from the behavior model to subsystems in the architecture, the result will look like Figure 9.15.

The connectedness of the resulting picture may be good or bad, depending on the component allocation decisions that were made up to this point. My first reaction to this architecture is that it is not as clean as I would like it. The collaborations around the Top Dialogue and the collaborations that span multiple layers need further attention.

Note in Figure 9.13, that most of the subsystems have opaque tops. Two were left transparent to show how the subsystem interfaces were derived from the message interfaces of their constituents. This is very important. Once we have determined the interface of a subsystem, regardless of the technique used, the subsystem should become a black box to everything outside its boundaries. Some

*Real
subsystems
are opaque.*

Figure 9.15
Architecture
diagram
showing com-
munication
between
subsystems

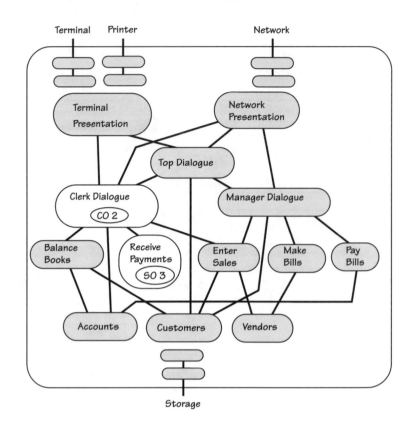

authors have suggested that subsystems are just logical groupings of objects and have no real identity of their own. The reason given for this suggestion is that the only things that do any real work are the objects. This is like saying that a VME board is not a real component because the only things that do any real work are the chips. Having transparent subsystems also implies that there is only one level of encapsulation, and that is at the lowest level component. Describing large systems in terms of their smallest component is not conducive to achieving any of the design goals for the system. If software is to become anything more than thousands of lines of code, we must have multiple levels of opaque components.

A second note is that the device subsystems have no messages assigned. Commonly, at least when I do it, the behavior modeling is carried out at the semantic level of the application. The interface subsystems, virtual devices, and the like, have semantics that are at a different level from the application. Shlaer and Mellor [SHL92] have emphasized this point by placing the application in a different domain from the interface concerns. The result of modeling only at the semantic level of the application is that the lower level subsystems do not have any behavior allocated to them. This can be remedied by carrying out a separate modeling exercise at the semantic level of the interface subsystems.

9.4.2 Organizing Messages into Channels

We now have subsystems with many individual messages connecting them to other subsystems. Handling the messages individually in the specification and evaluation activities that follow is not convenient, so I recommend that the messages be organized into channels. The term *channel* comes from the Mascot specification and is very similar to the notion of a contract described in Wirfs-Brock [WIR90]. The idea is to organize the messages into cohesive groups and to give each group a name. By defining and naming the channels separately from the subsystems that use them we can make the channels part of the architecture specification, in much the same way that a hardware bus specification is separate from the cards that use the bus. Having bus specifications separate from the subsystems in software systems provides the same benefits that separate bus specifications provide in hardware: modularity, encapsulation, reuse, and testability are all facilitated.

The specification for a channel consists of the following elements: a name, message content including both control and information flows, the medium it is carried in, and the representation of the control and information flows in that medium. An example is shown in Table 9.1.

Channel	Message Content	Medium	Representation
Hard Copy	Print (a Document)	C++ messages	C++ messages and instances of C++ classes
	QueueStatus returns (list of document names)		
	StatusOf (document name) returns (status description)		
	Cancel (document name)		
	Pause (document name)		

Table 9.1
Sample channel specification

A channel with a medium of C++ messages can only be used between subsystems that are implemented as C++ classes. If the medium had been, say, UNIX streams, then the channel could only be used between UNIX tasks and the representation section would have to detail how the messages and information flows would be described entirely in terms of data. Only dumb data can be transmitted over streams. The description of the representation is essential if the channel specification is to be separate from the subsystems that use the channel.

A channel has both content and a medium.

The simplest approach to nominating channels is to group all the messages that connect two subsystems into a single channel. This is entirely adequate if there are few messages and if all the messages deal with the same general topic. If the messages are concerned with more than one topic, such as normal access and administrative access, two or more channels may be nominated. See Chapter 10.

Channels provide encapsulation of the subsystems.

The message names that were appropriate in the behavior model for a specific application may not be general enough to support the change cases. In this case, a more sophisticated approach to specifying channel content may be needed. The technique is to construct a set of messages to use for channel specification that are general enough to allow interpretation as any of the specific messages needed in any of the change cases. By looking at the actual behavior model messages and the change cases the interface is supposed to support, more generic messages can be developed. For example, consider the situation in an inventory system of an accounting application for a manufacturing company where the messages between a service subsystem and a model subsystem consist of the following:

- AddPartAssembly (assembly name)
- AddTo (assembly name, aPart ID)
- FindPartsBy (assembly name) returns (parts list)

If one of the change cases that the architecture was supposed to support was conversion to a retail system, then channels with "findPartsBy (assembly name)" will not survive the change. If the channels have to change, then all the subsystems that use the channels will also have to change. By considering the original messages and the change case, we might nominate the following, more robust interface for the subsystems:

- AddCategory (category name)
- AddTo (category name, name, anItem)
- FindItemsByAttribute (category name, type) returns (item list)

Channel content can be designed like any other part of the system.

The original message names can still be used within each subsystem. The responsibility for translating between the generic, external messages, and the messages relevant to the internal components of a subsystem should fall to the interface machinery of the subsystem. Earlier in this section I described how the choice of medium affects the representation of the messages and arguments in a channel. The need to provide for translation and interpretation of messages received from outside a subsystem point up the need for interface machinery inside subsystems. In fact, subsystems will have an internal architecture that looks much like one being described here. The internal architecture of individual subsystems can be developed by applying the same set of techniques we have described up to this point.

The final output of the architecture nomination process is an architecture specified as an assembly of subsystems connected by separately specified channels. I want to reemphasize a very important point about subsystem channels. Even though their message content was derived from the messages of the components allocated to the subsystem, once we assign channels to subsystems, the internals of the subsystem become invisible to anything outside the subsystems. Once we have assigned

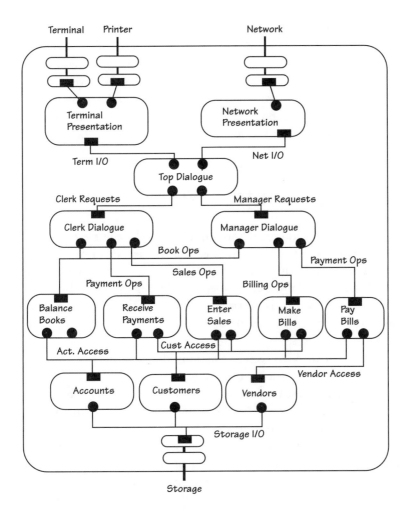

Figure 9.16
Architecture diagram showing named channel subsystems

channels to a subsystem, we could go so far as to replace the internals with spaghetti assembly code, if we wanted, and have no effect on the external users of the subsystem. Channels hide the contents of subsystems.

A final architecture specification diagram is shown in Figure 9.16.

9.4.3 Summary of Allocating Behavior

We have just used a technique of allocating behavior by component to subsystems in the architecture. It is one way of allocating behavior and defining interfaces for subsystems. Its primary advantage is that the behaviors and message interfaces of the components were derived directly from the user requirements. The behavior of our architecture specification is exactly as good and complete as our behavior model, so we can say that the architecture specification will meet the user requirements.

The suggestion that we should describe the communication between subsystems as collections of messages, or channels, is not common in software methods, but it provides a sound basis for much standardization and reuse of subsystems.

Whether the architecture specification will still meet the development sponsor requirements will be addressed when we evaluate the architecture. Whether this architecture is sufficient to support the desired degree of reuse across multiple products the development sponsor was looking for will have to be addressed in separate projects.

9.5 EVALUATE ARCHITECTURES

The architecture specification is the specification for the complete system. The system in turn, is supposed to meet the needs of its users and of its development sponsors. If we allocated the behavior from use cases to behavior model components, and then allocated those components to the architecture subsystems, the use case diagrams can be used to demonstrate how each of the user requirements will be met. This should be a sufficient demonstration that the architecture will also meet the run-time requirements.

When we evaluate the architecture with channels we evaluate the behavior allocation decisions.

In our first cut at the architecture, we derived an architecture that we believed could support the change cases, but we were guessing about the connections between subsystems. Now, we have allocated behavior model components which explicitly defined the connections between subsystems. Depending on the connections between components and how we allocated them, the modularity of the architecture may have changed. It is important, then, that we carefully evaluate our architecture specification to see if it can adequately support the change cases.

Questions for the evaluation

To do that, we can walk through applying each change case to the architecture specification and ask if the system can gracefully accommodate the change. We can now ask all three evaluation questions since we have channel specifications. The three questions that should be asked of each change case are:

1 Which subsystems will be impacted by the change?

2 Can the changes be made without affecting the external interface of the impacted subsystems?

3 Are there behaviors and information in the impacted subsystem that are not related to the change?

The goal is to have a very small number of subsystems affected by any change case, to have no changes in external interfaces, and to have all the behaviors and information in a subsystem be related to the change. This is a qualitative activity, and requires that the people doing the evaluation be familiar with the operation of each subsystem.

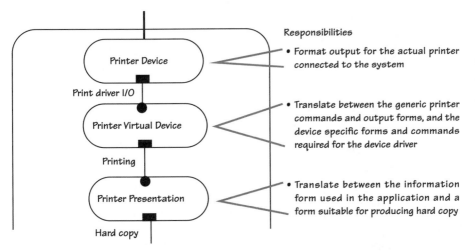

Responsibilities

Printer Device

• Format output for the actual printer connected to the system

Print driver I/O

Printer Virtual Device

• Translate between the generic printer commands and output forms, and the device specific forms and commands required for the device driver

Printing

Printer Presentation

• Translate between the information form used in the application and a form suitable for producing hard copy

Hard copy

To carry out the evaluation we need a diagram that shows the subsystems, the channels that connect them, a brief description of their responsibilities, and the message names and information flows that make up the channels between subsystems. This kind of specification is shown in Figure 9.16.

In the first pass through the architecture evaluations, there was much discussion about nominating new subsystems. All of those ideas apply here. I would like to describe the new element we now have—the channel interfaces. What follows are some examples of change case evaluations that focus on the channel interfaces of the subsystems.

9.5.1 Change Case Evaluation
Involving Platform and Peripherals

We put device and virtual-device subsystems in the architecture in order to isolate the application level subsystems from the effects of changes in the platform. The role of the channels of those subsystems is to enforce that isolation.

For this discussion, assume we have the following system architecture at a printer port, Figure 9.17, with the channel definitions shown in Table 9.2.

Channel	Message Content	Medium	Representation
Printing	PrintLine (a Line) returns (status), formFeed returns (status)		

Table 9.2
Printer device channel

The change cases affecting the virtual printer subsystem might be to support both character and graphics printers.

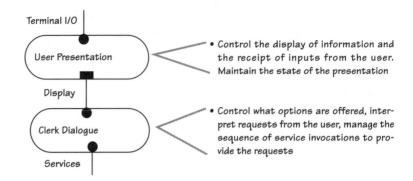

If we chose to isolate the effects of changing printer types in the Printer Virtual Device subsystem, then that would be the impacted subsystem mentioned in question 1. The responsibilities allocated to the virtual printer sound like it can satisfy Question 3 also. That leaves the interface issue in Question 2. The message content of the Printing channel is well equipped to handle character printers. But, a change to graphics printing would require a change to the channel content. The messages are not robust enough to hide the change. The semantic level of the messages is too low. Since the messages are far from being able to handle graphics, we should go all the way back to the behavior model for the printing activity to come up with a new set of messages that are capable of handling both text and graphics output.

9.5.2 Change Case Evaluation Involving Presentations

Change cases involving the look and feel of the presentation and the presentation platform (windowing system) are concerned with responsibilities that are usually allocated to the presentation subsystems, so we can expect to isolate those changes in the presentation subsystem. To evaluate if that is the case we need to look at the interface between the presentation and the rest of the application. Consider the architecture fragment in Figure 9.18 and channel specification in Table 9.3.

Table 9.3
Channel for a presentation subsystem

Channel	Message Content	Medium	Representation
Display	CreateMenu (name, item list), createPopUpDiaogue (name, control list), createTearOffMenu(name, item list), …		

If the change case involves changing the presentation look and feel and porting to other windowing systems, then there is an immediate problem with the messages in the Display channel. They expose the nature of the look and feel with messages like, createTearOffMenu(name, item list). When the Presentation subsystem is changed to another kind of presentation, the external channel, Display will also have to change. The change will then propagate back into the dialogue subsystems. The semantic level of the messages should be higher to isolate the details of the presentation inside the Presentation subsystem. An example of messages that would provide better encapsulation are messages like: offerOptions (name, item list) or requestChoice(name, option list).

These examples of interface evaluations emphasize the fact that having the right components is not enough to ensure that the system will be well behaved in the face of change. It is also necessary that the behavior be allocated appropriately and that the message names chosen effectively hide the contents of their subsystems.

9.5.3 Making the Changes

I have described a process for evaluating an architecture specification, and it should not be much of a surprise when some problems are found during the evaluation. When they are found, they should be corrected. Changes that involve changing message names should be made by revisiting the behavior model. Changes that involve only reallocating, that is, moving a complete component from one subsystem to another do not require revisiting the behavior model. This is the best incentive I know of for having a well formed architecture before starting any detailed behavior modeling. Chapter 10 shows both kinds of changes being made.

Fixing architecture problems may require fixing behavior allocation problems.

9.5.4 Evaluation Summary

An explicit evaluation of the architecture specification to determine if the system it describes meets the run-time requirements should not be necessary as long as the behavior modeling task supports direct traceability to the run-time requirements. Evaluation of the architecture for its ability to support the change cases is carried out by applying each change case to the architecture. The question of which subsystems, will be affected by the change is addressed by matching the responsibilities of the subsystems with the responsibilities affected by the change case. The question of whether the effects of the change will spread beyond those initial subsystems is addressed by deciding whether the internal changes will result in changes to the external interface. If the interface changes, then all users of that subsystem must change. A more robust interface should be developed, or components should be reallocated, to keep the effects of that change contained within one subsystem.

If you don't evaluate the decisions, it doesn't make any difference how you did the work.

The importance of documenting the build-time requirements and evaluating the system architecture for its ability to meet them cannot be overstated. It is only with the practice of evaluating designs against instances of extension and change that designers can deliver on the promises of ease of development, extension, and maintenance that have been made for software technology since time immemorial.

9.6 ALLOCATION ACROSS HARDWARE BOUNDARIES

Up to this point, I have described a process for deriving a system architecture from the point of view that there are no hardware boundaries that we have to worry about. I have found that to be a very useful assumption when looking at a system for the first time. But at some point, the allocation to hardware, to tasks, or to anything that requires a change in communication medium, must be made. Because this allocation to hardware and software boxes will have some definite architectural implications I would like to discuss it here.

A real system lives in real implementation enclosures.

The architectural goal is to arrange the software architecture so that when the hardware changes, the effect on the system is minimal. This is not to say that it is desirable for the architect to be unaware of where things are allocated. Crossing a hardware boundary has some costs associated with it, including time and bandwidth. The designer must be aware of the cost implications of the allocation decisions. I make this point to counter the implication that using technologies like an Object Request Broker or distributed objects, makes the physical location of resources irrelevant to everyone, including the designer. It should be irrelevant to most of the application subsystems, but it cannot be irrelevant to the designer of the system. I am about to describe a process in which the allocation decisions are made explicitly by the designer. The criteria for a successful design is that the effects of the allocation decisions are carefully isolated in a small number of subsystems.

The basis for this discussion is a recognition of the fact that software subsystems cannot span any memory-space boundary. Every hardware boundary is also a boundary of a software subsystem. At the network level, the hardware architecture consisting of computers on a network is also the software architecture. Inside a single computer, each task provided by the operating system also represents the boundary of a software subsystem.

Assume that we have an architecture diagram like Figure 9.19, where the boundary is the system boundary, and no hardware or task boundaries are considered. Assume further that the hardware configuration has already been selected, as is often the case. Also assume that some of the change cases involve implementing the system on different hardware configurations.

This system is actually going to be implemented on a client/server hardware architecture. The server side is a multitasking system, like UNIX. As always, there are a great many ways the system functionality can be distributed across any given set of hardware nodes. Our job as designers of the system is to evaluate the alternatives and propose the best solution.

Designing for the final product saves much rework.

I have found that the architecture diagram is a useful vehicle for making and evaluating those allocation decisions. If our boxless system architecture accounts for the complete system, then any allocation of that system to hardware will have to contain exactly the same set of subsystems. If we have been careful to ensure that

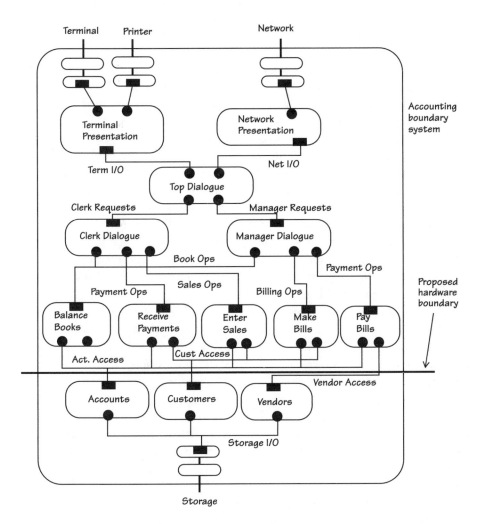

Figure 9.19
Architecture
diagram
showing the
proposed
allocation to
hardware
nodes

our architecture subsystems are small enough, we should not have to divide any of the subsystems when we allocate them to different hardware configurations. (It's not terrible if we have to divide a subsystem or any other component, it's just some work that we can avoid.)

The technique for allocation to hardware is to draw the hardware boundaries on the architecture diagram. There are two issues that need to be addressed: What kind of interface machinery must be provided? Where do we place the boundary?

9.6.1 Interface Machinery

Assume that we place the hardware boundary between the services and the model subsystems, as shown in Figure 9.19. That is, we will allocate the user interface and all the "application logic" to the client machine and the system state model to the server machine.

Interface machinery at hardware boundaries is the same as interface machinery at software subsystem boundaries.

The communication medium between hardware nodes, a network, is very different from the medium between subsystems inside a node, messages in a programming language, or pipes and streams in an operating system. Therefore, an appropriate interface should be provided. That interface might consist of device, virtual device, and presentation subsystems. This kind of machinery serves to raise the level of semantics up to something closer to the application level. I said earlier, that it was very important that the application not be aware of the physical distribution of the other subsystems. To achieve that goal, we must add a surrogate subsystem on each side of the boundary to provide the interface of the subsystem that got allocated to the other side of the boundary. The primary behavior of the surrogate subsystems is concerned with passing requests between their application side and their communication side. The surrogate subsystem is the presentation for the communication across hardware boundaries. The architectural result of these considerations is shown in Figure 9.20.

Location transparency is a run-time, not a design-time property.

By using the technique of explicitly adding interface machinery wherever a hardware boundary (or any other kind of boundary) crosses a communication channel in our architecture, we achieve the goals of having a distributed system and of isolating most components from any knowledge of the distribution. None of the existing subsystems is aware of the distribution. As far as they are concerned, they are always talking down the same channel with the same messages. The designer, on the other hand, is intimately aware of the distribution. The content of the channel is known and the physical media being used for transport are known. Thus, the ability of the selected medium to carry the required traffic can be evaluated and the cost of the communication can be calculated. This kind of information should play a very important role in evaluating alternative behavior distribution schemes.

This is the third behavior allocation decision we have seen.

Having placed the software subsystems in the hardware architecture nodes, it is a separate decision as to how to implement the software subsystems. In most systems, much of the behavior of the device and virtual device subsystems, as well as the presentation, is often provided by the operating system. In UNIX, for example, the file metaphor can serve as a common presentation for file, stream, and network connections. I would not recommend making the UNIX file interface visible in a presentation subsystem interface (remember the change operating systems change case discussed early) but much of the functionality of low-level interfaces is already available. Even when there are components available, I recommend that the architecture design be carried all the way to the edge of the system. The advantage is that with a complete design document, the impacts of the design decisions can be evaluated. In the example just cited, showing the presentation subsystems and their interfaces would allow the impact of making the UNIX file system interface visible to be evaluated.

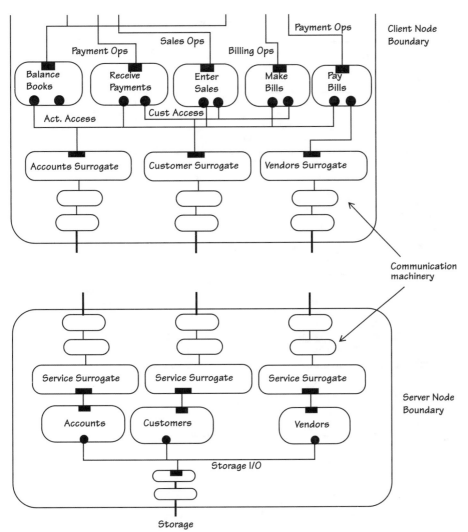

Figure 9.20
Architecture diagram fragments for the client and server hardware nodes

9.6.2 Placing the Boundaries

Behavior allocation decisions can be made in many ways. A big advantage of making the behavior allocation decisions on the architecture diagram is that the consequences of each decision are immediately obvious. Figure 9.21 shows our generic architecture with several alternative schemes for distributing the system across two kinds of hardware nodes. For purposes of this discussion, I will name the two nodes *user node* and *support node*. The names were chosen to avoid implying any particular behavior allocation.

Some of the implications of each of these allocation decisions are as follows:

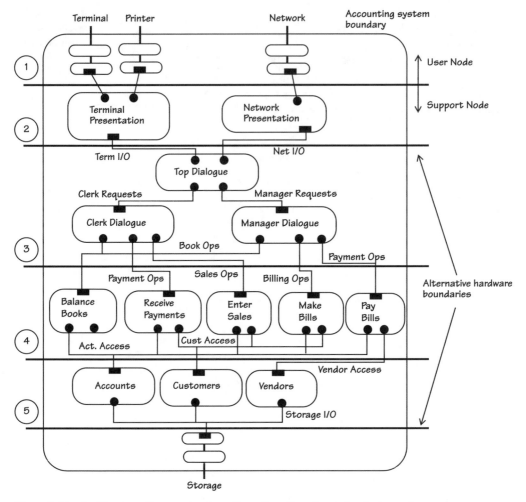

Figure 9.21 Architecture diagram showing alternative allocation to hardware nodes

1 *Host dumb terminal*   Allocating only the virtual device subsystems to the user node results in a dumb terminal behavior for the user node. If there were only one support node, we would have the classic mainframe host terminal system architecture. The message traffic between the nodes consists of screen level display commands and information. The traffic will be steady because every user command can result in requiring significant changes be made to the presentation.

2 *Smart terminal*   Placing the boundary so that the presentation subsystems are on the user node results in a smarter terminal than in the previous case, perhaps with semantics slightly above an X Terminal. The message traffic will consist of commands at the level of display elements. Traffic will be less steady than in

THE SOFTWARE SYSTEM ARCHITECTURE TASK I CHAPTER 9

the previous case because the presentation can cache much of the information it is displaying.

3   *Control client, application server*   Placing dialogues on the user node makes a client that is aware of the application. The support node becomes a function server or a service provider. The message traffic will consists of request for services and returns of the requested information.

4   *Application client, component server*   Placing the hardware boundary between the services and the model subsystems places all of the application logic on the user node. The support server becomes an intelligent component server, or the host for an enterprise model. This arrangement can effectively provide a high level of integrity and consistency to multiple users of the domain model. The message traffic will consist of requests that look like the access requests extracted from the use cases in the system state modeling task.

5   *Application client, database server*   When the hardware boundary is placed below the model subsystem, the user node will contain almost all the intelligence in the system, while the support server will be left with relatively "dumb" data. If a relational database were being used, the message traffic between hardware nodes might consist of SQL requests. This is the kind of allocation that is supported by most database vendors. It has the distinct disadvantage that most of the intelligence that could impose consistency and integrity on the information being stored is presumedly located on the multiple client nodes.

The end result of the behavior allocation decisions will be a software architecture for each of the hardware nodes. For the application client, the two component server options described above are shown in Figure 9.20.

Which allocation is "best?" It depends on the nature of the user and support node hardware, the communication medium and what other applications need to share the information. I can say that placing the hardware boundary too close to either edge, as in the dumb terminal option (1) or the dumb database option (5) are probably less desirable than the other options. The reason is that in those extreme options all of the processing are concentrated in one node.

The difference between host terminal and client-server systems is just behavior allocation.

If a system state model subsystem was designed assuming a single thread, single user environment, there will be some additional machinery needed to manage the multiple requests that may be generated in a multiuser system. This machinery could take the form of an additional dialogue subsystem resident with the model subsystems to ensure orderly access to the model subsystems.

9.6.3 Allocation to Non-Hardware Subsystems

Other units of implementation can be used to enclose subsystems. Those units include heavyweight processes in multitasking operating systems, lightweight processes (threads) provided in some operating systems and programming languages,

A DLL is also a subsystem implementation enclosure.

DLLs and OLEs of some operating systems (OS/2, Windows). Any of these enclosures can be used as subsystem boundaries. The mechanics of defining the internal architecture of each of them is the same as described above for subsystems bounded by hardware. The internal architecture of the interface subsystems will be the same: device, virtual device and presentation (surrogate) subsystems are entirely appropriate. The difference from the hardware bounded subsystem is that the interface subsystems will be translating to UNIX streams, mail boxes, or OLE function calls, rather than to Ethernet.

It is easier in the nonhardware subsystems to violate the encapsulation provided by the subsystem. I strongly recommend that you resist the temptation to do so. The problem is that in most nonhardware enclosures there are multiple communication mechanisms available. In heavyweight tasks, for example, interprocess communication (pipes, streams, etc.) can provide strong encapsulation, but shared memory is available as a back door into the subsystem. When a thread defines the boundary, the front door communication medium is the mail box, but synchronous function calls or message sends are also available. It is much more difficult to maintain or test the integrity of a subsystem when requests can sneak in a back door. My suggestion is that a single communication medium be selected to provide the enclosure for a subsystem, and that no other communication mechanisms be used, even if they are available.

Examples of subsystems enclosed by tasks and threads are shown in Chapter 10.

9.6.4 Summary of Allocation to Hardware

The process of distributing architecture subsystems across hardware nodes is made easier if the granularity of the subsystems is small enough so that the carefully designed subsystems will not have to be broken apart. A convenient vehicle for documenting and evaluating the allocation decisions is an architecture diagram with the system boundary as the diagram boundary.

Hardware boundaries can be drawn in many ways, but wherever a boundary crosses a communication channel, appropriate interface subsystems should be provided. Those subsystems should include a device at the hardware boundary, a virtual device for portability and presentation. Surrogate subsystems should be provided on each side to carry the interface, or channel, that the local subsystems need. Multiple surrogates could share the same presentation, for example, when many channels will be carried over the same network.

The evaluation of alternative allocation decisions should look at the processing load required of each node and the ability of the communication medium to carry the required traffic. Another consideration is the ability to handle multiple threads, or users, when the allocation decisions result in multiple users being serviced by a single processor.

9.7 ARCHITECTURE SUMMARY

Software architecture was defined as a collection of subsystems that are real units of implementation. A complete architecture specification includes the boundary of the system, connections that cross the boundaries, subsystems, how the subsystems are connected, and channels that make the connections.

In addition to specifying how the system is to be assembled, the architecture can be the basis for design and implementation assignments and the framework for integration of the parts. The architecture is evaluated primarily against its ability to support the change cases. It is the place in the design where we address the emergent, build-time requirements.

By shaping the architecture to meet the build-time requirements, we arrived at an architecture that uses six different kinds of subsystems. Each kind of subsystem serves to isolate and contain a different kind of change case.

Allocating behavior to the architecture subsystems can be done by allocating subsystems from the behavior modeling task or by doing the behavior model directly on the architecture subsystems. The former was recommended. The advantage of separating behavior modeling from architecture development is that the user requirements and development sponsor requirements can be addressed separately and explicitly. Interfaces between subsystems could be derived directly from the interfaces developed in the behavior-modeling activity.

Identifying and allocating behavior, then evaluating the allocation has been a common thread.

Distributing the architecture subsystems across hardware boundaries was described as a separate activity from defining the overall system architecture. The steps involved were placing the boundary and adding interface machinery for each channel the crossed the boundary. Surrogate subsystems were recommended on each side of the boundary to provide these channels. This approach maintained location transparency for the subsystems, but forced the designer to explicitly recognize, and hopefully to evaluate, the cost of communicating across the hardware boundary.

At the end of the architecture design process, we should have an architecture diagram for each unit of implementation, and we should be able to demonstrate that the architectures in the diagrams can support the build-time change cases.

CHAPTER 10

Architecture Example

CONTENTS

10.1 Specifying a Boundary and Ports   260

10.2 Nominating Subsystems   261

10.3 Evaluating the Preliminary Architecture   270

10.4 Allocating Model Components to Architecture   274

10.5 Evaluating the Detailed Architecture (Boxless)   286

10.6 Allocating Architecture Subsystems across Hardware Boundaries   295

10.7 Implementation Increments   309

In this example, we will develop and evaluate an architecture for our video store system. The first architecture we develop will be for the entire system, ignoring for the present any physical distribution. Distribution will be addressed later. For reasons that were amply discussed in Chapters 7 and 9, I will select the high-test architecture framework with service subsystems.

Two levels of detail will be shown.

There are two phases to architecture development. One phase is the development of a preliminary architecture to serve as a basis for initial feasibility evaluations and as input to the detailed behavior-modeling task. This preliminary architecture is typically the output of the initial design study. The other phase is the refinement of the architecture, which can be done when the results of the detailed behavior modeling are completed, and which is the output of later design studies. This example will follow that sequence of phases. In the initial nomination of architecture subsystems, I will assume that the user and development sponsor requirements have been documented, that a simple system state model is available, and that a simple service model was done.

Inputs to the Preliminary Architecture Task

- *Run-time requirements*   See the use case text in the example section for requirements in Chapter 6.
- *Build-time requirements*   See the change case list in the requirements example in Chapter 6.
- *System state model*   See the state element list in the system state task example in Chapter 6.
- *Behavior model*   See the service list in the behavior identification and allocation task example in Chapter 8.

The primary constraint on subsystem nominations is that they be fixed; they are created at start-up and remain in place for as long as the system runs. With this constraint and the above information as inputs, we can make our first nominations for subsystems in the system architecture.

10.1 SPECIFYING A BOUNDARY AND PORTS

Always design toward the big picture.

The boundary for the first architecture is the logical boundary of the system. The ports will not be physical ports, but will be terminals for the actors and connections to peripherals that the system must support. We start by drawing the box and labeling it the *logical system boundary.* Ports can be nominated by looking, first, at the list of actors. One port for each kind of actor is a reasonable starting place. The number of ports can be reduced if we know that several actors will share the same physical terminal, or will use the same kind of terminal interface. For this example, I will assume that the manager and bookkeeper will use the same terminal and that the clerks will use different terminals. Because the system will grow to multiple stores, I will show the bookkeeper connected to the system by a network. The manager may use either a local terminal or network connection. (That is a little awkward, but I want to show mixing and matching of presentations and physical devices.) I have found it helpful to show which external actors will be connected through each port.

Another source of ports that cross a system boundary is the peripherals. For this system the peripherals that come to mind are one or more printers and the physical disk for the database. For starters, I will assume that there will be two kinds of printers on the system: one for reports and one for bar codes that the stock-clerk uses. The system boundary now looks like Figure 10.1.

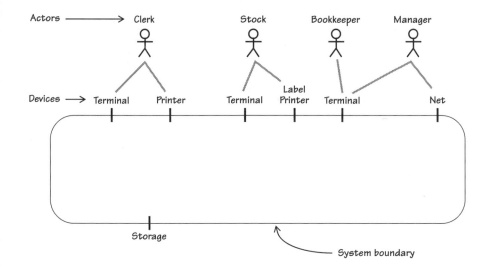

Figure 10.1
Architecture
diagram
showing
system bound-
ary, ports on
the bound-
ary, and
external
actors

10.2 NOMINATING SUBSYSTEMS

The general architecture framework I have selected calls for device, virtual device, and presentation subsystems for interfaces to the outside world, with dialogue, service, and model subsystems in the center of the application. There are others that I could have used but I chose this framework because I know that I can support most of the change cases. Regardless of the framework chosen, the selection of the framework should be a conscious decision.

Start with a template.

10.2.1 Interface Subsystems

The easiest subsystems to nominate are the low-level interface subsystems at the boundary of the system. Since our system boundary is just a logical boundary, specifying the interface subsystems is not terribly significant. Even without a physical boundary, the interface subsystems facilitate discussions of portability and peripheral changes, so I think it is worth while to put them in. I recommend nominating two for each port—a device subsystem to deal directly with the physical port and a virtual device to isolate the application from the ports (Figure 10.2).

Provide for platform independence.

10.2.2 Presentation Subsystems

Presentation subsystems are responsible for sending things to the outside world, so they are associated with a port and their behavior is dependent primarily on the nature of the device connected to the port, or ports, they are serving. There should be at least one per port, unless two ports share the same presentation (for example if the connection is a network with several different kinds of actors on the other end).

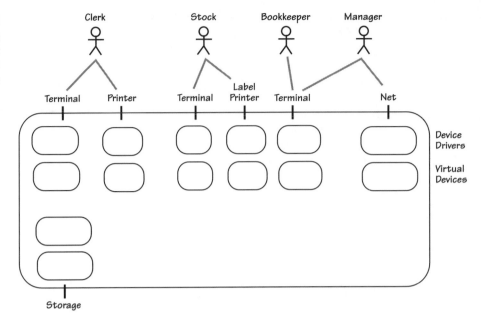

Figure 10.2
Adding
device driver
subsystems to
the ports

Presentation subsystems are appropriate for any interface that requires significant translation between the forms on the inside and forms on the outside. Printers, networks, and databases are examples of external systems that can use separate presentation.

Provide for
appearance
independence.

In this system I will nominate one presentation for each of the terminal ports. The network port may have several kinds of devices connected to it (for example storage systems and remote users). For now, I will assume that the presentation needed for the remote users is different from the presentation needed for local terminals, so I will nominate a remote user presentation and a storage presentation to serve the network port. When the design is firmed up, these nominations can be changed with little effect on the neighboring subsystems (Figure 10.3).

We have now completed the cocoon that isolates our application from changes and details of the outside world and the platform. All of the subsystems nominated up to this point should have interfaces with semantic levels below that of the main application. These subsystems are relatively easy to nominate because they are so directly connected to the ports and external devices.

The subsystems that follow should all use semantics from the application domain. The categories of those subsystems result from my decision of which kind of general architecture structure to use. The order of the nomination is not important, but I usually do the model subsystems first.

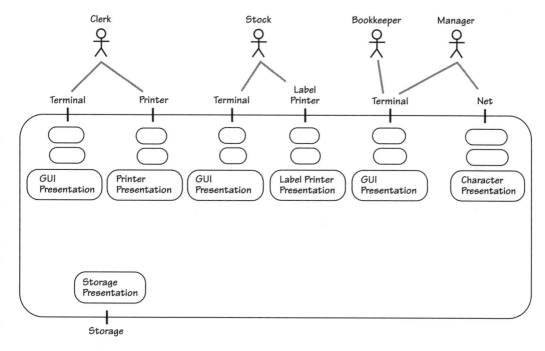

Figure 10.3   Adding presentation subsystems to the ports

10.2.3 Model Subsystems

The model subsystems provide a home for the system state components. The model subsystems are a good place to allocate behaviors related to looking up specific components and creating new system state components. Basically, they provide entry points into the system state model for the rest of the application. At this stage, i.e. without detailed static or behavior model results, the best we can do is to guess at what the main entry points are. We can check those guesses with some collaboration-responsibility modeling on the architecture, but full evaluation of the choices will have to wait until the results of the detailed behavior modeling task are available.

Provide a place to keep the system state.

For our example, the most common access seems to be looking up, renting, or returning rental items. In most of those access requests, the kind of the item will be known (video, CD, VCR, etc.), so it seems reasonable to make the top-level of access the kind of item. I will nominate a model subsystem of Inventory with separate channels for Tapes, CDs, Equipment, or Sale Items. That should satisfy the routine access requests.

Separate subsystems for customers and transactions should provide access for administrative and accounting use cases. I am guessing that I may want to provide separate hardware systems for the inventory clerk and for the sales clerk. I may then

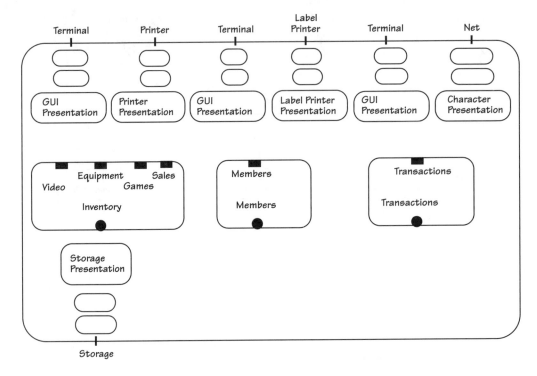

Figure 10.4 Adding model subsystems to the architecture

want to provide the inventory clerk with a separate system. To handle those two configurations, I would nominate separate subsystems for inventory and customer information. The price I will pay for that convenience in configuring the hardware systems is that I will have to manage the customer-inventory dependencies across the subsystem boundaries.

In drawing the picture, my habit is to put the model subsystems across the bottom of the architecture diagram, as shown in Figure 10.4. There is no magic in that arrangement, except that I happen to like it, and it helps remind me of the kind of subsystem with which I am dealing.

Designing for portability impacts all allocation decisions.

In addition to nominating the subsystems, we should have some idea of their contents and responsibilities. I mentioned earlier that they will hold the system state components and can serve system state components to whomever asks for them. On the other side of the model subsystems we have database interface machinery. My design decision is that there should be no explicit database dependencies in the model subsystems. The model subsystems and their contents should be responsible for maintaining their own state as long as that state can be determined with information available within the model itself.

All of those opinions on the behaviors of the model subsystems represent behavior allocation nominations. They are not final specifications and will have to be confirmed by evaluation against the external requirements that our system is supposed to support.

10.2.4 Dialogue Subsystems

Dialogue subsystems carry out the mapping between the events and requests from outside actors, on one hand, and the services and resources inside the system on the other. Services that are visible to the actor may be provided by coordinating the outputs of several of the internal service subsystems. Dialogue subsystems may be associated with the actor they serve or with the services they coordinate. I could nominate dialogues for the external actors they serve, such as manager, sales clerk, and stock clerk. Or, I could nominate dialogues for the services they control, such as check in/out or take inventory. The problem is that if dialogues are actors, different actors may invoke the same service, which means the service-related control information would be replicated. If dialogues are services, then the actor-specific control information would have to be replicated in the service-specific components. The choices for resolving the conflict are to choose one and merge and replicate the other control aspects as needed or to use two layers of dialogue subsystems. The two-layer approach, illustrated in Figure 10.5, is usually cleaner, particularly if the sequence of actions is the same regardless of who is doing them.

Provide for actor independence.

For this example, I will assume that the basic operations are always the same, regardless of who the actor is. I will nominate a separate dialogue for each kind of actor, and one for each major action sequence. The actor dialogues will include sales clerk, stock clerk, manger, and accountant. The usage-sequence dialogues are check out, check in, inventory access, sales, reporting, and administration.

This arrangement of subsystems was arrived at with some written ideas on my part of what kinds of responsibilities they will have. The actor dialogues will be responsible for indicating which services are available to their respective users, interpreting the users' requests and for invoking the appropriate sequence of control signals to have those requests carried out. The action-sequence dialogues will be responsible for actually managing the interaction between user and the system while the user is checking out a video or adding to inventory. They will also be responsible for invoking the proper sequence of internal services to provide the external services the user is requesting.

This behavior allocation will leave the actor dialogues with little to do except be "menu servers" for the actors, which may be all right. Another problem arises when we look at the ability of the action-sequence dialogues to support multiple users. The state of each user in the sequence of checking out videos, for example, will have to be maintained separately. In that case, the sequence dialogues would have to be replicated for each user, which was the situation I was trying to avoid in nominating

The decisions get more complicated as we move away from the boundary.

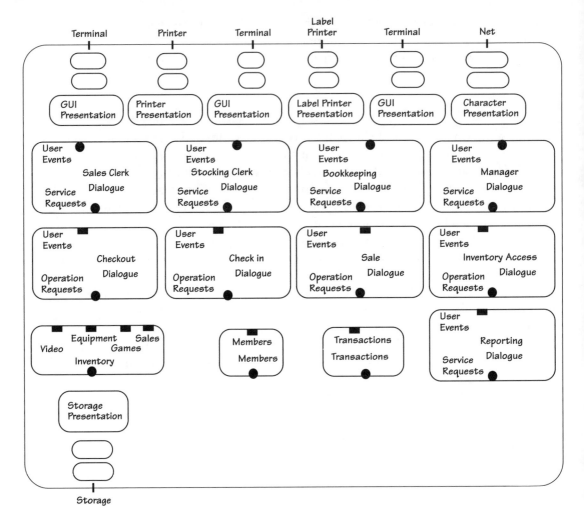

Figure 10.5 Adding two layers of dialogue subsystems to the architecture, one layer for actors and one layer for the services being used

the service dialogues in the first place. This line of thinking leads to the conclusion that the main unit of configuration is the actor. Perhaps the architecture should reflect that fact. Since it looks like the service-sequence dialogue information will have to be replicated for multiple users in any case, the responsibilities originally allocated to the action-sequence dialogues could be reallocated to the actor dialogues. This will leave us with a single level of dialogue subsystems (Figure 10.6).

The responsibility description is now as follows: "The actor dialogues are responsible for all dialogue management with each kind of user." Each dialogue subsystem will be configured with the controls appropriate for that actor. The dialogue will invoke the appropriate sequence of service and resource requests to provide the

ARCHITECTURE EXAMPLE | CHAPTER 10

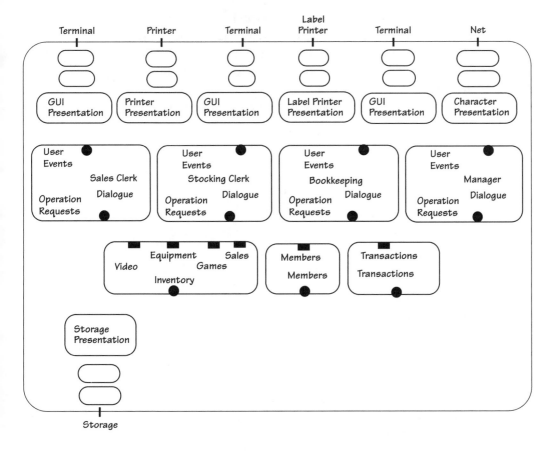

Figure 10.6 Adding one layer of dialogue subsystems to the architecture—dialogues associated with actors

requested service. Note that I have renamed the interface ports on the application side of the new dialogue subsystems to be the same as the ports on the former service dialogue subsystems. At this stage, the names and numbers of ports are just a guess, but they correctly reflect the fact that the functionality formerly allocated to the service-dialogue subsystems has not been reallocated to the actor-dialogue subsystems.

The preceding thought process demonstrates the kind of work needed to arrive at systems that are, in fact, easy to extend and modify. The extensions and changes must figure prominently in all behavior allocation decisions.

10.2.5 Service Subsystems

The last kind of subsystems called for in the template I selected are the service subsystems. There is nothing intrinsically "last" about them, but I usually leave them to the end because I find them easier to nominate at the time. By the process

Provide for functional extensions.

of elimination, the service subsystems will be responsible for whatever is not handled by the dialogue or model subsystems that border the service subsystems and which have already been defined. This process is subject to the additional constraint that the service subsystems must provide the units of functional growth, change, and configuration.

The following list of services from the behavior model is the reasonable place to start:

- Services
- Process Queries
- Change Inventory
- Administer Members
- Administer Cash Drawer:
- Check Inventory
- Change Users
- Define Reports
- Process Bills

I will nominate each as a service subsystem in the architecture (Figure 10.7).

When we developed the services list, thought was given to handling extensions, so I can take the service subsystem identities as good enough for now. However, having the picture to look at made a problem visible: namely, how to arrange the channels between the dialogues and the service components. Changing which services are available to an individual actor, and adding new services in the future, are common change cases. Those changes will take place on either side of the channels that connect the services to the dialogues. The question is, do we need one channel (that is, one set of messages) for each kind of service subsystem, or can we use the same channel for all service subsystems?

The advantage of the one-channel approach is that adding a new service will not require changes to the external interfaces of the dialogue subsystems. Whether it requires changes to the internal interfaces of the dialogue subsystems depends on where we allocate the responsibility for keeping the lists of available actions for each service subsystem. The most flexible arrangement would be for the service subsystems to provide the command choices to the dialogues. This would make adding a new service a matter of registering the service with the dialogues that will offer that service. This behavior allocation scheme should be kept in mind when we allocate the detailed behavior components to the architecture subsystems.

Always design for the big picture. We have completed our first pass at the nominations for a system architecture. A key aspect of the process was the continual reference to the growth and change

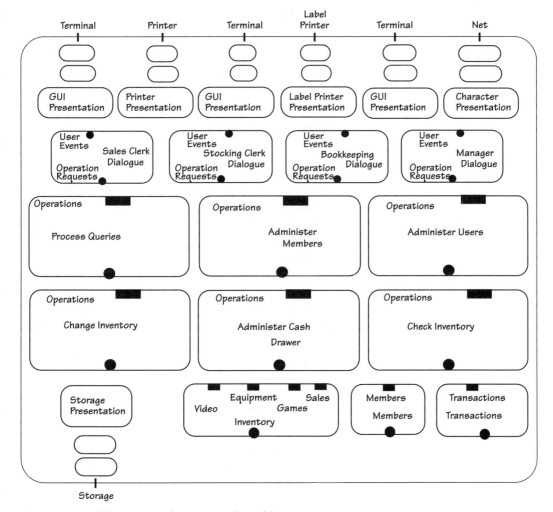

Figure 10.7 Adding service subsystems to the architecture

issues. This method is appropriate because it is in the definition of the system architecture that the "ility" attributes (maintainability, extensibility, modularity) get designed into the product. By being aware of the change cases while we are nominating subsystems and allocating responsibilities, we increase the likelihood that the design is as modular as it needs to be. Being good engineers, however, requires that we explicitly demonstrate that our design nominations meet all the requirements. For that reason, we should carry out the evaluation described next.

10.3 EVALUATING THE PRELIMINARY ARCHITECTURE

The inputs to the preliminary architecture included use cases and change cases, a simple system state model, and a service list for a behavior model. If the only behavior model available is the service model, then the evaluations we can do at this point consist of qualitative walkthroughs of the use and change cases on the architecture.

10.3.1 Completeness

Simple evaluations, done early, are very helpful.

As a first check, I suggest that the architecture diagram be examined for general completeness. Some of the things that are readily visible include whether there is sufficient machinery provided to handle the external actors and peripherals, and whether all the connections that cross the system boundary are accounted for. When there are multiple actors, we should see that there is a representative of each of the major types of actors. In the diagram in Figure 10.7, the path from external actor through the actor dialogue subsystems is pretty clear.

The other aspect of completeness that can be easily evaluated is whether all the "things" that the system manipulates have been accounted for. Here, there are some problems. For example, the existence of a cash drawer, users, and reports are implied by the names of the service subsystems that are supposed to manipulate them. Those things do not appear in the model subsystem names. I can add them as model subsystems.

The next question is, whether these new model components need to be separated from the services that manipulate them? There are two criteria for separating a service subsystem from its model. One is whether there is more than one service that accesses the model and the other is whether the service and the model might be changed at different times. Evaluating on the first criteria requires a more detailed behavior model than we have right now, so to be safe, I will keep the service subsystems separate from the model subsystems. I can collapse them into their service subsystems if later evaluation shows that they are tightly coupled (Figure 10.8).

10.3.2 Evaluating against User Requirements

Evaluating the ability of the architecture to provide the use cases can be done by walking through the use cases. I recommend that this be done quickly. If the walkthroughs are done in great detail, the effort is equivalent to doing a collaboration-responsibility behavior model with the subsystems as objects. While this is feasible, it reduces the independence of things that address the user requirements (the behavior model) and things that address the development sponsor requirements (the architecture). So these walkthroughs should be very brisk.

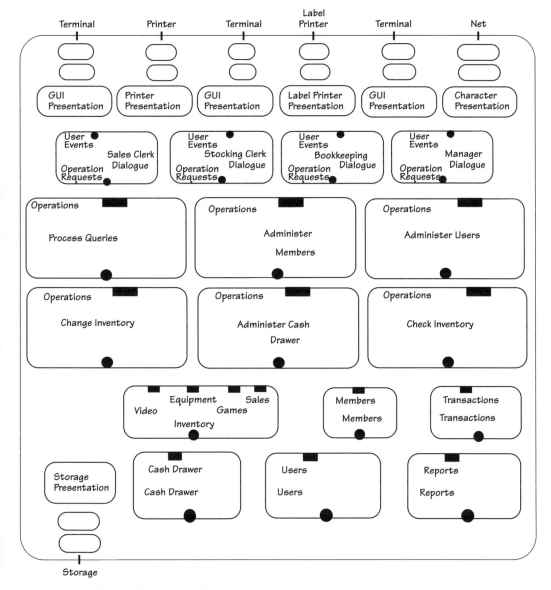

Figure 10.8 Adding additional model subsystems to the architecture

The use cases and their actors are listed in Table 10.1.

The question is, for each use case, can we start with an actor and see a path through the subsystems that looks like it will provide the required behavior? At this stage *looks like* means that the subsystem names imply they can do what is needed. Take for example the use case for renting a video (Figure 10.9).

	Manager	Bookkeeper	Sales	Stock
Query inventory for a title	X		X	X
Open membership	X		X	
Rent a tape, or other item			X	
Return a tape			X	
Sell an item			X	
Verify membership	X		X	
Request list of over due items	X		X	
Request a list of all rented items	X		X	
Add new titles, copies to inventory				X
Remove old titles				X
Check actual inventory against system inventory			X	
Request reports	X	X		
Request daily activity summary	X	X		
Request inventory listings	X		X	X
Request activity summaries	X	X		
Administer users	X			
Administer members	X		X	
Administer member rental limits	X			
Request member activity	X		X	
Edit inventory item	X			
Edit types and categories	X			
Administer specials	X			
Close and reconcile cash drawer	X		X	
Start the cash drawer	X		X	

Table 10.1
List of use case titles sorted by actor sources

The walkthrough thought process might go like this. The Rent a video use case begins with the Sales Clerk. The Presentation and Sales Clerk Dialogue subsystems should handle the direct interaction with the user. The queries about the video and whether the customer is a member can be handled by the Process Queries

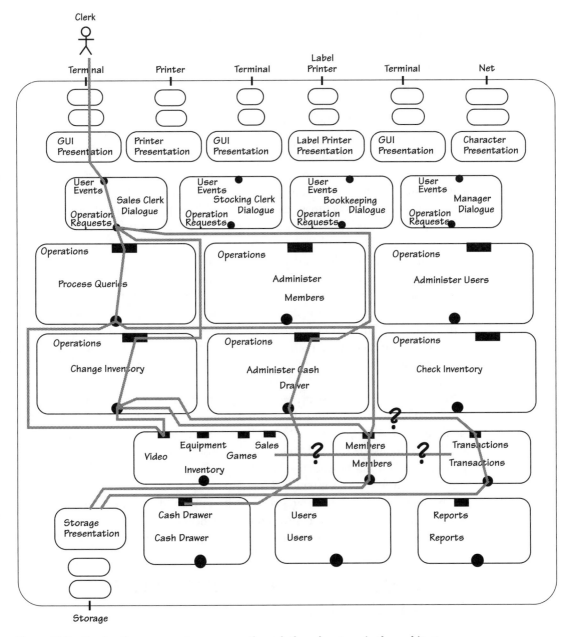

Figure 10.9 Tracing the response to a use case through the subsystems in the architecture

subsystem talking to the Inventory and Customers subsystems. For the actual rental transaction, it looks like the only path is through the Change Inventory subsystem. None of the other services look like they "know" enough to help out with rentals.

Renting a video requires modifying inventory, marking the customer and recording the transaction. The problem is that Change Inventory does not sound like it should be involved in changing customers and transactions. So, how do we modify the current, implied behavior to provide this use case?

Before addressing that question, the remainder of the use case can be handled by having the Sales Clerk Dialogue handle keeping the bill of sale items and totals. The payment can be handled by having the dialogue communicate with the Administer Cash Drawer service.

Structure is dictated by the change cases.

Returning to the problem of getting the model updated with the rental transaction, the actual rental behavior could be allocated at least three different ways: the dialogue subsystem could manipulate the video, customer, and transaction objects directly; the Change Inventory subsystem could be expanded to handle the coordination of video, customer, and transaction objects; or the Inventory model itself could be responsible for updating all the necessary components. Which of the three possibilities should be chosen depends on the rules for making a rental change. If, for example, the rental rules and the associations that must be updated can change with the actor or with the store in which the video is rented, then the first option looks like the best because the dialogue will change when the store or actor change. If the rental rules are part of the basic business rules for this system and only change when the business changes, then the third option looks best. If I wanted to use the second option, having a service manage the updating, then I would want to have it called out as a separate service subsystem.

For now, I will assume that the rental algorithm changes only when the business is changed. I can use the third allocation option: I will give the customer and videos involved in a transaction to the Inventory subsystem and let it and the system state model be responsible for updating all the necessary components and relationships. This decision should be documented as an additional responsibility in the description of the Inventory subsystem and the system state model objects.

The above discussion illustrates the activities involved in evaluating and modifying an architecture diagram. It also shows the benefits that can be achieved with this kind of analysis, even at this very preliminary stage of the design.

10.4 ALLOCATING MODEL COMPONENTS TO ARCHITECTURE

This is the detailed architecture development.

The architecture, up to this point, has been shaped primarily by the change cases. The user required behavior has not been accounted for in any very explicit way. In the previous section, it was assumed that there was no detailed behavior model available. Here, that model is available. We have available a complete set of object specifications which, when taken together, provide all of the behavior and information required by the users. The form of those specifications should be either collaboration responsibility specifications or interface views.

Our task now is to merge the architecture and behavior models to produce a system that successfully addresses both the user and development-sponsor requirements. The process requires a set of behavior allocation decisions. Inputs are the list of objects from the static and behavior models and the architecture subsystem nominations. The results of my allocation decisions are shown in two ways: each analysis model component is followed by the names of the architecture subsystems to which I allocated them (Table 10.2); and each architecture subsystem is followed by the analysis model components it contains (Table 10.3).

The architecture subsystems are as follows:

1 Sales clerk dialogue

2 Stocking clerk dialogue

3 Bookkeeping dialogue

4 Manager dialogue

5 Process queries

6 Change inventory

7 Administer members

8 Administer cash drawer

9 Check inventory

10 Change users

11 Define reports

12 Process bills

13 Inventory

14 Members

15 Transactions

16 Cash drawer

17 Users

18 Reports

Subsystem	Behavior model components
Dialog Components	
Cash drawer dialogue	Sales clerk dialogue, manager dialogue
Inventory dialogue	Stocking clerk dialogue
Item administration dialogue	Manager dialogue
Limit administration dialogue	Manager dialogue

Table 10.2

Allocation of behavior model components

**Table 10.2
Allocation of
behavior
model
components
(continued)**

Subsystem	Behavior model components
Member administration dialogue	Sales clerk dialogue, manager dialogue
Membership dialogue	Sales clerk dialogue, manager dialogue
Query dialogue	Sales clerk dialogue, stocking clerk dialogue, manager dialogue, bookkeeping dialogue
Rental dialogue	Sales clerk dialogue, manager dialogue
Report dialogue	Sales clerk dialogue, stocking clerk dialogue, bookkeeping dialogue, manager dialogue
Return dialogue	Sales clerk dialogue, manager dialogue
Sales dialogue	Sales clerk dialogue, manager dialogue
Special administration dialogue	Manager dialogue
Stocking dialogue	Stocking clerk dialogue
Top dialogue	Sales clerk dialogue, stocking clerk dialogue, bookkeeping dialogue, manager dialogue
Type administration dialogue	Manager dialogue
User administration dialogue	Manager dialogue

Service Components

Check-in	Change inventory
Check-out	Change inventory
Edit categories	Change inventory
Edit inventory	Change inventory
Edit limits	Change inventory
Edit members	Administer members
Edit specials	Change inventory
Edit users	Change users
ID server	Inventory
Inventory accumulator	Check inventory
Inventory adder	Inventory
Inventory deleter	Inventory
Lookup service	Process queries
Pricer	Change inventory
Report engine	Process queries
Report formatter	Process queries
Translator	Process queries, administer members, administer users, change inventory, define reports, process bills

Subsystem	Behavior model components
Model Components	
Active transactions	Transactions
Cash drawer	Cash drawer
Cash drawer activity log	Cash drawer
Category	Inventory
Category list	Inventory
Inventory	Inventory
Item	Inventory
Limit	Inventory
Limit list	Inventory
Member	Members
Member list	Members
Report	Reports
Report list	Reports
Sale item	Inventory
Special	Inventory
Special list	Inventory
Transaction log	Transactions
Transaction	Transactions
User	Users
User List	Users

Table 10.2
Allocation of
behavior
model
components
(continued)

Subsystem	Behavior model components
Sales clerk dialogue	Cash drawer dialogue, member administration dialogue, membership dialogue, query dialogue, rental dialogue, report dialogue, return dialogue, sales dialogue, top dialogue
Stocking clerk dialogue	Inventory dialogue, query dialogue, report dialogue, top dialogue
Bookkeeping dialogue	Report dialogue, top dialogue, query dialogue
Manager dialogue	Cash drawer dialogue, member administration dialogue, membership dialogue, query dialogue, rental dialogue, report dialogue, return dialogue, sales dialogue top dialogue, item administration dialogue, limit administration dialogue, type administration dialogue, user administration dialogue

Table 10.3
Content of
architectural
subsystems

Table 10.3
Content of
architectural
subsystems
(continued)

Subsystem	Behavior model components
Process queries	Lookup service, report engine, report formatter
Change inventory	Check-in, check-out, edit categories, edit inventory, edit limits, edit specials, prices
Administer members	Edit members
Administer cash drawer	
Check inventory	Inventory accumulator
Change users	Edit users
Define reports	
Process bills	
Inventory	ID server, inventory adder, inventory deleter, category, category list, inventory, item, limit, limit list, sale item, special, special list
Members	Member, member list
Transactions	Transaction log, active rentals
Cash drawer	Cash drawer, cash drawer activity log
Users	User, user list
Reports	Report script, report list

10.4.1 Organizing Channels

Channel content comes from the interface views allocated to each subsystem.

With the allocation decisions made, we can derive the interfaces for the architecture subsystems directly from the model components that were allocated to each subsystem. Each message whose receiver object is in a different subsystem from its sender object becomes part of the interface between the subsystems holding the sender and the receiver objects. A sample of the process is shown in Figure 10.10.

The messages between Sales Clerk Dialogue and Change Inventory include startCheckOut "itemID, customerName," itemAvailable "itemID," and record "aTransaction." The messages between Change Inventory and Inventory include InStock "itemID," and return "inventoryItem." If the process is repeated for all allocated objects, we will have the "real" collaborations and interfaces as dictated by the object allocation decisions I made. The subsystem collaborations that result from the allocation of the objects in the example are shown in Figure 10.11. Only subsystems that have an object allocated to them are shown. The example does not include all use case models. The lines in the figure indicate that there is some communication between the subsystems. By looking at the Interface views, we can

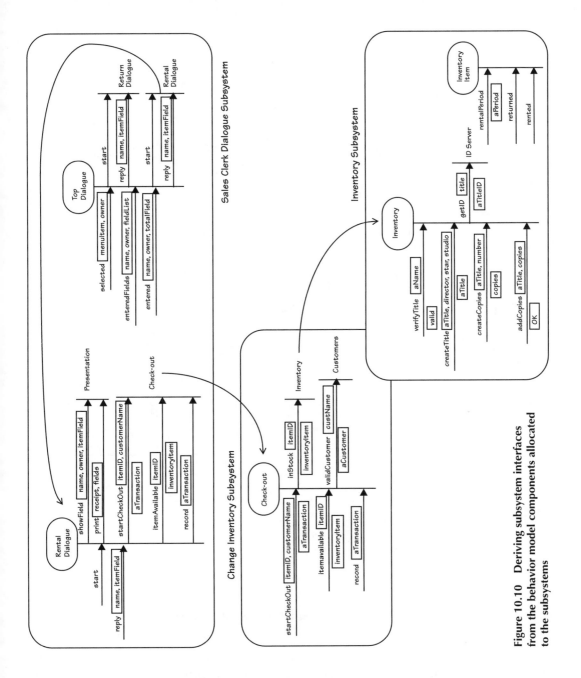

Figure 10.10 Deriving subsystem interfaces from the behavior model components allocated to the subsystems

populate those lines with actual messages. Note that I removed the channel connector symbols from the subsystems. I did that because, at this point, there are no channels. There are just messages that need to be carried between subsystems. Organization into channels will come next. Figure 10.12 shows the collected subsystem interfaces.

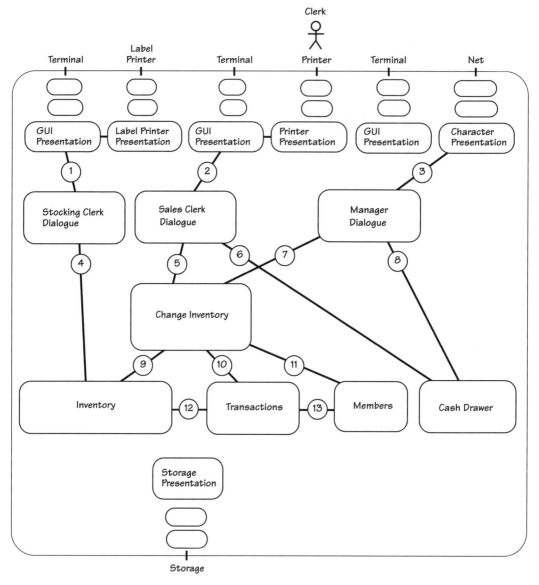

Figure 10.11 Deriving subsystem collaborations from the behavior model components allocated to the subsystems

Channels deserve some design attention, too.

This collection gives us a view of the messages that we have not seen before. Look at interfaces 1, 2, and 3 in Figure 10.12. We have gone to some trouble to separate the presentation components from the rest of the application. The motive was that presentations may be reusable within this application and even across multiple applications. If that is to happen, the interface to all the presentation components must be the same. Looking at the interfaces to our three GUI presentation

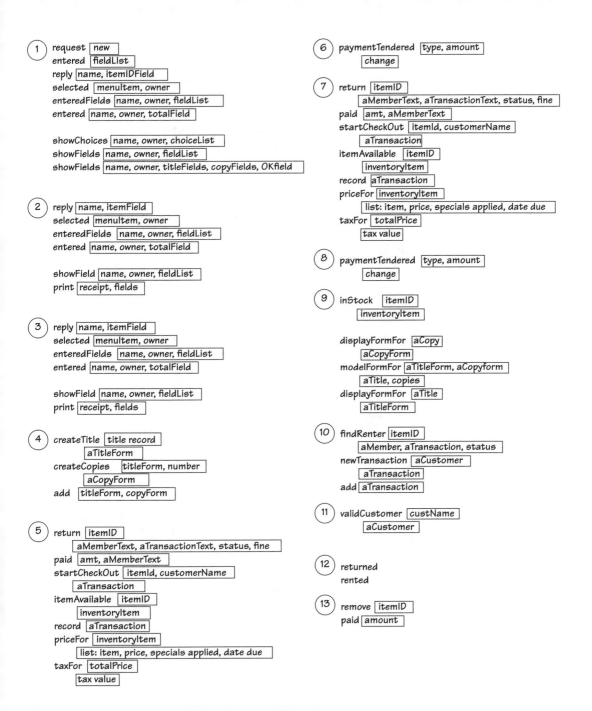

① request new
entered fieldList
reply name, itemIDField
selected menuItem, owner
enteredFields name, owner, fieldList
entered name, owner, totalField

showChoices name, owner, choiceList
showFields name, owner, fieldList
showFields name, owner, titleFields, copyFields, OKfield

② reply name, itemField
selected menuItem, owner
enteredFields name, owner, fieldList
entered name, owner, totalField

showField name, owner, fieldList
print receipt, fields

③ reply name, itemField
selected menuItem, owner
enteredFields name, owner, fieldList
entered name, owner, totalField

showField name, owner, fieldList
print receipt, fields

④ createTitle title record
aTitleForm
createCopies titleForm, number
aCopyForm
add titleForm, copyForm

⑤ return itemID
aMemberText, aTransactionText, status, fine
paid amt, aMemberText
startCheckOut itemId, customerName
aTransaction
itemAvailable itemID
inventoryItem
record aTransaction
priceFor inventoryItem
list: item, price, specials applied, date due
taxFor totalPrice
tax value

⑥ paymentTendered type, amount
change

⑦ return itemID
aMemberText, aTransactionText, status, fine
paid amt, aMemberText
startCheckOut itemId, customerName
aTransaction
itemAvailable itemID
inventoryItem
record aTransaction
priceFor inventoryItem
list: item, price, specials applied, date due
taxFor totalPrice
tax value

⑧ paymentTendered type, amount
change

⑨ inStock itemID
inventoryItem

displayFormFor aCopy
aCopyForm
modelFormFor aTitleForm, aCopyform
aTitle, copies
displayFormFor aTitle
aTitleForm

⑩ findRenter itemID
aMember, aTransaction, status
newTransaction aCustomer
aTransaction
add aTransaction

⑪ validCustomer custName
aCustomer

⑫ returned
rented

⑬ remove itemID
paid amount

Figure 10.12   Message content of the subsystem collaborations

subsystems, we see similarity in the messages, but they are not exactly the same. A single set of messages should be chosen. These new messages should be mapped back to the behavior model objects and taken back to the relevant interaction diagrams. The diagrams should be redone using the new message sets for the components.

Stocking Clerk Dialogue has an interface with Inventory because of my decision to allocate the Inventory Adder component to the Inventory subsystem. It has resulted in inconsistent communication patterns: Sales Clerk Dialogue uses Change Inventory to manipulate Inventory, while the Stocking Clerk Dialogue goes directly to the Inventory subsystem. Inventory Adder is a problem that should be fixed.

The requests for translation services in interface 9 are another artifact of putting Inventory Adder in Inventory. As a result the messages in 9 are not very cohesive.

The point of the discussion above is to indicate the value of taking this interface-centered approach. Many inconsistencies were found that could well have gone unnoticed if the message interfaces were not explicitly visible.

After determining that the messages are sufficient and consistent, they should be organized into channels. The named channels are as an important part of the architecture as the subsystems. The channels are the basis for subsystem reuse within a single application and across multiple applications.

Channel Definitions

Consider examples of channel definition. The first is a channel for the Presentation subsystems. The goal is to have a single channel for all subsystems. To arrive at that channel, I will combine the messages from interfaces 1–3 in Figure 10.12 into one consistent superset of the current messages. It looks like "entered" and "selected" should be sufficient on the input side. On the output side, "showChoices," "showFields," and "Print" should cover the ground. All of these messages will use "fields" as arguments. Given the simplicity of the message names, the field objects will have to carry a significant amount of information about allowable operations on the fields and perhaps some relative geometry information.

I will nominate two channels, Presentation Input and Presentation Output. Their specification might look like Table 10.4.

	Channel	Message Content	Type[a]	Medium[a]
Table 10.4 Channel specification for prasentation subsystems	Presentation Input	Entered (name, owner, fieldList) Selected (choiceField, owner)	Synchronous or asynchronous	
	Presentation Output	ShowChoices (name, owner, choiceFieldList) ShowFields (name, owner, fieldList) Print (owner, fieldList)	Synchronous or asynchronous	

a. The Type and Medium parts of the channel specification will have to wait until the decisions about allocation to implementation units have been made. The same message content can be implemented on many media.

The other example is taken from the messages in interfaces 5–8. These messages are concerned with getting rental items checked in and out. In the current design, the check-in and check-out behaviors are housed together in the same subsystem. If that were always the case, it would be appropriate to create one channel called Check in/out. In large video stores, however, check-in is carried out using a separate work station. Because of that possible future configuration, I will nominate two separate channels, Check-in Channel and Check-out Channel. I will also add in the payment message and will change the behavior allocation so that payment is routed through the Change Inventory subsystem Table 10.5.

Table 10.5
Channel
specificaiton
for applica-
tion-level
channels

Channel	Message Content	Type[a]	Medium[a]
Check-Out Channel	StartCheckOut (itemID, customerName) returns (aTransaction)	Synchronous or asynchronous	
	ItemAvailable (itemID) returns (inventoryItem)		
	PriceFor (inventoryItem) returns (list: item, price, specials applied, date due)		
	Completed (aTransaction)		
	PaymentTendered (type, amount) returns (change)		
Check-In Channel	Return (itemID) returns (aTransaction)	Synchronous or asynchronous	
	Paid (amount, memberText)		
	Completed (aTransaction)		
	PaymentTendered (type, amount) returns (change)		

a. The Type and Medium parts of the channel specification will have to wait until the decisions about allocation to implementation units have been made. The same message content can be implemented on many media.

In adding the payment handling behaviors to the change inventory subsystem, another problem came to light. The name I gave to the service subsystem that handled the inventory change requests was "Change Inventory." Because of that name, I originally allocated the responsibility for coordinating inventory users and transactions to the dialogue subsystem. This resulted in complex dependencies in the dialogue subsystems. I reallocated the transaction coordination responsibility to the Change Inventory subsystem, but now it was doing more than changing inventory: the name was a bad choice. Because the name of a subsystem, or any component, influences the kinds of responsibilities that will be allocated to it, it should be adjusted as the role of the component changes during the allocation and evaluation process. In this example, the new name, which I believe better reflects the kinds of responsibilities I want to allocate to the subsystem, is "Process Product Transactions."

A flexible, effective design takes a lot of work.

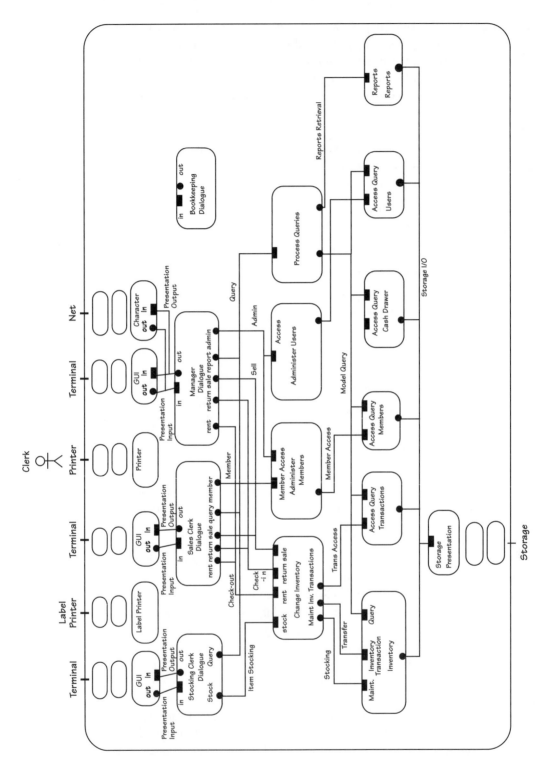

Figure 10.13 Architecture diagram for the video store system showing the named channels connecting the subsystems

With that name I feel more comfortable allocating responsibilities to it for handling all of the processing required to handle transactions related to products.

A complete architecture diagram with all channels named is shown in Figure 10.13.

The content of each channel is shown in Table 10.6.

Table 10.6
Channel
specifications

Channel	Message Content	Type[a]	Medium[a]
Check-Out	StartCheckOut (itemID, customerName) returns (aTransaction)		
	ItemAvailable (type, name, attribute-value list) returns (inventoryItem)		
	PriceFor (inventoryItem) returns (list: item, price, specials applied, date due)		
	Completed (aTransaction)		
	PaymentTendered (type, amount) returns (change)		
Check-In	Return (itemID) returns (aTransaction)		
	Completed (aTransaction)		
	Paid (amount, memberText)		
	PaymentTendered (type, amount) returns (change)		
Presentation Input	Entered (name, owner, fieldList)		
	Selected (choiceField, owner)		
Presentation Output	ShowChoices (name, owner, choiceFieldList)		
	ShowFields (name, owner, fieldList)		
	Print (owner, fieldList)		
Sell	StartSale (itemID) returns (aTransaction)		
	Completed (aTransaction)		
	ItemAvailable (itemID) returns (inventoryItem)		
	PriceFor (aTransaction) returns (list: item, price, specials applied)		
	PaymentTendered (type, amount) returns (change)		
Stocking	Add (type, itemText) returns (itemID, status)		
	Remove (itemID) returns (status)		

Table 10.6
Channel
specifications
(continued)

Channel	Message Content	Type[a]	Medium[a]
Item Stocking (example of interface that will not survive the port to equipment rental)	CreateTitle (title record) returns (aTitle)		
	CreateCopies (aTitle, number) returns (status)		
	Add (aTitle, copy list) returns (status)		
	Delete (copy list) returns (status)		
	GetItem (itemID) returns (anItem)		
Transfer	GetItem (itemID) returns (anItem)		
	ReplaceItem (anItem) returns (status)		
Query	Find (itemID, queryID, criteria List) returns (queryID, item list)		
	TypesAvaialble (queryID) returns (queryID, item type list)		
Storage I/O	GetDescriptionFor (type, name, attribute-value list) returns (description list)		
	GetConnectedDescriptionsFor (type, name, attribute-value list) returns (description list)		
	GetObject (ID) returns (anObject)		
	GetConnectedObjects (ID) returns (collection of objects)		
	SaveDescription (type, name, description) returns (status)		
	SaveObject (anObject) returns (status)		
Report Retrieval	GetTitlesFor (category) returns (title list)		
	GetReport (category, title) returns (report script)		

a. The Type and Medium parts of the channel specification will have to wait until the decisions about allocation to implementation units have been made. The same message content can be implemented on many media.

10.5 EVALUATING THE DETAILED ARCHITECTURE (BOXLESS)

The three questions that should be asked of each change case walkthrough are:

1 Which subsystems are directly impacted by the change case?
2 Can the interface channels remain unchanged through the change case?
3 Are there behaviors and information in the impacted subsystems that are not directly related to the change case?

10.5.1 Portability Evaluation

Portability is the easiest evaluation to make.

Change Database

Only the Storage Presentation subsystem should be impacted. The Storage channel has no messages that are dependent on the particular database used, so it should remain unchanged when the database is changed. Storage Presentation should have no behaviors that are not connected with moving things between the database and the application. I conclude that this architecture can adequately support this change case.

Change Presentation

This evaluation is the same as the previous example, but applied to the user presentation subsystems. The conclusion should be the same.

Change Computer Platforms

This evaluation is a superset of the previous two change cases. None of the behaviors mentioned in the behavior modeling task and none of the subsystem interfaces appear to have any dependency on the platform or the operating system. By itself, this implies that there should be no impact of changing the platform or the operating system on any of the main application subsystems. To ensure that this is the case we should specify that there can be no operating system calls in any of the application-level subsystems. Operating system, and, thus computer platform, dependencies should be limited to the device and virtual device subsystems at the system boundary. For subsystems implemented as operating-system tasks, which have not yet been decided, the scheduling of the tasks is probably provided by the operating system. The application code inside the subsystems should have little or no exposure to the scheduling functionality.

If these constraints can be met, the system should support the Change Platform change case quite well.

10.5.2 New Configurations, Reuse

Configure for an equipment rental system   Potentially, a large change for the system. In fact, it is large enough that it should probably be handled with a separate design study. For this example, I will use this change case to demonstrate some points about robustness in channels. Looking at the architecture in Figure 10.13, the overall structure should be adequate. Clearly, the things in Inventory will change, but it might be possible to reuse the Inventory subsystem itself and the service subsystems. So, for this change case, we might assume that the Inventory Subsystem will be most affected by the change.

The second question is, will the channels hide the change? Looking at the Item Stocking channel, we see messages like "createTitle" and "createCopies." These messages are not appropriate for the equipment rental system, so the answer is that the current channel will not hide the change. One fix is to make a new set of messages that can be interpreted in either domain. The "generic" channel messages could be interpreted back to the specific domain messages by the interface machinery inside each subsystem. The generic messages that might work in both domains are shown in Table 10.7.

Table 10.7
Application
specific and
generic mes-
sage names

Video Store Domain Messages	Generic Domain Messages
CreateTitle (title record) returns (aName)	CreateName (name record)
CreateCopies (aTitle, number)	CreateItem (aName, number)
Add (aTitle, copy list) returns (status)	Add (aName, item list)
Delete (copy list) returns (status)	Delete (item list)
GetItem (itemID) returns (anItem)	GetItem (itemID)

10.5.3 Extensions

Add custom report definition capability: defining reports at run-time requires that the user be able to see all of the things that can be reported on. The subjects of the reports will not change. I would implement this change case by adding a new service subsystem, called Define Reports. This service subsystem would have the needed access to all the model subsystems.

Are there any existing subsystems that would be impacted by the addition of this new service? Without doing a behavior model for the use case of defining a report, which would be a good idea, it appears that defining reports would have a fairly complex user dialogue. I would expect that there should be a change to any dialogue subsystem that needs to offer the report definition capability to its users. There is already a repository for reports in the system. It would be very convenient if the form of the script for canned reports were the same as the form for the custom reports. So the answer to the questions seems to be that only the dialogue subsystems will be impacted by the addition of the new service.

Can the existing interfaces hide the change case? The convention established in this design is to provide a separate channel on the dialogue subsystems for each major operation. Following this convention would mean that adding the new service would require a new channel, Report Definition, on each dialogue subsystem that wishes to offer the service. On the other side of the new service, it looks like the existing Query channel, which all model subsystems offer, should be sufficient to allow the Define Reports subsystem to obtain the "meta data" it needs, about what can be reported on.

Finally, Define Reports needs to be able to manipulate the report scripts in the Reports subsystem. The only channel available for Reports is Report Retrieval, which has getTitles and getReport messages. These are not sufficient for creating and editing reports. I would like not to have to change model subsystems, or their channels, when services are added, so I will have to fix these channels now to support this future service. There are two choices for the fix: add more messages to the existing channel, or create a new channel. There are not a great many new messages needed, but I find the idea of separating normal operations from editing operations appealing, so I will add a new channel, called Edit Reports. As a first guess about message content, I will nominate, getTitles, getReport, returnReport, and addReport. With these messages as suggestions, I should return to the behavior model and describe the interactions necessary to actually carry out report definition.

Changes in the architecture may result in changes in the behavior allocation model.

The bottom line for this change case is that I need to fix one existing subsystem, Reports, now to support the change. I have decided that when the change is made it will require adding dialogue components and a new channel to one or more dialogue subsystems. No changes should be necessary in any other subsystem.

10.5.4 Integration

Integrate with accounting system   Integration with other systems, an accounting system in this case, is a very common requirement and change case for systems. The corporate accounting system would appear as another actor or as a data interface to our video store system. I will assume that the accounting system will only be interested in the financial transactions in the video store. It would be nice if the change case could be handled without changing any of the existing application-level subsystems, for example, by altering only the Storage Presentation subsystem. This subsystem already has detailed knowledge about the objects being stored and

Future changes can have a big impact on current structure.

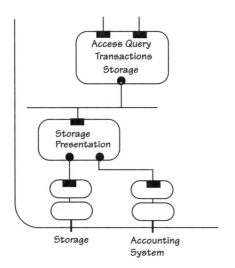

Figure 10.14
Integration with the accounting system using a storage presentation

Figure 10.15

Integration
with the
accounting
system using
an accounting
presentation
subsystem

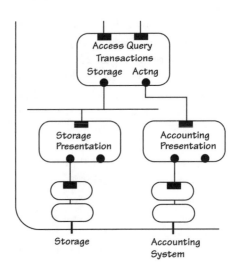

retrieved; perhaps we could add some extra behaviors about recording the appropriate transactions for the accounting systems as they pass through for regular storage.
While that avoids changing the Transactions subsystem, it does mix storage concerns with accounting integration concerns (Figure 10.14).

Another possibility would be to add a new presentation for the new actor or data
interface. The Accounting Presentation subsystem would be a peer to the present
Storage Presentation. This would separate the storage and integration concerns, but

Figure 10.16

Integration
with the
accounting
system using
a storage
dialogue

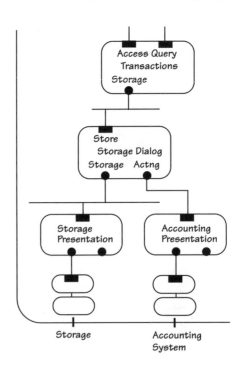

ARCHITECTURE EXAMPLE | CHAPTER 10

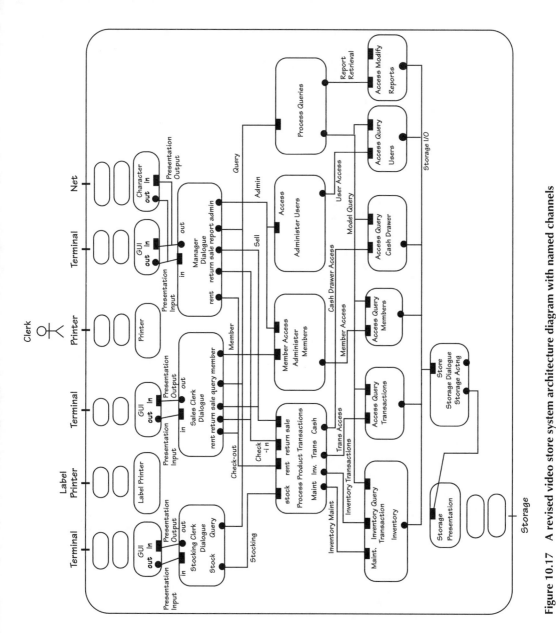

Figure 10.17 A revised video store system architecture diagram with named channels

it would require a change to the Transactions subsystem to be able to talk to the new presentation (Figure 10.15).

Yet a third possibility is to add a dialogue subsystem explicitly to handle routing decisions. This would be particularly appropriate if there were several future integrations with different outside systems. The dialogue subsystem would be the component that would absorb all the changes required for integrations with other sources and sinks of information (Figure 10.16).

The third option, adding a Storage Dialogue, does the best job of localizing the effects of change cases that involve directing information to other places, although none of the options offered is terribly disruptive. The final nomination, therefore, is to include the Storage Dialogue in the initial system architecture to support the future change case of integration with the accounting system.

The architecture diagram including all the changes discussed to this point is shown in Figure 10.17. The revised channel specifications are shown in Table 10.8. As we still have not assigned subsystems to actual implementation units, the Type and Medium fields of each channel specification are still empty.

Table 10.8 Revised channel specifications

Channel	Message Content	Type	Medium
Presentation-Dialogue Level Channels			
Presentation Input	Entered (name, owner, fieldList)	Synchronous or asynchronous	
	Selected (choiceField, owner)		
Presentation Output	ShowChoices (name, owner, choiceFieldList)	Synchronous or asynchronous	
	ShowFields (name, owner, fieldList)		
	Print (owner, fieldList)		
Dialogue-Service Level Channels			
Administration	GetNames (type) returns (name list)	Synchronous or asynchronous	
	GetItem (type, name) returns (item)		
	Return (type, item) returns (status)		
	DeleteItem (type, item) returns (status)		
	AddItem (type, item) returns (status)		
Check-in Channel	Return (itemID) returns (aTransaction)	Synchronous or asynchronous	
	Completed (aTransaction)		
	Paid (amount, memberText)		
	PaymentTendered (type, amount) returns (change)		
Check-out Channel	StartCheckOut (itemID, customerName) returns (aTransaction)	Synchronous or asynchronous	
	ItemAvailable (type, name, attribute-value list) returns (inventoryItem)		
	PriceFor (inventoryItem) returns (list: item, price, specials applied, date due)		
	Completed (aTransaction)		
	PaymentTendered (type, amount) returns (change)		

Channel	Message Content	Type	Medium
Member	Verify (a name) returns (member status)		
	Edit (member name) returns (member form)		
	Return (member form) returns (status)		
	Remove (member name, ID) returns (status)		
	NewMember returns (new member form)		
	AddNew (member form) returns status		
Query	GetReportNames returns (report name list)		
	RunReport (report name) returns (field list)		
	ExecuteQuery (query text) returns (field list)		
Sell	StartSale (itemID) returns (aTransaction)		
	Completed (aTransaction)		
	ItemAvailable (itemID) returns (inventoryItem)		
	PriceFor (aTransaction) returns (list: item, price, specials applied)		
	PaymentTendered (type, amount) returns (change)		
Stocking	Add (type, itemText) returns (itemID, status)		
	Remove (itemID) returns (status)		

Table 10.8
Revised
channel
specifications
(continued)

Service-Model Level Channels

Channel	Message Content	Type	Medium
Cash Drawer Access	CashTransaction (amount, amountTendered) returns (change)		
	CashIn (amount) returns (balance)		
	CashOut (amount) returns (balance)		
	Balance returns (balance)		
Inventory Maintenance	CreateName (name record) returns (aName)		
	CreateItem (aName, number)		
	Add (aName, item list) returns (status)		
	Delete (item list) returns (status)		
	GetItem (itemID) returns (anItem)		
Inventory Transactions	GetItem (itemID) returns (anItem)		
	ReplaceItem (anItem) returns (status)		

Table 10.8
Revised
channel
specifications
(continued)

Channel	Message Content	Type	Medium
Member Access, Transaction Access, User Access	GetNames returns (name list)		
	Get (name) returns (item)		
	Put (item) returns (status)		
	Add (item) returns (status)		
	Delete (item) returns (status)		
	GetTemplate (type) returns (template)		
Model Query	Find (itemID, criteria List) returns (item list)		
	TypesAvaialble ( ) returns (item type list)		
Report Retrieval	GetTitlesFor (category) returns (title list)		
	GetReport (category, title) returns (report script)		
Storage I/O	GetDescriptionFor (type, name, attribute-value list) returns (description list)		
	GetConnectedDescriptionsFor (type, name, attribute-value list) returns (description list)		
	GetObject (ID) returns (anObject)		
	GetConnectedObjects (ID) returns (collection of objects)		
	SaveDescription (type, name, description) returns (status)		
	SaveObject (anObject) returns (status)		
Edit Reports (future)	GetTitles returns (title list)		
	GetReport (report name) returns (report script)		
	ReturnReport (report script) returns (status)		
	AddReport (report script) returns (status)		

To this point, an architecture has been specified that is not concerned with how the system is allocated to its actual implementation units. Allocation to hardware and other implementation subsystems is discussed next.

There are no right answers, only trade-offs.

You may notice that this is not a perfect design. My intention is not to show a perfect design but to demonstrate a process for evaluating designs and for finding and fixing problems. This example is full of problems, some of which we have talked about, a few which have been fixed, and some which have been left as exercises for the interested reader. The fact that the interested reader can find additional problems with the design is a indication of the effectiveness of the notations and the techniques.

10.6 ALLOCATING ARCHITECTURE SUBSYSTEMS ACROSS HARDWARE BOUNDARIES

It is very common for the basic hardware architecture decisions to be made very early in any project. In this example, a typical hardware selection would be to have PC or point-of-sale workstations for users and a single server per store (for the single store case). Options for multiple stores and multiple servers will be discussed in the evaluation section.

A decision that is often made early in a project is the selection of a communication medium for the hardware components. For computers the usual medium is a network. The selection of which one is often dictated by local standards. If the choice has not been made, it can be left until the behavior allocation to hardware has been completed and the capacity demand is known. In this example, we will use a very common hardware architecture: one or more servers serving multiple workstations or point-of-sale systems. The hardware architecture is pictured in Figure 10.18.

Now make the system real.

Every hardware boundary is also the boundary for a software subsystem, so the hardware architecture, showing computers connected by a network, is also the top-level software architecture picture. We can now allocate software subsystems to the hardware-architecture subsystems.

The distribution of the system functionality to hardware units is a behavior allocation decision. In this case, the behavior units being allocated are the subsystems of the boxless architecture. I have two design goals in allocating subsystems: one is to balance the processing evenly between client and server; the other is to provide a consistent view of inventory to all users. A direct way to achieve the latter is to provide a single inventory model for all users, that is, put the model subsystems on the server machine. A way to achieve the former is to put everything else on the client machines.

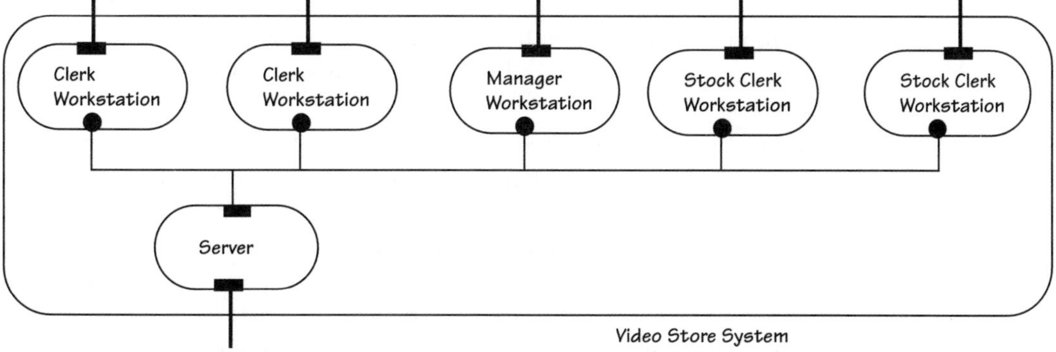

Figure 10.18   Architecture diagram showing hardware nodes as subsystems

10.6.1 Workstation Architecture

With that as a starting point, the next question is: How should we configure work-stations for each type of user? All workstations could be set up to handle all users. In that case, each workstation would have available all subsystems except the model subsystems. That is not very interesting for demonstration purposes, so I will try another approach. I can configure each workstation for a specific user. The dialogue subsystems were set up to serve all the needs of each kind of user, so they will fit nicely on each workstation. Because of my decision to keep the services on the client side, some of the service subsystems will have to be replicated on the client machines. Workstation architectures (without the necessary machinery at the boundaries) are shown in Figure 10.19.

Add Interface Machinery

Add interface machinery wherever a channel crosses a hardware boundary. To complete each architecture, we must add the appropriate interface machinery to handle each channel that crosses the boundary. In order to preserve the location independence of the application subsystems, the interface machinery should provide a message interface that exactly matches the one they used when all subsystems were inside the same "box." There are two ways to provide the needed interface. One is to provide surrogate subsystems to represent the subsystems on the other side of the hardware boundary. In our example, the Transaction Processing subsystem has channel connections to Inventory, Transactions, Members, and Cash Drawer, all of which cross the enclosing boundary. Thus, we could provide a row of surrogate subsystems to hide the connections to the remote subsystems. Each would have the same channel connections as the "real" subsystems, but the internal behaviors would be concerned entirely with passing requests between the local Transaction Processing subsystem and the local communication machinery (Figure 10.20).

A second way to provide the needed interface is to provide a single dialogue subsystem that provides exactly the channel connections needed. I chose to designate this new subsystem as a "dialogue" subsystem because it is concerned with the conversation between the service subsystems and the model subsystems. Of course, it does not communicate directly with the model subsystems; it relays messages to and from whatever communication machinery is appropriate. An example is shown in Figure 10.21.

Whichever way is chosen to provide the required channels to the service subsystems, there remains the need for additional interface subsystems to provide local platform independence. At least two should be used: a presentation and a virtual device. If the communication medium between hardware nodes is a network, for example, we may choose to isolate the network-specific aspects in the virtual communication device. That would leave the presentation with the responsibility of matching incoming messages with the original, outgoing request. These components are shown in Figure 10.21.

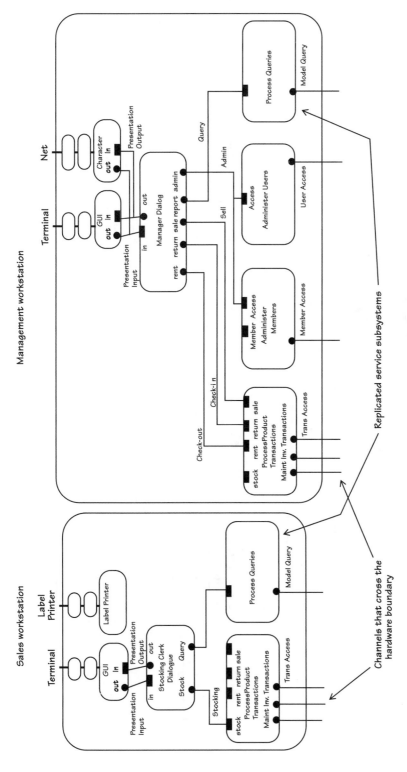

Figure 10.19 Architectures of the hardware nodes showing the initial allocation of subsystems to each node

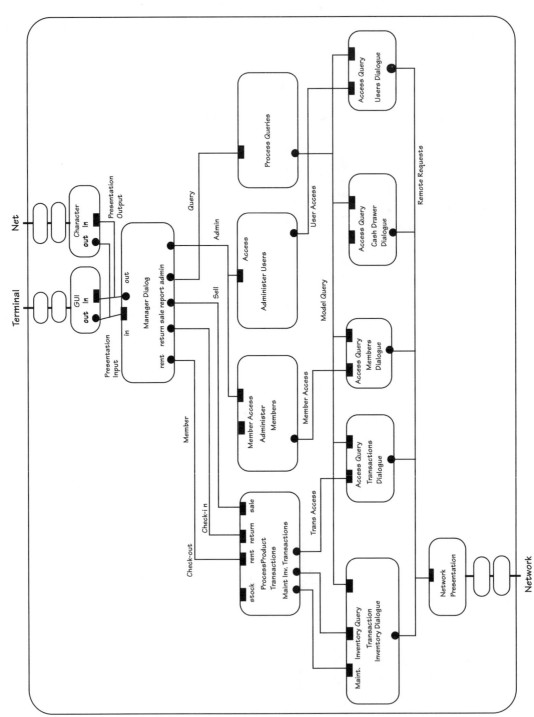

Figure 10.20   Architecture of the manager workstation node with interface subsystems added

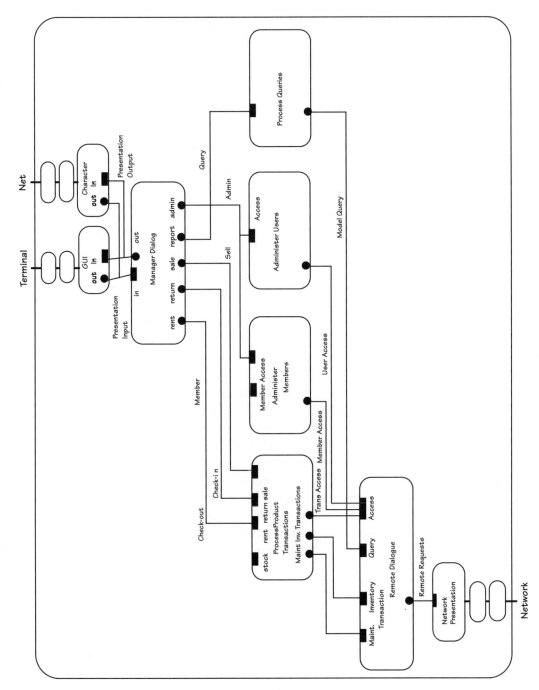

Figure 10.21 Architecture of the manager workstation node with alternative interface subsystem structure

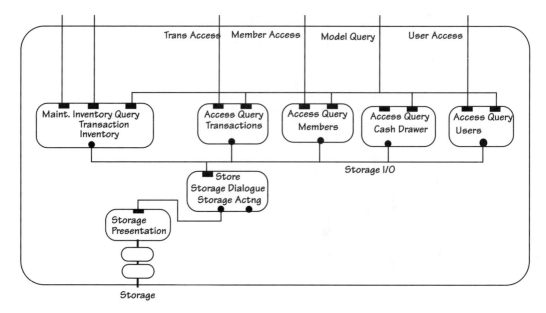

Figure 10.22   Architecture of the server node with the initial allocation of subsystems

10.6.2 Server Architecture

Before considering allocation of the subsystems in the workstation to specific implementation units, I would like to look at the server architecture. The initial subsystem allocation decision put the model subsystems in the server. The initial view of the server machine with the subsystems allocated to it is shown in Figure 10.22.

Engineering decisions should be defensible.

In looking at Figure 10.22, a problem is immediately obvious. The Cash Drawer subsystem was intended to maintain the state of a cash drawer for a single point-of-sale terminal. Each sales workstation will have its own cash drawer. While it is certainly possible to maintain the state of multiple cash drawers on one or more central servers, it seems more natural to keep the state of the local cash drawer on the local machine. *Seems more natural* is not a very good justification for an engineering decision, so I should do better before I reallocate and replicate the Cash Drawer subsystem.

One consideration is, who uses the Cash Drawer subsystem and how often? Each sales workstation will access the cash drawer at least once for every sale or rental transaction. Also, a manager may want a report of the current cash position for the entire store from time to time. Locating the Cash Drawer subsystem on the server would facilitate making the manager's report, but it would penalize every rental transaction with a cross-network access. If I allocate a Cash Drawer to each sales work station, I will save the routine accesses, but I will have to provide for the reporting functionality. To minimize the cross-network accesses, and to provide an interesting discussion about maintaining information integrity in a distributed system, I will allocate a separate Cash Drawer subsystem to each local workstation. (I will return to this discussion after finishing the discussion of the overall server architecture.)

Returning to the problem of the software architecture on the server computer, we must now provide the machinery to receive the messages arriving from multiple users and return the requested results. The physical port for those messages is the network connection on the server computer. My preferred architectural structure for interfaces consists of device, presentation, and dialogue subsystems. The device-type subsystems to handle the port can be added with little effort. The dialogue and presentation subsystems will take a little more effort.

The situation is more complex in the server than it was in the client workstations because the server must handle multiple users working on a single inventory model. To be more accurate, the situation requires developing a complete architecture for a system whose boundary is the edge of the server computer cabinet. We have a few of the subsystems given as inputs. Some of the external actors (the client systems, in this case) and some of the subsystems of the architecture are given by the previous work. In addition, there are new actors that were not considered in the initial big-system view of the architecture. The new actors could include a network administrator and a database administrator. If those actors had been included in the original requirements (they were not in this example), they could be moved to the server system. In this case, they were not included in the original requirements, so the engineering process should be repeated to develop the additional subsystems needed in the server system to support the new use cases. That activity will be left as an exercise for the interested reader. The end result is shown in Figure 10.23.

An interesting issue that can be addressed using an architecture diagram as the vehicle, is how to maintain the quality and integrity of distributed information. The allocation of Cash Drawer subsystems to each clerk workstation and the requirement to provide a manager with a consistent view of the cash position of the entire store provides the motivation for this discussion. (I do not recall that there was an explicit use case for providing the manager with a store-wide cash position, but it sounds like it should be a requirement.) Having chosen to allocate the responsibility for keeping the state of each local cash drawer to each local work station, I will now choose to allocate responsibility for maintaining the state of the collective cash drawer for the store to the server. With this choice, how do I provide the manager with a consistent view of the state of the distributed cash drawers?

Detailed design can uncover missing requirements.

Assume that a design goal is to minimize message traffic between clients and servers, and that the managers' requests for store-wide cash information are much less frequent than transactions on the individual workstation. I can satisfy the design requirement by having the store cash drawer on the server, ask for the current state of each of the workstation cash drawers when it needs the information. This "polling on demand mechanism" seems appropriate for the assumed conditions. Had the relative frequencies of the two kinds of requests been different, then some

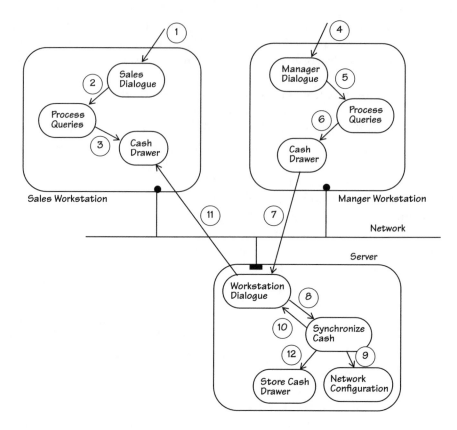

other mechanism should be used. Figure 10.24 shows an X-ray view of how requests to a local cash drawer and requests of the collective cash drawer are handled with the design choices I have made.

Discovering and fixing problems in architecture diagrams is much cheaper than discovering the problems at code or testing time.

After drawing Figure 10.24, I discovered that it had a problem. It was an honest problem of the type that occurs frequently in real work. I realized that by suggesting that the local cash drawers be located on the workstations and that store cash drawer be located on the server, I had divided a subsystem. In the original boxless architecture I showed only one cash-drawer subsystem, to which I allocated all the cash-drawer objects. In allocating subsystems to hardware boxes, I decided that I wanted to separate two things that I originally put in the single, Cash Drawer subsystem. An indication of the problem surfaced when I tried to fill in the message flows for Figure 10.23. I have no messages to populate channels 7–11 because, in the original allocation, there was only one cash drawer component. I did not account for having multiple cash drawers.

The problem here is that the cash-drawer subsystem selected for the initial architecture was too big. The solution is to go back to the place where the subsystems were nominated, renominate smaller subsystems, and reallocate the behavior model objects to the new subsystems. This process is not as disruptive as it sounds if a multiproject approach is being used. In that situation, the problem would be discovered

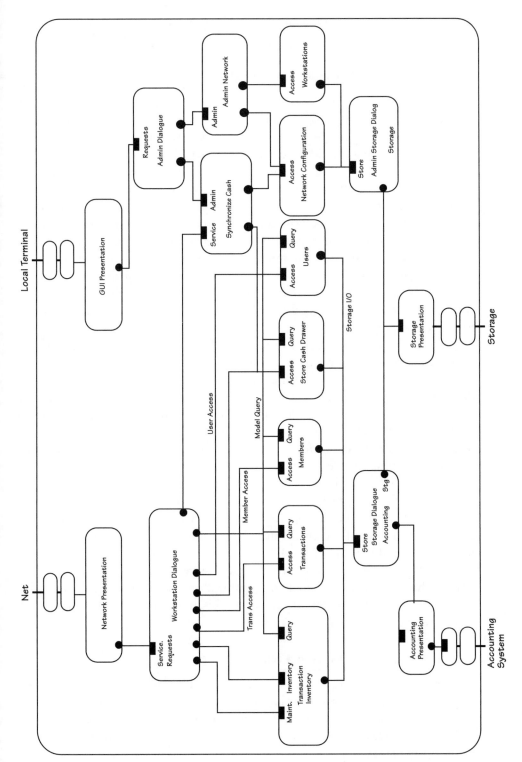

Figure 10.24 Complete server architecture

in an early design study and would be fixed in a subsequent, more detailed design project.

10.6.3 Evaluating Traffic Between Nodes

Demand summing is not covered, but it's necessary to evaluate channel demand.

If the project is detailed and formal, it may be possible and desirable to calculate the actual communication capacity demand for the channels that cross hardware boundaries. Summing the demand for all the messages that use a channel (using an appropriate summing algorithm to account for actual usage patterns) allows us to evaluate whether a particular communication medium will be sufficient. The ultimate source of information about invocation frequency is the use cases. To make the calculation, we need a way to trace backward from the message in a channel, through its invocations in the behavior model, and back to its use case source. The use case documentation can indicate how often a user will invoke the use case. The behavior model (for example, an interaction diagram) can indicate how often the message is sent in each use case. Combining the frequency that the use case is performed by a single user, the number of users, and the number of times the message is sent in each use case, we can calculate how often the communication medium will have to carry the message.

If we also know the size of the information flows that accompany each message from the date or object dictionary, we can calculate the total communication capacity demand for each message. (Of course, all of this infers that all aspects of the design were documented in a very formal and thorough manner.) Combining the message rates with their "sizes" for all the messages carried over a single physical medium, an Ethernet network for example, gives the total capacity demand for the medium. This can be compared with the available capacity to determine whether the selected medium is adequate.

In our example, the channels that cross the network include all of the Service-Model Level channels shown in Figure 10.17, except Cash Drawer Access. These channels will be carried over a network, Ethernet in this example, so we can specify the medium and type for each channel. The medium is Ethernet, and the type is, necessarily, asynchronous (Table 10.9).

I will leave it as an exercise for the interested reader to carry out the actual calculation. I have never encountered any organization that documents designs with enough detail to support that calculation. I think it is a good idea, but don't think many people find it very useful.

10.6.4 Allocating to Tasks in a Node

Tasks are subsystem enclosures.

The subsystems from the boxless architecture have been allocated to hardware subsystems (nodes). The external channels and their logical content have been determined. Inside computer systems, there are often other kinds of enclosures available which we can use as subsystems. These include tasks or processes provided by the operating system.

Channel	Message Content	Type	Medium
Inventory Maintenance	CreateName (name record) returns (aName)	Asynchronous	Ethernet
	CreateItem (aName, number)		
	Add (aName, item list) returns (status)		
	Delete (item list) returns (status)		
	GetItem (itemID) returns (anItem)		
Inventory Transactions	GetItem (itemID) returns (anItem)	Asynchronous	Ethernet
	ReplaceItem (anItem) returns (status)		
Member Access, Transaction Access, User Access	GetNames returns (name list)	Asynchronous	Ethernet
	Get (name) returns (item)		
	Put (item) returns (status)		
	Add (item) returns (status)		
	Delete (item) returns (status)		
	GetTemplate (type) returns (template)		
Model Query	Find (itemID, criteria List) returns (item list)	Asynchronous	Ethernet
	TypesAvaialble ( ) returns (item type list)		
Report Retrieval	GetTitlesFor (category) returns (title list)	Asynchronous	Ethernet
	GetReport (category, title) returns (report script)		

Table 10.9 Channel specifications with type and medium

It is possible, of course, to implement the server node, as shown in Figure 10.24, as a single task. In that case, the subsystems shown in the diagram would be implemented in constructs available in a programing language, such as instances of classes in C++ or Smalltalk.

For purposes of this example, assume that there is some incentive for using multiple tasks on the server. I will describe the process of allocating subsystems to a UNIX task and developing an internal architecture for the task subsystem.

Assume that the model subsystems will be in a single task and that the network I/O, storage I/O, and administrative subsystems will each have their own task. The task boundaries are shown in Figure 10.26.

The communication media inside a node include whatever interprocess communication the operating system provides. On UNIX, for example, the choices include remote procedure calls, sockets, pipes, and streams. When we consider the internal architecture of a task subsystem, the interface machinery we add will translate between the interprocess medium chosen and the programming language messages used inside the task subsystem. My nomination for a task-level subsystem architecture for the model subsystem is shown in Figure 10.27.

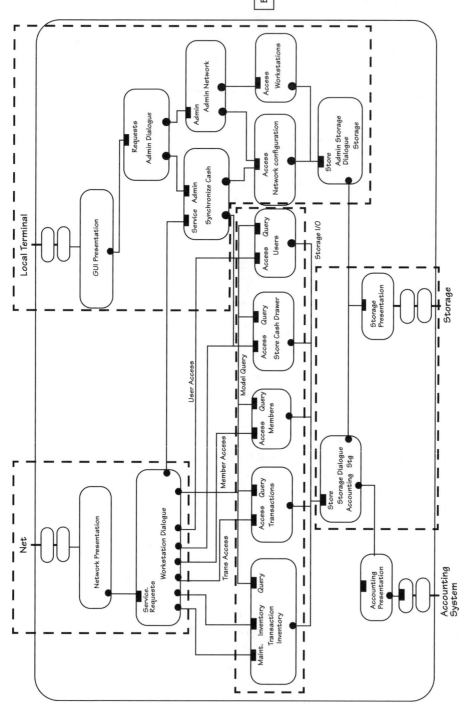

Figure 10.26 Allocation of subsystems to tasks on the server node

ARCHITECTURE EXAMPLE | CHAPTER 10

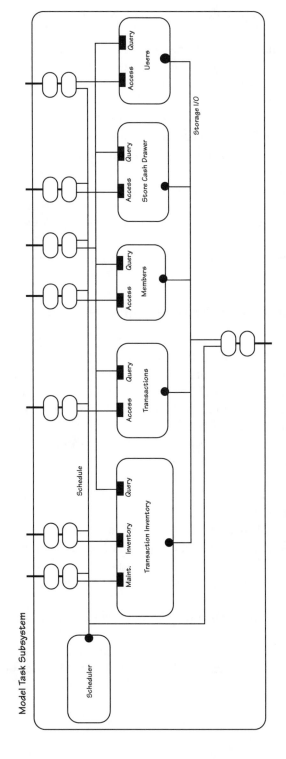

Figure 10.27 Internal architecture of the model task subsystem showing scheduler and interface subsystems

I have chosen to provide one external UNIX stream for each of the channels in the server-level architecture. Streams are cheap, and keeping them separate saves me the trouble of multiplexing all the channels into one stream and then demultiplexing them on the other side. The two little boxes shown on each stream do the reading and writing to the stream (the one closest to the boundary) and translate between the text in the stream and the C++ messages in the subsystems.

Real subsystem enclosures may introduce the need for additional components.

I have added a language-level subsystem to the task architecture, called Scheduler. Its responsibility is to watch the stream presentations and manage the sequence that they execute. This effectively schedules the execution of the model subsystems. Throughout this process I have been very careful in preventing contamination of any of the original subsystems with any knowledge of where they are implemented. The Scheduler carries the knowledge that the subsystem are actually in a synchronous environment and that they are being scheduled based on the presence of messages.

Had I chosen to multiplex all the channels into one stream, the multiplexer unit could have served as a scheduler.

10.6.5 Summary of the Subsystem Allocation Process

The overall process consisted of nominating a set of subsystems that describe the entire system. Those nominations are evaluated against the external goals for the system and we convinced ourselves that our nominations would, in fact, satisfy all the external requirements. Once the nominations were confirmed, we started allocating the subsystems to higher level subsystems, such as hardware nodes and operating-system tasks. (The example showed the mechanics of carrying out the allocations, but did not discuss the reasoning for those decisions.) No matter how we allocated the original subsystems, we could be confident that the system would still meet the external requirements.

I was very careful not to alter the original subsystems when they were allocated to various higher level subsystems.

While I did not make it an explicit design decision, an important decision was made in the assumption about the implementation-level of the original subsystems. In this example, I preserved their identity down to the code-level subsystems. I could have chosen to specify that the smallest unit I want to deal with is the heavy-weight task.

It is important to note that this allocation process depends on choosing the granularity of the boxless architecture subsystems correctly. *Correctly* cannot be easily predicted, so a multiple-project approach is recommended. The early, informal architecture study projects should provide information on the correct degree of granularity.

10.7 IMPLEMENTATION INCREMENTS

A cut at implementation increments was made in the behavior model section. However, now, with an architecture diagram in hand, we can see the complete implementation landscape and suggest a more complete list of implementation increments. These increments can be stated in terms of the subsystems that compose each increment. The sequence of increments proposed in the behavior model section can be retained: front end (A, in Figure 10.28), back end (B, in Figure 10.29), and middle (C, in Figure 10.28). In order for the front end to actually work, we can see in the architecture diagram in Figure 10.30 that we need the lower level interface machinery in place. Because of the value of letting users and managers operate a system, I will include the low-level interface components in the first increment.

The second, or parallel, increment consists of the model subsystems *(B)*. Here, I will not include the low-level storage interface machinery in the increment. That means we should make the storage interface machinery its own increment, which we can add in at any time (D, in Figure 10.29). The network interface machinery can be developed at any time (E, in Figures 10.27 and 10.28).

The third set of increments is the service subsystems *(C)*. To enforce the rule against use-coupling, we should be able to set up systems with just one service subsystem at a time.

In order to execute increment A, a separate component, perhaps a test harness would have to be provided to supply the channels that cross the boundary of the increment. Likewise, if increment B were constructed next or in parallel, then test subsystems would have to be provided to exercise the channels that cross the increment boundary. When increment C is constructed it could be connected to increment A for exercising. It could also be connected directly to increment B because the channels leaving C are exactly the channels entering B. The whole system could be run on a single machine for initial testing.

An architecture diagram for increment A is shown in Figure 10.30. The only subsystems are those in increment A and the harness for the dialogue subsystem.

There are no communications between subsystems in increment C, so it should be easy to build and exercise the service subsystems one at a time.

The E increments that contain the network interface machinery can be built separately and exercised independently of the other application subsystems. Again, test machinery would have to be provided to exercise the application-side channels. When the application increments A, B, and C, and the network increments, E, are ready, the application increments can be assembled and the systems run over the network.

Without the subsystems in the storage increments, D, test subsystems would be provided to feed the model subsystem's canned information. If increment D were available, the system would be able to handle live information.

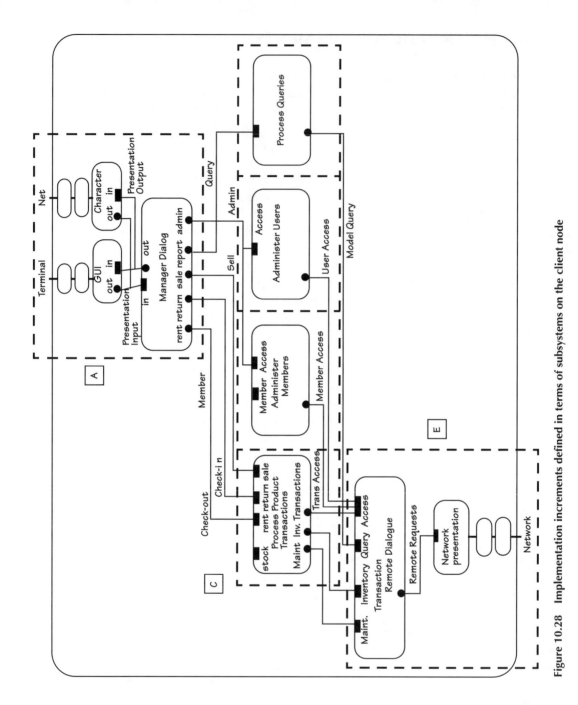

Figure 10.28   Implementation increments defined in terms of subsystems on the client node

The increments described above require a significant amount of test machinery to exercise them. That would be acceptable if the project called for building test machinery. However, if extensive test machinery were not called for, another

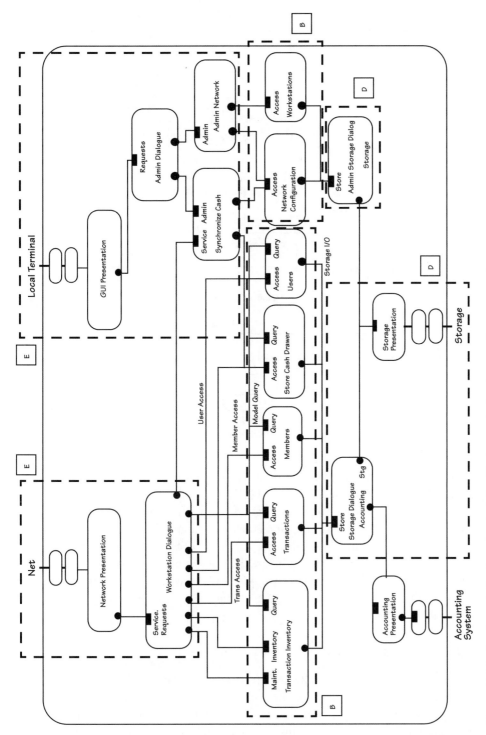

Figure 10.29 Implementation increments defined in terms of subsystems on the server node

Figure 10.30
Architecture
of increment
A shown as a
standalone
system

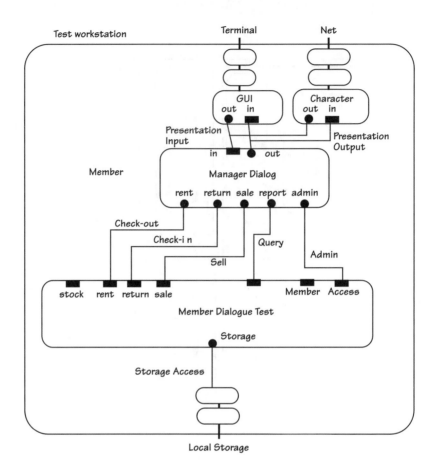

sequence of increments could be used: each increment would run from front to back. The increment map is shown in Figure 10.31 and Figure 10.32.

Increment *A* could be run on a single machine. It would be capable of making inventory transactions. The other increments *B*, *C*, and *D*, which provide administrative services, could be added sequentially. The network administration increment, *E*, could be developed before the rest of the system was actually installed on a network. Finally, increment *F* would allow the system to be installed on a network. In this sequence, the increments are bigger, but they do not require separate test machinery to exercise.

10.7.1 Project Sequence

To emphasize the role that the architecture specification has in a development project, I would like to describe the sequence in a project where the system being designed was being implemented. The design should be carried to the point where the interfaces for all the subsystems are firmly established, as shown in this example.

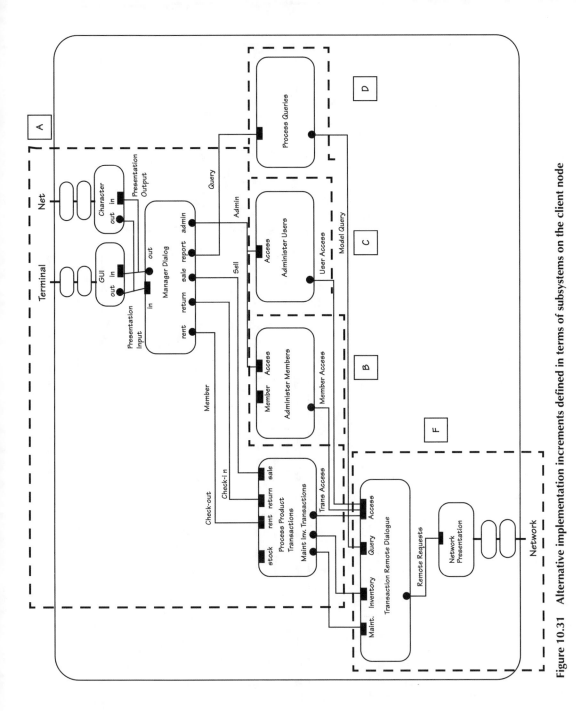

Figure 10.31 Alternative implementation increments defined in terms of subsystems on the client node

Only then should the individual increments be turned over to the implementation groups for construction.

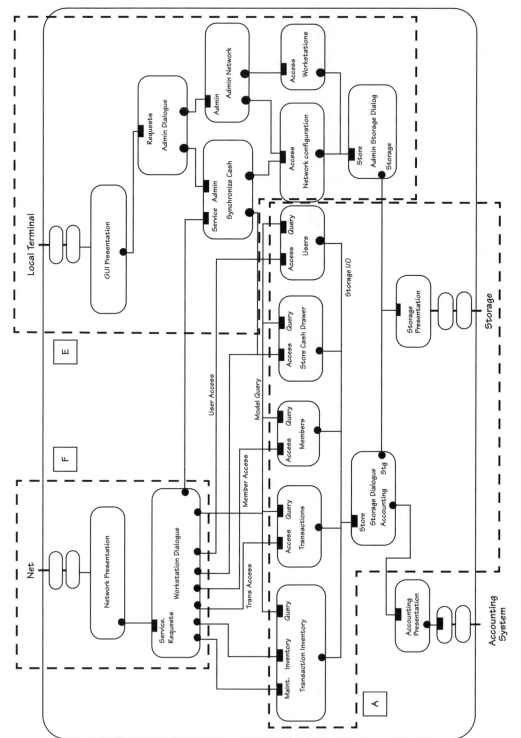

Figure 10.32   Alternative implementation increments defined in terms of subsystems on the server node

CHAPTER 11

The Behavior Description Task

CONTENTS

11.1 Introduction   315
11.2 Behavior Description   316
11.3 Constraints   316
11.4 References   318
11.5 Evaluation   318

11.1 INTRODUCTION

Two questions need to be addressed in this chapter. One is, what is behavior description? The other is, why is this chapter so short? I will begin with why the chapter is so short. Most people have biases that effect what they do and how they do it. I have described other people's bias in Chapter 1 and in the methodology comparison in Appendix B. I, too, have a bias that accounts for why the chapter is so short. My particular bias in the area of software design is toward the structure of software systems. Most of the content of this book is aimed at arriving at the structure, or architecture, of a software system. I confess to being less interested in the details of describing behavior after it is identified and allocated in an appropriate structure. So, the reason this chapter is short is that behavior description is not necessary to arrive at a system architecture. This does not mean that it is not important or that it should not be given adequate attention. It just means that I was not eager to write about it in this book. The subject is covered very well in a number of other works, some of which are listed at the end of this chapter.

A confession

Figure 11.1
Subtasks and work products in behavior description

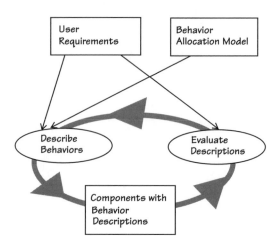

11.2 BEHAVIOR DESCRIPTION

How is the behavior carried out?

Behavior description accounts for the internal logic needed to carry out the behaviors previously allocated to the components. A good definition of the activity can be provided by kinds of notations that are used. Behavior description is notated with state models, pseudo code, structured English, and programming languages. Having a sufficient behavior description is essential for carrying the architecture design into implementation. It is also necessary for any detailed evaluations of system performance and throughput (Figure 11.1).

The behavior description task is separated from the behavior identification and allocation task for reasons that were covered in Chapter 2. The details of how a particular behavior will be carried out and the logic required are very sensitive to which attributes and other behaviors have been allocated to the component. So, it is very important that the behavior allocation remains fixed after the behavior is described. Changes to the behaviors allocated to a component will often require changing the behavior descriptions, which we should avoid doing again.

11.3 CONSTRAINTS

I would like to offer a few comments on constraints on the process of describing the behavior and then refer the reader to other sources that describe the techniques in more detail.

Behavior description should not change allocation or interface.

The scope of each behavior description should be strictly limited to a single component. All interactions between components should have been described completely in the behavior identification and allocation task. The behavior description should only have to account for how to handle messages received by the component and how to produce the messages sent. Of course, it is possible that in

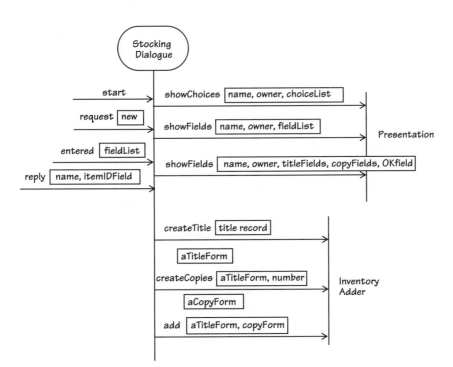

Figure 11.2

Example of an interface view of a component

doing the behavior description for a component you might discover that something is missing. When that happens, you should return to the behavior identification and allocation task to fix the problem and then describe the internal behavior. The reason for this is that the behavior allocations were carefully designed to address many kinds of requirements. Changing the allocation to address a local concern without considering the larger context of the decision could undo some of the earlier decisions.

The requirements for the behavior description are contained in the run-time requirements documents, in particular, the use cases, the rules and algorithms, and some of the nonfunctional requirements. In behavior allocation operation, the responsibility for implementing the functionality implied in those external requirements was distributed over one or, usually, more components of the system. How that behavior was distributed should be indicated by the message interfaces of each component. The task is to decide what internal logic is needed to implement each of the received messages in the components interface and how to produce each of the sent messages (Figure 11.2).

Some of the behavior needed in a component will come from internal considerations. Some of the behavior will be dictated by the external requirements. The need for the internal behavior should be indicated by the message names and responsibilities allocated to the component. Reference should be made to the external requirements when the behavior of the component is implementing some part of the external requirements. In the Stocking Dialogue component shown in Figure 11.2, the rules and implied behaviors for what choices to make available to the user will be dictated by the use cases. The details of the behaviors needed to get those choices sent to the Presentation and to collaborate with the Inventory Adder are based on the behavior allocation decisions that were made earlier.

11.4 REFERENCES

Instructions for describing behavior are provided in several sources. In *Structured Analysis* [YOR89], it is covered in chapters called "Process Specification" and "State Transition Diagrams." In Shlaer and Mellor [SHL92] it is covered in the chapters "Dynamics of Relationships" and "System Dynamics." Rumbaugh [RUM91] covers the topic in chapters titled "Dynamic Modeling" and "Functional Modeling."

This chapter and the chapters in the books mentioned above all nominally address the same topic: how to describe the behavior of an object. There are some differences in approach, however, that might make it difficult to simply pick up Shlaer or Rumbaugh and apply their techniques to describing object behaviors as in this book. The reason is that "events" in the Shlaer and Rumbaugh examples are events that occur in the real world. *Events* as we use the term are inside the system.

For those interested in understanding this more precisely, I can illustrate the difference with our Stocking Dialogue Component example in Figure 11.2. The behavior being described in this example is the response to the events that our Stocking Dialogue must respond to. In order to use the state transition techniques in the Shlaer and Rumbaugh books, the following translations must be kept in mind. In place of the events referred to in Shlaer and Rumbaugh, use the messages received by the Stocking Dialogue. For the events generated in Rumbaugh's state diagrams, substitute the messages sent by the Stocking Dialogue. Operations and functions referred to in Shlaer and Rumbaugh are the behaviors of the Stocking Dialogue.

11.5 EVALUATION

Evaluation of the behavior descriptions is usually a manual operation. People have to read through the descriptions, look at the environment of the component as indicated in the interaction diagrams, look at the external requirements, and decide if the descriptions provided will do the job. Simulation or execution of the descriptions is possible if the descriptions were written in an executable programming language.

CHAPTER 12

Conclusion

CONTENTS

12.1 Summary   319
12.2 The Critical Ideas   323
12.3 The Big Picture   324
12.4 Next Steps   324

12.1 SUMMARY

The Essential Tasks produce documents which describe the engineering decisions needed to arrive at the design of a software system. Each task is bounded by the requirements it addresses and by the evaluations of the output which demonstrate that the requirements have been successfully addressed. The Essential Tasks are summarized in the following outline:

A. Document External Requirements

    1. Run-Time Requirements Task

        • Inputs:
            User context
            Scope of the system
            User need
            System context

- Outputs:
    Goals and expectations for the system
    Functional requirements
    Rules and algorithms
    Control and information interfaces
    Constraints and other nonfunctional requirements

- Notations:
    Use cases
    Text

2. Build-Time Requirements Task

- Inputs:
    Development context
    Development sponsor needs
    Scope of the project

- Outputs:
    Goals and expectations in the development context
    Instances of growth and change
    Development constraints

- Notations:
    Change cases
    Text

B. Address Run-Time Requirements

- Inputs:
    User requirements
    Development sponsor requirements (minor)

- Outputs:
    Set of components which, taken together, can provide the
    run-time requirements

1. System State Model

- Requirements addressed:
    System state needed to provide run-time requirements

- Inputs:
    Use cases
    Rules and algorithms
    Information interfaces
    Change cases

- Outputs:
  System state content and structure

- Evaluations:
  Can the state model support the access requests generated in providing the run-time requirements?
  Can the state model structure support the changes to the state resulting from the build-time requirements?

- Notations:
  List information objects
  Object-attribute-relationship diagrams

2. Behavior Identification and Allocation Task

- Requirements addressed:
  Provide behavior content and structure sufficient to meet run-time requirements

- Inputs:
  Use cases
  Rules and algorithms
  Nonfunctional requirements
  System state model

- Outputs:
  Set of components with message interfaces. Functionality implied by message names can account for all user-required behaviors and information flows.

- Evaluations:
  Are all use cases and algorithms accounted for, and is local coupling and cohesion on components satisfactory?

- Notations:
  Collaboration-responsibility diagrams
  Object interaction diagrams
  Component interface diagrams

3. Behavior Description Task

- Requirements addressed:
  Provide logic to correctly implement functions, rules, and algorithms called for in run-time requirements

- Inputs:
  Set of components with message interfaces
  Static structure of the domain

- Outputs:

  Set of components with message interfaces and internal behavior descriptions that can account for all user-required behaviors and information flows

- Evaluations:

  Compare behavior descriptions with run-time requirements

- Notations:

  State transition diagrams (not described in this book)

  Flow charts

  Structured English

C. Address Build-Time Requirements

- Inputs:

  Change cases

  User constraints

  System context

  Set of components with message interfaces

- Outputs:

  System architecture

1. System Architecture Task

- Requirements addressed:

  Build-time emergent properties

  Run-time emergent properties

- Inputs:

  Change cases

  User constraints

  System context

  Set of components with message interfaces

- Outputs:

  System architecture

- Evaluations:

  Can architecture support the change cases?

  Can run-time emergent properties be demonstrated?

- Notations:

  Mascot-like architecture diagrams

12.2 THE CRITICAL IDEAS

There are a number of ideas presented in this book which seem to me to be critical to achieving the kinds of results that are promised and looked for in attempts to improve software development processes:

- *Document build-time requirements*   Documenting the build-time requirements, change cases, as peers of the run-time requirements, use cases, is necessary to delivering systems that have good build-time performance characteristics. Documenting them is the necessary first step toward designing good build-time properties in software systems.

- *Using build-time requirements to evaluate system structure*   The run-time requirements impose no constraints on the allocation and distribution of behavior in the system. The structure of the behavior and information in the system, as determined by the behavior allocation decisions, directly impacts the build-time properties of extensibility and maintainability. Thus, the build-time requirements can be used to evaluate the system structure. The structure of the complete system is its architecture, so the build-time requirements are the primary evaluation criteria for the architecture.

- *Address run-time and build-time requirements in separate aspects of the system design*   The idea that build-time and run-time requirements could be addressed in separate tasks and the results merged together to produce a complete system, makes the task of addressing all the requirements much easier.

- *Evaluating software design documents*   Earlier, in Chapter 1, I introduced the importance of having measurement tools in addition to production tools in delivering products that meet their requirements. I have tried to implement that idea by emphasizing the importance of deriving evaluation criteria for every document from the external requirements and then applying those criteria to the documents. Identifying the evaluation criteria against external requirements as an important part of the design process had the effect of reducing the importance of (capital-*M*) Methodologies. If the evaluations are in place, then what particular diagrams are drawn becomes less important. The process can be defined entirely by the evaluations that must be made.

- *Making behavior identification and allocation an explicit decision*   Recognizing that identifying and allocating behavior in a system establishes limits on the modularity potential of the entire system and determines the complexity of the behavior descriptions needed to implement the behaviors, is very important. That recognition provides an opportunity to explicitly address system modularity at a fundamental level.

- *Interface views*   Drawing interface views was a natural extension of the interaction diagram and has proven to be a very useful way of looking at components of the system. The interface views facilitate making local behavior coupling and cohesion evaluations on the components. They also make it easy to derive subsystem interfaces directly from the behavior model components allocated to the subsystems.

- *Standard architectures*   With the architecture shaped by the build-time requirements, and with almost everyone's build-time requirements being the same, software system architectures can have the same form. This idea has important ramifications for component reuse and the software components industry. It was first proposed, to my knowledge, by Michael Jackson [JACK82].

12.3 THE BIG PICTURE

More than design techniques are needed to deliver quality products.

I have been careful to set the scope of the Essential Tasks. We have a tendency in this industry to ascribe macroscale results to microscale tools and processes. In the big picture, each software product is a subsystem to the product at the next level up the product hierarchy. At each level of the product hierarchy, there is a hierarchy of processes that keep products flowing to the market. That process hierarchy begins with the techniques and notations in the tool boxes of the people who design and implement single products. Those tasks are applied in projects to make a single build-time change in a product. A product is moved through its life cycle in a process defined by a sequence of projects. Somewhere, above the individual product lifecycles, there is a process that looks at the needs of multiple products and returns common architectures and resalable parts.

The Essential Tasks presented here are the tools in the tool box belonging to the engineer who designs a single level of a software product. They are very important to the successful execution of the higher level processes, but they do not describe the higher level processes. The fact is that all of the processes in the hierarchy must be effectively executed in order to achieve the macroscale benefits most organizations want.

12.4 NEXT STEPS

I believe that carrying out the Essential Tasks as described here in development projects would result in significant improvements in the run-time and build-time properties of the systems produced, compared to the average system produced today. I believe this because the suggestions made here are patterned very closely on practices in the hard-product industries where they have worked well. Imagine, for a moment, what would happen if a small group in a development organization convinced their managers that they should try the approaches described here on their next project. They would receive approval and proceed to conduct the engineering part of the project with all the demonstrations and evaluations I have recommended. The product would get coded and delivered and placed in service. Everyone would declare victory and celebrate. Then some flinty-eyed manager would ask, "Are we better off now compared to doing it the old way?"

I must confess that this is a hard question to answer. Making that comparison requires that measurements be available from past projects and products. If the measurements are available, then some way of accounting for differences in the size of the current and past projects is needed. It is not helpful to observe that the old project took 50 person-years and the new one took 28 person-years. The difference could be due to any combination of factors: from better design techniques perhaps, but also perhaps a better programming language, better people, or a smaller project. The question about whether we are better off with a new technique is hard to answer because there is not a good way to measure the intrinsic size of a software system.

So, after making a big deal about the importance of knowing the goals for an activity and measuring the outputs against the goals, I am unable to recommend a way to directly measure the impact of applying the Essential Tasks. In spite of the lack of measurements for the process described here, I still heartily recommend that the build-time requirements be documented, that behavior content be evaluated against run-time requirements, and that the system structure be described in static subsystems and evaluated against build-time requirements.

Summary of Essential Tasks

This summary provides a condensed version of the techniques contained in this book.

Basic Principles

- Document the external goals for each activity and measure the output of the activity against those goals.

- Evaluate all engineering decisions against the goals those decisions are supposed to address.

- Always evaluate the results of any engineering decision before those results are used in another decision.

- Use run-time requirements to evaluate behavior and information. Use build-time requirements to evaluate allocation of that behavior, and the structures and architecture of the system.

- All items that are to be evaluated together must be visible at the same time in the design documentation.

A.1 THE ESSENTIAL TASKS

Figure A.1 shows the flows and dependencies among the techniques in developing a single-level design of a system.

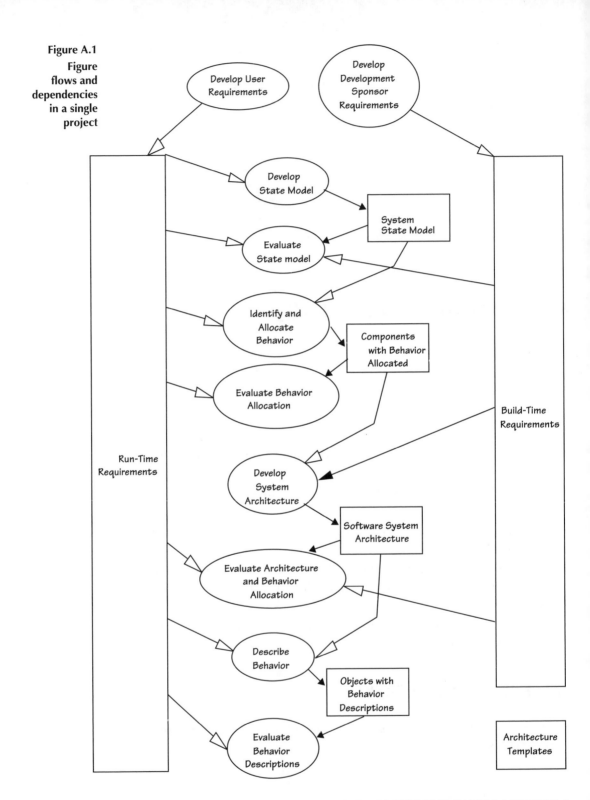

Figure A.1
Figure flows and dependencies in a single project

Develop User Requirements

Develop Development Sponsor Requirements

Develop State Model

System State Model

Evaluate State model

Identify and Allocate Behavior

Components with Behavior Allocated

Evaluate Behavior Allocation

Run-Time Requirements

Build-Time Requirements

Develop System Architecture

Software System Architecture

Evaluate Architecture and Behavior Allocation

Describe Behavior

Objects with Behavior Descriptions

Evaluate Behavior Descriptions

Architecture Templates

A.1.1 User Requirements Task

Goals

Document the needs of users of the system. These needs impinge on the system while it is running. The needs should be stated in a manner that can be understood and verified by user authorities. The form should also be useful as the input and the source of evaluation criteria for the information and functionality of the system.

Inputs

Document the scope and context for the system, policies, and rules the system must adhere to or implement, relevant policy and rule documents, sample reports and files that will cross the system boundary, user authority designations, and communication protocols or conventions the system must support.

Outputs

Statement of all the run-time requirements the system must support: users' and user-sponsor's goals and expectations, users' functional requirements, control interfaces, information interfaces, rules and algorithms the system will implement, and user constraints.

Actions

Document each of the outputs in the chosen techniques. Information comes from user authorities. These can be people on the team with the required experience or people in the user domain designated as authorities.

Evaluations

Evaluation is, necessarily, entirely by manual reviews with the relevant parties.

Notations

Documenting user functional requirements

- *Textual, functional requirements*   Document the functions that the systems will provide to its users. The point of view is from "inside" the system. The form is difficult for users to review, and is difficult to use to drive engineering decisions.

- *Use cases (and event cases)*   Document the users (human and machine) that interact with the system and the individual uses each makes of the system or the events that the system must respond to. The point of view is from "outside" the system. The form is easy for domain authorities to review because it describes their actual usages. The form lends itself well to use with engineering tasks.

- *Rules and algorithms*   The rules and algorithms the system is expected to implement are documented as textual descriptions.

Documenting nonfunctional requirements

- *Goals and expectations*   Users' and user-sponsor's goals and expectations and user constraints are described in textual descriptions.
- *Control interfaces*   These interfaces include user interfaces and other messaging interfaces the system must support. Documentation techniques include sample screens and interface prototypes for user interfaces and state models and protocol specifications for other messaging interfaces

A.1.2 Development Sponsor Requirements

Goals

Document the build-time changes that the system must support. The form should be understandable by the development sponsor authorities, should be usable as an input to the engineering decisions that go into the system, and should serve as s source of evaluation criteria for the structure of the system.

Inputs

Describe the development and enhancement context for the product, development sponsor authority designations, growth and enhancement needs of the users of the target product, and plans for related products and systems.

Outputs

Describe the build-time changes the system must support: the change cases. These include ports, service additions, alternative configurations, other systems to be supported, requirements for incremental implementation, and anticipated integrations with other systems. The development-sponsor requirements constitute a product plan for the system being engineered.

Actions

Describe, in text, each change that must be made as a unit—a change case. Sources of changes include the expectations of the target users of the system, technology trends, related systems being developed in the organization, and other potential users (besides the target users) of the system. This information is gathered from interviews with user authorities, development-sponsor authorities, and strategy and planning documents in the development organization.

Evaluations

Evaluations are by manual reviews with the development-sponsor authorities. Decisions about which change cases to support should be based on the priorities of the development organization and the economic costs and benefits of each change case.

Notations

Change cases are documented with text that includes the name and description of the changes involved.

A.1.3 System State Task

Goals

Document all the content and structure of state elements that the system needs in order to provide the required information and functionality to its users. All the state elements included should be described with words drawn from the application domain. The resulting model should support the access requests that the rest of the system will make. It should also be able to be gracefully extended as the system grows and changes.

Inputs

Describe the use cases, change cases, information interface elements, policy, and algorithm requirements.

Outputs

Describe the names and descriptions of the state elements that the system must maintain, static or structural relationships between the elements, and content (attributes) of the elements.

Actions

Derive evaluation criteria from the inputs: access requests and object additions. Nominate state elements and nominate relationships and attributes.

Evaluations

Walk through access requests on the structure. If the model cannot support the access request or does it in a clumsy way, add state elements and relationships, add attributes, or promote/demote attributes to objects. Walk through state model change cases. If adding a new kind of state element causes significant structural change to the model, nominate new elements and relationships so that the change will have less impact.

Figure A.2
**"Object/entity,
attribute,
relationship"
diagram
notation**

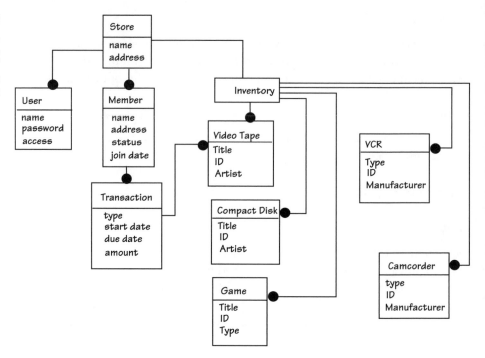

Notations

Use entity-relationship-like diagrams, such as Rumbaugh object model, or Shlaer-Mellor information model. Any diagram that shows objects, attributes, and relationships is sufficient (Figure A.2).

A.1.4 Behavior Identification and Allocation Task

Goals

Name all the behaviors and information needed to provide the user-required functionality, and allocate those behaviors to components of the system. The allocation should be such that the system can gracefully support the growth and change required of it.

Inputs

Describe the use cases, rules and algorithms, constraints, system state model, and architectural forms for the system (templates).

Outputs

Describe the set of system components with behaviors and attributes. This set of system components, taken together, can provide all of the run-time requirements.

Actions

Select a template for the system structure to guide the nomination of additional system elements. For each required usage (use case) nominate a set of elements to provide the use case. Nominate the behaviors (functions, messages) that will provide the use case and implement the required rules and algorithms. Allocate them to sender and receiver elements. Collect the complete interface for each element resulting from all the individual allocations. Complete specification of the behavior interface including both the control aspects (message or function names) and information flows (arguments and returns).

Evaluations

Evaluation against the user requirements is done by providing a walkthrough of the use case on the system elements that provide the use case. Local evaluations for coupling and cohesion can be carried out. Evaluation against the external development sponsor requirements can be carried out only on the complete subsystem structure of the system (the architecture). That evaluation must wait until the behavior elements have been allocated to subsystems.

Notations

Class-responsibility-collaboration card (CRC cards) modeling is an informal documentation technique (because there is no record of the individual walkthroughs). Object interaction diagrams (Objectory) and event traces (Rumbaugh) provide more formal documentation (Figure A.3). Both of these document control flows, but not information flows. Adding information flows to object interaction diagrams makes them excellent vehicles for documenting behavior identification and allocation decisions. Cohesion and coupling evaluations on individual objects are facilitated with an object interface view (Figure A.4).

A.1.5 Behavior Description Task

Goals

To describe the operation of the behaviors named in the identification and allocation phase, above. To account for the logic necessary to implements the rules, algorithms, and use cases in the user requirements.

Figure A.3
Object inter-action diagram notation

Use case name: Add new titles

If the clerk selects "add," the system requests the title. The clerk enters the title and the system verifies that it is a current title and requests the number of items being added.

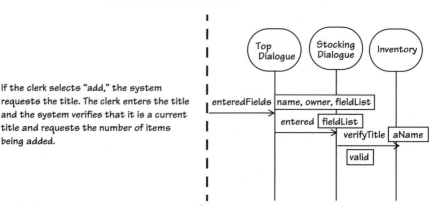

Inputs

Describe elements from the behavior identification and allocation phase, use cases, rules and algorithms

Outputs

Describe behavior descriptions (logic) for all of the behaviors identified in the previous activity.

Figure A.4
Interface view notation

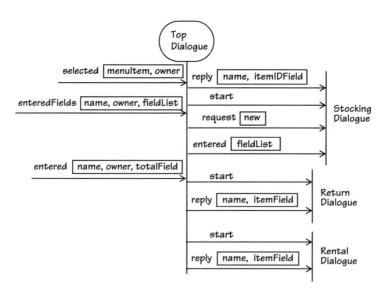

Actions

Given the external behavior requirements and the context of each message (the element to which it is allocated), describe the logic and conditionals needed to carry out the behavior. Each description should be limited to the scope of the system element to which the behavior was allocated.

Evaluations

Evaluation is by manual walkthrough of the logic descriptions against the run-time requirements.

Notations

Notations include state transition diagrams, truth tables, pseudo code, logic flow diagrams, Structured English, and programming languages.

A.1.6 Architecture Task

Goals

Describe the implementation building block structure of the complete system. The architecture specification consists of the system boundary, the communication channels that cross the boundary and the subsystems, and their connections, that compose the system. If the specified subsystems are created and connected according to the architecture specification, the system will run.

Inputs

Describe the development-sponsor requirements (change cases), user requirements, external actors, output of static and behavior identification and allocation activities, above, list of available architecture templates.

Outputs

Describe the subsystem structure of the target system, specified to a level of detail sufficient to address the needs of the project. System specifications may include communication channel specifications for each subsystem, responsibility descriptions for subsystems, internal specifications for subsystems, and allocation of subsystems to hardware and other implementation units.

Actions

Select a form for the architecture, if not already selected. Select the physical boundary for the architecture diagram. Indicate all physical communication channels that cross the boundary. Populate the selected template with subsystem nominations. Provide interface subsystems for each channel and for each type of actor. Using the behavior and static model outputs, nominate application-level subsystems. If the selected system boundary includes hardware, or other memory boundaries, then nominated subsystems may be allocated to those units. Each set of subsystem nominations should be evaluated against external requirements before any further allocation, decomposition ,or description of the subsystems is undertaken.

Evaluations

- *Against user requirements*   If the behavior allocation to the architecture subsystems was carried out by allocating static and behavior-model elements to the subsystems, no further evaluation against user requirements is needed (assuming the static and behavior models were evaluated against user requirements). If no previous demonstration was done, then evaluation of the architecture is by walking through each of the use cases on the architecture diagram. When problems are found, behavior and information should be reallocated.

- *Against development sponsor requirements*   Walk through each of the change cases. Ask three questions of each change case: 1) How many subsystems are directly impacted? 2) Does the external interface of the impacted subsystems change? 3) Is there information and behavior in the impacted subsystems not directly related to the change case? The optimum answers are 1) one, 2) no, and 3) no. If problems are found, the semantic level of interfaces can be changed, behavior and information reallocated, and subsystems may be renominated.

Notations

Responsibility Driven Design (Wirfs-Brock) and Objectory (Jacobson) both offer subsystem diagrams, but in both cases, communication channels, particularly those outbound from a subsystem, are not well handled, and a system boundary is not part of the diagrams. Mascot and ROOM notation handle channels much better, but still lack a system boundary (Figure A.5).

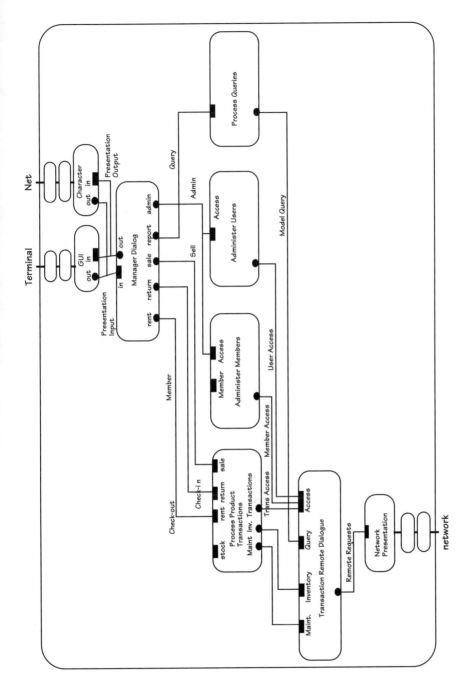

Figure A.5 Software subsystem architecture notation

Methodology Comparison

B.1 SOFTWARE METHODOLOGIES

A software design methodology is a set of instructions for how to analyze and design software systems. Many methodologies have been published over the years. Some of the authors, well known in the industry, include Yourdon, Constantine, Gane and Sarsen, Ward and Mellor, Hatley, Booch, Rumbaugh, Wirfs-Brock, and Jacobson. There are dozens of others. The content of some of the major methodologies is shown in Table B.1.

Methodologies are conveyed in books, CASE tools, and training courses. Writers of methodologies set out to provide a complete set of instructions for designing software. This, in itself, presents a problem for most users of the methodology. Most organizations are using a less than complete set of techniques in their process, so a comprehensive methodology is a big change. The expectation that the methodology is the next "silver bullet" adds to the difficulty that methodologies have in meeting the needs and expectations of their users.

On the average, a methodology describes a portion of one kind of software development project. That project is one that begins with a need for a new automated system and ends with the delivery of a working system that meets the need. The methodology provides instructions covering activities that begin after the need has been recognized, or after the need has been documented in requirements, and ends just before coding begins or just before the design is expressed in programming language features. The instructions call for a comprehensive set of documents and a single level of formality throughout the project. The same set of diagrams seems to be called for on all projects that use the methodology.

Table B.1   Work products in methodologies

Name	Structured A & D	RDD	Shlaer/Mellor	Objectory	Unified Method	OMT (original)
Reference	[YOR89]	[WIR90]	[SHL92]	[JAC92]	[BOO95]	[RUM91]
Work				Use cases	Use cases	Problem statement
	Entity-relationship	Hierarchy	Information model	Entity object model	Class diagram	Object model
Product	Data flow	CRC cards	State model	Analysis object model	Message trace	Data flow
	State transition	Class specification	Process description	Interaction diagram	Object message	State model
	Structure chart			State model	State mode	
	Processor model	Subsystem collaboration	Subsystem model	Subsystem structure	Module (file) diagram	
	Task model		Domain model		Platform diagram	

Methodologies often show a data or function bias that matches the practice bias in the industry out of which the methodology grew. Traditionally, function and data were strongly separated in software development. Perhaps because of that tradition, people and their practices tend to have a bias toward one or the other of those aspects of a system. It has been my observation that in the commercial data processing world, the bias is toward information, while in the technical software world (telecommunication, machine control), the bias is toward function. The strength of these biases was brought home to me by two incidents that happened at about the same time. I was working with a client on a digital telephone switch. In developing the architecture diagrams, the engineers refused to show any connections to the system database, or to the data stores present on each card in the switch. One of the required design notations on the project was the object interaction diagram. I recommended that both message names and information flows be shown in the diagram. The engineers could not bring themselves to show information flows on those diagrams. The rationale was that when information is needed, "we'll just get it."

Shortly afterward, I conducted a design course for a group of commercial data processing developers who were getting started in object-oriented design. I introduced the object interaction diagram and recommended that both message names and information arguments be shown on the diagram. One person in the course refused to write down the message names. The only thing worth thinking about was the data flows. These two incidents serve as a reminder to me of how strong the data and function biases can be.

The bias has not been noticeably reduced with the introduction of object technology. The data people still spend most of their design time on the static object model and the function people still spend most of their time on the object interaction diagrams (without information flows) and on state charts. The impact of these biases is that one aspect of the system gets more attention at the expense of the other. It is common, in my experience, for a development team to use only one diagram in designing their systems. When the data bias is active, the one diagram is an entity-relationship diagram or a static object model. When the function bias is active, the diagram used is the structure chart or the object interaction diagram. The bottom line is that a significant fraction of the system design decisions are not documented and are probably made in the context of writing the code.

Many of the organizations that agonize over the selection of "The Methodology" to use appear to expect that, after choosing "The Methodology," their products and economics will be significantly improved.

In listening to conversations about methodologies, one can easily get the impression that they are very different from each other, perhaps even mutually exclusive. Consider the wars between advocates of structured analysis and design, information engineering, and the various sects of object enthusiasts. These apparent, large differences between methodologies are troubling. It seems that if all the methodologies are talking about designing the same thing, a software system, then there should be a thread of common issues that they address.

So the average methodology suffers from several problems. On one hand, common interpretations of the methodology make it appear to be too formal and too inflexible for most organizations. On the other, there are often unreasonable expectations placed on the methodology about the benefits that will accrue when the right set of diagrams are drawn.

B.2 METHODOLOGIES AND THE ESSENTIAL TASKS

With a list of Essential Tasks, and some Basic Principles to guide their application, I would like to address two questions: Are they as different from one another as they seem, and do they provide a sufficient foundation for a successful development practice?

The reason any individual or organization starts using, or changes, their design methodology is to gain some improvement in the quality or economics of their software product. It is appropriate, then, that method comparisons should be based on the ability of the method to support improving the product. Methodologies, of course, cannot actually do anything by themselves and even the perfect method cannot make up for inexperienced or incompetent people or processes. But, if we can identify a list of tasks and work product categories that must be present in a development process in order to address the desired properties, then we could use that list as a basis for comparing methodologies.

We have such a list in the Essential Tasks and Basic Principles. The tasks cover documenting the external goals and then addressing each of the major aspects of a system: state, behavior, and system structure. The principles call for evaluating the artifacts of each task against the external goals. If a design methodology does not include those things, it is very difficult to see how it can contribute to the improvements in the attributes of a software product.

To make the comparison, I propose to use the Essential Tasks as the framework for comparing methodologies. By grouping the work products of each methodology into the categories of the Essential Tasks, we can see more similarities between the methodologies than differences. The Basic Principles will be used to evaluate the instructions for each task in the methodology for their effectiveness in evaluating the decisions being made.

I will use the term *external evaluations* to refer to evaluating a document against criteria derived from the external requirements for the system. External requirements are specific to each system being developed. There are other criteria used to guide the decision-making process and to evaluate the results. Those are, by symmetry, *internal evaluations*. Internal evaluations are made using criteria that are not connected to the specific system under design. Examples include: use 7 ± 2 functions in any one level of a data flow diagram, the structure chart should be onion-shaped, the inheritance tree should be closer to square rather than deep and narrow or wide and shallow, and identify subsystems by minimizing communication across each subsystem boundary. The internal evaluations are helpful only to the extent that they help the system meet its external requirements. The only way we can tell if they did help is to evaluate the design, however it was arrived at, against the external requirements and properties. For this reason, the evaluation criteria I will apply to software methodologies is whether they call for external evaluations.

The methods considered here include:

- Structured Analysis and Structured Design [YOU89]
- Objectory [JAC92]
- Responsibility Driven Design [WIR90]
- Object Modeling Technique (OMT) [RUM91]
- Object-Oriented Analysis (Shlaer-Mellor)[SHL92]

B.2.1 Structured Analysis and Structured Design

Structured Analysis provides good coverage of the Essential Tasks. The architecture notations are briefly covered in the section on Follow On Issues. The data flow diagrams produced in the essential model, which constitute the first step in the description of applying the process, are used as the description of the requirements. Those same diagrams are then carried directly into the later analysis and design activities. From the point of view of the Basic Principles, this mixes the statement of the external needs the system is to meet with the decisions about the content and structure of the system itself. The context diagram with its data flows and event lists called for in the environmental model, which follows the essential model, is a much better statement of the requirements on the system because it is not stated in terms of decisions made by the analyst. Documentation of build-time requirements and any explicit evaluation for extensibility is missing. The documents described in the structured analysis and structured design method include the following:

- Data flow diagram
- Entity-relationship diagram
- Data dictionary
- Structured English
- Context diagram
- Event list
- State transition diagram
- Process specification
- Processor model
- Tasks

Table B.2 shows where these documents fit in the Essential Tasks:

Essential Task	Notation, Products	External Evaluation
User Requirements	Context diagram, event list	
Development Sponsor Requirements	Not documented	
System State	Entity-relationship diagram, data dictionary	None
Behavior Identification & Allocation	Data flow diagram, structure chart	None
Behavior Description	State transition diagram, structured English	None
Architecture	Process specification, processor model, tasks	None

Table B.2
Structured
Analysis

B.2.2 Responsibility-Driven Design

Responsibility-Driven Design offers good coverage of the Essential Tasks. The notation used for both the system state and the behavior identification and allocation is rather informal—the CRC card. While no documentation of either run-time or build-time requirements is called for, the scenarios used in the walkthroughs during allocation are effective documents of the user functional requirements.

Work products developed in this design method include the following:

- Class-responsibility-collaboration cards
- Hierarchy graphs
- Collaboration graph
- Contract specifications
- Subsystem graphs and collaborations
- Contract signatures

Table B.3 shows where these documents fit in the Essential Tasks:

	Essential Task	Notation, Products	External Evaluation
Table B.3 **Responsibility** **Driven Design**	User Requirements	Not included	
	Development Sponsor Requirements	Not documented	
	System State	CRC cards, class hierarchy diagram	None
	Behavior Identification & Allocation	Responsibility, contract description, signatures	Scenario walkthroughs
	Behavior Description	Contract descriptions	None
	Architecture	Subsystem diagrams	None

B.2.3 Object-Oriented Analysis (Shlaer-Mellor)

Object-Oriented analysis (Shlaer-Mellor) provides good coverage of the Essential Tasks. There is more attention given to architecture issues than in most methods. I use *architecture* as I have defined it here. There is an architecture domain in Shlaer-Mellor that is used differently. The domains and subsystems correspond to system architecture as I have used the term. The event list qualifies as a statement of external functional requirements. Instances of change are not explicitly documented.

The work products used in this method include the following:

- Event list
- Domain chart
- Information (entity-relationship) model
- State model
- Object communication model
- Subsystem communication diagram
- Action flow diagram
- Object access diagram
- Process diagram
- Process descriptions

Table B.4 shows where these documents fit in the Essential Tasks:

Essential Task	Notation, Products	External Evaluation	
User Requirements	Event list		**Table B.4**
Development Sponsor Requirements	Not documented		**Shlaer-Mellor**
System State	Entity-relationship model	None	
Behavior Identification & Allocation	Action flow diagram, process table, object access model	Event modeling	
Behavior Description	State model for objects, action descriptions	None	
Architecture	Domain diagrams, subsystem models	None	

B.2.4 Object Modeling Technique (OMT)

Object Modeling Technique (OMT) calls for a Problem Statement as the only statement of external requirements. It uses scenarios of external access to develop the Dynamic Model. OMT is one of the very few methods that calls for an explicit operation to allocate behaviors to objects. Operations identified in the Dynamic Model and the Functional Model are explicitly allocated to the objects identified in the Object Model. System architecture as subsystems associated with hardware is briefly mentioned. There is no explicit documentation of build-time requirements or evaluation for extensibility.

Work products in this method include the following:

- Problem statement
- Scenarios
- Event lists
- Static object model
- State transition diagram
- Data flow diagram
- Function description
- Event trace
- Object model with operations.

Table B.5 shows where these documents fit in the Essential Tasks:

Table B.5
OMT Method

Essential Task	Notation, Products	External Evaluation
User Requirements	Problem statement, scenarios, event list	
Development Sponsor Requirements	Not documented	
System State	Entity-relationship model	None
Behavior Identification & Allocation	Data flow diagram, event trace	Scenario model with event trace
Behavior Description	State model, function descriptions	None
Architecture	Subsystems	None

As I write this, Rational Corporation is in the process of integrating the methodologies of Booch, Rumbaugh and Jacobson. That will result in the addition of use cases as a means of documenting functional requirements of users.

B.2.5 Objectory

Objectory is a mature and formal method. Of the methodologies compared here, it is the only one to explicitly call for different kinds of objects (entity, control and interface). As we will see later, this is important in achieving a changeable system. The practice of documenting user functional requirements as use cases and then using the use cases explicitly throughout the analysis and design process is a contribution from Objectory that is being adopted by many other methodologies. No build-time requirements are documented.

Work products called for in Objectory include the following:

- Use case description and model
- User interface specification
- Entity object model
- Analysis object model
- Interaction diagram
- Subsystem diagram
- Object specifications
- Traceability documents

Table B.6 shows where these documents fit in the Essential Tasks:

Table B.6 Objectory

Essential Task	Notation, Products	External Evaluation
User Requirements	Use cases, use case requirements	
Development Sponsor Requirements	Not documented	
System State	Entity Object model	None
Behavior Identification & Allocation	Interaction diagram, analysis object model	Each diagram associated with a use case
Behavior Description	State model	None
Architecture	Package and subsystem diagram	None

B.2.6 Summary of the Comparison

The methodologies do, in fact, address a common set of concerns when viewed in terms of how they support the Essential Tasks. The emphasis given to each task varies, with the system architecture getting the least attention, but they are reasonably complete. For those methodologies that have not embraced use cases, the documentation of run-time requirements is usually done indirectly. Documentation of build-time requirements is consistently absent. With the exception of using use cases or event lists to drive the behavior models, there is no explicit evaluation of the analysis and design documents against the external requirements.

I believe that a significant advance in consistency between methodologies can made by adding build-time requirement documentation to all methodologies and evaluating every work product category against the external requirements.

These additions can easily be made by users of any methodology. They require no major restructuring of the methodology or of the tools that may support it.

The result of making these additions would be, I believe, a rapid convergence on a single set of instructions for developing software products, that is convergence to a single methodology. The evaluations will quickly indicate inadequate notations (assuming the evaluations are executed effectively).

The general purpose software engineer's tools box should have the following compartments in it:

- Run-time requirements
- Build-time requirements
- System state
- Evaluations of system state against run-time and build-time requirements
- Behavior identification and allocation
- Behavior descriptions
- Evaluations of behavior descriptions against run-time and build-time requirements
- System architecture

The presence of the evaluations for each Essential Task list would remove much of the burden of delivering a good design now borne by the detailed instructions for the task. This is because if errors are made, there is a place to catch them and make changes before the errors propagate to other areas of the design. The engineer will quickly learn how to deliver a good design.

Most methodology books look a great deal like this book in that they spend most of their pages describing how to do individual tasks. That does not mean that this book should be considered to be a methodology book. I think it indicates that most books with the label of methodology are really closer to tool descriptions than to process descriptions. I think both descriptions are needed. People need to know how to use the individual tools of their trade, and they need to know how to apply those tools in many situations to accomplish a desired result.

Bibliography

[BEC89] K. Beck and W. Cunningham, "A Laboratory for Teaching Object-Oriented Thinking," *OOPSLA*, 1989.

[CHU95] L. Chung, B. Nixon, and E. Yu, "Using Non-Functional Requirements to Systematically Select Among Alternatives in Architectural Design," *Proceedings of the First International Workshop on Architectures of Software Systems* Pittsburgh: Carnegie Melon University, 1995.

[COX92] B. Cox, *The Industrial Software Revolution* IEEE Software, November 1992.

[GAC95] C. Gacek, A. Abd-Ailah, B. Clark, and B. Boehm, "On the Definition of Software System Architecture," *Proceedings of the First International Workshop on Architectures for Software Systems* D. Garlan, ed., Pittsburgh: Carnegie Mellon University, 1995, p. 85.

[GAM95] E. Gamma, R. Helm, R. Johnson, and J. Vlissides, *Design Patterns*, Reading, MA: Addison-Wesley, 1995.

[GAR93] D. Garlan and M. Shaw, "An Introduction to Software Archiecture," *Advances in Software Engineering and Knowledge Engineering*, Vol. 1, World Scientific Publishing Company, 1993.

[GAR95] D. Garlan, "What is Style," *Proceedings of the First International Workshop on Architectures of Software Systems*, Pittsburgh: Carnegie Melon University, 1995.

[EME95] D. Emery and R. Hillard, "Architecture, Methods and Open Issues," *Proceedings of the First International Workshop on Architectures of Software Systems* Pittsburgh: Carnegie Melon University, 1995.

[HOF95] C. Hofmeister, R. Nord, and D. Soni, "Architectural Descriptions of Software Systems," *Proceedings of the First International Workshop on Architectures of Software Systems* Pittsburgh: Carnegie Melon University, 1995.

[HUM89] W. Humphry, Kitson, and Kasse, *The State of Software Engineeing Practice: A Preliminary Report*, Carnegie-Mellon University: Software Enginering Institute, CMU/SEI-89-TR-1, DTIC, Number ADA 206573, February 1989.

[IEEE95] *IEEE Software*, November 1995.

[JAC87] I. Jacobson, "Object Oriented Development in an Industrial Environment," *OOPSLA '87 Conference Proceedings*, ACM 1987. ACM order number 548871.

[JAC92] I. Jacobson, M. Christerson, P. Jonsson, and G. Overgaard, *Object-Oriented Software Engineering*, Reading, MA: Addison-Wesley, 1992.

[JACK82] M. Jackson, "Two Pairs of Examples in the Jancson Approach to Systems Development," *15th Hawaii International Conference on Systems Sciences* January 1982.

[KAN95] S. Kan, *Metrics and Models in Software Quality Engineering* Reading, MA: Addison-Wesley, 1995.

[KOZ95] W. Kozaczynski, "Software Components, the Building Blocks of System Architectures," *Proceedings of the First International Workshop on Architectures of Software Systems* Pittsburgh: Carnegie Melon University, 1995.

[KRU94] P. Krutchen and C. Thompson, *Proceedings TRI-Ada '94*, Baltimore MD, 1994.

[KRU95] P. Krutchen, "The 4+1 View Model of Architecture," *IEEE Software*, November 1995.

[MAG95] J. Magee and J. Kramer, "Modeling Distributed Software Architectures," *Proceedings of the First International Workshop on Architectures for Software Systems* Pittsburgh: Carnegie Mellon University, 1995.

[MAS87] *The Official Handbook of MASCOT Version 3.1*, Issue 1, Computing Division, Worcestershire: Royal Signals and Radar Establishment, 1987.

[MEZ95] G. Mezaros, "Software Architecture in BNR," *Proceedings of the First International Workshop on Architectures of Software Systems* Pittsburgh: Carnegie Melon University, 1995.

[PAR79] D. Parnas, "Designing Software for Ease of Extension and Contraction," *IEEE Transactions of Software Engineering*, Vol. SE-5, No. 2, March 1979, pp. 128–138.

[PAUL95] F. Paulish, "Pattern-Oriented Software Archiecture," *Proceedings of the First International Workshop on Architectures of Software Systems* Pittsburgh: Carnegie Melon University, 1995.

[REC91] E. Rechtin, *Systems Architecting*, New York: Prentice Hall, 1991.

[RUM91] J. Rumbaugh, M. Blaha, W. Premerlani, F. Eddy, and W. Lorensen, *Object-Oriented Modeling and Design* Englewood Cliffs, NJ: Prentice Hall, 1991.

[SEL94] B. Selic, G. Gullekson, and P. Ward, *Real-Time Object-Oriented Modeling* New York: Wiley, 1994.

[SHAW95] M. Shaw, "Comparing Architectural Design Styles," *IEEE Software*, November 1995.

[SHAW96] M. Shaw, *Software Architectures*, Englewood Cliffs, NJ: Prentice Hall, 1996.

[SHL92] S. Shlaer and S. Mellor, *Object Lifecycles-Modeling the World in States*, Englewood Cliffs, NJ: Prentice Hall, 1992.

[VAN95] F. Van der Linden and J. Muller, "Creating Architectures with Building Blocks," IEEE Software, November 1995.

[VIC95] A. Vickers and J. McDermid, "ArCATECH-An Architectural Construction and Analysis Technique for Real-Time Systems," *Proceedings of the First International Workshop on Architectures for Software Systems*, Pittsburgh: Carnegie Mellon University, 1995.

[WIR90] R. Wirfs-Brock, B. Wilkerson, and L. Wiener, *Designing Object-Oriented Software*, Englewood Cliffs, NJ: Prentice Hall, 1990.

[YOU89] E. Yourdon, *Modern Structured Analysis*, Englewood Cliffs, NJ: Prentice Hall, 1989.

Index

Numbers in italics refer to examples

A

access requests 85, 90, 92, *97, 113*
actor 54, 63, *72*
architecture notation 6, 15, 18, 213, *271, 284*
    channel specification notation 243, *283*
architecture task, subtasks 42
    behavior allocation to subsystems
        217, 239, *274*
    channels, deriving 240, *278*
    evaluation, detailed architecture 246, 248,
        286, 304
    evaluation, preliminary architecture
        16, *218,* 237, 246, *270*
    subsystem allocation to hardware
        250, 255, 295, *304*
    subsystem architecture 296,
    subsystem, nominating 217, 227, *261*
architecture 2, 15
    bottom-up 9
    boundaries in 18, 214, *253, 295*
    boxless 226, 250
    definition 9, 17
    elements of 12
    evaluation of 16, 246
    generic 224
    hardware, relationship to 14
    impact on behavior allocation 129, 135,
        162
    layers in 217, 220, 222
    ports, communication 15, 18, *260*
    style 5
    template 129, 214, 225
  attribute 89, 90

B

basic mechanism 137
Basic Principles 11, 17, 26
Beck, Kent 133
behavior description 43, 315, 333
    logic 316
    rules and algorithms in 317
behavior identification and allocation 42,
  121, *161*
    architecture, effect on 122, 129, 137, 217
    cohesion in 127, 142, 149, *171*
    components, kinds of 122
    control flows 135, 333
    coupling in 127, 143, *177*
    information flows 135, 333
    interface profiles 125, 137, *179*
    services 44, 152, *201*
    use coupling 126, 144
behavior identification and allocation notation
    collaboration graphs 150, *197*
    CRC cards 147, *196*
    interaction diagrams 133, *174*
    interface views 124, *178, 185*
behavior identification and allocation task,
  subtasks 331
    allocating behaviors to subsystems
        217, 237, *274*
    allocating messages to components
        11, 136, 148, *164, 189*
    allocating subsystems to hardware and
        processes 250, 255, *295*
    behavior, identifying and allocating
        131, 136, 148, *161, 189*

behavior identification and allocation task, subtasks *(continued)*

    components, nominating 129, 135, 148, 155, *161*

    evaluation, behavior allocation 127, 132, 149, *175, 196*

    evaluation, in architecture 127, 218, 249, *289*

    evaluation, local 127, 132, 139, *177*

    service model 44, 153, *201*

Booch, Grady 88

boundary

    hardware 250

    system 226

branches, iterations, in behavior allocation 138

build-time properties 12

    measurements 36

business object model 83

C

change case 213, 215, 231, 246

    definition 63

    questions for evaluation 246

    and service subsystems 233

channel specification 243, *285*

Chung 7

cohesion 149

cohesiveness, behavior alloaction 142

collaboration 149

    connectedness 150

collaboration graph 151, *197*

collaboration responsibility modeling 127, 147

    notation 147

communication medium 250, 256

completeness, behavior allocation 142

complexity 2, 32

component

    dialogue 123

    interface profile 124, *178, 185*

    model 123

    presentation 123

component *(continued)*

    service 123

    size 136

connectedness, subsystem 241

CORE method 55

CRC cards 147, *196*

Cunningham, Ward 133

D

data model 83

database 84

    as an actor 54

dependency, behavior allocation 142

development process 31

    hardware 32

    software 34

development process, chunks 34

    architecture 37

    code 37

    cross product 34

    design 37

    integration 37

    project 36

    prototype 38

dialogue/control components, in behavior allocation 131

distributed objects 250

domain object model 83, 217

E

efficiency, in system state 90

emergent properties 20, 23, 29, 211

entity model 83

entry points, as subsystem identifiers 234

essential task

    behavior description 43

    behavior identification and allocation 42

    build-time requirements 41

    run-time requirements 40

    software system architecture 42

essential task *(continued)*
    system state 41
    definition 38
evaluation criteria
    architecture 213
    system state, 86, 90
evaluation of
    architecture 16, 246
    behavior allocation 127, 132, 149,
        175, 196
    behavior allocation in architecture
        127, 218, 249, *289*
    behavior allocation, local evaluation
        127, 132, 139, *177*
    build-time requirements 67
    detailed architecture 246, 248, *286*, 304
    external requirements 52, 60, 67
    preliminary architecture 16, *218*, 237,
        246, *270*
    run-time requirements 60
    system state 85, 89, 104, 108
    use cases 60
external requirements 27, 51
    architecture, role in evaluation 218, 246,
        270, 286
    behavior allocation, role in evaluation
        127, 132, *175, 208*
    change cases 62, *80*
    developer role 50
    development sponsor role 50
    evaluation, use in 11, 28
    system state, role in evaluation 85, 90, *96*
    use cases 55, *73*
    user role 49
    user sponsor role 49
external requirements task, subtasks
    see requirements task
    build-time requirements 50, 61, *80*
    evaluation of 52, 60, 67
    run time requirements 49, 53, *73*

F

feasibility study 237
function 152
functional requirements 55

G

Gacek 7
gauges 26

H

hardware architecture, relationship to
    software 14
hardware boundary, locating 253
hardware node, software architecture for 255

I

incremental implementation 156
increments
    nominating 157, *182*
    project 37
information flows 149
information model 83
inheritance 140
interaction diagram 143, *174, 184*
interface components,
    in behavior allocation 130
interface profile type 125, 142
interface view 125, *178, 186*

J

Jacobson 133, 145, 156

K

Krutchen 5

M

Mascot diagram 18, 213
measures 26

medium, physical communication 252
Mellor, Steve 242
memory space 14
message interface 124
message name 141, 249
    consistency 141
    control part 136
    information part 136
message naming 138
methodology
    architecture in 8, 220
    improving 45
methodologies
    comparison 339
    Object Modeling Technique (OMT) 346
    Objectory 55, 88, 123, 133, 152, 347
    Responsibility Driven Design (RDD) 344
    Shlaer-Melor 345
    Structured analysis and Design 343

N

naming responsibilities, consistency 156
notations
    channel specification 243, *285*
    collaboration graph 151, *197*
    CRC cards 147, *196*
    interaction diagram 143, *174*, *184*
    interface view 125, *178*, *186*
    object diagram 85, 87, *108*, *111*, *112*
    pseudo code 335
    service model *210*
    state transition diagram 335
    Structured English 335
    system architecture 214, *266*, *284*, *291*
    truth table 335

O

object diagram 85, 87, *108*, *111*, *112*
Object Modeling Technique (OMT) 346
Object Request Broker 250
Objectory 55, 88, 123, 133, 152, 347

P

Parnas, David 156, 157
patterns 6, 9, 10
performance 20
peripherals, as actors 227
ports 226
process, hardware development 32
process, software development 34
process formality 44
process level
    cross product 34
    product 35
    project 36
product, levels of 31
projects, software development
    essential tasks in 38
    projects, kinds of 36
properties 29
pseudo code 335

R

Rechtin 3, 15
relationships 90
    system state 89
reliability 20
requirements task, build-time subtasks 61
    change cases 62, *80*
    constraints, development sponsor 66, *81*
    evaluation of 67
    scope 61, *80*
requirements task, run-time subtasks 53
    algorithms 60, *79*
    constraints, user sponsor 60, *80*
    control interface 58, *78*
    evaluation of 60
    function requirements 55, *73*
    information interface 59, *79*
    nonfunctional requirements 60, *80*
    rules and algorithms 60, *79*
    scope 53, *72*
    use cases 55, *73*
    user interface 58, *78*

responsibility 148
  generic 215
Responsibility Driven Design (RDD) 344
reuse 20
role, definition 54
ROOM 18

S

semantic level 52, 225, 227, 248, 249
  in state element description 89
  system state 91
service components
  from use cases 155
  in behavior allocation 131
service model, evaluation 158
service modeling 44, 127, 153, *201*
Shaw, Mary 4
Shlaer, Sally 242
Shlaer-Melor methodology 345
simulation 318
size, system 325
software industry 26
stake holders 48
  build-time 50
  run-time 49
state element 84, 86, 90
  definition 88
  naming 89
state transition diagram 335
Structured Analysis and Design 343
Structured English 335
subsystem 12
  allocating behavior 237
  allocating components 238
  allocating functions 238
  allocating responsibility 235
  allocation to hardware 250
  allocation to non-hardware 255
  bottom up 9
  device, semantic level 242

subsystem *(continued)*
  device driver 224
  dialogue control 230
  dialogue controller 224
  dialogues, identifying 230
  hardware 13
  implementation 252
  interfaces 240
  model, identifying 233, 234
  model subsystem 225
  nomination 227
  physical 213
  presentation 224, 228
  service subsystems 225, 232
  size 227, 251
  software 13
  surrogate 252
  virtual device 228
system architecture 214, *266, 284, 291*
system boundary 15
system integration 21
system state 84, 93
  change cases 85
  efficiency 92
  element, in model subsystems 233
  element, and service subsystems 232
  evaluation 85, 90
  evaluation criteria 86
  extensions and additions 93
  in behavior allocation 129
  interchangeability 90
  notation 85, 87
  sufficiency 91
system state notation 134, *174, 184*
system state task, subtasks
  attributes, nominating 90, *102*
  evaluation criteria 86, 90, *96*
  evaluation of 85, 89, *104, 108*
  relationships, nominating 90, *102*
  state elements, nominating 89, 99, *105*

T

tangibility, system 19
top down 22
truth table 335

U

use cases 55, 136, 138
    behavior, use in nominating 131, 134,
       148, *164, 190*
    developing 55, 138, *73*
    evaluation , use in 139, *175, 208*
    evaluation of 60
    services, use in nominating 155, *202*
use coupling 126, 144

V

Van der Linden 7
views 3
    of architecture 3, 5, 15
    and controllers 217
    interface 125, 140, *178*

W

Wirfs-Brock, Rebecca 9, 133, 243